SRA® MATH
Explorations and Applications

85°

Stephen S. Willoughby
Carl Bereiter
Peter Hilton
Joseph H. Rubinstein
Co-author of Thinking Story® selections **Marlene Scardamalia**

SRA McGraw-Hill

Columbus, Ohio

A Division of The McGraw-Hill Companies

SRA/McGraw-Hill

A Division of The **McGraw·Hill** *Companies*

Copyright © 1998 by SRA/McGraw-Hill. All rights reserved.
Except as permitted under the United States Copyright Act,
no part of this publication may be reproduced or distributed
in any form or by any means, or stored in a database or
retrieval system, without prior written permission from the
publisher.

Printed in the United States of America.

Send all inquiries to:
SRA/McGraw-Hill
250 Old Wilson Bridge Road, Suite 310
Worthington, OH 43085

ISBN 0-02-687857-7

2 3 4 5 6 7 8 9 VHP 02 01 00 99 98 97

Contents

Whole Numbers and Integers 2

■ Application   ▲ Revisiting

Contents

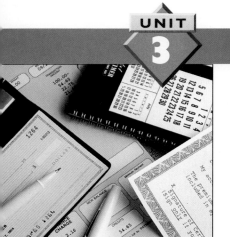

■ Application   ▲ Revisiting

Contents

UNIT 4 — Fractions and Mixed Numbers   236

■ Application   ▲ Revisiting

Contents

UNIT 5 — Algebra Readiness   340

■ Application   ▲ Revisiting

Contents

UNIT 6 — Geometry   436

■ Application   ▲ Revisiting

Contents

Resources

■ Application   ▲ Revisiting

Dear Student,

You'll find a lot of things in this *Math Explorations and Applications* book. You'll find stories with Mr. Muddle, Ferdie, Portia, Manolita, Marcus, and their friends, whom you may remember from earlier years.

You'll find games that will give you a chance to practice and put to use many of the skills you will be learning.

You'll find stories and examples that will show you how mathematics can help you solve problems and cut down on your work.

You'll be reading and talking about many of the pages with your class. That's because mathematics is something people often learn together and do together.

Of course, this book isn't all fun and games. Learning should be enjoyable, but it also takes time and effort. Most of all, it takes thinking.

We hope you enjoy this book. We hope you learn a lot. And we hope you think a lot.

The Authors of *Math Explorations and Applications*

UNIT 1

Whole Numbers and Integers

REVIEWING ARITHMETIC

- measurement

- place value

- basic operations

- negative numbers

- multiplying integers

SCHOOL TO WORK CONNECTION

Decorators use math . . .

A decorator spends only part of the time looking for things that clients want in their homes. A lot of time is spent in people's homes measuring floors for carpeting, rooms for furniture, furniture for fabric, and walls for wallpaper. Wallpaper and fabric come in rolls of a certain width, and decorators must decide how much to buy.

3

Measuring and Visualizing

Kim and Paul wanted to tile the floor of their clubhouse. They decided to measure the floor to see how many tiles they would need.

But one end of their meterstick had been broken. It looked like this:

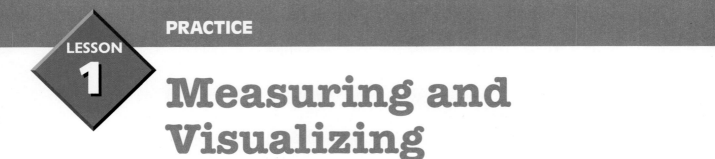

They used the stick anyway. Paul measured the length of the clubhouse. He was able to fit the stick along the length of the room about five times with a little room left over. But he still didn't know how long the room was. Can you help him?

◆ The stick is broken at the 99-centimeter mark. About how long is the broken meterstick?

◆ If the stick were not broken, how many centimeters would there be in five lengths of the stick? (There are 100 centimeters in a meter.)

◆ How many centimeters are there in five lengths of the broken meterstick? Try to figure this out in your head.

Paul said the clubhouse floor is five sticks long plus about 5 centimeters.

◆ How many centimeters is that?

Kim used the broken meterstick to measure the width of the clubhouse.

She started at one wall and marked off 99 centimeters.

Then she moved the stick and marked off another 99 centimeters.

Then she moved the stick again and marked off another 99 centimeters.

◆ How many centimeters has she marked off so far?

Then Kim tried to mark off another 99 centimeters. But there was not enough room.

◆ How could you measure the last section?

Kim measured the last section. It was 60 centimeters long.

◆ How many centimeters wide is the clubhouse?

Suppose the meterstick was broken at the 98-centimeter mark.

◆ How many centimeters long would five lengths of the stick be?

Now try these in your head.

Suppose the meterstick is broken at this centimeter mark:	How long would this many lengths be in centimeters?
1 97	4
2 95	6
3 92	3

Work in groups. Measure the length and width of your classroom with a regular meterstick. Compare your results with those of other groups.

Save your results in your Math Journal. You'll need them for Lesson 13.

◆ LESSON 1 Measuring

Alan was stacking cubes. He made one stack three cubes high. Then he put four more cubes around the bottom cube. When he looked at the pile of cubes from the south, it looked like this.

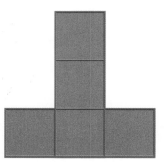

When he looked at the stack of cubes from the west, it looked just the same.

Using graph paper, Alan kept track of how many cubes were in each stack looking down from above. He called this a map.

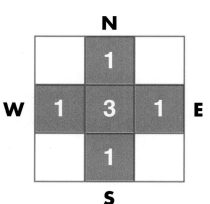

Alan decided to put four more cubes in the design. On his "map" his record looked like this.

◆ How did that change the view from the south?

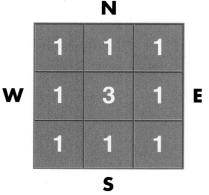

◆ How did the view from the west look?

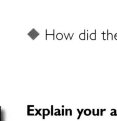

Explain your answers to these two questions in your Math Journal.

A different stack of cubes looked like this from the south:

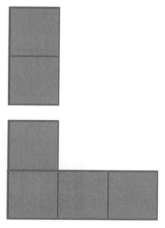

And like this from the west:

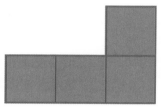

◆ Draw a "map" of this stack. Are there any other possible maps that could make those two views?

For another stack the view from the south was this:

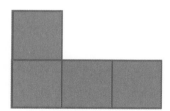

And the view from the west was this:

◆ How many cubes are in this stack? Are you sure?

◆ What is the maximum number of cubes that might be in the stack?

◆ What is the minimum number possible?

Draw a map for the maximum number and a map for the minimum number of cubes that could be in this stack.

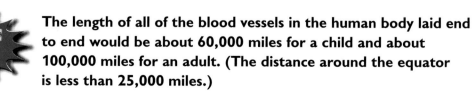

The length of all of the blood vessels in the human body laid end to end would be about 60,000 miles for a child and about 100,000 miles for an adult. (The distance around the equator is less than 25,000 miles.)

Place Value

When the 1990 Census was taken, the total population of the United States was estimated to be 248,709,873. This lesson will show you how to read that number, and other numbers, by using place value.

Millions   Thousands

hundreds	tens	ones	hundreds	tens	ones	hundreds	tens	ones
2	4	8	7	0	9	8	7	3

This number is two hundred forty-eight million, seven hundred nine thousand, eight hundred seventy-three.

The 2 stands for 2 hundred millions.	200,000,000
The 4 stands for 4 ten millions.	40,000,000
The 8 stands for 8 millions.	8,000,000
The 7 stands for 7 hundred thousands.	700,000
The 0 stands for 0 ten thousands.	0
The 9 stands for 9 thousands.	9,000
The 8 stands for 8 hundreds.	800
The 7 stands for 7 tens.	70
The 3 stands for 3 ones.	3

The value of each place is ten times that of the place to the right: *tens* are ten times *ones*, *hundred thousands* are ten times *ten thousands*, and so on.

Write the numbers in standard form.

1 9000 + 500 + 40 + 3

2 6000 + 700 + 80 + 9

3 70,000 + 200 + 3

4 3 + 500 + 20,000

5 20 + 9000 + 50,000

6 2 + 300 + 200,000

7 4000 + 70 + 30,000 + 1

8 6 + 50 + 8000

Copy and complete the number sequences.

9 3995, 3996, ■, ■, ■, ■, ■, 4002

10 5678, 5679, ■, ■, ■, ■, ■, 5685

11 9996, 9997, ■, ■, ■, ■, ■, 10,003

12 6098, 6099, ■, ■, ■, ■, ■, 6105

Roll and Regroup A Number Game

Players: Two or more
Materials: One 0–5 cube, one 5–10 cube
Object: To make the greatest number
Math Focus: Addition facts, place value, regrouping, and mathematical reasoning

RULES

1. Draw boxes on your paper like this: ⬜ ⬜ ⬜
                                               hundreds tens ones

2. The first player rolls both cubes. Every player writes the sum of the cubes in the hundreds box, the tens box, or the ones box.

3. The cubes are rolled twice more, and each time every player writes the sum of the numbers in one of the remaining boxes.

4. After the three rolls, the players find the value of their numbers, regrouping where necessary.

5. The player who makes the greatest number is the winner of the round.

SAMPLE GAME

Numbers rolled:		David wrote:			Maria wrote:			Corrine wrote:		
5 3	First roll		8				8	8		
8 3	Second roll	11	8			11	8	8		11
10 4	Third roll	11	8	14	14	11	8	8	14	11

David regrouped 11 hundreds, 8 tens, and 14 to get 1194.
Maria regrouped 14 hundreds, 11 tens, and 8 to get 1518.
Corrine regrouped 8 hundreds, 14 tens, and 11 to get 951.
Maria won this round.

Can you describe the strategies you used to play this game? Write each idea in your Math Journal.

◆ **LESSON 2   Place Value**

To determine the winners of many Olympic races, participants' times are measured using decimals. For example, in the 1996 Summer Olympics, Gary Neiwand won the cycling sprint in 10.129 seconds. This is how you use place value to read decimal numbers like this one.

tens	ones	tenths	hundredths	thousandths
1	0	1	2	9

This number is ten and one hundred twenty-nine thousandths. Another way to say it is ten point one two nine.

The 1 stands for 1 ten.	10.
The 0 stands for 0 ones.	0.
The 1 stands for 1 **tenth.**	0.1
The 2 stands for 2 **hundredths.**	0.02
The 9 stands for 9 **thousandths.**	0.009

We can tell the place value of any **digit** in a number by the **decimal point.** The decimal point is always between the ones and the tenths place.

On both sides of the decimal point, each place has a value ten times that of the place to the right.

5	5	5	5	5

The purple 5 stands for 5 thousandths.	0.005
The orange 5 stands for 5 hundredths.	0.05
The blue 5 stands for 5 tenths.	0.5
The red 5 stands for 5 ones.	5.
The green 5 stands for 5 tens.	50.

What does the 7 stand for in each of these numbers? Show it in two ways. The first one has been done for you.

13 363.721   **7 tenths, 0.7**   14 635.567   15 457.318

16 567.105   17 749.956   18 892.713

19 971.324   20 214.271   21 639.257

Write in standard form.

22 2 tenths, 4 hundredths, 6 thousandths

23 3 tenths, 3 hundredths, 5 thousandths

24 3 tenths, 5 hundredths, 0 thousandths

25 4 tenths, 0 hundredths, 9 thousandths

26 0 tenths, 6 hundredths, 4 thousandths

27 2 tenths, 7 hundredths, 0 thousandths

28 5 tenths, 0 hundredths, 3 thousandths

29 0 tenths, 0 hundredths, 4 thousandths

30 7 ones, 4 tenths, 2 hundredths

31 6 ones, 8 hundredths, 7 thousandths

Write in standard form.

32 0.7 + 0.05 + 0.002

33 0.03 + 0.005 + 0.1

34 0.009 + 0.02 + 0.5

35 0.6 + 0.03 + 0.001

36 0.007 + 0.9 + 0.06

37 0.3 + 0.007

38 0.02 + 0.004

39 0.08 + 0.7 + 0.002

40 2 + 0.6 + 0.04

Sometimes we put 0s in places to the right of the decimal point to help make the arithmetic easier. This is helpful when we are comparing decimals.

Which is greater, 0.94 or 0.904?

We can put a 0 after 0.94, making it 0.940, so that both decimals have the same number of places after the decimal point. (0.940 has the same value as 0.94, assuming we know that 0.94 is precise to the thousandths place.)

Now it is easier to see that 0.940 is greater than 0.904.

Copy each pair of numbers but replace ● with <, >, or =.

41 0.9 ● 0.009

42 0.5 ● 0.50

43 0.32 ● 0.23

44 0.63 ● 0.613

45 0.498 ● 0.4

46 9.35 ● 9.53

47 0.479 ● 0.5

48 8.0 ● 0.8

49 8.78 ● 8.8

50 0.71 ● 0.7

51 0.06 ● 0.59

52 3.28 ● 2.34

53 0.42 ● 0.419

54 0.5 ● 0.62

55 0.2 ● 0.195

Estimating with Fractions

Not all amounts can be expressed as a whole number. In this lesson you will use **fractions** and **mixed numbers** to make estimates.

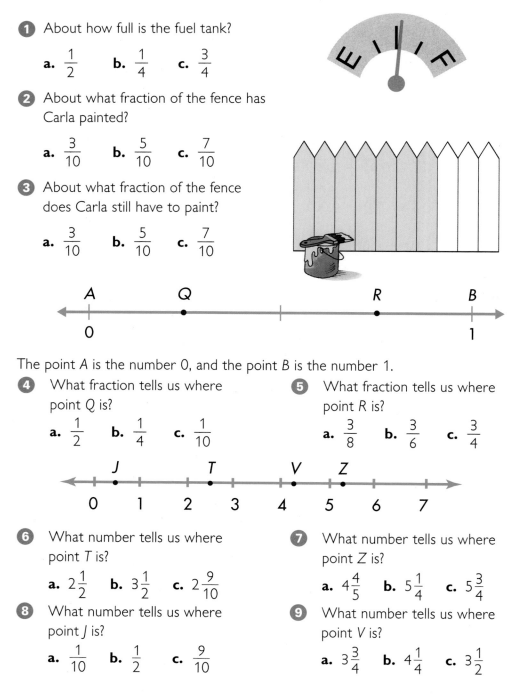

1 About how full is the fuel tank?

   a. $\frac{1}{2}$ **b.** $\frac{1}{4}$ **c.** $\frac{3}{4}$

2 About what fraction of the fence has Carla painted?

   a. $\frac{3}{10}$ **b.** $\frac{5}{10}$ **c.** $\frac{7}{10}$

3 About what fraction of the fence does Carla still have to paint?

   a. $\frac{3}{10}$ **b.** $\frac{5}{10}$ **c.** $\frac{7}{10}$

The point A is the number 0, and the point B is the number 1.

4 What fraction tells us where point Q is?

   a. $\frac{1}{2}$ **b.** $\frac{1}{4}$ **c.** $\frac{1}{10}$

5 What fraction tells us where point R is?

   a. $\frac{3}{8}$ **b.** $\frac{3}{6}$ **c.** $\frac{3}{4}$

6 What number tells us where point T is?

   a. $2\frac{1}{2}$ **b.** $3\frac{1}{2}$ **c.** $2\frac{9}{10}$

7 What number tells us where point Z is?

   a. $4\frac{4}{5}$ **b.** $5\frac{1}{4}$ **c.** $5\frac{3}{4}$

8 What number tells us where point J is?

   a. $\frac{1}{10}$ **b.** $\frac{1}{2}$ **c.** $\frac{9}{10}$

9 What number tells us where point V is?

   a. $3\frac{3}{4}$ **b.** $4\frac{1}{4}$ **c.** $3\frac{1}{2}$

Solve these problems.

10 A concert will last two hours. Can the entire concert be recorded on an audiotape that plays $\frac{3}{4}$ of an hour on each side?

11 Ms. Dimitrov was driving from Sayville to Oceanside. She drove about $\frac{1}{3}$ of the way in one hour and used 10 liters of gasoline.

   a. At that speed about how long will the trip take?

   b. About how much gasoline will she use on the entire trip?

12 About $\frac{3}{10}$ of Earth's surface is land. About what fraction is water?

13 Arturo sleeps about eight hours each day.

   a. About what fraction of the day is that?

   b. About what fraction of a week does Arturo sleep?

   c. About what fraction of a year does Arturo sleep?

   d. About what fraction of a year is Arturo awake?

14 There are 29 people in Chitra's class. Eighteen voted to have their class party on Tuesday, and the rest voted for Wednesday. Did the majority vote for Tuesday?

15 A portable tape player that usually sells for $40 is on sale for $27.95. Is that more than $\frac{1}{4}$ off the regular price?

16 What is the sale price of the headphones?

17 Sarah invited 15 people to a party, and 12 people came to it. Did over $\frac{2}{3}$ of the people she invited attend the party?

SALE
Regularly $30
NOW
1/3 off

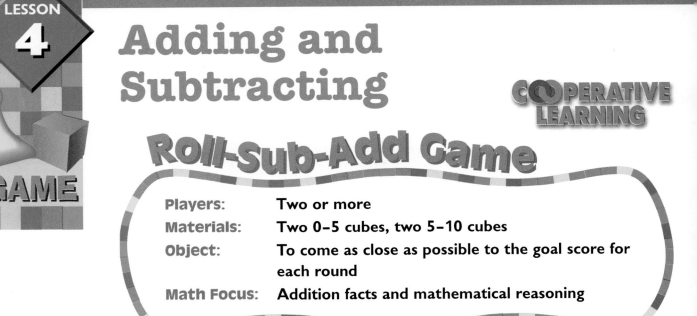

LESSON 4

GAME

Adding and Subtracting

Roll-Sub-Add Game

COOPERATIVE LEARNING

Players:	Two or more
Materials:	Two 0–5 cubes, two 5–10 cubes
Object:	To come as close as possible to the goal score for each round
Math Focus:	Addition facts and mathematical reasoning

RULES

1. The first player rolls all the cubes and makes a score as close to 0 as possible. To do this, he or she may add, subtract, or both. The player uses the number on each cube once and only once. Two or three cubes may be put together to make a multidigit number.

2. Other players take turns following the same procedure.

3. The player whose score is closest to 0 is the winner of the round.

4. For the second round the goal is changed to 1, but the rules remain the same. The goal is increased by 1 for each new round.

5. The game ends when the goal of 10 (or some other agreed-upon number) has been reached or when time has run out.

SAMPLE GAME

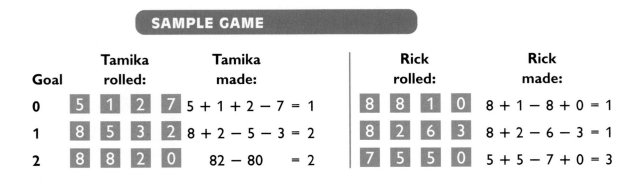

Goal	Tamika rolled:	Tamika made:		Rick rolled:	Rick made:
0	5 1 2 7	$5 + 1 + 2 - 7 = 1$		8 8 1 0	$8 + 1 - 8 + 0 = 1$
1	8 5 3 2	$8 + 2 - 5 - 3 = 2$		8 2 6 3	$8 + 2 - 6 - 3 = 1$
2	8 8 2 0	$82 - 80 = 2$		7 5 5 0	$5 + 5 - 7 + 0 = 3$

Solve for *n*. Watch the signs.

1 $7 + 8 = n$ **2** $n = 2 + 7$ **3** $7 + 7 = n$ **4** $n = 6 + 5$

5 $13 - 4 = n$ **6** $n = 17 - 7$ **7** $n = 8 + 9$ **8** $12 - 8 = n$

9 $8 + 5 = n$ **10** $n = 16 - 9$ **11** $n = 15 - 6$ **12** $4 + 7 = n$

13 $10 + 10 = n$ **14** $n = 7 + 5$ **15** $15 - 5 = n$ **16** $n = 7 + 6$

17 $15 - 9 = n$ **18** $n = 6 + 6$ **19** $n = 9 + 7$ **20** $n = 10 - 3$

21 $2 + 8 = n$ **22** $n = 15 - 8$ **23** $n = 14 - 8$ **24** $n = 12 - 9$

25 $13 - 7 = n$ **26** $n = 14 - 7$ **27** $12 - 4 = n$ **28** $6 + 4 = n$

29 $18 - 9 = n$ **30** $n = 13 - 8$ **31** $9 + 6 = n$ **32** $11 - 7 = n$

33 $10 + 6 = n$ **34** $n = 9 + 9$ **35** $11 - 8 = n$ **36** $n = 10 + 9$

37 $8 + 8 = n$ **38** $n = 4 + 4$ **39** $n = 5 + 9$ **40** $11 - 2 = n$

Add or subtract. Watch the signs.

41 $\begin{array}{r} 5 \\ + 5 \\ \hline \end{array}$ **42** $\begin{array}{r} 4 \\ + 9 \\ \hline \end{array}$ **43** $\begin{array}{r} 18 \\ - 8 \\ \hline \end{array}$ **44** $\begin{array}{r} 17 \\ - 9 \\ \hline \end{array}$ **45** $\begin{array}{r} 2 \\ + 9 \\ \hline \end{array}$

46 $\begin{array}{r} 16 \\ - 8 \\ \hline \end{array}$ **47** $\begin{array}{r} 9 \\ + 3 \\ \hline \end{array}$ **48** $\begin{array}{r} 17 \\ - 8 \\ \hline \end{array}$

49 $\begin{array}{r} 16 \\ - 6 \\ \hline \end{array}$ **50** $\begin{array}{r} 16 \\ - 7 \\ \hline \end{array}$ **51** $\begin{array}{r} 15 \\ - 7 \\ \hline \end{array}$

52 $\begin{array}{r} 8 \\ + 4 \\ \hline \end{array}$ **53** $\begin{array}{r} 14 \\ - 5 \\ \hline \end{array}$ **54** $\begin{array}{r} 16 \\ - 10 \\ \hline \end{array}$

55 $\begin{array}{r} 14 \\ - 9 \\ \hline \end{array}$ **56** $\begin{array}{r} 13 \\ - 9 \\ \hline \end{array}$ **57** $\begin{array}{r} 12 \\ - 5 \\ \hline \end{array}$

58 $\begin{array}{r} 6 \\ + 8 \\ \hline \end{array}$ **59** $\begin{array}{r} 3 \\ + 8 \\ \hline \end{array}$ **60** $\begin{array}{r} 11 \\ - 6 \\ \hline \end{array}$

SELF ASSESSMENT

Are You Shiny or Rusty?

On this page did you get

Very shiny	54 or more right
Shiny	48–53 right
A bit rusty	42–47 right
Rusty	Fewer than 42 right

Keep in shape by practicing your number facts for addition and subtraction.

LESSON 5

GAME

Multiplying and Dividing

COOPERATIVE LEARNING

Multifact Game

Players:	**Two or more**
Materials:	**Two 0–5 cubes, two 5–10 cubes**
Object:	**To make a score that is closest to 25**
Math Focus:	**Multiplication facts, multidigit addition and subtraction, and mental arithmetic**

RULES

1. Take turns rolling all four cubes. Make two multiplication problems from any of the numbers rolled. Each number may be used once in each problem. For example, if you roll 7, 2, 3 and 5, you could make 7 × 2 and 3 × 2, but you could not make 3 × 3.

2. Find the products of both problems, and add or subtract them to get your score for the round.

3. The player whose score is closest to 25 wins the round.

SAMPLE GAME

Juan rolled:

Juan made:
3 × 7 and 3 × 2
He added the products.
His score was 27.

Emily won this round.

Sam rolled:

Sam made:
4 × 6 and 6 × 8
He subtracted the products.
His score was 24.

Emily rolled:

Emily made:
5 × 5 and 9 × 0
She added the products.
Her score was 25.

Solve for *n*. Watch the signs.

1 $56 \div 7 = n$ **2** $n = 5 \times 5$ **3** $n = 7 \times 7$

4 $6 \times 8 = n$ **5** $n = 9 \times 4$ **6** $8 \times 9 = n$

7 $8 \times 4 = n$ **8** $n = 80 \div 8$ **9** $n = 54 \div 6$

10 $45 \div 5 = n$ **11** $n = 72 \div 9$ **12** $50 \div 5 = n$

13 $60 \div 6 = n$ **14** $n = 64 \div 8$ **15** $9 \times 7 = n$

16 $3 \times 8 = n$ **17** $n = 9 \times 3$ **18** $n = 48 \div 8$

19 $45 \div 9 = n$ **20** $n = 72 \div 8$ **21** $32 \div 4 = n$

22 $36 \div 9 = n$ **23** $n = 2 \times 9$ **24** $n = 9 \times 6$

25 $35 \div 5 = n$ **26** $n = 60 \div 10$ **27** $24 \div 8 = n$

28 $30 \div 6 = n$ **29** $n = 63 \div 7$ **30** $n = 5 \times 9$

Multiply or divide. Watch the signs.

31 $\begin{array}{r} 2 \\ \times\ 7 \\ \hline \end{array}$ **32** $7\overline{)70}$ **33** $9\overline{)63}$ **34** $\begin{array}{r} 7 \\ \times\ 5 \\ \hline \end{array}$ **35** $\begin{array}{r} 6 \\ \times\ 6 \\ \hline \end{array}$

36 $8\overline{)56}$ **37** $7\overline{)49}$ **38** $8\overline{)40}$ **39** $\begin{array}{r} 7 \\ \times\ 8 \\ \hline \end{array}$ **40** $4\overline{)36}$

41 $\begin{array}{r} 8 \\ \times\ 5 \\ \hline \end{array}$ **42** $\begin{array}{r} 10 \\ \times\ 10 \\ \hline \end{array}$

43 $9\overline{)54}$ **44** $\begin{array}{r} 8 \\ \times\ 2 \\ \hline \end{array}$

SELF ASSESSMENT

Are You Shiny or Rusty?

On this page did you get

Very shiny   44 or more right

Shiny   39–43 right

A bit rusty   34–38 right

Rusty   Fewer than 34 right

Keep in shape by practicing your number facts.

45 $7\overline{)42}$ **46** $9\overline{)81}$

47 $\begin{array}{r} 10 \\ \times\ 6 \\ \hline \end{array}$ **48** $\begin{array}{r} 8 \\ \times\ 8 \\ \hline \end{array}$

LESSON

6

GAME

Applying Basic Facts

Cubo

COOPERATIVE LEARNING

Players:	Two or more
Materials:	Two 0–5 cubes, two 5–10 cubes
Object:	To score as close to 21 as possible
Math Focus:	Mental arithmetic with all four operations

RULES

1. Roll all four cubes on each turn.

2. Use any combination of the four operations (addition, subtraction, multiplication, and division) on the numbers rolled to make a number as close to 21 as possible. Use the number on each cube once and only once. (If two cubes have the same number, you must use both.)

If you rolled:	You could make these scores:	By doing these operations, for example:
3	19	$6 - 3 = 3$; $3 \times 6 = 18$; $18 + 1 = 19$
6	23	$3 \times 6 = 18$; $18 + 6 = 24$; $24 - 1 = 23$
6	21	$6 - 1 = 5$; $5 \times 3 = 15$; $15 + 6 = 21$
1	21	$6 - 3 = 3$; $6 + 1 = 7$; $3 \times 7 = 21$

3. The player who scores 21 or closest to it is the winner of the round.

OTHER WAYS TO PLAY THIS GAME

1. Make the goal a number other than 21.

2. Use more or fewer than four cubes.

3. Choose a set of numbers (0 to 10, 10 to 20, and so on), and try to make all the scores in the set. (It may not be possible to make every score.)

Solve for *n*. Watch the signs.

1. $7 \times 8 = n$
2. $n = 17 - 8$
3. $14 - 6 = n$
4. $7 + 8 = n$
5. $n = 36 \div 9$
6. $7 + 7 = n$
7. $49 \div 7 = n$
8. $n = 15 - 9$
9. $4 \times 6 = n$
10. $16 - 7 = n$
11. $n = 5 + 4$
12. $n = 12 - 5$
13. $4 + 9 = n$
14. $4 \times 8 = n$
15. $10 - 4 = n$
16. $7 \times 9 = n$
17. $0 + 7 = n$
18. $n = 3 + 8$
19. $7 \times 6 = n$
20. $n = 0 \times 8$
21. $18 - 9 = n$
22. $5 + 9 = n$
23. $7 - 0 = n$
24. $n = 8 \times 8$
25. $10 + 8 = n$
26. $n = 0 \div 8$
27. $15 - 9 = n$
28. $9 + 8 = n$
29. $8 \times 3 = n$
30. $15 \div 3 = n$
31. $n = 48 \div 8$
32. $n = 9 + 7$
33. $4 + 8 = n$
34. $n = 81 \div 9$
35. $n = 35 \div 7$
36. $n = 12 - 6$
37. $n = 6 \times 6$
38. $12 - 9 = n$
39. $n = 30 \div 6$

40. $n = 19 - 10$
41. $45 \div 9 = n$
42. $n = 8 \times 9$
43. $n = 12 - 8$
44. $n = 54 \div 6$
45. $n = 6 + 7$
46. $8 \times 5 = n$
47. $9 - 3 = n$
48. $5 \times 5 = n$
49. $n = 5 + 5$
50. $8 + 8 = n$

SELF ASSESSMENT

Are You Shiny or Rusty?

Very shiny   45 or more right
Shiny   40–44 right
A bit rusty   35–39 right
Rusty   Less than 35 right

Keep in shape by practicing your number facts for addition, subtraction, multiplication, and division.

Mental Arithmetic

You've learned about place value and have practiced your number facts. In this lesson you'll put it all together to solve problems mentally.

Solve for the variable. Do the problems in your head. Then write the answers.

1 $4 \times 4 = n$ **2** $40 \times 4 = n$ **3** $3 + 9 = x$

4 $30 + 90 = n$ **5** $30 + 95 = y$ **6** $6 \div 3 = x$

7 $60 \div 3 = n$ **8** $600 \div 3 = r$ **9** $10 \times 10 = m$

10 $10 \times 100 = n$ **11** $8 + 7 = x$ **12** $8 \times 7 = n$

13 $80 \times 7 = y$ **14** $100 - 20 = r$ **15** $100 - 25 = n$

16 $37 + 10 = n$ **17** $37 + 100 = m$ **18** $3700 + 1000 = t$

19 $3700 + 100 = n$ **20** $3700 + 10 = z$ **21** $16 - 9 = n$

22 $16 - 10 = y$ **23** $16 - 11 = x$ **24** $16 - 12 = r$

25 $160 - 120 = t$ **26** $160 - 115 = n$ **27** $16 \times 10 = m$

28 $16 \times 5 = s$ **29** $16 \times 2 = n$ **30** $16 \times 1 = y$

Solve these problems.

31 Anna wants to purchase a bicycle that costs $139.95. If she can save $2.50 per week, how many weeks will it take to save enough money?

32 A theater has 5000 seats. There are two performances a day, and about $\frac{1}{2}$ of the seats are used at each performance. About how much money would the theater collect each day if tickets cost

   a. $2 each?

   b. $3 each?

   c. $2.50 each?

State	Area (square kilometers)
Montana	376,991
Massachusetts	20,300
Missouri	178,446
Ohio	106,067

GEOGRAPHY CONNECTION

Arizona is the state directly west of New Mexico. It looks to be about $\frac{3}{4}$ or $\frac{4}{5}$ the size of Montana. Since the area of Montana is 376,991 km², you could estimate the area of Arizona to be about 300,000 km².

Use the map and the chart to estimate the area in square kilometers of the following states. In each problem four areas are given in square kilometers, but only one is correct. Choose the correct area.

33 New Mexico   **a.** 150,289   **b.** 314,334   **c.** 105,321   **d.** 567,402

34 Georgia   **a.** 150,010   **b.** 472,809   **c.** 210,450   **d.** 102,946

35 Pennsylvania   **a.** 46,315   **b.** 256,947   **c.** 116,083   **d.** 437,231

36 Oklahoma   **a.** 392,025   **b.** 53,702   **c.** 108,257   **d.** 177,877

37 Texas   **a.** 45,327   **b.** 678,358   **c.** 392,621   **d.** 192,849

38 Connecticut   **a.** 12,550   **b.** 194,327   **c.** 56,240   **d.** 376,294

◆ **LESSON 7 Mental Arithmetic**

Mr. Muddle's Extra-Large Problems

Part 1

"How is your T-shirt business doing?" Manolita asked. "Not too well," said Mr. Muddle. "People like my T-shirts, but often they don't buy any. They say they can't find any that fit."

Willy looked through the piles of T-shirts neatly stacked on the counter.

"No wonder," Willy said. "You have a few medium T-shirts, and all the rest are small. You need some large and extra-large sizes. That's what most people buy."

"Something must be wrong," said Mr. Muddle. "The company is supposed to send me the same number of every size."

Mr. Muddle opened a box that had just come. Sure enough, it held 36 small, 36 medium, 36 large, and 36 extra-large T-shirts.

"Maybe you should order more of some sizes than others," Marcus said. "I have an idea. For the next week ask all the customers who come in what sizes they want. Write down what they tell you."

Mr. Muddle did just that. Here is the record he showed Marcus the next week:

Tuesday	Ⓧ Ⓧ Ⓛ Ⓛ L M Ⓧ Ⓧ Ⓧ Ⓜ S Ⓛ Ⓧ XL Ⓛ Ⓢ Ⓧ XL Ⓛ L Ⓜ Ⓜ XL Ⓛ Ⓢ L XL Ⓧ Ⓜ Ⓧ Ⓛ L Ⓛ
Wednesday	Ⓧ L L Ⓧ XL Ⓧ Ⓧ Ⓢ Ⓛ Ⓧ Ⓛ M Ⓜ Ⓛ Ⓛ Ⓢ Ⓜ L Ⓛ Ⓜ XL Ⓛ Ⓧ M XL Ⓜ Ⓛ S Ⓛ Ⓧ Ⓧ
Thursday	L Ⓧ Ⓛ Ⓧ L Ⓧ L Ⓜ Ⓧ Ⓛ Ⓧ Ⓜ Ⓛ XL Ⓛ Ⓛ Ⓢ L Ⓧ Ⓛ S L Ⓜ Ⓛ Ⓧ L Ⓜ Ⓛ XL Ⓜ Ⓛ Ⓧ M
Friday	Ⓢ L Ⓧ Ⓛ XL Ⓧ XL Ⓛ Ⓢ L Ⓛ Ⓧ M Ⓛ Ⓜ L Ⓧ Ⓜ Ⓛ L Ⓛ M Ⓧ Ⓛ Ⓛ Ⓜ Ⓧ S Ⓛ M Ⓧ L Ⓜ L Ⓛ Ⓧ Ⓧ XL Ⓢ
Saturday	L Ⓧ XL Ⓧ L Ⓢ L XL XL L Ⓜ L XL XL Ⓜ L Ⓛ L XL M L Ⓢ L Ⓜ XL XL L Ⓜ L S M XL XL Ⓢ L XL L Ⓜ XL XL XL XL Ⓜ M XL L Ⓢ L Ⓜ L XL L Ⓜ L Ⓜ L XL XL XL L Ⓢ L Ⓜ L XL XL XL L XL XL
Monday	Ⓢ XL XL L L XL M Ⓜ L XL XL L XL XL Ⓜ XL XL XL L Ⓢ L L Ⓜ L L Ⓜ L L

"What are the circles for?" Manolita asked.

"They mark my star customers," Mr. Muddle answered. "Each one of them bought a T-shirt."

. . . to be continued

Work in groups. Discuss how you figured out your answers. Compare them with other groups.

1 If each new box holds the same number of each size, how could Mr. Muddle end up with only small and medium T-shirts?

2 Figure out from Mr. Muddle's record how many people wanted each size of T-shirt. How many T-shirts of each size did he sell that week?

3 What do you think of Mr. Muddle's way of keeping a record? Show a better way to do it.

4 Look at the record of T-shirts sold on Saturday and Monday. How are those days different from the other days? How could you explain this difference?

5 How many large and extra-large T-shirts could Mr. Muddle have sold that week if he had had enough for everyone who wanted one?

LESSON 8

Multidigit Addition

For a popular concert, 83,576 tickets were sold on the first day. On the second day 19,806 tickets were sold. How many tickets were sold? To find out, find the **sum** of 83,576 and 19,806.

$$83{,}576 + 19{,}806 = ?$$

Remember:

83,576 + 19,806	Line up corresponding digits.
1 83,576 + 19,806 2	Add the digits in the ones place. $6 + 6 = 12$ Write 2. "Carry" 1.
1 83,576 + 19,806 82	Add the next column. $1 + 7 + 0 = 8$ Write 8.
1 1 83,576 + 19,806 382	Add the next column. $5 + 8 = 13$ Write 3. Carry 1.
11 1 83,576 + 19,806 3,382	Add the next column. $1 + 3 + 9 = 13$ Write 3. Carry 1.
11 1 83,576 + 19,806 103,382	Add the next column. $1 + 8 + 1 = 10$ Write 10. There were 103,382 tickets sold.

Add. Use shortcuts when you can.

1   86
     + 86

2   75
     + 98

3   46
     + 53

4   207
     + 359

5   617
     + 849

6   86
     + 731

7   500
     + 700

8   406
     + 79

9   342
     + 658

10 305
     + 609

11 2346
     + 7654

12 346
     + 235

13 5000
     + 2476

14 4962
     +   1

15 8219
     +   1

16 5999
     +   1

17 99,999
     +   1

18 99,999
     +   2

19 60
     + 20

20 80
     + 70

21 800
     + 700

22 8000
     + 7000

23 493
     +   7

24 493
     + 507

25 1493
     + 3507

Solve these problems.

26 Lin's family went on vacation for 21 days near Cape Canaveral, Florida. When they got back, Lin gave Fred five NASA postcards for his postcard collection. How many postcards does Fred have now?

27 Lin's family began their vacation on June 25. What was the last day of their vacation?

28 Lin had 98 seashells in her collection. During her vacation she found 14 shells on the beach. How many shells does she have now?

◆ LESSON 8 Multidigit Addition

$356 + 829 + 54 = ?$

There are many ways to add more than two numbers.

One way is to add the numbers in pairs.

$$\begin{array}{r} 356 \\ +\ 829 \\ \hline 1185 \end{array}$$ Add one pair.

$$\begin{array}{r} 1185 \\ +\ \ \ 54 \\ \hline 1239 \end{array}$$ Then add the other number to that sum.

It's not necessary to add the numbers in order. For example, to add $999 + 667 + 1$, first add $999 + 1$ to get 1000. Then it's easy to add $667 + 1000$ to get 1667.

Another way is to add the numbers in a column.

$$\begin{array}{r} 1 \\ 356 \\ 829 \\ +\ \ 54 \\ \hline 9 \end{array} \longrightarrow \begin{array}{r} 11 \\ 356 \\ 829 \\ +\ \ 54 \\ \hline 39 \end{array} \longrightarrow \begin{array}{r} 11 \\ 356 \\ 829 \\ +\ \ 54 \\ \hline 1239 \end{array}$$

The second method is usually faster.

Add. How many can you do without using paper and pencil?

29. $42 + 57 + 64 = \blacksquare$

30. $250 + 250 + 250 + 250 = \blacksquare$

31. $843 + 71 + 64 = \blacksquare$

32. $9473 + 8597 + 6492 + 2179 = \blacksquare$

33. $4000 + 5000 + 7000 = \blacksquare$

34. $150 + 250 + 150 + 250 = \blacksquare$

35. $123 + 456 + 789 = \blacksquare$

36. $29 + 39 + 50 = \blacksquare$

37. $25 + 25 + 25 + 25 = \blacksquare$

38. $999 + 999 + 999 = \blacksquare$

39. $9999 + 9999 + 9999 = \blacksquare$

40. $1001 + 1002 + 999 + 998 = \blacksquare$

41. $480 + 310 + 612 = \blacksquare$

42. $528 + 63 + 816 = \blacksquare$

43. $375 + 400 + 125 = \blacksquare$

44. $705 + 208 + 413 = \blacksquare$

Add. How many can you do without using paper and pencil?

45	46	47	48	49
750	979	300	55	402
750	365	300	55	508
750	489	350	+ 55	311
+ 750	685	+ 5		+ 203
	+ 944			

50	51	52	53	54
777	625	473	722	391
888	450	695	278	523
+ 999	175	+ 829	410	+ 754
	+ 250		+ 306	

PROBLEM SOLVING

Solve these problems.

55 Chan, Rachel, and Jody collect postcards. Jody has 80. So does Rachel. Chan has 42. How many do they have all together?

56 Lauren, Kim, and Brandon also collect postcards. Lauren has 15 more than Kim, who has 23 more than Brandon. Brandon has 56. How many do they have all together?

57 The Blue Flags played three home games last week. On Monday about 3000 people were at the game. On Wednesday about 5000 people watched them play. About 11,000 people were at Saturday's game. About how many tickets were sold for the games last week?

58 For their next home game the Blue Flags have sold about 4500 regularly priced tickets, about 1200 student tickets, and about 1500 senior citizen tickets. About how many tickets have been sold?

Multidigit Subtraction

For a new magazine the publisher printed 50,026 copies. Of those, 39,478 were sold. How many were not sold? To find out, subtract 39,478 from 50,026.

$$50,026 - 39,478 = ?$$

Remember:

$$\begin{array}{r} \mathbf{50,026} \\ -\ \mathbf{39,478} \end{array}$$	Line up the corresponding digits. Subtract the digits in the ones place. It is not possible, because 6 is less than 8. Look for the next nonzero digit in the **minuend.** It's the 2. Remember, the minuend is the number from which another number is subtracted.
$$\begin{array}{r} {}^{1\ 16} \\ \mathbf{50,02\!\!\!/6} \\ -\ \mathbf{39,478} \end{array}$$	Regroup the 2 tens and 6 to make 1 ten and 16.
$$\begin{array}{r} {}^{1\ 16} \\ \mathbf{50,02\!\!\!/6} \\ -\mathbf{39,478} \\ \hline 8 \end{array}$$	Now subtract the ones. $16 - 8 = 8$ Write 8.
$$\begin{array}{r} {}^{1\ 16} \\ \mathbf{50,02\!\!\!/6} \\ -\ \mathbf{39,478} \\ \hline 8 \end{array}$$	Subtract the tens. It is not possible, because 1 is less than 7. Look for the next nonzero digit in the minuend. It's the 5.
$$\begin{array}{r} {}^{\ \ \ \ 11} \\ {}^{4\ 9\ 9\ 1\ 16} \\ \cancel{\mathbf{50,02\!\!\!/6}} \\ -\ \mathbf{39,478} \\ \hline 8 \end{array}$$	Regroup the 500 hundreds and 1 ten to make 499 hundreds and 11 tens.
$$\begin{array}{r} {}^{\ \ \ \ 11} \\ {}^{4\ 9\ 9\ 1\ 16} \\ \cancel{\mathbf{50,026}} \\ -\ \mathbf{39,478} \\ \hline 10,548 \end{array}$$	Now finish the subtraction. There were 10,548 unsold copies.

Subtract. Use shortcuts when you can.

① 94 − 37	② 68 − 43	③ 127 − 85	④ 249 − 37	⑤ 645 − 79
⑥ 63 − 62	⑦ 100 − 1	⑧ 800 −300	⑨ 432 −431	⑩ 703 −504
⑪ 1000 −999	⑫ 1600 −700	⑬ 1800 −500	⑭ 1800 −501	⑮ 1800 −510
⑯ 407 −349	⑰ 506 −247	⑱ 3007 −1248	⑲ 1000 − 1	⑳ 4091 −1095
㉑ 1000 − 2	㉒ 100 − 3	㉓ 18,000 −7,000	㉔ 500 −400	㉕ 2400 −900
㉖ 63 − 37	㉗ 630 −370	㉘ 6300 −3700	㉙ 63,000 −37,000	㉚ 63,005 −37,005

Solve these problems.

㉛ The world's highest mountain is Mount Everest, 8848 meters above sea level. The highest mountain in North America is Mount McKinley, 6194 meters above sea level.

    a. How much higher than Mount McKinley is Mount Everest?

    b. How far apart are the two mountains?

㉜ The lowest point on Earth is the Dead Sea, 397 meters below sea level. The lowest point in North America is Death Valley, 86 meters below sea level. How much lower is the Dead Sea than Death Valley?

◆ LESSON 9   Multidigit Subtraction

Solve these problems. Use shortcuts when you can.

33 386 +249	**34** 548 −267	**35** 4705 +3846	**36** 4705 −3846	**37** 2783 +4596
38 10,000 +3,507	**39** 10,000 −3,507	**40** 4567 −3456	**41** 4567 +3456	**42** 750 −250
43 750 +250	**44** 1000 −250	**45** 1000 − 1	**46** 6450 +3275	**47** 3450 +6275
48 10,000 −2,500	**49** 638 −495	**50** 208 −129	**51** 3003 − 4	**52** 897 + 6
53 375 625 + 100	**54** 4050 3720 1000 +8975	**55** 50 50 25 + 25	**56** 6297 3426 9351 +7644	**57** 453 2974 5190 + 68

Solve these problems.

58 Angelo lives 15 kilometers from the city of Sioux Falls. Janine lives 10 kilometers from Sioux Falls.

  a. Who lives farther from Sioux Falls?

  b. How much farther?

  c. How far apart do Angelo and Janine live?

59 Anya lives 6 miles from her friend Douglas and 4 miles from her friend Tarrah.

  a. What is the farthest distance apart Douglas and Tarrah could live?

  b. What is the closest Douglas and Tarrah could live?

60 Mr. Warren has seven cats, five dogs, and about 100 chickens on his farm. How many eggs do the chickens lay each day?

Solve these problems.

Ms. Arbuncle wants to buy a car. She has checked the prices of three used cars. The Hubmobile sells for $7843, the Folkwagon sells for $8209, and the Ritzwheel sells for $9078. But Ms. Arbuncle also wants to purchase insurance, which will cost $2053 for the Hubmobile, $1704 for the Folkwagon, and $1577 for the Ritzwheel.

61 How much will she have to pay to buy the Hubmobile with the insurance she wants?

62 How much will she have to pay for the Folkwagon with the insurance she wants?

63 How much will she have to pay for the Ritzwheel with the insurance she wants?

64 Ms. Arbuncle has $10,000 to spend on a car and insurance. Are there any of the cars she cannot afford to buy with the insurance she wants? If so, which can she not afford to buy?

65 For those cars she can afford, how much money will Ms. Arbuncle have left after she pays for the car and insurance?

LESSON 10 Addition and Subtraction Applications

Road atlases provide the highway distances between places on a map. Travelers can use this information to plan their trips.

This map shows driving distances in miles between selected cities in the United States.

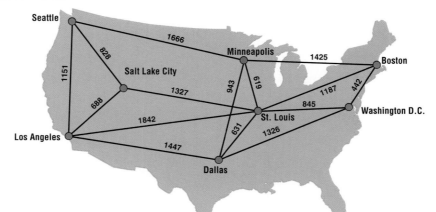

GEOGRAPHY CONNECTION

Use the map to answer these questions.

1 How many miles is it from Los Angeles to Salt Lake City?

2 How many miles is it from Los Angeles to St. Louis if you go through Salt Lake City?

3 How many miles is it from Los Angeles to St. Louis if you go through Dallas?

4 If you were going from Dallas to Washington, D.C., how much farther would it be to go through St. Louis?

5 If you were going from Dallas to Minneapolis, how much farther would it be to go through St. Louis?

6 Suppose you were going from Dallas to Boston and you wanted to visit St. Louis and Washington, D.C.

    a. Would it be shorter to visit St. Louis first or Washington, D.C., first?

    b. How many miles shorter?

7 How many miles is a round trip from Seattle to Los Angeles and back to Seattle?

8 Which round trip is shorter:

  a. Minneapolis–Dallas–St. Louis–Minneapolis?

  b. Minneapolis–St. Louis–Dallas–Minneapolis?

9 Put the following trips in order from shortest to longest:

  a. Dallas–Minneapolis–Boston

  b. Dallas–St. Louis–Boston

  c. Dallas–Washington, D.C.–Boston

10 Put the following trips in order from shortest to longest:

  a. Los Angeles–Seattle–Minneapolis

  b. Los Angeles–Salt Lake City–St. Louis–Minneapolis

  c. Los Angeles–Dallas–St. Louis–Minneapolis

11 How many miles long is the shortest path from Los Angeles to Washington, D.C., as shown on the map?

12 How many miles long is the shortest path from Seattle to Dallas shown on the map? Do you think this is the shortest possible path between Seattle and Dallas?

13 Suppose you were going from Seattle to St. Louis.

  a. Would it be shorter to go through Minneapolis or Salt Lake City?

  b. How much shorter?

Challenge: Plan a trip that is less than 3000 miles and includes as many of the cities on the map as possible. The trip can start in any city and end in any city (not necessarily the one in which you start). Compare your answer with others in the class.

Superchallenge: (Use a calculator to help you with this problem, but think and plan before you calculate.) Plan a trip that lets you visit all eight cities on the map. The total distance should be as short as you can make it. You need not return to the original city.

◆ LESSON 10 Addition and Subtraction Applications

Texas Distances	
From/To	**Miles**
Austin–Dallas	195
Dallas–Houston	246
Houston–Austin	186
Houston–El Paso	769

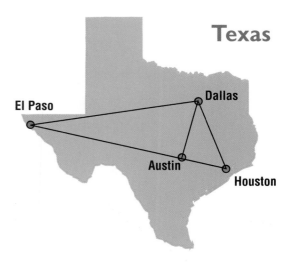

Texas

Solve these problems using the table and the map above.

14 How far would you travel if you drove from Austin to Dallas to Houston and then back to Austin?

15 You take the trip described in problem 14. If you drive at an average speed of 50 miles per hour, about how many hours would you spend driving?

16 If during your trip from Austin you had a meeting in Dallas that lasted for three hours and a dinner in Houston that lasted for two hours, about how long would the entire trip take?

17 If you left Austin at 5:00 A.M., about what time would you get back to Austin?

18 How long is the drive from El Paso to Houston and back?

19 If you drove 50 miles per hour from El Paso to Houston and back, about how many hours would you spend driving? Assuming you drive ten hours each day, how many days would that be?

20 You are planning to drive from Dallas to Houston. You expect your average speed will be 50 miles an hour and that you will make a 30-minute stop for lunch. What is the latest you could leave to be in Houston by 2:00 P.M.?

GAME

C○○PERATIVE LEARNING

Players:	**Two or more**
Materials:	**Two 0–5 cubes, two 5–10 cubes**
Object:	**To get the sum closest to but not over 1000**
Math Focus:	**Place value, multidigit addition, and mathematical reasoning**

RULES

1. Roll all four cubes. If you roll a 10, roll that cube again.

2. Combine three of the numbers rolled to make a three-digit number.

3. Roll all four cubes again. Make a second three-digit number and add it to your first number.

4. You may stop after your second roll, or you may make another three-digit number and add it to your previous sum. You may roll and add as many times as you want.

5. The player whose sum is closest to but not over 1000 is the winner.

SAMPLE GAME

Anita rolled:

5	3	4	6

3	6	7	2

Anita wrote:

$$643$$
$$+\ 327$$
$$970$$

Anita stopped.

Miguel rolled:

0	5	9	1

3	7	7	1

8	2	3	9

Miguel wrote:

$$519$$
$$+\ 137$$
$$656$$
$$+329$$
$$985$$

Miguel stopped after his third roll.

Miguel was the winner.

MATH JOURNAL

Can you describe how you played this game? Write your strategies in your Math Journal.

Powers and Multiples of 10

Because our number system is based on 10, there are many shortcuts for working with powers of 10. In this lesson you'll learn a quick way to multiply by a power or a multiple of 10.

$26 \times 1000 = ?$

Remember:

26×1000	Count the 0s in the power of 10. A power is the product of the multiplication of a number by itself. $1000 = 10 \times 10 \times 10$. It is the third power of 10. There are three 0s.
26	Write the number being multiplied: 26.
26,000	Write three 0s to the right of 26.

Multiply.

1. 3×10
2. 3×100
3. 45×100
4. 45×1000

5. 1000×78
6. 10×78
7. 100×5
8. $10,000 \times 5$

9. 989×10
10. 100×989
11. 6789×10
12. 100×6789

13. 63×100
14. 63×1000
15. $10,000 \times 51$
16. 51×1000

$7 \times 800 = ?$

Remember:

7×800	Count the 0s in the multiple of 10. There are two 0s.
7×800	Multiply the nonzero digits. $7 \times 8 = 56$
56	Write 56.
5600	Write two 0s to the right of 56.

Multiply.

17. 9×60
18. 9×600
19. 7×700
20. 7×7000

21. 300×4
22. 3000×4
23. 40×6
24. 4000×6

25. 5×700
26. 70×5
27. 9×90
28. 9000×9

29. 20×8
30. 80×2
31. 8×200
32. 8000×2

36 • Whole Numbers and Integers

$90 \times 700 = ?$

Remember:

90×700	Count the 0s in both factors. There are three 0s.
90×700	Multiply the nonzero digits. $9 \times 7 = 63$
63	Write 63.
63,000	Write three 0s to the right of 63.

Be careful when the product of the nonzero digits has a 0.

80×50	There are two 0s.
40	8×5
4000	Write two 0s to the right of 40.

Multiply.

33. 40×20
34. 400×20
35. 30×400
36. 30×4000

37. 90×30
38. 90×3000
39. 10×100
40. 8×1000

41. 90×70
42. 100×63
43. 27×10
44. 70×700

45. 60×700
46. 20×50
47. 200×50
48. 60×600

49. 60×60
50. 80×90
51. 800×900
52. 4×500

53. 40×50
54. 90×60
55. 900×6
56. 100×100

57. 10×70
58. 100×11
59. 12×100
60. 60×4

61. 40×60
62. 600×40
63. 40×600
64. 500×80

65. 50×30
66. 8×7000
67. 50×1000
68. 60×800

Solve these problems.

69. There are about 50 books on each of the 20 shelves in the classroom. About how many books are on the shelves?

70. Will 1000 books in the school library fit onto 40 shelves that can hold up to 30 books each?

◆ **LESSON 11** Powers and Multiples of 10

THINKING STORY

Mr. Muddle's Extra-Large Problems

Part 2

You may want to refer to the earlier part of this Thinking Story on pages 22–23.

"I think we've solved your problem, Mr. Muddle," said Willy. "To have enough of every size, you should get about 60 extra-large, 60 large, 30 medium, and 15 small T-shirts each week."

"Oh, dear," said Mr. Muddle. "That's too many. There are 144 T-shirts in a box. To get what you say I need, I'd have to buy two boxes a week. I can't afford to do that every week. See how much they cost!"

Mr. Muddle showed his friends the price list.

Quality T-Shirts Price List (All prices subject to change.)		
Number of Boxes	Price	You Save
1	$576.00	
2	$1,120.00	$32.00
3	$1,670.00	$58.00
4	$2,200.00	$104.00

Each additional box, add $520.00. Above prices are for boxes with one shirt size. Add $30.00 per box for boxes with mixed size.

"It won't cost you more money to buy two boxes instead of one," said Manolita. "This price list says it will cost you $32 less."

. . . to be continued

Work in groups. Discuss your answers and how you figured them out. Then compare your answers with those of other groups.

① Is Manolita right in saying two boxes cost less than one box?

② If Mr. Muddle had enough money and enough storage space, what would be the cheapest way for him to buy T-shirts?

③ If Mr. Muddle can never afford to buy more than two boxes at a time, what would be a good way for him to order T-shirts? Will he need to order two boxes every week to have enough of every size?

④ How much money will Mr. Muddle save if he orders one box of a single size and one box of mixed sizes, instead of two boxes of mixed sizes?

Multidigit Multiplication

At every game of the seven-game home stand, the stadium was filled to capacity. Tickets were sold for all 47,826 seats. How many tickets were sold for the home stand? You can multiply to find out.

$7 \times 47,826 = ?$

Remember:

$$\begin{array}{r} 47,826 \\ \times\qquad 7 \\ \hline 2 \end{array}$$

$7 \times 6 = 42$
Write 2.
Remember the 4.

$$\begin{array}{r} 47,826 \\ \times\qquad 7 \\ \hline 82 \end{array}$$

$7 \times 2 = 14$
Add 4 and get 18.
Write 8. Remember the 1.

$$\begin{array}{r} 47,826 \\ \times\qquad 7 \\ \hline 782 \end{array}$$

$7 \times 8 = 56$
Add 1 and get 57.
Write 7. Remember the 5.

$$\begin{array}{r} 47,826 \\ \times\qquad 7 \\ \hline 4782 \end{array}$$

$7 \times 7 = 49$
Add 5 and get 54.
Write 4. Remember the 5.

$$\begin{array}{r} 47,826 \\ \times\qquad 7 \\ \hline 334,782 \end{array}$$

$7 \times 4 = 28$
Add 5 and get 33.
Write 33.

There were 334,782 tickets sold.

Check to be sure that your answer makes sense.
The answer should be more than $7 \times 40,000$, which is 280,000.
The answer should be less than $7 \times 50,000$, which is 350,000.
The number 334,782 is between 280,000 and 350,000.

Multiply. Check to be sure that your answers make sense.

1 73
× 5

2 56
× 8

3 83
× 7

4 59
× 9

5 47
× 4

6 41
× 6

7 609
× 6

8 753
× 4

9 821
× 8

10 537
× 7

11 987
× 1

12 430
× 3

13 700
× 5

14 5
× 700

15 400
× 9

16 60
× 8

17 8
× 60

18 500
× 9

19 40
× 80

20 90
× 60

21 600
× 80

22 70
× 9000

23 800
× 800

24 70
× 70

25 500
× 20

26 630
× 7

27 63
× 7

28 6300
× 70

29 6300
× 700

30 700
× 63

Solve these problems.

31 Sharifa has $35. She wants to treat five friends to a baseball game. Each ticket costs $4.95. Does she have enough money?

32 A school has 80 students and 14 adults going on a field trip. Can the students be put into 14 groups with no more than six students in each group?

33 A theater group is selling tickets to a play for $7 apiece. The theater can seat 200 people. If the show is a sell-out, how much money will the group collect?

◆ LESSON 12 Multidigit Multiplication

To multiply by a multiplier with more than one digit, follow the procedure as in the example on page 40. Put the ones digit of each **partial product** below the digit of the multiplier you are using.

$537 \times 47{,}826 = ?$

47,826 × 537 ─────── 334782	Multiply by the ones digit. Write this partial product (334,782) so that its ones digit (2) is in the ones column.
47,826 × 537 ─────── 334 782 1 434 78	Multiply by the tens digit. Write this partial product (143,478 tens) so that its ones digit (8) is in the tens column.
47,826 × 537 ─────── 334 782 1 434 78 23 913 0	Multiply by the hundreds digit. Write this partial product (239,130 hundreds) so that its ones digit (0) is in the hundreds column.
47,826 × 537 ─────── 334 782 1 434 78 23 913 0 ─────── 25,682,562	Add the partial products.

Check to be sure that your answer makes sense.

    The answer should be more than $500 \times 40{,}000$, which is 20,000,000.

    The answer should be less than $600 \times 50{,}000$, which is 30,000,000.

    25,682,562 is between 20,000,000 and 30,000,000.

So the answer makes sense.

Multiply. Check your answers to be sure they make sense.

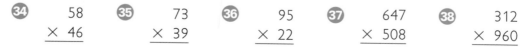

34	58 × 46	**35**	73 × 39	**36**	95 × 22	**37**	647 × 508	**38**	312 × 960

Multiply. Check your answers to be sure they make sense.

㉟ 26	㊵ 584	㊶ 584	㊷ 584	㊸ 584
× 71	× 8	× 10	× 80	× 88

㊹ 584	㊺ 742	㊻ 742	㊼ 742	㊽ 742
× 800	× 100	× 6	× 600	× 606

㊾ 742	㊿ 832	⑤ 368	㉜ 368	㉝ 3680
× 60	× 502	× 79	× 790	× 790

(39) 26 × 71 (40) 584 × 8 (41) 584 × 10 (42) 584 × 80 (43) 584 × 88

(44) 584 × 800 (45) 742 × 100 (46) 742 × 6 (47) 742 × 600 (48) 742 × 606

(49) 742 × 60 (50) 832 × 502 (51) 368 × 79 (52) 368 × 790 (53) 3680 × 790

Watch the signs.

(54) 5103 − 746 (55) 5103 + 746 (56) 5103 × 746 (57) 1000 − 648 (58) 1648 − 1000

(59) 1000 + 648 (60) 1000 × 648 (61) 2000 − 648 (62) 2000 × 648 (63) 648 + 200

(64) 512 + 47 (65) 512 − 47 (66) 512 × 7 (67) 512 × 4 (68) 512 × 47

Solve these problems.

(69) Last week, José swam 20 laps of the pool on Monday, Tuesday, Wednesday, and Thursday. He swam 30 laps on both Friday and Saturday.

   a. How many laps did he swim all together?

   b. If each lap is 50 meters, how far did José swim last week?

(70) José is swimming in a smaller pool in which laps are 40 meters. He plans to swim twice as many laps on Monday, Tuesday, Wednesday, and Thursday as he did last week, and the same number of laps as last week on Friday and Saturday.

   a. How many laps will he swim this week if he follows his plan?

   b. How many meters will he swim this week?

Applying Multiplication

You can make a diagram on grid paper to help you solve problems involving area. In this lesson you'll see how to use a diagram to plan an arrangement of tiles on a floor.

Remember that Paul and Kim measured the floor of their clubhouse so they could tile it. The floor is 500 centimeters long and 357 centimeters wide. The tiles they want to buy are square. Each tile is 25 centimeters on a side. Paul and Kim made this diagram to plan how to arrange the tiles.

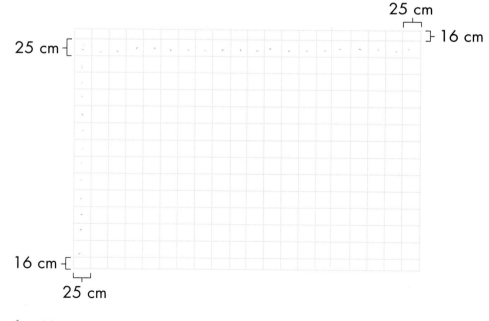

◆ How many whole tiles will they put down?

◆ How many tiles will they need to cut?

◆ How many tiles will they need to purchase?

The tiles that Kim and Paul want to buy come in boxes of 24. Each box costs $8.00.

◆ How many boxes will they need to buy?

◆ How many extra whole tiles will they have?

◆ How much will the tiles cost (not including tax)?

◆ **Challenge:** If you were tiling your classroom floor, how many tiles would you need if each tile were 25 centimeters by 25 centimeters? (If you have already measured your classroom, use those results.)

Solve these problems.

1 Roger wants to make five kites. For each kite he needs two unbroken bamboo strips—one that is 60 centimeters long and one 80 centimeters long. Bamboo strips are 100 centimeters long and cost 75¢ each.

a. How many bamboo strips does Roger need to buy?

b. How much will it cost him (not counting the tax)?

2 Ms. Yamato is planning to buy carpeting for her living room. The carpeting she likes is 5 meters wide and costs $59.95 a meter. Her living room is 7 meters long and five meters wide.

a. How much carpeting should she buy?

b. How much will it cost?

3 There are 26 students in Rebecca's class who are going to a soccer game. The tickets are $6.75. Rebecca said that it will cost $17.55 for everyone to go. Was she right? Explain how you can tell.

4 Andre is putting baseball cards into an album. He bought 11 packs of 12 cards each to put in the album. Each page has spaces for nine cards, and Andre has 15 empty pages.

a. How many cards does Andre have to put in the album?

b. Will all of the cards fit in the album?

c. How many empty spaces or how many leftover cards will Andre have after he puts the cards in the album?

◆ **LESSON 13** Applying Multiplication

Roll a Problem Game

C**OO**PERATIVE LEARNING

GAME

Players:	**Two or more**
Materials:	**One 0–5 cube**
Object:	**To get the greatest product**
Math Focus:	**Multidigit multiplication, place value, and mathematical reasoning**

RULES

1. Use blanks to outline a multiplication problem on your paper, like this:

$$\begin{array}{r} \underline{\quad\quad} \; \underline{\quad\quad} \\ \times \; \underline{\quad\quad} \; \underline{\quad\quad} \\ \hline \end{array}$$

2. The first player rolls the cube four times.

3. Each time the cube is rolled, write that number in one of the blanks in your outline.

4. When all the blanks have been filled, find the product of the two numbers.

5. The player with the greatest product wins the round.

OTHER WAYS TO PLAY THIS GAME

1. Try to get the least product.

2. Multiply a one-digit number and a three-digit number.

3. Multiply two three-digit numbers.

4. Use a 5–10 cube. If you roll a 10, roll that cube again.

5. Instead of a cube, use ten slips of paper numbered 0 through 9. The first player draws the slips one at a time from a container.

MATH JOURNAL

If you played the game again, would you use the same strategy? In your Math Journal, write about the strategies you used.

In each problem two of the answers are incorrect and one is correct.
Choose the correct answer. Discuss your methods for finding the
answers. What methods worked best?

5 23×29 **a.** 967   **b.** 367   **c.** 667

6 17×77 **a.** 1309   **b.** 6309   **c.** 1609

7 49×92 **a.** 3508   **b.** 4508   **c.** 5508

8 63×36 **a.** 2868   **b.** 2268   **c.** 3868

9 89×32 **a.** 1848   **b.** 2348   **c.** 2848

10 $6973 - 3937$ **a.** 1336   **b.** 336   **c.** 3036

11 $6973 + 3937$ **a.** 8910   **b.** 10,910   **c.** 3910

12 947×21 **a.** 19,887   **b.** 17,887   **c.** 1887

13 327×32 **a.** 40,464   **b.** 10,464   **c.** 1464

14 821×89 **a.** 73,069   **b.** 83,069   **c.** 16,069

15 456×52 **a.** 20,002   **b.** 2372   **c.** 23,712

16 593×42 **a.** 204,906   **b.** 34,906   **c.** 24,906

17 $3377 + 167$ **a.** 3544   **b.** 5044   **c.** 5344

18 $1871 - 1387$ **a.** 1484   **b.** 484   **c.** 84

19 $1812 - 1776$ **a.** 136   **b.** 1036   **c.** 36

20 $367 + 274$ **a.** 641   **b.** 341   **c.** 441

21 413×211 **a.** 67,143   **b.** 77,143   **c.** 87,143

22 387×195 **a.** 85,465   **b.** 75,465   **c.** 87,465

23 $2492 - 363$ **a.** 2129   **b.** 2329   **c.** 1929

24 $1540 + 12,249$ **a.** 27,649   **b.** 2789   **c.** 13,789

Mid-Unit Review

Write the numbers in standard form.

1 5000 + 600 + 80 + 5

2 8000 + 200 + 30 + 9

3 4000 + 50 + 1

4 30,000 + 600 + 20

5 5 + 800 + 400,000

6 0.6 + 0.04 + 0.005

7 0.03 + 0.006 + 0.1

8 0.008 + 0.3

9 3 tenths, 5 hundredths, 3 thousandths

10 0 tenths, 7 hundredths, 2 thousandths

Copy each pair of numbers but replace ● with > , <, or =.

11 3.9 ● 4.1

12 0.6 ● 0.06

13 0.778 ● 0.8

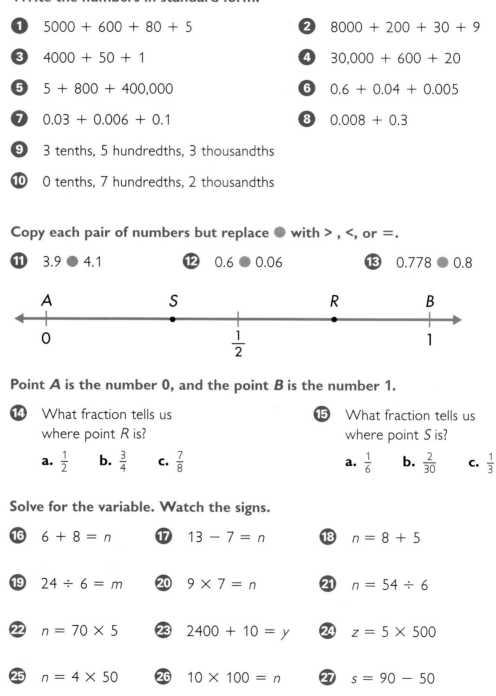

Point A is the number 0, and the point B is the number 1.

14 What fraction tells us where point R is?

    a. $\frac{1}{2}$ **b.** $\frac{3}{4}$ **c.** $\frac{7}{8}$

15 What fraction tells us where point S is?

    a. $\frac{1}{6}$ **b.** $\frac{2}{30}$ **c.** $\frac{1}{3}$

Solve for the variable. Watch the signs.

16 $6 + 8 = n$

17 $13 - 7 = n$

18 $n = 8 + 5$

19 $24 \div 6 = m$

20 $9 \times 7 = n$

21 $n = 54 \div 6$

22 $n = 70 \times 5$

23 $2400 + 10 = y$

24 $z = 5 \times 500$

25 $n = 4 \times 50$

26 $10 \times 100 = n$

27 $s = 90 - 50$

Add or subtract. Use shortcuts when you can.

28
```
  100
−  27
```

29
```
 2100
+  70
```

30
```
 2000
−   6
```

31
```
 5000
+3034
```

32
```
 4001
 2000
 2020
+3980
```

33
```
 6999
+   1
```

34
```
 3006
+2238
```

35
```
 65,000
−30,334
```

36
```
 400
 200
+209
```

37
```
 5000
 2359
+3034
```

Multiply.

38
```
  800
×  60
```

39
```
  100
× 100
```

40
```
  700
×  80
```

41
```
 1000
×  24
```

42
```
  539
×   7
```

43
```
  67
×  9
```

44
```
  832
×  15
```

45
```
  302
×  46
```

46
```
  730
×  50
```

47
```
  306
×  80
```

Choose the correct answer.

48 17 × 248   **a.** 4206   **b.** 4216   **c.** 42,106

49 8305 − 2919   **a.** 5386   **b.** 11,224   **c.** 6386

50 3206 + 3811   **a.** 6917   **b.** 7117   **c.** 7017

51 314 × 62   **a.** 19,468   **b.** 17,928   **c.** 16,828

52 928 − 359   **a.** 531   **b.** 1287   **c.** 569

53 853 + 2496   **a.** 1099   **b.** 3349   **c.** 3029

Solve these problems.

54 Art hiked for about 6 hours. About what fraction of the day is that?

55 Of the 32 students in Corrine's class, 14 are wearing sneakers today. Are the majority of her classmates wearing sneakers?

Division

Mrs. Katz has 24 oranges to put in packages to sell in her store. She wants to put the same number of oranges in each package, but no more than six will fit in a package.

◆ How many ways can Mrs. Katz package the oranges so that there are none left to sell individually?

Divide.

1 7)56   **2** 6)42   **3** 8)72   **4** 9)36   **5** 3)17

6 8)66   **7** 4)24   **8** 7)50   **9** 6)34   **10** 5)43

11 9)63   **12** 3)20   **13** 7)35   **14** 8)48   **15** 3)21

16 9)81   **17** 7)58   **18** 6)47   **19** 6)53   **20** 4)38

21 8)75   **22** 8)64   **23** 4)22   **24** 5)25   **25** 4)31

26 7)49   **27** 9)64   **28** 7)38   **29** 9)86   **30** 8)32

Besides the United States and Canada, other countries whose basic unit of money is called the dollar include Australia, Liberia, New Zealand, and Singapore.

Often in real life the answer to division problems must be interpreted. In this lesson you'll explore situations that call for different ways to interpret answers in division problems.

Frank made 30 cupcakes. He put them in boxes to sell at a bake sale. Only four fit in a box.

◆ How many boxes will he fill?

◆ How many cupcakes will be left over?

◆ What can he do with them?

There are 30 members of the Rocky Hill Ski Club. They are planning to go skiing at High Hills Ski Center next weekend. With all the skis and gear, only four persons can go in one car.

◆ How many cars will they need to take?

◆ Why can't they take $7\frac{1}{2}$ cars?

Bonita has a board that is 30 centimeters long. She wants to divide it into four equal pieces to make a square frame. She wants the frame to be as large as possible.

◆ How long should she make each of the small pieces?

◆ Will part of the board be left?

◆ LESSON 14   Division

Ms. Chen gave Donald, Carlos, Rose, and Dorothy 30 bananas that weren't eaten at the school picnic. She told them to share the bananas equally.

◆   How many whole bananas did each one get?

◆   In order to share equally and use all the bananas, what must they have done with the last two bananas?

◆   How many bananas did each one get?

Pat has a rock collection. She has boxes that are 4 centimeters high to hold individual rocks. There are 30 centimeters between the shelves on which she stacks the boxes.

◆   How many boxes can she stack on a shelf?

◆   How much space will be left over?

◆   Can she use the leftover space to stack more rocks?

For each of these problems, we did the same division problem:

$$4\overline{)30}$$

But we looked at the answers differently in each case. We obtained as possible answers:

$$7 \text{ R2, } 8, 7.5, 7\tfrac{1}{2}, 7$$

Whenever you divide to find the answer to a problem, you must decide which is the right answer. Sometimes you'll round up or down to the nearest whole number; sometimes you'll show the remainder; sometimes you'll use a fraction or a decimal answer. There may even be other possibilities for the answer to the problem or the way to present it. It all depends on the situation.

Solve the following problems. Write a short sentence as an answer to each problem, giving your answer and your reason for choosing that answer.

31 All 1032 students from the Worthington School must be taken by bus on a field trip. No more than 40 students are allowed on one bus. How many busses will be needed?

32 Mr. Alonzo has 1032 pieces of construction paper that he wants to divide equally among the 40 people in his class. How many pieces should each person get?

33 Mr. Alonzo has 1032 marbles that he wants to divide equally among the 40 people in his class. How many marbles should each person get?

34 The total cost of a party was $1032. Each of the 40 people at the party had to pay an equal share of the cost. How much should each person pay?

35 Angie the tailor has 1032 inches of material with which to make vests. Each vest requires 40 inches of material. How many vests can she make?

36 The school board has told Ms. Miller, the principal, that she must have exactly the same number of students in each of the 40 classes in her school. There are 1032 students in the school. How many students should be in each class?

Dividing by a One-Digit Divisor

At a charity dinner, $18,432 was raised. The money is to be divided among seven charities. How much will each charity receive? Find out by dividing.

$18,432 \div 7 = ?$

$$7\overline{)18{,}432}$$

Since 1 is less than 7, start by dividing 18 by 7.
That is, use 18 as a partial dividend.
The **dividend** is the number to be divided.

$$
\begin{array}{r}
2 \\
7\overline{)18{,}432} \\
14 \\
\hline
4
\end{array}
$$

There are two, but not three, 7s in 18.
Write 2 above the 8.
Multiply 2 × 7 and write 14 below the 18.
Subtract 14 from 18, leaving 4.

$$
\begin{array}{r}
2\ 6 \\
7\overline{)18{,}432} \\
14 \\
\hline
4\ 4 \\
4\ 2 \\
\hline
2
\end{array}
$$

"Bring down" the next digit (4) and divide 44 by 7, getting 6.
Write 6 above the 4 you brought down.
Multiply 6 × 7 and write 42 below the 44.
Subtract 42 from 44, leaving 2.

$$
\begin{array}{r}
2\ 6\ 3 \\
7\overline{)18{,}432} \\
14 \\
\hline
4\ 4 \\
4\ 2 \\
\hline
2\ 3 \\
2\ 1 \\
\hline
2
\end{array}
$$

Bring down the 3.
There are three, but not four, 7s in 23.
3 × 7 = 21
23 − 21 = 2

$$
\begin{array}{r}
2\ 6\ 3\ 3 \\
7\overline{)18{,}432} \\
14 \\
\hline
4\ 4 \\
4\ 2 \\
\hline
2\ 3 \\
2\ 1 \\
\hline
2\ 2 \\
2\ 1 \\
\hline
1
\end{array}
$$

Bring down the 2.
There are three, but not four, 7s in 22.
3 × 7 = 21
22 − 21 = 1
The answer is 2633, but there is a remainder of 1.
Each charity will get $2633, with $1 left over.

Check to be sure that your answer is correct.

Multiply the quotient by the divisor and add the remainder.

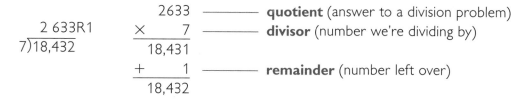

$$\begin{array}{r} 2\,633\text{R1} \\ \hline 7)18{,}432 \end{array}$$

$$\begin{array}{r} 2633 \\ \times \quad 7 \\ \hline 18{,}431 \\ + \quad 1 \\ \hline 18{,}432 \end{array}$$

2633 —————— **quotient** (answer to a division problem)

7 —————— **divisor** (number we're dividing by)

1 —————— **remainder** (number left over)

The result should be the same as the dividend. It is, so the answer is correct.

Divide. If the answer is not a whole number, leave the remainder as shown in the example.

① 8)56

② 9)8271

③ 7)31,563

④ 5)7285

⑤ 4)832

⑥ 6)6120

⑦ 7)406

⑧ 9)6195

⑨ 5)935

⑩ 3)2343

⑪ 6)39

⑫ 8)1894

Solve these problems.

⑬ Mrs. Ortiz bought seven puppies for $875. She wants to know how much this is per puppy. How much did she pay for each puppy?

⑭ Mrs. Ortiz wants to sell six of the puppies and keep one.
  a. How much must she charge for each puppy so that she gets back her $875 but sells only six of them? (Assume that she will charge the same for each puppy.)
  b. If you were Mrs. Ortiz, what price would you charge for each puppy?

⑮ Mrs. Ortiz decides to keep two puppies instead of one.

  a. If she still wants to get back $875, how much must she charge for each puppy?

  b. Mrs. Ortiz is able to sell one of the five remaining puppies for $200. How much must she charge for the others to get a total of at least $875?

◆ LESSON 15 Dividing by a One-Digit Divisor

You've learned the procedure for long division. Now you'll review the procedures for short division.

$543,296 \div 7 = ?$

$7\overline{)543,296}$	7 is greater than 5. 54 is the next partial dividend.
$\begin{array}{r} 7 \\ 7\overline{)54^53,296} \end{array}$	$7 \times 7 = 49$ $54 - 49 = 5$ Write the 5 in front of the 3. 53 is the new partial dividend.
$\begin{array}{r} 7\ 7 \\ 7\overline{)54^53,^4296} \end{array}$	$7 \times 7 = 49$ $53 - 49 = 4$ Write the 4 in front of the 2. 42 is the new partial dividend.
$\begin{array}{r} 7\ 7\ 6 \\ 7\overline{)54^53,^4296} \end{array}$	$6 \times 7 = 42$ $42 - 42 = 0$ There's no need to write 0 in front of the 9. 9 is the new partial dividend.
$\begin{array}{r} 7\ 7\ 6\ 1 \\ 7\overline{)54^53,^429^26} \end{array}$	$1 \times 7 = 7$ $9 - 7 = 2$ 26 is the new partial dividend.
$\begin{array}{r} 7\ 7\ 61\ 3 \\ 7\overline{)54^53,^429^26} \end{array}$	$3 \times 7 = 21$ $26 - 21 = 5$ The answer is 77,613 with 5 left over. Depending on the situation, you might use 77,613 or 77,614.

Check your answer to be sure that it makes sense.

77,613 is a little less than 80,000.

$7 \times 80,000$ is 560,000.

543,296 is a little less than 560,000.

So the answer makes sense.

Compare the procedures for division (page 54) and short division (page 56).

◆ Make sure you get the same answer when you do a problem either way.

Solve these division problems. There are no remainders. Check your answers to be sure that they make sense.

16 49,380 ÷ 5   **17** 76,136 ÷ 8   **18** 47,016 ÷ 2

19 64,251 ÷ 3   **20** 9872 ÷ 4   **21** 33,282 ÷ 9

22 51,884 ÷ 7   **23** 82,734 ÷ 6   **24** 45,186 ÷ 6

25 25,581 ÷ 3   **26** 4356 ÷ 6   **27** 19,912 ÷ 8

Solve these problems.

28 Mr. and Mrs. Singh drove 3555 kilometers in the last five days. If they drove about the same amount each day, about how many kilometers did they drive each day?

29 Mr. and Mrs. Perez have a 1125 kilometer trip to make in two days. They want to drive about twice as far the first day as the second. How far should they drive the first day?

30 Three friends are making a 2070 kilometer trip over three days. They want to drive the same distance each day and share the driving equally. How far should each person drive on the first day?

LESSON 16

Dividing by a Multidigit Divisor

In this lesson you'll review a method for dividing by a multidigit divisor in which you first make an **approximation** of the answer.

$139,196 \div 73 = ?$

$73\overline{)139,196}$	It is sensible to first approximate an answer.
$70\overline{)139,196}$	Round 73 to 70.
$7\overline{)13,919.6}$	139,196 divided by 70 is the same as 13,919.6 divided by 7.
$\begin{array}{r} 1\,9 \\ 7\overline{)13,919.6} \end{array}$	The approximate answer is *about 1900.*

Now do the division.

$73\overline{)139,196}$	Since 73 × 1 is greater than 13, a 0 could be written above 3, but this isn't necessary. Use 139 as the partial dividend.
$\begin{array}{r} 1 \\ 73\overline{)139,196} \end{array}$	Estimate the quotient by mentally dropping the last digit of both divisor and partial dividend. Since 7 × 1 = 7 and 7 × 2 = 14, use 1 as your *trial quotient.*
$\begin{array}{r} 1 \\ 73\overline{)139,196} \\ \underline{73} \\ 66 \end{array}$	1 × 73 = 73 139 − 73 = 66
$\begin{array}{r} 1 \\ 73\overline{)139,196} \\ \underline{73} \\ 661 \end{array}$	Bring down the 1 and use 661 as the new partial dividend.

```
         1 9
  73)139,196
      73
      66 1
      65 7
          4
```

Since 7 × 9 = 63, try 9 as the next trial quotient.
9 × 73 = 657
If 657 were greater than 661, you'd cross out 9
and try 8.
661 − 657 = 4

```
       1 9 0
  73)139,196
      73
      66 1
      65 7
         49
```

Bring down the 9. Since 73 is greater than 49,
the next digit of the quotient is 0.
(It is essential to write this 0 to show that
there are no tens in the quotient. If you
omit the 0, the 9 in the hundreds place
might seem to be in the tens place.)

```
              6
       1 9 0 7̸
  73)139,196
      73
      66 1
      65 7
         496
         5̶1̶1̶
         438
          58
```

Bring down the 6.
Because 7 × 7 = 49, try 7 as the trial quotient.
Since 511 is greater than 496, 7 is too large.
Try 6.

Depending on the situation, 1907 or 1906 may be the best answer
to this problem. Clearly, 1907 is closer, because the remainder, 58,
is more than half of the divisor.

Check: Is 1907 close to 1900, the approximation we made first?
Yes, so the answer makes sense.

**The following problems have no remainders. Find the quotient in
each problem.**

1 2924 ÷ 86   **2** 33,696 ÷ 432   **3** 15,964 ÷ 52

4 28,569 ÷ 321   **5** 60,207 ÷ 61   **6** 29,240 ÷ 860

◆   Look around. Is there an easy way to do problem 6?

◆ LESSON 16 Dividing by a Multidigit Divisor

You know you can multiply by 10 easily. Multiplying by 100, 1000, and so on is equally easy ($7 \times 100 = 700$, $7 \times 1000 = 7000$, and so on).

You can also multiply by numbers like 25 easily. Think of 25 as $\frac{100}{4}$. Then, $25 \times 36 = \frac{100}{4} \times 36 = 100 \times \frac{1}{4} \times 36 = 100 \times 9 = 900$. So, to multiply 36 by 25, take $\frac{1}{4}$ of 36 (9) and write two 0s after it: 900.

Multiply 25×36 the usual way.

◆ Is the answer 900?

To multiply 50×36, you can use the fact that 50 is $\frac{100}{2}$.

◆ Try doing that multiplication the short way. What is your answer?

To multiply 75×36, remember that $75 = \frac{3}{4}$ of 100. Since $\frac{1}{4}$ of 36 is 9, $\frac{3}{4}$ of 36 is $3 \times 9 = 27$. Finally, $27 \times 100 = 2700$.

In a similar way you can see that $36 \times 5 = 36 \times \frac{1}{2} \times 10 = 18 \times 10 = 180$. Or, $36 \times 250 = 36 \times \frac{1}{4} \times 1000 = 9 \times 1000 = 9000$.

Similar procedures can be used to divide easily. For example, what is $700 \div 25$? Since $25 = \frac{100}{4}$, $700 \div 25 = 700 \div 100 \times 4 = 7 \times 4 = 28$.

Do the following multiplication and division problems, using shortcuts whenever possible.

7 $18 \div 2$ **8** 18×5 **9** $38 \div 2$ **10** 38×5

11 $17 \div 2$ **12** 17×5 **13** 335×2 **14** $335 \div 5$

15 $24 \div 4$ **16** 24×25 **17** 24×50 **18** 24×75

19 $92 \div 4$ **20** 92×25 **21** 92×50 **22** 92×75

23 $96 \div 4$ **24** 96×25 **25** 96×50 **26** 96×75

27 96×250 **28** 96×750 **29** 92×250 **30** 6×4

31 $600 \div 25$ **32** 9×4 **33** $900 \div 25$ **34** 11×4

35 $1100 \div 25$ **36** 64×25 **37** 64×75 **38** 65×25

Solve the following multiplication and division problems, using shortcuts whenever possible. Find the value of *n* in each case.

39 $10 \times 76 = n$

40 $100 \times 76 = n$

41 $25 \times 76 = n$

42 $50 \times 76 = n$

43 $75 \times 76 = n$

44 $1000 \times 428 = n$

45 $250 \times 428 = n$

46 $750 \times 428 = n$

47 $500 \times 428 = n$

48 $107{,}000 \div 250 = n$

49 $321{,}000 \div 428 = n$

50 $214{,}000 \div 500 = n$

51 $32{,}528 \div 19 = n$

52 $20{,}093 \div 71 = n$

53 $167{,}162 \div 83 = n$

54 $44 \times 25 = n$

55 $44 \times 50 = n$

56 $44 \times 75 = n$

57 $196 \div 4 = n$

58 $196 \times 25 = n$

59 $196 \times 50 = n$

60 $196 \times 75 = n$

61 $14 \div 4 = n$

62 $14 \times 25 = n$

63 $14 \times 50 = n$

64 $14 \times 75 = n$

65 $18 \div 4 = n$

66 $18 \times 25 = n$

67 $50 \times 18 = n$

68 $75 \times 18 = n$

Solve these problems.

69 Douglas has been saving all of the quarters he has received in change for the past several months. He has 38 quarters.
   a. How many cents worth of quarters does he have?
   b. What are his quarters worth in dollars and cents?

70 The 76 sixth graders at William McKinley School are raising money for a computer. If each student raises $50, how much money will they raise?

71 The Census Bureau projects that by 2050, the United States population will be 394,000,000.
   a. If that population were distributed evenly among the states, how many people would live in each state?
   b. Do you think the population will be distributed evenly among all the states? Why or why not?

◆ LESSON 16 Dividing by a Multidigit Divisor

Solve these problems.

72 Ms. Lopez drives to work each day, about 250 days a year. The round trip is 36 miles. About how many miles does she drive to and from work in a year?

73 Ms. Lopez records the reading on her odometer at the beginning of each year. Last year on January 1 the odometer read 43,298. This year on January 1 the odometer read 56,037. How many miles did she drive all together last year? About how much of that was for something other than going to and from work?

74 Ms. Lopez believes her car gets an average of about 25 miles per gallon. Approximately how many gallons of gas did she use last year?

75 The last four times Ms. Lopez bought gas, she recorded the mileage shown on her odometer and also how much gas she bought. Here is her record. Use it to calculate her average mileage on a gallon of gas for as many of the times as is possible. Why can you not find the average for the first time she bought gas? Do you need the number of gallons she put in the car for the first time? Explain.

Odometer reading:	62,573	62,873	63,113	63,437
Gallons gas bought:	11	12	10	12

76 Ms. Okamoto is about to make a 450-mile trip. She filled her 16 gallon gas tank, and she wants to refill it when it is half full.

a. Assuming her car continues to get about 25 miles per gallon, after how many miles should she plan on stopping for gas?

b. About how many times will she need to stop for gas on her trip?

Roll a Problem Game (Division)

COOPERATIVE LEARNING

GAME

Players:	**Two or more**
Materials:	**One 0–5 cube**
Object:	**To get the greatest quotient**
Math Focus:	**Multidigit division, place value, and mathematical reasoning**

RULES

1. Outline a division problem on your paper, like this:

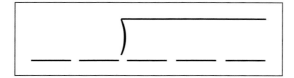

2. The lead player rolls the cube. Write the number in any of the five blanks.

3. The lead player rolls the cube again. Write the number in any of the remaining blanks. Zero may not be written in the first blank, except when it comes on the last roll.

4. Repeat step 3 until all the blanks are filled.

5. Divide the three-digit number by the two-digit number. Carry out the division as far as necessary to see who has the greatest quotient.

6. The player with the greatest quotient wins.

OTHER WAYS TO PLAY THIS GAME

1. The least quotient wins. Zero may not be written in the first blank under the division sign except when it comes on the last roll.

2. Change the number of digits in the divisor or the dividend.

3. Use a 5–10 cube. If a 10 is rolled, roll that cube again.

4. Instead of a cube, use ten numbered cards or slips of paper.

Division Applications

In this lesson you'll use what you know about arithmetic to solve problems mentally.

Solve these problems in your head. Then write the answers.

1 30 × 3   **2** 60 × 3   **3** 600 × 3

4 1800 ÷ 3   **5** 1800 ÷ 30   **6** 1800 ÷ 300

7 16 + 10   **8** 160 + 5   **9** 160 + 15

10 175 − 15   **11** 12 ÷ 12   **12** 24 ÷ 12

13 48 ÷ 12   **14** 4 × 12   **15** 5 × 12

16 50 × 12   **17** 600 ÷ 12   **18** 60 ÷ 12

19 60 ÷ 6   **20** 60 ÷ 3   **21** 2 × 75

22 150 ÷ 75   **23** 150 ÷ 50   **24** 150 ÷ 25

25 300 ÷ 25   **26** 3000 ÷ 25   **27** 3025 ÷ 25

28 4 × 25   **29** 4 × 250   **30** 1000 ÷ 4

For each problem several answers are given, but only one is correct. Choose the correct answer.

31 How many minutes are there in one week?

    a. 1,000,000
    b. 39,475
    c. 10,080
    d. 100,800

32 Ms. Abdul's salary is $27,120 per year. How much does she earn each month?

    a. $22,600
    b. $2260
    c. $312
    d. $3120

Solve these problems.

33 Mr. DeAngelo sold 1012 pairs of shoes in the 22 days he worked last month. About how many pairs of shoes did he sell each day?

34 Mr. Peterson found an old recipe for 24 loaves of bread. He wants to use the recipe to make two loaves of bread. The original recipe calls for 36 kilograms of flour and 156 grams of salt.

   a. How much flour should he use?

   b. How much salt should he use?

35 Eva has 320 pictures that she took during the summer. She puts her pictures in an album, 12 on a page. How many pages will she need for these pictures?

36 Sara is planning a backpacking trip. The trip is for six days, and she can hike about 15 kilometers a day. About how many kilometers can she cover during the entire trip?

37 Francesca's scout troop is chartering a bus to go to summer camp. The cost of the bus is $196. There are 35 scouts going to camp. How much will each scout pay for her trip?

38 For a cookout at camp, Francesca's troop plans on having two hot dogs and two hot dog buns for each of the 35 scouts. Hot dogs come in packages of ten, and hot dog buns come in packages of eight. How many packages of hot dogs and hot dog buns does the troop need?

39 Mr. Kim earns $12 an hour. He just received a paycheck for $936. How many hours did he work during that pay period?

◆ LESSON 17 Division Applications

Solve these problems.

40 Matt read an 888-page book in 37 hours last month. About how many pages per hour is that?

41 Matt counted the number of words on three different pages of the book that looked typical to him. There were 483 words on one of the pages, 503 words on a second page, and 511 words on the third page.

    a. About how many words do you think there are in the entire book?

    b. About how many words per hour did Matt read?

    c. About how many words per minute is that?

42 Ms. Whitman has a large rectangular lawn that is 374 feet long and 285 feet wide. She wants to put fertilizer on the lawn. Each bag of fertilizer is supposed to cover 5000 square feet. How many bags of fertilizer should she buy? If each bag of fertilizer costs $5, how much will she spend on fertilizer?

43 An airplane flew 2425 miles in five hours. What was its average speed in miles per hour?

44 Don and Juwan can plant an average of 80 seedling trees in an hour. They intend to plant 400 trees on each acre of their property.

    a. How long will they need to complete one acre?

    b. How many hours will they need to plant trees on all 160 acres of their property?

    c. How many trees will they plant on the 160 acres?

    d. If they plant trees for 12 hours each day, how many days will they need to complete the job?

45 Don and Juwan's property is in the shape of a rectangle composed of squares 1 acre in area. The property is 16 squares long and 10 squares wide. On each acre they are planting 400 trees in the shape of a square, with 20 trees on each side. Viewed from above, the trees will be in the shape of a rectangle. How many rows of trees will there be, and how many trees will be in each row?

Roll and Divide Game

Players:	**Two or more**
Materials:	**Two 0–5 cubes, two 5–10 cubes**
Object:	**To create a division problem without a remainder but with the greatest divisor**
Math Focus:	**Mental arithmetic (multiplication and division)**

RULES

1. The first player rolls all four cubes and uses one or two of the numbers rolled as the digits of the dividend. (Neither the divisor nor the dividend can be 0, although each may contain a 0.) Another number rolled is used as the divisor. The answer cannot have a decimal or fractional part. There cannot be a remainder. A player's score is 0 if he or she cannot follow this rule to make a problem.

2. The other players follow the same procedure.

3. In each round the player with the greatest divisor wins and starts the next round. If two players have the same divisor, the player with the greater quotient wins.

SAMPLE GAME

Round 1:

Miguel rolled: `0` `4` `7` `9` He made: $49 \div 7 = 7$. His divisor was 7.

Judith rolled: `5` `6` `0` `6` She made $60 \div 6 = 10$. Her divisor was 6.

So Miguel won this round.

Round 2:

Miguel rolled: `4` `4` `8` `8` He made: $48 \div 8 = 6$. His divisor was 8.

Judith rolled: `10` `10` `5` `0` She made: $510 \div 10 = 51$. Her divisor was 10.

Judith won this round.
(She could also have used $100 \div 10 = 10$ or $10 \div 10 = 1$.)

LESSON
18

Arithmetic Applications

In this lesson you'll use what you know about addition, subtraction, multiplication, and division to solve these problems.

Solve these problems.

1 Juanita earns $2.50 per hour mowing lawns. How much will she earn for eight hours of work?

2 For most people adult height is about double the height at the age of two. Philip was 87 centimeters tall when he was two years old. About how tall would you expect him to be when he is 21?

3 Mr. Redhawk earns $33,600 a year but is paid once a month. How much does he earn each month?

4 Mr. Goldstein earns $2541.67 each month. Before he is paid, deductions are made for taxes ($612), insurance ($228), and savings ($42.75). What is his take-home pay each month?

5 At $30,500 per year, how much does Mr. Goldstein earn in a week?

6 Which job has a higher annual salary, one that pays $21,000 per year or one that pays $425 each week?

7 Which job has a higher annual salary, one that pays $1100 every two weeks or one that pays $2300 each month?

8 Mr. Ramirez earns $31,200 per year. Mrs. Ramirez earns $2600 each month. What is the total of their annual salaries?

9 Mrs. Kelly has $1678.56 in her checking account. She has the following bills: electricity, $31.74; gas, $43.82; telephone, $26.59; grocery store, $207.57; service station, $57; doctor, $235; rent, $600; and insurance, $145. Does she have enough money in her checking account to pay her bills?

10 If Mrs. Kelly's checking-account balance is $1678.56 and she writes checks for a total of $1346.72, how much money will she have left in her checking account?

11 Arturo's class is going to the state capital. The cost to charter a bus is $116.64. If the 18 students share the cost equally, how much will each student pay?

12 Sofi had 750 stamps in her collection. She traded 25 stamps with Jerome, swapping one for one. How many stamps does she have now?

13 Sofi has her stamps in an album with 50 pages. If the same number of stamps were on each page, how many would be on a page?

14 Deanna saved in her bank account exactly half of the money she received for her birthday. She deposited $37.50 in her savings account. How much money did she receive?

15 Deanna wants to use the other half of her birthday money to buy a book for $5.95, a CD for $14.97, and a necklace for $18.50. Can she afford all three purchases?

◆ **LESSON 18** Arithmetic Applications

Mr. Muddle's Extra-Large Problems

Part 3

THINKING STORY

You may want to refer to earlier parts of this Thinking Story on pages 22–23 and 38–39 to refresh your memory.

Mr. Muddle counted the T-shirts in his store. He found that he had 26 medium, 87 small, and none at all of the large and extra-large sizes.

"I'd better order some more T-shirts right away," he said. He took an order form out of his desk.

"How many shirts of each size did you say I need each week?" Mr. Muddle asked.

"You need 60 extra large, 60 large, 30 medium, and 15 small," Marcus answered.

"How can I get that number?" Mr. Muddle muttered. "This order form is so confusing. I used to just write a "1" in the bottom box. Then everything was taken care of for me. I know! I'll write a "2" in the box instead. Then I'll be sure to get enough of every size."

"I have a better idea," said Manolita. "Just order one box of large T-shirts and one box of the extra-large size. That way you'll save money."

"I think you need a long-term plan," said Marcus.

. . . to be continued

Quality T-Shirts Order Form

Orders are accepted for boxes only. Each box contains 12 bags of 12 T-shirts. Show number of bags of each size per box, or save money by ordering only one size per box.

Single Sizes

Size	Number of Boxes
Small	_____
Medium	_____
Large	_____
X-Large	_____
	[ ]

Total

Price $_____

(see current price list)

Mixed Sizes

Number of Bags
(Each column must add up to 12.)

	First Box	Second Box	Third Box
Small			
Medium			
Large			
X-Large			

Number of boxes   [ ]

Price $_____

(include extra charge for mixed boxes)

Easy Ordering Method:

Enter the total number of boxes you want. Don't bother to fill out the rest of the form. We will ship equal numbers of each size, packed to save you the most money.

Number of boxes   [ ]

Work in groups. Discuss your answers and how you figured them out. Compare your answers with others.

1 What will happen if Mr. Muddle writes a "2" in the bottom box? What do you think of that way of ordering?

2 What would happen if Mr. Muddle wrote a "4" in the bottom box?

3 What is good and what is bad about Manolita's idea?

4 Work out an ordering plan for Mr. Muddle that will cover the next four weeks. Mr. Muddle can't afford to order more than two boxes at a time. Save him as much money as you can. Be sure that he always has enough T-shirts of every size.

5 A **super challenge** question: Why doesn't the order form have room for more than three boxes of mixed sizes?

LESSON 19

Using Your Calculator

A calculator is a useful tool. To use your calculator effectively, you need to know what its special features are. Answer as many of the following questions as you can. Some of them may not apply to your calculator.

1 What is the greatest number your calculator is able to display?

2 What happens if the answer to a problem you give the calculator has more digits than the calculator display can show (for example, the problem 7,777,777 × 8,888,888)?

3 What is the difference between the ⁰ⁿ/ₐc and ᶜᴱ/c keys?

4 How can you store a number in the calculator's memory? How can you display a number already in the memory?

5 What does the ¹/x key do?

6 Can your calculator display fractions? If so, how?

7 Can your calculator add and subtract fractions? If not, can you use your calculator to check your answers when you add and subtract fractions? How can you do this?

8 Does your calculator round to the last decimal place it shows? (Hint: Find 2 ÷ 3. How does this tell you whether the calculator rounds?)

9 Does your calculator "remember" more digits than it shows? How might you find out this information?

GAME

Key Keys Game

C**OO**PERATIVE LEARNING

Players:	**One or more**
Materials:	**One calculator per player**
Object:	**To reach a given number using only permitted keys**
Math Focus:	**Mental arithmetic (all four operations), using a calculator, and mathematical reasoning**

RULES

1. Choose several keys ("permitted keys") including one number.

2. Try to get the display to show another number you select. See who can get to the selected number with the fewest steps. (You don't have to push ▣ after each operation.)

SAMPLE GAME

Min and Oliver chose these keys: ＋, －, ✕, ÷, ＝, 7

They wanted to reach the number 22.

Min reached 22 in ten steps:

7, ÷, 7, ＋, 7, ＋, 7, ＋, 7, ＝
Oliver won the round.

Oliver reached 22 in eight steps:

7, 7, ＋, 7, 7, ÷, 7, ＝

Can you do these? Count your steps.

1. Permitted keys: ＋, －, ✕, ÷, ＝, 8

   Try to reach: **a.** 24   **b.** 11   **c.** 19   **d.** 640   **e.** 2   **f.** 56

2. Permitted keys: ＋, －, ✕, ÷, ＝, 9

   Try to reach: **a.** 45   **b.** 81   **c.** 82   **d.** 360   **e.** 4   **f.** 98

   Permitted keys: ＋, －, ✕, ÷, ＝, 5

   Try to reach: **a.** 25   **b.** 550   **c.** 280   **d.** 165   **e.** 11   **f.** 13

LESSON 20

Calculator or Mental Arithmetic?

Are all problems quicker to solve with a calculator? Have a race to find out.

COOPERATIVE LEARNING

Do this with a partner. One of you must use a calculator; the other, any other method. The player using a calculator must press all the keys indicated. See how fast each of you can find the answers.

1 $7 \times 8 = n$ **2** $70 \times 8 = n$ **3** $700 \times 8 = n$

4 $7000 \times 8 = n$ **5** $7 \times 80 = n$ **6** $7 \times 800 = n$

7 $7 \times 8000 = n$ **8** $70 \times 80 = n$ **9** $700 \times 80 = n$

10 $70 \times 800 = n$ **11** $700 \times 800 = n$ **12** $7000 \times 8000 = n$

13 $7 + 8 = n$ **14** $70 + 8 = n$ **15** $7 + 80 = n$

16 $7000 + 80 = n$ **17** $8 - 7 = n$ **18** $80 - 7 = n$

19 $8000 - 70 = n$ **20** $8000 - 700 = n$ **21** $90 \times 700 = n$

22 $600 \times 80 = n$ **23** $5000 \times 800 = n$ **24** $50 \times 600 = n$

25 $900 \times 600 = n$ **26** $5 \times 90 = n$ **27** $80 \times 80 = n$

28 $600 \times 70 = n$ **29** $700 \times 7 = n$ **30** $100 \times 80 = n$

31 $600 \times 60 = n$ **32** $40 \times 800 = n$ **33** $56 \div 7 = n$

34 $560 \div 70 = n$ **35** $5600 \div 700 = n$ **36** $5600 \div 7 = n$

37 $5600 \div 70 = n$ **38** $810 \div 9 = n$ **39** $810 \div 90 = n$

40 $4900 \div 70 = n$ **41** $640 \div 80 = n$ **42** $50 \times 50 = n$

43 $500 \times 5 = n$ **44** $50 + 50 = n$ **45** $50 + 5 = n$

46 $500 + 5 = n$ **47** $50 - 40 = n$ **48** $50 - 4 = n$

49 $500 - 4 = n$ **50** $30 \times 900 = n$ **51** $300 \times 90 = n$

◆ Which person finished first? Did most of the pairs have the same winner?

MATH JOURNAL

How can you decide when it would be faster to use a calculator or to use mental arithmetic? Record your strategies in your Math Journal.

Approximation Game

COOPERATIVE LEARNING

GAME

Players:	**Three or more**
Materials:	**One calculator for the lead player**
Object:	**To get the most points by making close approximations**
Math Focus:	**Place value, using a calculator, and mathematical reasoning**

RULES

1. Make a game form like this:

Round	Approximation	Point for Correct First Digit	Points for Correct Number of Digits	Score for Round
1				
2				

2. Decide how many rounds will be played. List them on the game form and add a space at the bottom for the total.

3. The lead player writes a problem on the board (for example, 73 × 59) and uses the calculator to find the answer.

4. Each player writes an approximate answer on the game form.

5. The lead player rounds the correct answer to a number with only one nonzero digit and writes it on the board, saying the first digit and the number of digits in the answer.

6. Look at your approximation and score yourself as follows: one point for the correct first digit and two points for the correct number of digits. Record your points on your game form.

If your approximation was:	And the correct answer is:	Then you would score:
4000	3652 → 4000	three points
50,000	44370 → 40,000	two points
900	9231 → 9000	one point

7. The player with the greatest total score at the end of the game is the winner.

◆ LESSON 20 Calculator or Mental Arithmetic?

In this lesson you'll use your approximating skills and number sense to find correct answers and tell when answers don't make sense.

In each case two of the answers are clearly wrong and one is correct. Choose the correct answer. Watch the signs!

52	843 × 629 =	**a.** 53,427	**b.** 530,247	**c.** 5,300,427
53	5043 × 75 =	**a.** 3725	**b.** 37,825	**c.** 378,225
54	86,658 ÷ 429 =	**a.** 202	**b.** 2562	**c.** 22,602
55	73,492 + 876 =	**a.** 15,468	**b.** 159,168	**c.** 74,368
56	642 × 593 =	**a.** 38,706	**b.** 380,706	**c.** 3,800,706
57	3487 − 94 =	**a.** 2647	**b.** 3393	**c.** 3581
58	3487 × 94 =	**a.** 327,778	**b.** 247,778	**c.** 467,778
59	3487 + 94 =	**a.** 3393	**b.** 128	**c.** 3581
60	3478 ÷ 94 =	**a.** 37	**b.** 4	**c.** 420
61	954 × 8 =	**a.** 762	**b.** 7632	**c.** 8062
62	57 × 68 =	**a.** 3876	**b.** 2876	**c.** 4876
63	475 × 71 =	**a.** 33,725	**b.** 27,725	**c.** 41,725
64	29 × 32 =	**a.** 98	**b.** 928	**c.** 9298
65	24 × 1765 =	**a.** 4260	**b.** 63,260	**c.** 42,360
66	28,764 ÷ 423 =	**a.** 728	**b.** 7	**c.** 68

Solve these problems.

67 A school has 20 classes. Each class has 25, 26, 27, or 28 students. Are there more than 600 students in the school?

68 Karim has $150.00. Does he have enough money to buy six concert tickets that cost $24.50 each?

Solve these problems.

69 Patty can read about 45 pages per hour in the book she's reading. The book has 1231 pages and she is now on page 92. Using a calculator, she decides she will have to spend 253 hours reading before she finishes the book. Do you agree? If not, about how long do you think it will take for her to finish the book?

70 Chiyo runs 5 miles each morning, every day of the year. She believes she will run about 1800 miles in a year. Do you agree? If not, about how many miles do you think she will run in a year?

71 Carlos pays 25 cents to ride the bus to school each day and 25 cents to ride it home. He goes to school about 180 days each year. About how much does he spend to ride the bus each year?

72 Joe has $20. He wants to buy some ballpoint pens that cost $1.98 each. About how many of the pens can he buy?

73 Mary, Mike, and Mavis are all twelve years old. Mary estimates that she has been alive for 4400 days. Mike believes he's been alive for 44,000 days, and Mavis estimates she's been alive for 440 days. Tell whether each estimate is reasonable and why you think so.

74 Jin wants to buy a jacket for $89, a pair of slacks for $73, and two shirts for $21 each. He has $300 to spend. Does he have enough money to buy all of these clothes? If not, about how much more money does he need? If he does have enough, about how much extra money will he have left after buying the clothes?

75 Jin had been saving about $30 a week towards his new clothes. He thought it would take him four months to save $300. Was he correct? If not, about how many months did it take?

LESSON 21

Rounding

Which number is easier to work with, 88,978 or 90,000?

Multiples of 10, 100, 1000, and so on are usually easier to work with than most other numbers. So when we are estimating or approximating, we often round numbers to a multiple of 10, 100, and so on.

We may round to the nearest multiple below. We call that **rounding** down. Or we may round to the nearest multiple above. We call that rounding up. Sometimes we round to the nearest multiple. How much we round and in what direction depends on the problem we are trying to solve.

Let's practice rounding to the nearest multiple.

Round 1248 to the nearest 10, 100, and 1000.

To the nearest 10: Since 48 is between 40 and 50, but closer to 50, 1248 rounds to 1250.

To the nearest 100: Since 248 is between 200 and 300, but closer to 200, 1248 rounds to 1200.

To the nearest 1000: Since 1248 is between 1000 and 2000, but closer to 1000, it rounds to 1000.

Round 45 to the nearest 10.

The number 45 is between 40 and 50 and is equally close to both. Most people use the rule to round up. So to round 45 to the nearest ten, we can round 45 up to 50. Sometimes how we round depends more on the situation than on following a rule. We will see an example of this on page 80.

Round 62.2 to the nearest whole number.

The number 62.2 is between 62 and 63 but closer to 62.

Round each of the following numbers to the nearest million.

1. 73,474,362
2. 1,973,425
3. 14,298,755

4. 645,043,171
5. 73,500,000
6. 211,000

7. 800,000
8. 73,500,001
9. 95,724,000

Round each of the following numbers to the nearest hundred thousand.

10. 73,474,362
11. 106,876
12. 53,493

13. 525,672
14. 1,263,000
15. 6,539,000

16. 472,311
17. 251,998
18. 832,599

19. How many possible correct answers are there to problem 5 above? What are they? Look at problems 10, 5, and 1, and explain why it might not be a good idea to round a number first to the nearest hundred thousand and then to the nearest million.

Round each of the following numbers to the nearest whole number.

20. 73.65
21. 81.04
22. 0.73
23. 6.52

24. 0.31
25. 56.4
26. 56.5
27. 17.09

28. 56.6
29. 0.49
30. 4.52
31. 0.65

32. 417.8
33. 6.85
34. 12.49
35. 10.06

Round each of the following numbers to the nearest hundred.

36. 843.6
37. 589.702
38. 1111
39. 9999

40. 500
41. 47
42. 53
43. 672

44. 888
45. 447
46. 2763
47. 364.9

48. 74
49. 1859
50. 739
51. 802

◆ LESSON 21 Rounding

How much we round and whether we round up or down depends on the problem we are trying to solve.

Example:

Mr. and Mrs. Taylor and their three children have been at the amusement park most of the day, and Mr. and Mrs. Taylor have about $20 left to spend. Jack asks his parents if the whole family can go on the cable car, which costs $3.35 per person. Mrs. Taylor thinks, "$3.35 is less than $4. Five times $4 is $20. Five times $3.35 will be less than $20. So we have enough money."

If Mrs. Taylor had rounded $3.35 down to $3.00, she would have known that five tickets for the ride would be more than $15, but she would not have been sure that they were less than $20. Notice that rounding to $3.00 is rounding to the nearest dollar but that it is not as useful as rounding up in this situation.

Discuss solutions to the following questions. Try to find solutions that avoid paper and pencil calculations.

◆ Jessica is traveling to Endville, 2089 kilometers away. She wants to spend three days driving. About how far should she plan to drive each day?

◆ Carlos is going to make 24 stuffed animals for a bazaar. He needs 90 centimeters of fabric for each animal. Will he have enough fabric if he buys 18 meters (1800 centimeters) of fabric? 24 meters (2400 centimeters) of fabric?

◆ Frances saved $23.57. Packages of sports cards are on sale for $2.47 each. Does Frances have enough money to purchase ten packs? seven packs?

Explain how to solve each of the following without actually doing the paper and pencil calculations.

52 Mr. Hilton has a $20 bill, three $5 bills, and less than a dollar of change in his pocket. He wants to spend $4.98 on milk, $22.89 on meat, and $4.53 on vegetables. Does he have enough money to do that?

53 Jeremy can run for a long time at a rate of about 7.2 miles per hour. He wants to run 27.4 miles in less than four hours. Will he be able to do that?

54 Maria can ride her bicycle for long periods of time at an average speed of 12 miles per hour. She wants to ride 50 miles in less than five hours. Will she be able to do it?

55 Brittany can ride her bicycle for long periods of time at a rate of about 18 miles per hour. She wants to ride 100 miles in no more than five hours. Will she be able to do it?

56 If Mrs. Littman drives her car an average of 53 miles an hour for 8 hours and 17 minutes, will she go farther than 200 miles? Will she go farther than 400 miles? Will she go farther than 600 miles?

LESSON 22

Using Negative Numbers

In many real-life situations we need to describe things using numbers that are less than 0. In this lesson you'll review how to identify and name these negative numbers.

◆ Can you think of times when it might be useful to use numbers less than 0?

Suppose the temperature is 10°C and it goes down 15°C. What will the temperature be?

| Temperature: 10°C | Goes Down 15°C | Temperature: 5° below 0° |

We can then write this problem in this way: 10 − 15 = (−5)
−5 is read "negative 5."

We often call a temperature of 5° below 0°C a temperature of −5°C.

You can show negative numbers on a number line.

Write the missing items.

	Temperature Before Change	Temperature Change	Temperature After Change
1	15°C	up 5°	▨
2	10°C	down 15°	▨
3	−5°C (5° below 0°C)	down 5°	▨
4	−10°C	up 2°	▨
5	−5°C	up 5°	▨

Diego's bank allows customers temporarily to have a negative **balance** in their accounts.

Diego's balance was $5. He then wrote a check for $15. What was his new balance?

We can write that problem in this way:

$$(5) + (-15) = (-10)$$

Diego's new balance was $-$$10.

Write the missing items.

	If Diego's balance was:	And he did this:	Then his new balance would be:
6	$15	deposited $5	■
7	$50	wrote check for $20	■
8	$5	wrote check for $25	■
9	–$25	deposited $25	■

Add or subtract. Watch for negative numbers.

10 10 + 20 **11** 10 − 20 **12** 20 − 20 **13** 15 − 20

14 15 − 25 **15** 0 − 25 **16** (−10) + 10 **17** (−10) − 10

18 7 − 16 **19** 16 − 7 **20** 12 − 4 **21** 4 − 12

22 8 − 3 **23** 8 − 8 **24** 8 − 10 **25** 8 − 14

26 (−6) + 1 **27** (−6) + 4 **28** (−7) + 13 **29** (−7) + 0

30 (−2) + 12 **31** 10 − 12 **32** 15 − 8 **33** 9 − 14

LESSON 23

Computing with Negative Numbers

Add or subtract. Do not use a calculator. Watch for negative numbers.

1. 100 − 50
2. 50 − 100
3. 100 − 200
4. 150 − 200

5. (−100) + 150
6. (−100) − 150
7. (−150) − 100
8. (−150) + 100

9. 0 − 250
10. 0 + 250
11. 75 − 100
12. 175 − 200

13. 125 − 50
14. 125 − 150
15. (−50) + 75
16. (−50) + 25

Look on your calculator for a key that looks like this ⁺⁄₋ or this ⁺⊖. You can use the ⁺⁄₋ key on a calculator to compute with negative numbers.

Look at these examples.

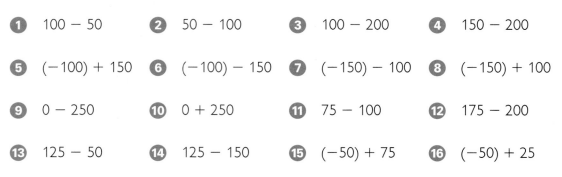

Problem:	Push:	
50 − 20	5 0 , − , 2 0 , =	30.
20 − 50	2 0 , − , 5 0 , =	−30.
(−40) + 30	4 0 , ⁺⁄₋ , + , 3 0 , =	−10.
(−5) − 20	5 , ⁺⁄₋ , − , 2 0 , =	−25.

17. Now use your calculator to do problems 1–16. See if you get the same answers you got before.

Use your calculator to explore subtracting a negative number.

FANTASTIC FACT

Mountains over 3280 feet above sea level cover over one fourth of Earth's land surface.

The chart below shows the highest and lowest points in each continent. The distances are measured from sea level. For example, a height of 29,028 feet means that the point is 29,028 feet above sea level. A distance of −1302 feet means that the point is 1302 feet below sea level.

Continent	Name and Place of Highest Point	Feet from Sea Level	Name and Place of Lowest Point	Feet from Sea Level
Asia	Mt. Everest (Nepal-Tibet)	29,028	Dead Sea (Israel-Jordan)	−1302
Africa	Mt. Kilimanjaro (Tanzania)	19,340	Lake Assal (Ethiopia)	−512
North America	Mt. McKinley (Alaska)	20,320	Death Valley (California)	−282
South America	Mt. Aconcagua (Argentina)	22,834	Valdes Peninsula (Argentina)	−131
Antarctica	Vinson Massif	16,864	not known	not known
Europe	Mt. El' brus (Russia)	18,510	Caspian Sea (Russia)	−92
Australia	Mt. Kosciusko (New South Wales)	7310	Lake Eyre (South Australia)	−52

Use the chart to solve these problems.

18 How high above sea level is Mount McKinley?

19 What is the difference in feet between the highest and lowest points on Earth?

20 What is the difference between the highest and the lowest points in North America?

21 How much higher is the highest point in Africa than the highest point in Europe?

22 How much lower is the lowest point in South America than the lowest point in Australia?

◆ **LESSON 23** Computing with Negative Numbers

Mr. Muddle's Extra-Large Problems

Part 4

You may want to refer to previous parts of this Thinking Story on pages 22-23, 38-39, and 70-71.

One day a woman walked into Mr. Muddle's T-shirt store. She said, "Mr. Muddle, I'm vice president of the Acme T-Shirt Company. I have an offer you won't be able to refuse. We will give you all the T-shirts you want, absolutely free! All you have to do is put a sign in your window that says 'We Proudly Sell Acme T-Shirts.'"

"Great," said Mr. Muddle. "Maybe at last I'll start to make money on my store."

"You'll be rich in no time," said the woman. "Would you like to place your first order right now?"

"You bet," said Mr. Muddle. "Since they're free, I'll take 1000 of each size."

"That's the spirit," said the woman. "Six thousand T-shirts!"

"You have six different sizes?" Mr. Muddle asked.

"Of course. Large, extra-large, small, extra-small, medium, and extra-medium. I guess you'll want the shirts made of our extra-special cloth. They will cost you only $2.95 a shirt. Believe me, it's worth it."

"All right," said Mr. Muddle. "Nothing but the best for my customers."

"Do you want any lettering on the T-shirts?"

"Oh, yes," Mr. Muddle said. "All my T-shirts say 'T-Shirt' across the front."

"That's 10¢ a letter . . . for seven letters . . . 70¢ a shirt."

"Seven letters? I count six," said Mr. Muddle.

"You forgot the hyphen in 'T-Shirt.' But what's another dime when the shirts are free? Then there's the delivery charge—$25 per delivery, large or small."

Mr. Muddle started to look worried. "That's strange. The other company delivers free."

"Ah, but we have same-day delivery. We deliver them the same day you get them."

"Oh, that's all right then," replied Mr. Muddle.

"Then there's the service charge—only $100 a month. That's all. Except for the sign, of course. You put it in the window: 'We Proudly Sell Acme T-Shirts.' It's $450."

"No," said Mr. Muddle. "I can't do it. I know I'd save lots of money if I sold Acme T-shirts. But I don't think I would feel proud anymore."

. . . the end

Work in groups. Discuss your answers and how you figured them out. Then compare your answers with those of other groups.

1 What is silly about the sizes Acme T-shirts come in?

2 About how much would each "free" Acme T-shirt cost Mr. Muddle? You may have to work hard on this problem. Salespeople like the vice president from the Acme T-Shirt Company don't make it easy to figure out what things really cost.

3 Would Mr. Muddle be better off getting his T-shirts from the Acme T-Shirt Company or staying with the other company? Explain your answer.

LESSON 24

Multiplying Positive and Negative Numbers

If you save $5 every week for 50 weeks, how much money will you have saved? Did you add 5 over and over until you got your answer, or did you use a quicker way to find the answer?

If you borrow $4 from a friend every week for seven weeks, how much will you owe your friend after the seven weeks?

Borrowing $4 is like saving negative $4 (−$4), and being in debt $28 is like having saved −$28. Because of this sort of thinking, we say that $7 \times -4 = -28$. Or, in general, a positive number times a negative number is a negative number.

You know that with positive numbers the order in which you multiply two numbers doesn't influence the product. For example, 7×8 is the same as 8×7. We would like that same rule to apply to all numbers, so we say that $-4 \times 7 = 7 \times -4 = -28$.

Find the value of *n* in each of the following problems.

1 $7 \times -3 = n$ **2** $4 \times -6 = n$ **3** $n = 9 \times -5$

4 $n = 20 \times -5$ **5** $48 \times -5 = n$ **6** $n = 50 \times -48$

7 $n = 25 \times -40$ **8** $n = 25 \times -80$ **9** $n = 80 \times -25$

10 $-3 \times 7 = n$ **11** $-6 \times 8 = n$ **12** $-80 \times 6 = n$

Find the value of *n* in each of the following problems.

⑬ $n = -5 \times 48$

⑭ $n = -25 \times 80$

⑮ $75 \times 80 = n$

⑯ $75 \times -80 = n$

⑰ $-80 \times 75 = n$

⑱ $250 \times -20 = n$

⑲ $-250 \times 20 = n$

⑳ $n = -750 \times 20$

㉑ $12 \times 6 = n$

㉒ $12 \times -6 = n$

㉓ $n = -6 \times 12$

㉔ $20 \times -50 = n$

㉕ $50 \times 20 = n$

㉖ $n = -10 \times 10$

㉗ $-100 \times 10 = n$

㉘ $45 \times 40 = n$

㉙ $n = -40 \times 45$

㉚ $60 \times 70 = n$

㉛ $60 \times -70 = n$

㉜ $n = 25 \times -8$

㉝ $-60 \times 12 = n$

㉞ $16 \times 4 = n$

㉟ $n = 11 \times -8$

㊱ $n = -7 \times 5$

㊲ Consider the following four multiplication problems:

$3 \times 4 = ?$ $3 \times -4 = ?$ $-3 \times 4 = ?$ $-3 \times -4 = ?$

What should the answer to the last problem be? Should it be the same as the answer to either the second or third problem? Why or why not? Discuss this with your friends. What do you think is a reasonable answer to the question "What is -3 times -4?" Would you choose the rule that the product of two negative numbers is positive, or that the product of two negative numbers is negative?

Because people find it most convenient to use the rule that a negative number multiplied by a negative number equals a positive number, most calculators have been programmed to follow this rule.

㊳ Write a problem that could be solved by multiplying a negative number by a positive number.

The lowest temperature ever recorded on Earth was −89°C (−129°F) at Vostok, Antarctica on July 21, 1983.

Unit 1 Review

Lessons 8, 9, 12, 15, and 16

Solve these problems. Watch the signs.

1   783
    + 246

2   4038
    − 896

3   5309
    × 73

4   6)‾7404‾

5   8)‾7704‾

6   4038
    + 896

7   5309
    − 4000

8   35)‾15,960‾

9   783
    × 246

10   4038
    × 89

11   9)‾3843‾

12   7)‾2247‾

13   5309
    + 4873

14   783
    − 246

15   8)‾8352‾

16   80)‾83,520‾

Lessons 13 and 20

In each problem two of the answers are clearly wrong and one is correct. Choose the correct answer.

17   728 × 542   **a.** 39,456   **b.** 394,576   **c.** 3,913,456

18   7523 × 806   **a.** 6,063,538   **b.** 663,538   **c.** 60,063,538

19   7523 + 803   **a.** 8326   **b.** 15,326   **c.** 5326

20   3014 − 876   **a.** 5862   **b.** 2138   **c.** 3962

21   47,705 ÷ 145   **a.** 9306   **b.** 4076   **c.** 329

22   2409 ÷ 73   **a.** 2113   **b.** 213   **c.** 33

23   682 × 47   **a.** 36,524   **b.** 32,054   **c.** 22,864

24   451 + 926   **a.** 1377   **b.** 5277   **c.** 13,477

25   8194 − 3475   **a.** 4719   **b.** 5321   **c.** 7429

26   90,272 ÷ 28   **a.** 32   **b.** 324   **c.** 3224

Lessons 22 and 24

Solve. Watch for negative numbers.

27 $5 + 20$ **28** $5 - 20$ **29** $(-5) + 20$

30 $(-5) - 20$ **31** $13 - 8$ **32** $8 - 13$

33 $(-13) - 8$ **34** $(-8) - 13$ **35** 5×-4

36 -3×6 **37** -2×1 **38** 7×-8

PROBLEM SOLVING

Solve these problems.

39 How many students are in 14 classes of 25 students each?

40 As many as 50 children can be transported on one ABC school bus. How many buses are needed to transport 342 children?

Lessons 9, 13, 17, 18, and 22

41 You can get 3 kilograms of dog food for $4.77 or 7 kilograms of the same dog food for $10.46. In which container does the dog food cost less per kilogram?

42 If the temperature is 15°C now, what will it be if it

a. goes down 5°C?

b. goes down 15°C?

c. goes up 8°C?

d. goes down 30°C?

15°
10°
5°
0°
-5°
-10°
°C

43 One kilogram of hamburger costs $4.19.

a. How much will 7 kilograms cost?

b. How much will 4 kilograms cost?

c. How much will 10 kilograms cost?

44 Leo has $12.00. With it he has to pay $1.20 for lunch five times next week and buy a notebook that costs $1.49. Does he have enough money so that he can buy a $5.00 ticket for the high school football game today?

45 Suki is crushing aluminum cans to send to the recycling center. She has about 600 cans to crush and can crush two cans every minute. About how long will it take Suki to crush all the cans?

LESSON
26

Unit 1 Practice

Add.

Lesson 8

① 3847
   + 6952

② 8340
   + 7396

③ 4783
   + 2875

④ 3872
   + 846

⑤ 7903
   + 3408

⑥ 9994
   + 9876

⑦ 403
   + 7828

⑧ 5743
   + 6921

Lesson 9

Subtract.

⑨ 5302
   − 461

⑩ 5871
   − 3942

⑪ 5003
   − 2769

⑫ 4872
   − 2171

⑬ 10,000
   − 3,462

⑭ 6047
   − 382

⑮ 43,571
   − 488

⑯ 2576
   − 1849

Lessons 8 and 9

Watch the signs.

⑰ 4321
   + 3456

⑱ 4321
   − 3456

⑲ 9878
   + 5676

⑳ 9878
   − 5676

㉑ 4823
   + 759

㉒ 6104
   − 586

㉓ 403
   − 397

㉔ 403
   + 397

Lessons 11 and 12

Multiply. Check your answers to be sure that they make sense.

㉕ 200
   × 4

㉖ 534
   × 9

㉗ 6395
   × 7

㉘ 308
   × 21

㉙ 78
   × 54

㉚ 69
   × 73

㉛ 59
   × 96

㉜ 879
   × 302

㉝ 607
   × 865

㉞ 703
   × 71

㉟ 300
   × 800

㊱ 2000
   × 90

Lesson 15 Divide. Answers will be whole numbers. There will be no remainder.

37. $8\overline{)4032}$ 38. $6\overline{)534}$ 39. $5\overline{)3915}$ 40. $7\overline{)59{,}479}$

41. $9\overline{)40{,}752}$ 42. $3\overline{)534}$ 43. $4\overline{)11{,}352}$ 44. $2\overline{)13{,}578}$

Lesson 16 Divide. Round decimal quotients to the nearest whole number.

45. $50\overline{)473{,}200}$ 46. $25\overline{)473{,}210}$ 47. $25\overline{)905}$

48. $25\overline{)700}$ 49. $25\overline{)6120}$ 50. $75\overline{)5750}$

Lessons 22 and 24 Watch the signs.

51. $5 + 10$ 52. $5 - 10$ 53. $(-5) + 10$ 54. $(-5) - 10$

55. $10 - 20$ 56. $10 + 20$ 57. $(-10) - 20$ 58. $(-10) + 20$

59. $7 - 8$ 60. $8 - 7$ 61. $(-7) - 8$ 62. $(-8) - 7$

63. 6×-9 64. -25×4 65. -30×70 66. 16×-5

Lessons 13 and 20 In each problem two of the answers are clearly wrong and one is correct. Choose the correct answer.

67. $438 \times 694 =$ **a.** 3372 **b.** 33,972 **c.** 303,972

68. $6805 \times 79 =$ **a.** 5595 **b.** 53,595 **c.** 537,595

69. $4567 \times 824 =$ **a.** 373,208 **b.** 3,763,208 **c.** 37,863,208

70. $6 \times 7863 =$ **a.** 478 **b.** 4718 **c.** 47,178

71. $597 \times 68 =$ **a.** 4596 **b.** 40,596 **c.** 401,596

72. $742{,}014 \div 78 =$ **a.** 9513 **b.** 95,413 **c.** 950,413

73. $291{,}312 \div 408 =$ **a.** 74 **b.** 714 **c.** 7314

74. $264{,}128 \div 64 =$ **a.** 427 **b.** 4127 **c.** 41,027

75. $46{,}890 \div 45 =$ **a.** 142 **b.** 1042 **c.** 10,342

76. $3145 \div 37 =$ **a.** 5 **b.** 8 **c.** 85

◆ **LESSON 26   Unit 1 Practice**

Lessons 9, 13, 17, 18, and 22

Solve these problems.

77 If 50 cubes (all the same weight) weigh 194 grams, how much does each cube weigh?

78 If 194 people each gave $50 to the local college, how much would the college get?

79 Mr. Muñoz's hens laid 194 eggs, but 50 of the eggs were broken in an accident. There are 12 eggs in a dozen. How many dozens of unbroken eggs did Mr. Muñoz have that he could sell?

80 Mary can read about 50 pages in an hour. One day she read a book that was 194 pages long, and then she spent an hour reading another book.

   a. About how many pages did she read that day?

   b. About how many hours did she read that day?

81 If you have to cook a 6-kilogram turkey about five hours at 170°C, how long and at what temperature would you cook two 6-kilogram turkeys?

82 If the temperature is 10°C, what will the temperature be

   a. when it goes down 10°C?

   b. when it goes up 10°C?

   c. when it goes down 20°C?

   d. when it goes down 5°C?

   e. when it goes down 25°C?

83 Tickets to the class play cost $1.98. About $240 has been collected so far. About how many people have bought tickets?

84 Jesse is preparing to mail flyers about the next club meeting. He can fold, staple, and put address labels on three flyers every minute. How long will it take him to finish 75 flyers?

85 Ms. Lee earns about $3200 each month. About how much does she earn each year?

Numbo Jumbo

Players:	Two
Materials:	None
Object:	To determine the other player's number
Math Focus:	Mathematical reasoning

RULES

1. The first player chooses and writes down secretly any two-digit number in which no digit is repeated. Numbers that start with 0 (such as 07) are acceptable.

2. The second player says a two-digit number.

3. The first player responds with the letter *T* for each digit the second player guesses correctly and has in the correct position, *P* for each digit the second player guesses correctly but has in the wrong spot, and *F* for each digit he or she guesses incorrectly.

4. Repeat steps 2 and 3 until the first player responds with *TT*.

   Here are some suggestions:

   A. The first player should announce *T*s first, then *P*s, and then *F*s to avoid giving information about the order of the digits.

   B. Both players should record every guess and every response.

SAMPLE GAME

Glenda wrote 94 on her paper and hid it from Michael.

Michael guessed: 57   46   68   Glenda responded: FF   PF   FF

Michael stopped to think. He said to himself "5, 7, 6, and 8 cannot occur. Four is in the ones place, so all I have to find is the other number."

Michael guessed: 01   93   94   Glenda responded: FF   TF   TT

ANOTHER WAY TO PLAY THIS GAME

Use three-digit numbers instead of two-digit numbers.

UNIT 1

Unit Test

Watch the signs.

1 356 × 78   **2** 356 − 78   **3** 356 + 78   **4** 1274 × 91

5 1274 + 91   **6** 1274 − 91   **7** 1274 ÷ 91   **8** 7990 ÷ 85

9 4007 − 2409   **10** 5386 + 825   **11** 679 × 48   **12** 11,984 ÷ 14

13 5992 ÷ 7   **14** 30,168 ÷ 9   **15** 52,824 ÷ 6   **16** 18,075 ÷ 5

In each problem two of the answers are clearly wrong and one is correct. Choose the correct answer.

17 4673 × 75,154   **a.** 351,194,642   **b.** 35,194,624   **c.** 3,904,624

18 672 × 4960   **a.** 33,120   **b.** 333,120   **c.** 3,333,120

19 716,103 ÷ 753   **a.** 951   **b.** 9451   **c.** 94,451

20 5,718,016 ÷ 1024   **a.** 584   **b.** 5584   **c.** 55,484

21 4673 + 75,154   **a.** 129,827   **b.** 12,827   **c.** 79,827

22 75,154 − 4673   **a.** 28,481   **b.** 70,481   **c.** 2481

Add or subtract. Watch for negative numbers.

23 (−5) + 5   **24** (−5) − 5   **25** (−5) − 10

26 13 − 7   **27** 7 − 13   **28** (−7) − 13

29 (−8) + 7   **30** (−8) − 7   **31** 8 − 7

32 −7 × 2   **33** 8 × 9   **34** 25 × −3

Solve these problems.

35 Gloria's checking-account balance was $63. Then she wrote a check for $73. What was her new balance?

36 Happy Cow Dairy sells milk in 2-liter cartons for $1.32 or in 10-liter cartons for $6.50. In which container does the milk cost less per liter?

37　At the Quick-Service store a liter of milk costs 73¢ and a loaf of bread costs 90¢. How much will John pay for 2 liters of milk and three loaves of bread?

38　Celia's class is making Thanksgiving nut cups for the hospital. The students can make 30 nut cups in ten minutes. How long will it take them to make 600 nut cups?

39　Mr. Chen wants the class to finish the nut cup project in five days. Will they finish on time if they work on the nut cups 30 minutes each day?

40　At the beginning of the day the odometer on the school bus showed 49,723 kilometers. At the end of the day the odometer showed 49,916 kilometers.

　　a. How many kilometers did the bus travel that day?

　　b. How much farther must the bus travel before the odometer shows 50,000 kilometers?

41　A Hubmobile car can transport six people. How many Hubmobile cars will be needed to transport 27 people?

42　A stationery store sells a box of 24 pencils for $1.98. Do you think the store will sell you one pencil for 6¢?

43　Tomás was born on April 29, 1985. In what year will he

　　a. graduate from high school?

　　b. be 30 years old?

　　c. be 75 years old?

44　Mr. Havel wants to fertilize his lawn. Each bag of fertilizer is supposed to cover 75 square feet. Mr. Havel's front lawn is 144 square feet and the back lawn is 200 square feet. How many bags of fertilizer will Mr. Havel need to buy (assuming he doesn't already have some)?

45　Vanessa stopped for lunch at a fast-food restaurant. She wanted a hamburger for $1.89, a salad for $1.29, and a lemonade for $0.89. She had $5 with her. Could she buy the lunch she wanted?

CLEVER COUNTING

People in all cultures and all times have needed to count. Different cultures develop different ways of expressing numbers.

The Romans developed a numeration system that we still see in use today. Originally, the Roman numerals for 1 through 10 were I, II, III, IIII, V, VI, VII, VIII, VIIII, and X.

◆ Do you see a possible connection between these symbols and finger counting? Explain.

Later the symbols IV and IX were used instead of IIII and VIIII. What does it mean when the "I" is written before the "V" and the "X"? Why do you suppose this change was made?

Try doing the following problems using only Roman numerals (don't convert to your usual system or use a calculator).

Use the Roman numerals, including L = 50, C = 100, D = 500, and M = 1000.

MMMMDLXXVI + MCCCCLXXII

MMMCCLXXVIII − MDCCCLXVIIII

CLXXXVIII × XVIII

Show all your work for these problems in Roman numerals.

Many other number systems have been used.

CULTURE	NUMBER SYSTEM BASED ON	REGION
Babylonians	60	Middle East
Mayans	20	South America
Yuki	8	North America
Nahuatl	addition	Central America
Hindu-Arabic	10	Asia
Computers	2	everywhere

Conduct library research to investigate these or other numeration systems, and do some calculations in those systems as well.

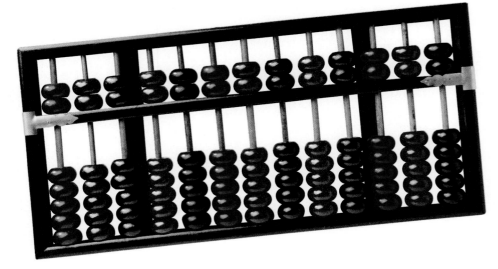

In your Math Journal discuss how difficult arithmetic is in our system, which uses place value as well as base 10, as compared with a system that does not use place value.

UNIT

2

Decimals and Exponents

UNDERSTANDING POWERS OF 10

- operations with decimals

- precision in measurement

- exponential notation

- counting outcomes

SCHOOL TO WORK CONNECTION

Gas station attendants use math . . .

The gas station attendant pumps gas that is measured to the nearest tenth of a gallon. The pump computes how many dollars and cents the customer owes for the gas. The customer chooses the type of gasoline according to price (given to thousandths of a dollar) or according to the octane rating (given as a percent).

Adding and Subtracting Decimals

You know how to add decimals—the same way you add whole numbers. Line up the decimal points to make sure you add thousandths to thousandths, hundredths to hundredths, and so on.

Examples:

0.38 + 0.25 = ?

$$\begin{array}{r} {\scriptstyle 1} \\ 0.38 \\ + \ 0.25 \\ \hline 0.63 \end{array}$$

Line up the decimal points.
Add.

0.937 + 0.3 = ?

$$\begin{array}{r} 0.937 \\ + \ 0.3 \\ \hline \end{array}$$

Occasionally, you may have to add decimals that don't have the same number of digits after the decimal point.

$$\begin{array}{r} 0.937 \\ + \ 0.300 \\ \hline 1.237 \end{array}$$

To help line up the digits, you may put 0s to the right of 0.3 so that both decimals have the same number of digits after the decimal point. You may do this because 0.3 and 0.300 have the same value. However, you may be indicating greater precision than is appropriate.

Subtraction with decimals is also the same as subtraction with whole numbers after you line up the decimal points.

Examples:

0.38 − 0.25 = ?

$$\begin{array}{r} 0.38 \\ - \ 0.25 \\ \hline 0.13 \end{array}$$

Line up the decimal points.
Subtract.

0.937 − 0.3 = ?

$$\begin{array}{r} 0.937 \\ -\ 0.300 \\ \hline 0.637 \end{array}$$

You may write 0s to help you in lining up decimal points, just as in addition.

Add or subtract. Watch the signs.

1 0.4 + 0.1   **2** 0.4 − 0.1   **3** 0.33 + 0.25

4 0.33 − 0.25   **5** 0.375 − 0.167   **6** 0.375 + 0.167

7 0.417 + 0.333   **8** 0.417 − 0.333   **9** 0.5 + 0.33

10 0.5 − 0.33   **11** 0.8 − 0.3   **12** 0.8 + 0.3

13 0.67 + 0.2   **14** 0.67 − 0.2   **15** 0.4 + 0.28

16 0.4 − 0.28   **17** 6.8 + 3.2   **18** 6.8 − 3.2

19 5.9 − 4.7   **20** 5.9 + 4.7   **21** 2.4 + 1.2

22 2.4 − 1.2   **23** 5.4 − 5.4   **24** 5.4 + 5.4

25 2.4 + 0.18   **26** 2.4 − 0.18   **27** 1 + 0.5

28 1 − 0.5   **29** 6.1 + 3.1   **30** 6.1 − 3.1

Solve these problems.

31 George has a piece of rope 5.5 meters long. He cut off a piece 2.4 meters long. How long is the remaining piece?

32 Mr. Engle bought three packages of ground beef at the store. They weighed 0.97 kilograms, 1.09 kilograms, and 2.00 kilograms. How much ground beef did he buy all together?

◆ **LESSON 27 Adding and Subtracting Decimals**

Solve these problems.

33 Sam works at Robert's Fast Food restaurant. A customer ordered two BIG BOB sandwiches for $1.98 each, a milkshake for $1.29, potato chips for $0.59, and a dessert for $1.09. He handed Sam a ten-dollar bill. Sam's cash register showed that the customer should receive $93.07 in change. Is anything wrong? What mistake do you think Sam may have made? How much change should the customer receive?

34 Abigail went to the grocery store to buy three containers of milk for $1.08 apiece, a head of lettuce for $1.27, a loaf of bread for $1.89, and some cheese for $2.53. She has a $50 bill, a $20 bill, a $10 bill, and a $5 bill in her pocket. Which should she give the clerk in order to receive the least amount of change? How much change should she receive?

35 Miguel has put the following ten items in his grocery basket so far: milk ($1.87), orange juice ($0.97), cottage cheese ($2.57), bread ($1.98), meat ($7.50), lettuce ($0.89), carrots ($1.84), crackers ($2.53), popcorn ($2.89), and bagels ($0.78). He has $28. Can he also afford to buy ice cream that costs $3.99? If he can't afford the ice cream, how much more money would he need to buy it? If he can afford the ice cream and buys it, how much change should he receive if he gives the clerk $28?

36 David had a balance in his checkbook of $342.05. He wrote a check for $73.16. What is his new balance?

37 Phyllis went to a discount art store to buy pictures to decorate her house. She wanted to buy five pictures for $4.99 each, three other pictures for $6.99 each, and a large picture for $24.98. She had $60 with her. Could she pay for all the pictures? If so, how much money would she have left after paying for them? If not, how much more money would she need in order to pay for the pictures?

Major Reductions Sale

Harder Roll a Decimal Game

GAME

Players:	Two
Materials:	One 0–5 cube, one 5–10 cube
Object:	To get the greater total score
Math Focus:	Place value, comparing decimal numbers, subtracting decimal numbers, and mathematical reasoning

RULES

1. Before play begins, agree on the number of rounds.

2. Roll the 0–5 cube. If a 0 is rolled, roll that cube again. Write a decimal point followed by as many blanks as the number rolled. If you roll a 3, you would write this: __ __ __.

3. Roll the 5–10 cube as many times as there are blanks in your decimal. If you roll a 10, roll that cube again.

4. Each time you roll the 5–10 cube, write that number in one of your blanks.

5. After both players have made decimals, subtract the lesser decimal from the greater decimal. Award the difference to the person who made the greater decimal.

6. After an agreed-upon number of rounds, add up your score. The player with the greater total is the winner.

SAMPLE GAME

Round	Andrea's Roll	Dan's Roll	Andrea's Score	Dan's Score
1	.76	.966		.206
2	.957	.676	.281	
3	.97775	.9665	.01125	
4	.8	.9576		.1576
5	.99	.866	.124	
6	.86855	.8875		.01895
Total			.41625	.38255

Andrea was the winner.

Applying Decimals

Solve these problems.

1 Dewayne had a $10 bill and spent some money at the grocery store. Now he has $3.47. How much money did he spend at the grocery store?

2 Abe is 1.60 meters tall. Last year he was 1.52 meters tall. How much has he grown since last year?

3 Winona has a board that is 2.50 meters long. If she cuts off 1.75 meters of the board, how much will be left?

4 Rosalind has a 2-kilogram bag of flour. She wants to bake a cake that uses 0.25 kilogram of flour, some bread that uses 1.5 kilograms of flour, and a batch of cookies that uses 0.35 kilogram of flour. Does she have enough flour?

5 Mr. Gonzales checked his odometer before he started driving this morning. It read 2545.3 miles. At noon it was 2563.7, and when he arrived home at 5 P.M., it was 2622.8. Did he drive more in the morning or the afternoon?

6 The balance in Sonia's checking account was $30.63. She then deposited $403.36. What was the new balance?

7 Darrell and Nathan timed each other in the 50-meter dash. Darrell took 10.7 seconds, and Nathan took 9.8 seconds. How much less time did Nathan take?

8 Mrs. Cooper went to the grocery store this morning. She wanted only five items: a loaf of bread for $0.75, a box of cereal for $2.79, a can of soup for $0.32, a pound of apples for $0.97, and a pineapple for $1.99. The clerk asked Mrs. Cooper for $10.24. Could that have been right? How can you tell?

Solve.

9 Philip wrote down the deposits and the amounts of the checks he had written all month, but he didn't bother doing the arithmetic. He started with a balance of $12.73. What was his balance at the end of the month? Was there ever a time when his balance was negative?

Amount of Check	Amount of Deposit	Balance
		12.73
10.00		
	148.57	
43.86		
102.78		
	100.00	
54.61		
83.07	200.00	
150.00		
5.00		

10 Two months later Philip's records looked like this. Find his balance at the end of that month.

Amount of Check	Amount of Deposit	Balance
		12.53
	148.57	
35.42		
90.00		
25.00		
	100.00	
8.57		
63.25	200.00	
150.00		
60.00		

◆ **LESSON 28** Applying Decimals

THINKING STORY

Efficiency Experts

Part 1

Ferdie, Portia, Manolita, and Marcus went into business as efficiency experts. That means they thought up quicker, easier, or cheaper ways to do things.

Their first customer was Mr. Eng. He said, "I have to wear glasses when I read, but not other times. As a result, my glasses are never where I need them. Suppose I am down in my workshop and I need to read the label on a can. But my glasses are in the living room, where I put them down after reading a book. If I sit down in the living room to read, then my glasses are sure to be upstairs in the bedroom. I'm always running around. Can you help me?"

The children thought about Mr. Eng's problem. Finally Manolita came up with an idea. "Why don't you buy four or five pairs of glasses? Leave them in different parts of the house. Then you won't have to walk so far to find a pair."

Mr. Eng tried the idea and said it worked fine.

The next customer was Mr. Breezy. He had a problem with keys. "I have six keys to different doors in my house and six keys to different doors in my dog-training school," he said. He showed them the key ring with the 12 keys on it. "All the keys look pretty much alike. I waste a lot of time trying different keys every time I want to lock or unlock a door."

"That's easy," said Ferdie. "Your problem is really the same as Mr. Eng's. You can solve it the same way. Just get four or five keys made for every lock. Put them on your key ring. Then each time you try a key, you will have four or five chances of getting the right one instead of only one chance."

"I have a different idea," said Portia. "Get two key rings—a silver ring for your house keys and a gold ring for your dog-school keys. Then you won't have to hunt through so many keys to find the right one."

"I don't see how that will help," said Ferdie. "He'll still have all the same keys as before."

. . . to be continued

Work in groups. Discuss your answers and how you figured them out. Then compare your answers with those of other groups.

1. What is another way of solving Mr. Eng's problem? In what ways is your idea better than or worse than Manolita's idea?

2. Would Ferdie's idea help Mr. Breezy? Why or why not?

3. Was Ferdie right when he said that Mr. Breezy would have more chances of getting the key on the first try? Give a reason for your answer.

4. Would Portia's idea help Mr. Breezy? Why or why not?

5. What is another way of solving Mr. Breezy's problem? In what ways is your idea better than or worse than Portia's idea?

LESSON 29

Decimals and Powers of 10

You know that the value of a digit's place in a number is ten times as much as the place to its right. So you can multiply by a power of 10 just by moving the decimal point to the right.

To multiply by 10, move the decimal point one place to the right. You may need to write in a 0.

Examples:

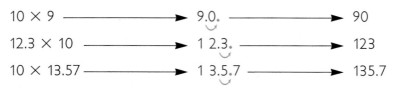

10 × 9 ⟶ 9.0. ⟶ 90

12.3 × 10 ⟶ 1 2.3. ⟶ 123

10 × 13.57 ⟶ 1 3.5.7 ⟶ 135.7

To multiply by 100, move the decimal point two places to the right. You may need extra 0s in writing your answer.

Examples:

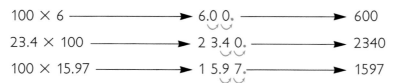

100 × 6 ⟶ 6.0 0. ⟶ 600

23.4 × 100 ⟶ 2 3.4 0. ⟶ 2340

100 × 15.97 ⟶ 1 5.9 7. ⟶ 1597

To multiply by any power of 10, count the number of 0s in the power of 10. Then move the decimal point that many places to the right. You may need to write in extra 0s.

Multiply.

1 10 × 1.9   **2** 1000 × 1.9   **3** 100 × 0.36

4 0.36 × 1000   **5** 1.96 × 10   **6** 1000 × 1.96

7 100 × 0.973   **8** 0.973 × 10,000   **9** 100 × 5.6

10 5.6 × 10,000   **11** 0.07 × 10   **12** 100 × 0.07

13 10 × 0.89   **14** 0.89 × 1000   **15** 10 × 23.7

16 1000 × 23.7   **17** 1.05 × 10   **18** 100 × 1.05

19 10 × 1.932   **20** 1.932 × 1000   **21** 19.32 × 10

You know that the value of a digit's place in a number is one-tenth the value of the place to its left. So you can divide by a power of 10 just by moving the decimal point to the left.

To divide by 10, move the decimal point one place to the left. You may need to write in a 0.

Examples:

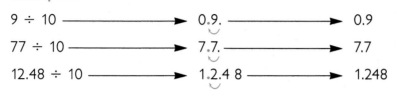

To divide by 100, move the decimal point two places to the left. You may need to write in extra 0s.

Examples:

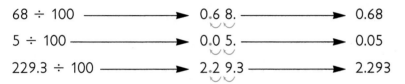

To divide by any power of 10, count the 0s in the power of 10. Then move the decimal point that many places to the left. You may need to write in extra 0s.

Divide.

22 33 ÷ 10

23 33 ÷ 100

24 7.5 ÷ 10

25 7.5 ÷ 100

26 19.6 ÷ 10

27 19.6 ÷ 1000

28 219.7 ÷ 10

29 219.7 ÷ 1000

30 0.3 ÷ 10

31 0.3 ÷ 100

32 1.05 ÷ 10

33 1.05 ÷ 100

34 20.3 ÷ 100

35 20.3 ÷ 10,000

36 0.02 ÷ 10

37 0.02 ÷ 100

38 5000 ÷ 10

39 5000 ÷ 1000

40 270 ÷ 1000

41 270 ÷ 10

42 27 ÷ 10

◆ LESSON 29   Decimals and Powers of 10

The basic unit of length in the metric system is the *meter*. Its symbol is *m*. The following table shows some metric units of length:

Unit	Symbol	Relationship to the Meter	Number of Meters
millimeter	mm	one-thousandth of a meter	0.001
centimeter	cm	one-hundredth of a meter	0.01
decimeter	dm	one-tenth of a meter	0.1
meter	m	one meter	1
dekameter	dam	ten meters	10
hectometer	hm	one hundred meters	100
kilometer	km	one thousand meters	1000

The *gram* is a metric unit of weight. Its symbol is *g*. Other metric units of weight correspond to the metric units of length. For example, a milligram is one thousandth of a gram.

◆   What are some other metric units of weight and their symbols?

◆   How are they related to the gram?

43   Use a computer or other means to draw and complete a table for metric units of weight.

The *liter* is a metric unit of capacity. Its symbol is *L*. Other metric units of capacity correspond to the metric units of length and weight.

◆   What are some metric units of capacity and their symbols?

◆   How are they related to the liter?

44   Use a computer or other means to draw a table, and complete the table for metric units of capacity.

The meter is defined as the distance travelled by light in a vacuum in $\dfrac{1}{299,792,458}$ of a second.

The meter is divided or multiplied by powers of 10 to produce the other metric units of length. For this reason it is easy to change from one unit of length to another in the metric system.

To convert from larger to smaller units, multiply by moving the decimal point right. To convert from smaller to larger units, divide by moving the decimal point to the left.

It is just as easy to change from one unit of weight or volume to another.

Example:	14 m = ■ cm	
Remember:	0.01 m = 1 cm	
	1 m = 100. cm	Multiply by 100.
	14 m = 1400. cm	Multiply by 100.
Example:	70 g = ■ kg	
Remember:	1000 g = 1 kg	
	1 g = 0.001 kg	Divide by 1000.
	70 g = 0.070 kg	Divide by 1000.
Example:	3.02 L = ■ mL	
Remember:	0.001 L = 1 mL	
	1 L = 1000 mL	Multiply by 1000.
	3.02 L = 3020 mL	Multiply by 1000.

Complete these conversions.

㊺ 3 m = ■ cm

㊻ 312 cm = ■ m

㊼ 2 kg = ■ mg

㊽ 300 g = ■ kg

㊾ 31.2 cm = ■ m

㊿ 500 mL = ■ L

(51) 1.5 L = ■ mL

(52) 200 mg = ■ g

(53) 50 mL = ■ L

(54) 4000 mm = ■ m

(55) 200 g = ■ kg

(56) 10 m = ■ dm

(57) 11 g = ■ mg

(58) 0.5 L = ■ mL

(59) 52.35 mg = ■ g

PROBLEM SOLVING

Solve this problem.

(60) Natasha has a pet hamster named Goldie. Natasha weighed and measured Goldie and found that the hamster weighs 120 grams and is 13 centimeters long.

a. What is Goldie's weight in kilograms?

b. What is Goldie's length in meters?

Multiplying Decimals and Whole Numbers

Jamal wants to buy seven jars of poster paint that cost $0.54 each. What will the total cost be?

$$7 \times 0.54 = ?$$

To find the answer, we could simply add 0.54 seven times:

$$7 \times 0.54 = 0.54 + 0.54 + 0.54 + 0.54 + 0.54 + 0.54 + 0.54$$
$$= 3.78$$

We can think of this another way. Write $0.54 as 54¢. Since 7 × 54 is 378, the total cost is 378¢. In dollars and cents, that is $3.78. So 7 × $0.54 is $3.78.

$$
\begin{array}{r} 54 \\ \times\ 7 \\ \hline 378 \end{array}
\qquad
\begin{array}{r} 0.54 \\ \times\ 7 \\ \hline 3.78 \end{array}
$$

Remember: **When you multiply a decimal by a whole number, multiply as though the decimal were a whole number, too. Then write the decimal point in the product as many places from the right as it is in the decimal factor.**

Example: 83 × 2.741

$$
\begin{array}{r} 2.741 \\ \times\ \ \ \ \ 83 \\ \hline 8\,223 \\ +\ 219\,28\ \ \\ \hline 227.503 \end{array}
$$

2.741 ◄──── This decimal point is three places from the right.

227.503 ◄──── So put this decimal point three places from the right.

Multiply.

1 2.4 × 7   2 0.6 × 5   3 0.65 × 5   4 3.65 × 5

5 0.1 × 8   6 2.1 × 8   7 0.4 × 6   8 0.04 × 6

9 3.2 × 3   10 43.2 × 3   11 20 × 0.8   12 22 × 0.8

Rosa was about to buy a package of dog treats at the supermarket.

"That can't be right," said Rosa.

◆ Why not?

DOG TREATS

Unit Price: $3.15 per kg
Weight: 2.35 kg
Price of Package: $17.40

Linda, Pablo, and Jim were shopping for a carpet. "I like that one," Linda told the saleswoman.

When the saleswoman asked the family how much carpet they needed, they said that the room was 4.62 meters long and 3.56 meters wide.

The saleswoman took out her calculator, pressed a few keys, and said, "That's 164.472 square meters."

"That can't be," said Jim.

◆ Why not?

In each case one answer is correct. Decide which one is correct without using a calculator.

13. $4.3 \times 6.4 =$ **a.** 2.752   **b.** 27.52   **c.** 275. 2

14. $2.5 \times 15.3 =$ **a.** 38.25   **b.** 382.5   **c.** 3825

15. $3.3 \times 3.3 =$ **a.** 1.089   **b.** 10.89   **c.** 108.9

16. $10.14 \times 10.51 =$ **a.** 1.065714   **b.** 10.65714   **c.** 106.5714

17. $1.04 \times 25.6 =$ **a.** 266.24   **b.** 26.624   **c.** 2.6624

18. $9.4 \times 11.8 =$ **a.** 110.92   **b.** 11.092   **c.** 1.1092

19. $17.5 \times 2.1 =$ **a.** 3675   **b.** 367.5   **c.** 36.75

20. $2.9 \times 2.9 =$ **a.** 0.841   **b.** 8.41   **c.** 84.1

21. $26.7 \times 10.2 =$ **a.** 272.34   **b.** 27.234   **c.** 2.7234

22. $62.3 \times 1.08 =$ **a.** 6728.4   **b.** 672.84   **c.** 67.284

23. $5.72 \times 34 =$ **a.** 19.448   **b.** 194.48   **c.** 1944.8

24. $18.6 \times 4.9 =$ **a.** 91.14   **b.** 911.4   **c.** 9114

25. $0.4 \times 1.3 =$ **a.** 0.052   **b.** 0.52   **c.** 5.2

Multiplying Decimals

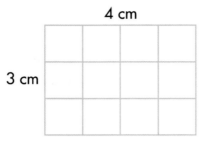

4 cm

3 cm

To find the area of a rectangle, multiply the length and the width. Your answer will be in square units. The area of the rectangle above is 3 centimeters × 4 centimeters, or 12 square centimeters.

Often we have to multiply two decimals when we are finding areas. Suppose we want to find the area of a rectangle that is 0.3 meter long and 0.25 meter wide. The area is 0.3 × 0.25 square meter.

Let's draw that rectangle in a square that is 1 meter on a side (1 square meter). The rectangle is yellow. See the illustration on the next page.

One side of the square is marked off in hundredths. The other side is in tenths. We want to find the area of the yellow rectangle. It is three tenths of a meter long and 25 hundredths of a meter wide.

◆   How many tenths in one whole?

◆   How many hundredths in one whole?

◆   How many small rectangles are there in the entire square?

◆   What part of the large square is each small rectangle?

◆   How many of the small rectangles are in the yellow rectangle?

◆   How did you find that?

The area of the yellow rectangle is $\frac{75}{1000}$ of a square meter, or 0.075 square meter. So we say that 0.3 × 0.25 is 0.075.

0.3 m

0.25 m

Notice that we found the number of small rectangles by multiplying two whole numbers (3 and 25). The size of each small rectangle is determined by the size of the units of the two factors: (tenths × hundredths = thousandths).

We can use this idea whenever we multiply two decimals. The number in the answer, if we ignore the decimal point, is the product of the numbers in the factors.

To place the decimal point, we look at the number of decimal places in each factor.

◆ LESSON 31 Multiplying Decimals

To multiply two decimals, multiply as though there were no decimal points. Then place the point in the answer as many places from the right as there are digits to the right of the decimal point in the two factors together. This is easier to understand with an example.

Example: $10.1 \times 3.48 = ?$

$$
\begin{array}{r}
3.4\,8 \\
\times \quad 1\,0.1 \\
\hline
3\,4\,8 \\
\times\,3\,4\,8\,0 \\
\hline
3\,5.1\,4\,8
\end{array}
$$

3.4 8 ◄——— This decimal point is two places from the right.
× 1 0.1 ◄——— This point is one place from the right.
3 5.1 4 8 ◄——— $2 + 1 = 3$ So place the point three places from the right in the answer.

The answer is 35.148.

Check to see that the answer makes sense. It should be more than 10×3 and less than 11×4. Is 35.148 between 30 and 44? Yes, so the answer makes sense.

Multiply. Check your answers to be sure they make sense.

1. 4×0.8
2. 0.4×0.8
3. 75×0.2
4. 7.5×0.2
5. 101×0.66
6. 1.01×6.6
7. 3.02×21
8. 0.302×0.21
9. 0.40×0.25
10. 0.04×0.25
11. 0.037×9
12. 3.7×0.09
13. 42×0.55
14. 4.2×5.5
15. 3.57×11
16. 35.7×1.1
17. 606×2.2
18. 6.06×0.22
19. 1.540×21
20. 1.540×0.21
21. 35×7.2
22. 3.5×72
23. 8.4×6.9
24. 0.84×0.69
25. 5.1×0.09
26. 51×0.9
27. 73.8×2.3
28. 7.38×23
29. 47×9.45
30. 4.7×9.45
31. 4.7×94.5
32. 75×10.3
33. 75×1.03

Solve these problems.

34 Antonio bought 12 cans of juice for $2.53 each. How much did he have to pay for them?

35 Jefferson's weekly paycheck is $243.57. How much does he receive in one year?

36 One pencil costs $0.57. How much will 20 pencils cost?

37 Patrick lives 0.7 miles from school. If he rides his bicycle to school and back every day from Monday through Friday, how many miles does he ride in a week?

38 Each of the Gumper quintuplets weighs exactly 51.3 kilograms. How much do they weigh all together?

39 Each of the Gumper quintuplets can jump across a puddle that is 3.74 meters wide. How wide a puddle can they jump all together?

40 Each of the Gumper quintuplets has $43.57 in her pocket. How much money do they have all together?

41 How much will it cost for the Gumper quintuplets to go to a movie if tickets cost $4.75 each?

42 The quintuplets have some coupons for the movie theater that say, "Buy one ticket, get another ticket free." Using the coupons, how much will it cost them to go to a movie?

Precision with Customary Measurements

Work in groups to measure the length of your classroom. Share your results with the class. Did each get the same result?

When you report a measurement, such as 3 feet 2 inches, people assume you believe the true measurement is closer to 3 feet 2 inches than to either 3 feet 1 inch or 3 feet 3 inches.

◆ What is the measurement exactly halfway between 3 feet 1 inch and 3 feet 2 inches?

◆ What is the measurement exactly halfway between 3 feet 2 inches and 3 feet 3 inches?

So if you say a length is 3 feet 2 inches, you mean that the length is between 3 feet $1\frac{1}{2}$ inches and 3 feet $2\frac{1}{2}$ inches.

In general you should be careful not to report a measurement that would give the impression it is more precise than it really is. So, to say the length of your school room is 27 feet, 3 and $\frac{5}{16}$ inches gives the impression you believe your measurement is correct to the nearest sixteenth of an inch.

◆ Were all of the class's measurements within $\frac{1}{16}$ inch of each other?

This is unlikely, given the usual methods of measuring and all the things that might go wrong as you are trying to measure the length of the room.

Solve these problems.

1 Suppose you hear that a new mall has opened 10 miles from your school.

   a. Do you think the mall is exactly 10 miles from your school?

   b. What is the closest the mall could be to school?

   c. What is the farthest the mall could be from school?

2 Suppose a county map reports a street is 52,799 feet long.

   a. What is the shortest length the street could have?

   b. What is the longest length the street could have?

Between what two measures would you assume the true measure is if somebody reported each of the following measurements?

3   3 feet 4 inches

4   5 yards, 2 feet, 7 inches

5   27 miles

6   27.3 miles

7   27.0 miles

8   7 inches

9   18 yards

10   54 feet

11   648 inches

12   8 feet

13   8 feet, 3 inches

14   6 miles

15 $4\frac{1}{2}$ feet

16   12 yards

17   37 feet

18   57 pounds

19   1216 gallons

20   13 years

21   Discuss the relationship between the three measurements in problems 9–11.

How would you report the measurements given below with the possible indicated error?

22   10 feet, possible error of $\frac{1}{2}$ foot

23   10 feet, possible error of $\frac{1}{2}$ inch

24   1 mile, possible error of $\frac{1}{20}$ mile

25   1 mile, possible error of $\frac{1}{2}$ yard

26   1 mile, possible error of $\frac{1}{2}$ foot

27   1 mile, possible error of $\frac{1}{2}$ inch

28   8 inches, possible error of $\frac{1}{2}$ inch

29   12 miles, possible error of 0.05 mile

30   9 yards, possible error of $\frac{1}{2}$ yard

31   9 yards, possible error of $\frac{1}{2}$ foot

LESSON 33

Reporting Metric Measurements

When we report a measurement, the number of decimal places we use gives an idea of how precise we think the measurement is.

Examples:

If we report:
6 meters

We believe the true measure is between 5.5 meters and 6.5 meters.

If we report:
6.0 meters

We believe the true measure is between 5.95 meters and 6.05 meters.

If we report:
6.00 meters

We believe the true measure is between 5.995 meters and 6.005 meters.

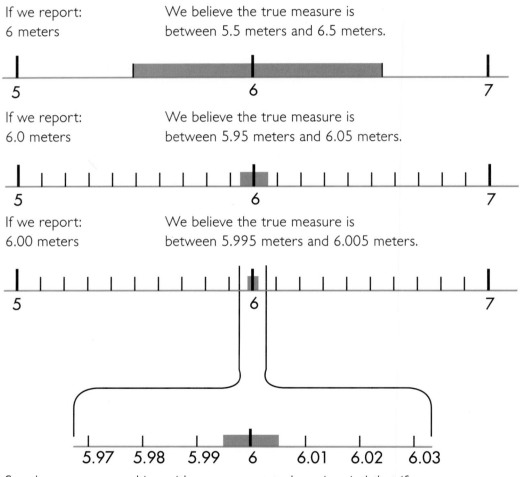

So when you are working with measurements, keep in mind that if you put 0s to the right of a decimal, then you are changing the meaning of that measurement.

What did the person who made the measurement believe was the true range of the measurement?

1. 4 centimeters

2. 7.0 kilometers

3. 5.00 meters

4. 8 decimeters

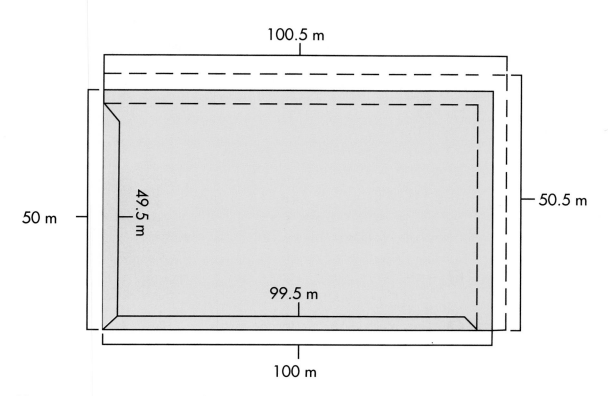

100.5 m

50 m

49.5 m

50.5 m

99.5 m

100 m

Hector measured the length of a rectangular field to be 100 m and the width to be 50 m.

Answer the following questions.

5 What are the perimeter and area of the field if Hector's measurements are exactly right?

6 If the true length and width of the field are 0.5 m greater than Hector's measurements, what is the true perimeter? What is the true area?

7 If the true length and width of the field are 0.5 m less than Hector's measurements, what is the true perimeter? What is the true area?

8 What are the greatest errors possible in Hector's figures for the perimeter and area of the field?

9 If Hector were measuring the area of the field to decide how much seed to buy and plant in the field, would he use the greatest possible area or the least possible area?

10 If Hector were measuring the area of the field to see if it was large enough to use as a playing field for some game, would he use the greatest possible area or the least possible area?

Solving Problems Using Decimals

Mr. Reilly is having carpet put in his living room. The room is 3.6 meters wide and 6.3 meters long.

The carpet he likes is 4.0 meters wide and costs $21.95 per running meter. He must buy a piece that is 4.0 meters wide, even though the room is not that wide.

1 How many running meters of carpet must Mr. Reilly buy?

2 How much will he pay for the carpet?

The salesman tells Mr. Reilly that he can have the store install the carpet for $3.25 per square meter of the room. Included in this service is trimming the piece of carpet to fit and attaching the carpet to the floor.

3 How many square meters are in the room?

4 How much will it cost if Mr. Reilly has the store install the carpet?

5 How much will it cost Mr. Reilly for the carpet and the installation?

Another carpeting store is having a sale on remnants, or pieces of carpeting that have already been cut. They are selling a piece of carpet that is 4.0 meters wide and 6.7 meters long for $19.95 per meter of length.

6 How much will this carpet remnant cost?

This store has an installation charge of $3.50 per square meter.

7 How much will it cost Mr. Reilly to have this store's employees install the carpet?

8 How much will it cost for the carpet and the installation from the second store?

9 Which store would charge less for the carpet and installation?

10 What other factors besides cost might Mr. Reilly consider in deciding where to buy his carpet?

Hannah Reilly liked the carpet her father bought so much that now she wants to carpet her room. Her room is a rectangle 3.2 meters wide and 4.8 meters long.

The carpet she likes is 4 meters wide and costs $18.50 per running meter. Today only, there's a big sale. This carpet is selling for half its regular price. Installation is $2.50 per square meter of the room.

11 How many running meters of carpet does Hannah need?

12 What will it cost to buy carpet for her room?

13 What is the area of the room in square meters?

14 What will it cost to have the carpet installed?

15 What is the total cost to carpet Hannah's room?

Hannah would like to take a few days to think about the carpet and make sure it's what she wants. After the sale ends, the carpeting will be back to its regular price and installation will be $3.25 per square meter.

16 How much more will the carpeting cost after the sale ends?

17 How much more will the installation cost?

18 How much more will the total cost to carpet Hannah's room be if Hannah places her order after the sale ends?

◆ LESSON 34 Solving Problems Using Decimals

Multiply. Look for patterns that will help you.

19 0.05 × 2   **20** 0.05 × 0.02   **21** 0.05 × 0.2

22 0.5 × 0.2   **23** 0.5 × 2   **24** 5 × 0.2

25 5 × 2   **26** 0.3 × 4   **27** 0.3 × 14

28 0.3333 × 0.3333   **29** 0.33333 × 0.33333   **30** 0.333333 × 0.333333

31 2 × 3   **32** 21 × 31   **33** 2.1 × 3.1

34 2.01 × 3.1   **35** 2.01 × 3.01   **36** 2.01 × 3.001

37 2.001 × 3.001   **38** 0.46 × 0.71   **39** 0.85 × 2.6

40 9.4 × 2   **41** 9.4 × 0.2   **42** 9.4 × 0.02

43 9.4 × 1.02   **44** 0.94 × 1.02   **45** 0.94 × 1.002

46 1.8 × 8.1   **47** 2.7 × 7.2   **48** 3.6 × 0.63

Do these problems in your head. Watch the signs.

49 72 × 10 = ■   **50** 7.2 × 10 = ■   **51** 72 ÷ 10 = ■

52 72 ÷ 100 = ■   **53** 1.5 × 10 = ■   **54** 1.5 × 100 = ■

55 1.5 × 1000 = ■   **56** 1.5 ÷ 10 = ■   **57** 1.5 ÷ 100 = ■

58 1.5 ÷ 1000 = ■   **59** 0.6 × 10 = ■   **60** 0.6 ÷ 10 = ■

61 50 ÷ 100 = ■   **62** 50 ÷ 1000 = ■   **63** 0.05 × 100 = ■

64 0.05 ÷ 10 = ■   **65** 1 ÷ 10 = ■   **66** 1 ÷ 100 = ■

67 0.01 × 100 = ■   **68** 0.01 × 1000 = ■   **69** 0.001 × 1000 = ■

70 650 ÷ 1000 = ■   **71** 650 ÷ 100 = ■   **72** 65 ÷ 10 = ■

73 6.5 × 100 = ■   **74** 0.65 × 100 = ■   **75** 6.5 ÷ 100 = ■

76 4.8 × 100 = ■   **77** 2.3 ÷ 100 = ■   **78** 0.79 ÷ 10 = ■

Make 25 Game

Players:	Two or more
Materials:	Two 0–5 cubes, two 5–10 cubes, a calculator
Object:	To get the product closest to 25
Math Focus:	Multidigit multiplication with decimal numbers and mathematical reasoning

RULES

1. Take turns rolling all four cubes. If you roll a 10, roll that cube again.

2. Use each number once to make two two-digit numbers whose product is close to 25. You may make decimals. Do not use a calculator or pencil and paper in making these numbers.

3. The player with the product closest to 25 wins the round. Use a calculator or pencil and paper for checking products only if necessary.

SAMPLE GAME

Alicia rolled:

`0` `1` `5` `7`

Alicia made this problem:

5.1 × 7.0

Yan rolled:

`1` `5` `5` `2`

Yan made this problem:

5.1 × 5.2

Alicia and Yan knew that 5.1 × 7.0 is about 35 and that 5.1 × 5.2 is only a little more than 25. So they knew that Yan was the winner of the round. If the products had been closer, Alicia and Yan could have checked them on a calculator.

Suppose you roll 1, 3, 7, and 9. How would you decide which numbers to make? Record your ideas in your Math Journal.

Understanding Division by Decimals

Kyle and his family were comparing the price of a sports drink in two stores. In the first store they could get a 4-liter container for $3.24. The unit price listed was 81¢ per liter, or $0.81 per liter.

In the second store there was no unit price listed, but they could get a 3.80-liter container for only $3.12.

◆ Which sports drink was less expensive per liter?

◆ How much less?

One way to solve the problem is to divide the price by the number of liters. In the first store the unit price could be calculated by dividing $3.24 by 4 or 324¢ by 4:

$$\begin{array}{r} 81 \\ 4{\overline{\smash{)}324}} \end{array}$$

So the sports drink costs 81¢ or $0.81 per liter at the first store. In the second store finding the unit price requires dividing 3.12 by 3.80:

$$3.80{\overline{\smash{)}3.12}}$$

◆ Do you think the answer is greater than $1 or less than $1 per liter?

Look at each of these division problems.

a. $3.80{\overline{\smash{)}3.12}}$ **b.** $38.0{\overline{\smash{)}31.2}}$ **c.** $380{\overline{\smash{)}312}}$

d. $3800{\overline{\smash{)}3120}}$ **e.** $0.380{\overline{\smash{)}0.312}}$ **f.** $38{,}000{\overline{\smash{)}31{,}200}}$

◆ Do you think they have the same answer?

◆ Estimate the answer.

Look at each of these division problems.

a. $4{\overline{\smash{)}32}}$ **b.** $40{\overline{\smash{)}320}}$ **c.** $400{\overline{\smash{)}3200}}$

d. $0.4{\overline{\smash{)}3.2}}$ **e.** $0.04{\overline{\smash{)}0.32}}$ **f.** $4000{\overline{\smash{)}32{,}000}}$

◆ What do you think is the relationship among their answers?

If you multiply or divide both the divisor and the dividend of a division problem by the same number, the quotient will be unchanged.

So if you know that 32 ÷ 4 = 8, then:

320 ÷ 40 = 8   3200 ÷ 400 = 8   3.2 ÷ 0.4 = 8   0.32 ÷ 0.04 = 8

For each of the following problems, write three more problems that would have the same answer.

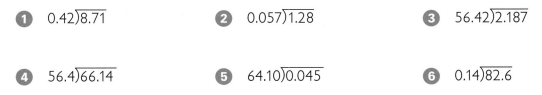

1 0.42)8.71   **2** 0.057)1.28   **3** 56.42)2.187

4 56.4)66.14   **5** 64.10)0.045   **6** 0.14)82.6

Approximate answers by short division if the decimal point of the divisor is between the first and second digit. If it is not, move it. Be sure also to move the point in the dividend the same number of places in the same direction.

Example:

0.42)8.71   It is hard to approximate because the decimal point isn't between the first and second digits.

0.4.2)8.7.1   Move the decimal point in both the divisor and dividend.

4)87.1   Round 4.2 to 4.

21
4)87.1   Divide to get the approximation, which is about 21.

(The actual answer to 8.71 ÷ 0.42 is about 20.74.)

Decide which answer is closest to the correct answer.

7 56.4)66.14   **a.** 0.117   **b.** 1.17   **c.** 11.7

8 0.057)1.28   **a.** 0.225   **b.** 2.25   **c.** 22.5

9 64.1)0.045   **a.** 0.07   **b.** 0.007 **c.** 0.0007

10 0.29)10.73   **a.** 37   **b.** 370   **c.** 3700

11 0.05)4.77   **a.** 9.54   **b.** 95.4   **c.** 954

12 0.4)72.24   **a.** 1806   **b.** 180.6 **c.** 18.06

LESSON 36

Dividing by Decimals

In a new housing development there are 6.852 acres of land. If each lot in the development is about 0.37 of an acre, how many lots can there be?

Divide to find the answer.

$6.852 \div 0.37 = ?$

$0.37\overline{)6.852} \longrightarrow 3.7\overline{)68.52}$ First approximate an answer.

$4\overline{)68.52}$ Round 3.7 to 4.

$\begin{array}{r} 17. \\ 4\overline{)68.52} \end{array}$ Do the short division. Stop when you get a reasonable approximation. The answer will be about 17.

Now do the division.

$0.37\overline{)6.852}$ Move the decimal point in the divisor to the right of the last nonzero digit.

$37\overline{)6.852}$ Move the decimal point in the dividend the same number of places in the same direction. Sometimes you will need to write extra 0s, but in this case you do not.

$37\overline{)685.2}$ Now the problem is in a form with which you can work.

$$\begin{array}{r} 18.5 \\ 37\overline{)685.2} \\ -\underline{37} \\ 315 \\ -\underline{296} \\ 192 \\ -\underline{185} \\ 7 \end{array}$$

Divide. Carry out the division to as many places as you need. Place the decimal point in the quotient directly above the new place of the decimal point in the dividend.

The 6.852 acres of land will hold about 18 lots, each about 0.37 of an acre.

Here is another method of dividing by a decimal with the same example.

Approximate the answer
by doing the short division.

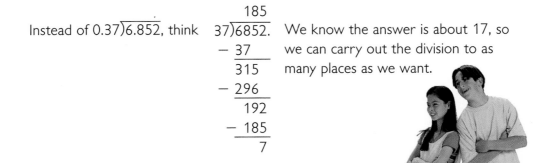

$$0.37)\overline{6.852} \longrightarrow 3.7)\overline{68.52} \longrightarrow 4)\overline{68.52}^{\,17.}$$

Now ignore the decimal point and divide.

Instead of $0.37)\overline{6.852}$, think

$$
\begin{array}{r}
185 \\
37)\overline{6852.} \\
-\;37 \\
\hline
315 \\
-\;296 \\
\hline
192 \\
-\;185 \\
\hline
7
\end{array}
$$

We know the answer is about 17, so we can carry out the division to as many places as we want.

Use the approximation (from the short division) to place the decimal point correctly in your quotient.

$$
\begin{array}{r}
18.5 \\
37)\overline{6852}
\end{array}
$$

Divide. Round quotients to the nearest hundredth.

Remember: To round to the nearest hundredth, you'll need to divide to thousandths. For example, if a quotient is 0.457, it rounds to 0.46.

1. $12 \div 0.4$
2. $999 \div 3.33$
3. $24.3 \div 0.27$

4. $125 \div 2.5$
5. $35 \div 7.2$
6. $0.384 \div 12$

7. $48 \div 0.16$
8. $81.54 \div 0.6$
9. $10.24 \div 12.8$

10. $8125 \div 1300$
11. $12.47 \div 1.4$
12. $16.18 \div 36$

13. $300 \div 0.75$
14. $2 \div 0.025$
15. $28 \div 4.5$

16. $512 \div 3.2$
17. $200 \div 56$
18. $21.6 \div 0.3$

19. $75 \div 15$
20. $560 \div 2.8$
21. $9.7 \div 0.64$

◆ LESSON 36   Dividing by Decimals

Solve these problems.

㉒ Melissa and Eric are making hand puppets for party favors. They use 0.25 meter of fabric for each puppet. They have four packages of fabric. Each package has 3 meters of fabric. How many hand puppets can they make?

㉓ Barry is building a fence 15 meters long on one side of his yard. He plans to put a fence post every 1.5 meters. How many fence posts does he need? (Hint: There must be a post at each end.)

㉔ Mikhail and his two brothers are evenly splitting the cost of a birthday gift for their mother. The gift cost $31.71, including tax. How much should each brother contribute?

㉕ Ms. Rasheed is knitting an afghan. She wants it to be 2 meters long. She can knit about 7.5 centimeters a day. About how many days will it take her to knit the afghan? (Hint: 7.5 centimeters = 0.075 meter)

㉖ Mr. Sato spent $43.78 for groceries on Thursday and $26.39 for groceries on Saturday. Did he spend more than $100 for groceries in those two days?

㉗ Dolores is in charge of collecting money for a class trip. The trip will cost $5.60 per student. So far, Dolores has collected $100.80. How many students have paid?

㉘ Gong Li works part-time at the local nursery. She earns $7.50 an hour. She has forgotten how many hours she worked last week, but she knows that she earned $187.50. How many hours did she work?

㉙ Mr. Rodriguez is a baker. He uses 0.4 kilogram of flour for each loaf of bread he makes. How many loaves of bread can he make from 100 kilograms of flour?

Watch the signs. Round quotients to the nearest hundredth.

③⓪ 43.78 + 26.39

③① 43.78 − 26.39

③② 5.7 × 1.3

③③ 4.2 ÷ 0.7

③④ 34.086 − 12.92

③⑤ 0.481 × 3.6

③⑥ 5.7 ÷ 1.3

③⑦ 2.801 + 35.64

③⑧ 6.401 × 0.32

③⑨ 1.024 ÷ 12.8

④⓪ 63 × 2.5

④① 48 − 1.8

④② 7.93 + 12.46

④③ 540 ÷ 12.6

④④ 54.2 − 36.4

Solve these problems.

④⑤ The regular annual subscription rate for a weekly magazine is $57.00. The newsstand price is $1.50 per issue. How much will a yearly subscription save compared with the newsstand price?

④⑥ The regular annual subscription rate for a monthly magazine is $36.00. A three-year subscription is available for $116.00. When might it be worthwhile to subscribe for three years?

④⑦ Marco used a calculator to multiply 34.5 by 74.1. His answer was 25,564.5. What, if anything, did Marco most likely do wrong?

④⑧ A one-bedroom apartment rents for $435 per month. How much is that per year?

④⑨ Kareem started a window-washing business. He estimates that to earn a good income, he needs to charge about $1.50 for each standard-sized window. On visiting the Crawford home, which has 30 windows, he told Mr. Crawford that he could wash all of the windows for $4.50. Does that seem to be a reasonable price? If not, what mistake do you think Kareem made?

Arithmetic with Decimals

Solve.

The floor of Alan's room is 3.6 meters long and 2.4 meters wide.

Alan wants to put tile on his floor. The chart shows the size and price of different square tiles he can buy.

Size (length of each side)	Price
0.1 meter	$0.10
0.2 meter	$0.36
0.3 meter	$0.81
0.4 meter	$1.35
0.5 meter	$2.00

1 What is the area of Alan's room?

2 What is the area of a 0.1-meter tile?

3 How many 0.1-meter tiles would he need?

4 What is the area of a 0.2-meter tile?

5 How many 0.2-meter tiles would he need?

6 Use a computer or other means to draw and complete the following chart. Which size of tile will be the least expensive for Alan? (He cannot cut the tiles, and he must cover the entire floor.)

Size of Tile	Area of Tile	Number of Tiles Needed	Price for Each Tile	Total Cost
0.1 meter	0.01 m²	864	$0.10	$86.40
0.2 meter	0.04 m²	216	$0.36	■
0.3 meter	■	■	■	■
0.4 meter	■	■	■	■
0.5 meter	■	■	■	■

"How thick is this piece of paper?" asked Inez. Here's how she solved the problem.

First she counted out 100 sheets of that kind of paper. Then she measured the thickness of the 100 sheets.

Inez found that 100 sheets are about 1.1 centimeters thick. Then she thought, "Since 100 sheets are about 1.1 centimeters thick, 1 sheet is about 0.011 centimeter thick. 0.011 centimeter is the same as 0.11 millimeter."

Solve these problems.

7 About how much does a paper clip weigh? (Hint: Weigh 100 paper clips.)

8 About how much does one facial tissue weigh? (Hint: Weigh a stack of tissues.)

9 About how much does one staple weigh? (Hint: Weigh a box of staples.)

Can you solve these problems without a hint?

10 About how much does one new piece of chalk weigh?

11 About how thick is the thickest paper you can find?

12 About how thick is the thinnest paper you can find?

To measure gold dust, the Egyptians used the amount that would fill a goose quill.

Mid-Unit Review

Add or subtract. Watch the signs.

1 2.4 + 0.6   **2** 0.844 + 0.666   **3** 0.844 − 0.666

Multiply.

4 2.7 × 10   **5** 0.46 × 1000   **6** 100 × 1.08

Divide.

7 27 ÷ 100   **8** 14.5 ÷ 1000   **9** 0.04 ÷ 10

Complete.

10 6 m = ■ cm   **11** 300 mg = ■ g   **12** 40 mL = ■ L

Choose the correct answer.

13 3.4 × 50
   a. 170
   b. 17
   c. 1.7

14 34 × 3.4
   a. 115.6
   b. 11.56
   c. 1.156

15 4.2 ÷ 3
   a. 140
   b. 14
   c. 1.4

16 2.3 × 5.08
   a. 116.84
   b. 11.684
   c. 1.1684

17 43.1 × 1.27
   a. 5.4737
   b. 54.737
   c. 547.37

18 24.6 ÷ 0.03
   a. 8.2
   b. 82
   c. 820

Solve.

19 6 × 2.7   **20** 0.203 × 0.06   **21** 1.720 × 41

Between what two measures would you assume the true measure is if somebody reported each of the following measurements?

22 4 yards   **23** 22.7 miles

How would you report the measurement given below with the possible indicated error?

24 20 feet, possible error of $\frac{1}{2}$ foot   **25** 2 miles, possible error of $\frac{1}{2}$ yard

For each of the following problems, write three more problems that would have the same answer.

26 0.42)8.88   **27** 0.65)4.128   **28** 33.5)0.906

Divide. Round quotients to the nearest hundredth.

29 0.38)77.52   **30** 5.6)952   **31** 0.012)64.8

32 0.28)4.97   **33** 3.34)48.3   **34** 0.07)98

35 4.5)58.5   **36** 14.3)68.2   **37** 0.23)75.21

Solve these problems.

38 Jessica went to the grocery store. She bought two containers of juice for $2.95 each, a box of cookies for $2.29, a loaf of bread for $1.39, and some vegetables for $3.25. She paid with a $10 bill and a $5 bill. How much change should she get from the cashier?

39 Ed's pet puppy, Alonzo, now weighs 5.80 kilograms. A year ago, Alonzo weighed in at 4.45 kilograms. How much weight did Alonzo gain?

40 Arthur is paid $635.85 a week. If he is paid the same amount every week, and then gets a bonus of one-week's salary, how much will he earn in a year?

41 Suki is collecting money for a class trip that will cost $7.25 per student. If she has collected $101.50 so far, how many students have paid?

Mr. Rodriguez is having carpet installed in his den. The room is a rectangle 4.2 meters wide and 5.8 meters long. The carpet he has chosen is 4.5 meters wide and costs $25.95 per running meter. He has to buy a piece that is 4.5 meters wide even though the room is not that wide. Installation costs $3.50 per square meter of the room.

42 How many running meters of carpet must Mr. Rodriguez buy?

43 How much will he pay for the carpet?

44 What is the area of the room?

45 How much will installation cost?

Keeping Sharp

Solve. Do as many problems as you can without paper and pencil.

1 $4 + 7 = \blacksquare$ **2** $\blacksquare = 100 + 200$ **3** $\blacksquare = 7 \times 8$

4 $80 \times 7 = \blacksquare$ **5** $25 + 26 = \blacksquare$ **6** $75 - 24 = \blacksquare$

7 $3 \times 3 \times 3 = \blacksquare$ **8** $5721 - 5721 = \blacksquare$ **9** $30 \times 30 = \blacksquare$

10 $27 \div 3 = \blacksquare$ **11** $\blacksquare = 6 \times 20$ **12** $\blacksquare = 6 \times 200$

13 $\blacksquare = 5 \times 200$ **14** $100 \div 5 = \blacksquare$ **15** $35 \times 10 = \blacksquare$

16 $3500 \div 10 = \blacksquare$ **17** $\blacksquare = 14 + 14$ **18** $\blacksquare = 140 + 140$

19 $\blacksquare = 140 + 139$ **20** $20 \times 20 = \blacksquare$ **21** $19 \times 20 = \blacksquare$

22 $35\overline{)700}$ **23** $25\overline{)800}$ **24** $3\overline{)750}$ **25** $30\overline{)750}$

26
$$357$$
$$+\ 243$$

27
$$250$$
$$250$$
$$250$$
$$+\ 250$$

28
$$9735$$
$$-\ 9734$$

29
$$10,000$$
$$-\ 9,999$$

In each problem two of the answers are clearly wrong and one is correct. Choose the correct answer.

30 $1.578 + 2.397$ **a.** 3.975   **b.** 39.75   **c.** 397.5

31 $10.632 - 2.977$ **a.** 0.7385   **b.** 73.85   **c.** 7.655

32 1.973×2.693 **a.** 53.13   **b.** 5.313   **c.** 0.5313

33 $16.31 \div 2.08$ **a.** 0.7841   **b.** 7.841   **c.** 78.41

34 10.25×12.55 **a.** 128.64   **b.** 1286.4   **c.** 12.864

35 $20.25 \div 4.45$ **a.** 455.1   **b.** 45.51   **c.** 4.551

Work in groups on this problem.

From the views shown here, decide the maximum and minimum number of cubes that could be in the stack of cubes. Use blocks or number cubes to build a stack of cubes that has these views.

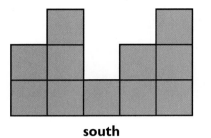

south

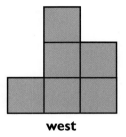

west

◆ How can you tell whether your stack has the maximum possible number of cubes?

◆ How can you tell whether your stack has the minimum possible number of cubes?

Draw "maps" like these showing the maximum and minimum number of cubes in each stack if you were looking down from above.

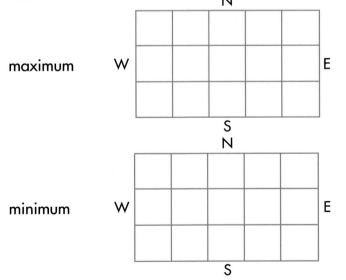

maximum

minimum

Using cubes, make up your own stacks, and draw pictures of the south and west views. Work with your group to determine the minimum and maximum number of cubes that could be in a stack that makes those views.

After you have completed several examples, exchange them with other groups to see if they get different answers. Then try to decide who has the better answers.

◆ **LESSON 38 Keeping Sharp**

Efficiency Experts

Part 2

M r. Schnitzel ran an old-fashioned butcher shop. He didn't sell meat already cut and wrapped in plastic. Instead, he asked customers what they wanted. Then he cut the meat for them. One day he went to the Efficiency Experts.

"Business is very good," Mr. Schnitzel said. "But I get tired running back and forth all day in my butcher shop. Could you help me find a way to operate my shop so that I won't have to walk so much?"

Marcus decided it was his turn to solve a problem. He drew a scale map of Mr. Schnitzel's shop. This is what it looked like:

Mr. Schnitzel's Butcher Shop

Scale: 1.5 cm = 1 m

Marcus watched Mr. Schnitzel waiting on customers. He took careful notes. This is what Mr. Schnitzel usually did:

1. Stand at counter and find out what customer wants
2. Go into freezer room and get meat
3. Take meat to chopping block and cut piece off
4. Take meat to scale, weigh it, and show it to customer
5. Take meat to wrapping table and wrap it
6. Hand wrapped meat over counter and get money
7. Go to cash register and ring up money
8. Give customer change
9. Go to chopping block and pick up meat that is left
10. Carry meat back into freezer room
11. Return to counter and talk to next customer

"I can see why you get tired," Marcus said. "I think that by moving a few things around we can save you a lot of steps."

. . . to be continued

Work in groups. Discuss your answers and how you figured them out. Then compare your answers with those of other groups.

❶ About how far does Mr. Schnitzel have to walk each time he goes through the 11 steps of serving a customer? (Note: Marcus's map is marked off in 1-meter squares. Estimate instead of measuring each distance.)

❷ Design a better way of placing things in Mr. Schnitzel's butcher shop. Draw a scale map to show where things go. The following things can be moved: counter, scale, chopping block, cash register, and wrapping table. The following cannot be moved: the door to the street and the freezer room door.

❸ With your new plan how far will Mr. Schnitzel have to walk to serve a customer?

❹ If Mr. Schnitzel has to walk about 3 kilometers a day inside his shop now, about how far will he have to walk each day with your plan?

LESSON 39

Exponents

Sometimes in solving problems we must repeatedly multiply by the same number.

ALGEBRA READINESS

If you know the edge of a cube is 4 centimeters long, you know there are 4 × 4 × 4 cubic centimeters in the whole cube.

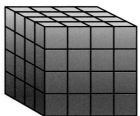

Suppose you have $500 in the bank and the bank pays 3% interest per year. To find the amount of money you have after one year, multiply $500 by 1.03. For each year that the money (the $500 and all the interest) stays in the bank, you find the amount of money you have at the end of the year by multiplying the amount at the beginning of the year by 1.03. To find how much money you have after four years, you can do this:

$$500 \times 1.03 \times 1.03 \times 1.03 \times 1.03$$

If you flip five coins (a penny, a nickel, a dime, a quarter, and a half dollar), there are many ways they could land. A few of the ways are shown in the chart. (**H** is for heads. **T** is for tails.)

	Penny	Nickel	Dime	Quarter	Half Dollar
First try	H	H	H	T	T
Second try	T	H	T	T	T
Third try	H	T	H	T	H
Fourth try	T	T	T	H	H
Fifth try	T	H	T	T	H
Sixth try	T	T	T	T	H

Since each coin must land in one of two possible ways, you can find out how many different ways the five coins could land by multiplying: 2 × 2 × 2 × 2 × 2.

Think about writing how to find the amount of money after eight years, or the number of different ways ten coins could land. Writing all of the factors could take a while.

To avoid writing so many factors, we write a small figure to the right of and slightly above the factor to show how many times that factor is used. The small figure is called an **exponent,** and the factor is called the **base.**

$4 \times 4 \times 4$ is written 4^3.

exponent

base ——— $4^3 = 4 \times 4 \times 4$

4^3 is read "4 to the third" or "4 cubed."

◆ Why might a number with an exponent of 3 be called "cubed"?

$1.03 \times 1.03 \times 1.03 \times 1.03$ is written 1.03^4.

exponent

base ——— $1.03^4 = 1.03 \times 1.03 \times 1.03 \times 1.03$

1.03^4 is read "1.03 to the fourth."

$500 \times 1.03 \times 1.03 \times 1.03 \times 1.03 = 500 \times 1.03^4$

$2 \times 2 \times 2 \times 2 \times 2$ is written 2^5.

exponent

base ——— $2^5 = 2 \times 2 \times 2 \times 2 \times 2$

2^5 is read "2 to the fifth."

When exponents are used to write numbers, we may say the number has been written in **exponential form.**

◆ Exponents are sometimes called powers. Can you see why 10, 100, 1000, and so on are called "powers of 10"?

If you flip 20 different coins, there are over 1,000,000 different ways for the coins to land.

◆ LESSON 39 Exponents

To evaluate a number written in exponential form, simply do the indicated arithmetic.

Examples:
$$4^3 = 4 \times 4 \times 4 = 64$$

$$500 \times 1.03^4 = 500 \times 1.03 \times 1.03 \times 1.03 \times 1.03$$
$$= 562.754 \text{ or } 562.75$$
(Use a calculator to check this.)

$$2^5 = 2 \times 2 \times 2 \times 2 \times 2 = 32$$

Evaluate these numbers.

1 2^5 **2** 2^{10} **3** 5^2 **4** 10^2 **5** 3^4

6 4^3 **7** 1^{10} **8** 1^{100} **9** 12^3 **10** 6^3

Write in exponential form. The first one has been done for you.

11 $5 \times 5 \times 5 \times 5 \times 5 \times 5 \times 5$ 5^7

12 $3 \times 3 \times 3 \times 3 \times 3 \times 3 \times 3 \times 3$

13 $10 \times 10 \times 10 \times 10$

14 $12 \times 12 \times 12$

15 $7 \times 7 \times 7 \times 7 \times 7$

Evaluate each of these. You may find it easier to evaluate the exponential part first and then multiply by the other factor.

Example: $7 \times 2^5 = 7 \times 32$ and $7 \times 32 = 224$

16 10×2^{10} **17** 7×5^2 **18** 6×10^2 **19** 7×3^4

20 7×4^3 **21** 10×1^{10} **22** 10×1^{100} **23** 4×10^3

24 5×10^3 **25** 7×10^8 **26** 6×10^4 **27** 3×10^7

Use a calculator to evaluate these.

28 1.05^{10} **29** 1.06^{10} **30** 1.07^{10} **31** 1.08^{10}

Use your calculator to help you answer the questions below. Before you calculate think about how using exponents can help you find answers.

You have two ancestors from one generation ago (your biological parents).

32 How many ancestors do you have from two generations ago (grandparents)?

33 How many ancestors do you have from three generations ago (great-grandparents)?

34 How many ancestors do you have from four generations ago?

35 How many ancestors do you have from ten generations ago?

36 How many ancestors do you have from 12 generations ago?

37 How many ancestors do you have from 13 generations ago?

38 How many ancestors do you have from 15 generations ago?

39 How many ancestors do you have from 18 generations ago?

If there are about 25 years between the births of parents and their children, your ancestors of ten generations ago were born about 250 years before you. So you had 1024 ancestors 250 years ago (not counting those from previous generations who were still alive).

40 How many ancestors did you have 500 years ago?

41 How many ancestors did you have 750 years ago? If your calculator cannot display this number, try to find a way to use your calculator to help you find the answer using paper and pencil.

42 Population experts estimate that there were fewer than 500,000,000 people on Earth until about 1600 A.D. Discuss this estimate in light of your answer to question 41.

LESSON 40

Counting Possibilities

Suppose you are walking down a path and you get to a place where the path splits into three paths. You must choose which of the three paths you will follow. You remember from the map that no matter which of the three paths you take, you will get to another place where the path splits into three. Then you will walk on to the end without further splits and without meeting any of the other paths. How many different places might you go?

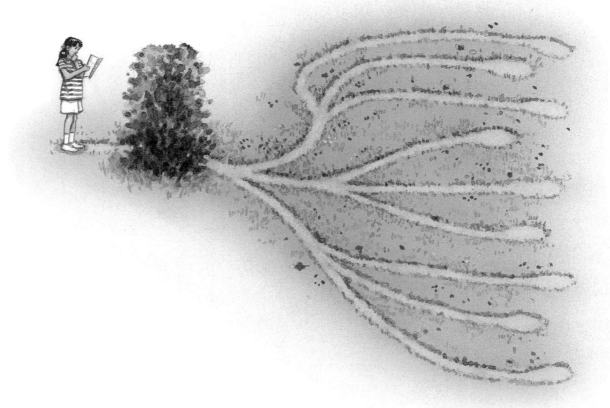

◆ Do you agree that you have 3 × 3, or nine different possible destinations?

◆ How could you express 3 × 3 using an exponent?

◆ Suppose each of the nine destinations leads to yet another place where the road splits into three paths. How many possible final destinations are there?

◆ How could you express this answer using an exponent?

Solve these problems.

1 If you know that a path splits into four paths, and then each of those splits into four paths, how many different destinations are possible?

2 If a path splits into two paths and then each of those splits into three paths, how many possible destinations are there?

3 Suppose you have four different colored shirts you can wear and three different colored slacks. How many different outfits are possible (assuming you don't care about color coordination)?

4 The school lunch menu has two kinds of drinks and four kinds of fruit. How many different combinations of a drink and fruit are possible?

5 If you roll a 0–5 number cube, how many possible numbers might appear? If you roll a 5–10 number cube, how many different numbers might appear? Suppose you roll both cubes together and record the number that each cube shows. How many possible number pairs are there with the 0–5 number written first? Some of those possible pairs are: (0,5), (0,6), (0,7), (0,8), (0,9), (0,10), (1,5), (1,6), and so on. How many of these are there all together? Try to explain how to get this result easily and why your procedure works. Discuss your procedure with other members of your class.

6 Suppose you have two 0–5 cubes, one painted blue and one painted green. (The numbers are painted in white.) How many possible sets of rolls are there if the number on the blue cube is always listed first?

7 If you roll a 0–5 number cube three times and keep track of the number showing each time, how many different ordered triples are possible? Those triples would include the following: (0,0,0), (0,0,1), (0,0,2), (0,0,3), (0,0,4), (0,0,5), (0,1,0), (0,1,1), (0,1,2), and so on.

8 Can you think of a way to use exponents to show your answer and process for problem 7? Show it.

LESSON 41

Writing Powers of 10

If you are multiplying by the same factor several times, there is an easy way to indicate that.

$7 \times 10 \times 10 \times 10 \times 10 \times 10 \times 10 = 7{,}000{,}000$

$7 \times 10 \times 10 \times 10 \times 10 \times 10 \times 10 = 7 \times 10^6$

Sometimes it is convenient to write 7,000,000.

Sometimes it is convenient to write 7×10^6.

7×10^6 is read "7 times 10 to the sixth."

Write each of the following by using an exponent.
(We call this the *exponential form.*)

Examples:

$600{,}000 = 6 \times 10^5$

$60 = 6 \times 10 \text{ or } 6 \times 10^1$

1 5000	**2** 200	**3** 40
4 8,000,000	**5** 3,000,000,000	**6** 80
7 700,000	**8** 40,000	**9** 800
10 9,000,000	**11** 4000	**12** 3000
13 600	**14** 400	**15** 30,000

Write in standard form.

16 5×10^8	**17** 3×10^5	**18** 8×10^1	**19** 10^2
20 4×10^7	**21** 2×10^2	**22** 5×10^2	**23** 10^3
24 8×10^6	**25** 7×10^4	**26** 8×10^3	**27** 10^1
28 9×10^3	**29** 6×10^9	**30** 10^5	**31** 10^4

The chart below shows basic information about the known planets in our solar system. Using a computer or other means, draw the chart but use exponential notation to show the distances. Save your completed chart because you will need it in the next lesson.

Our Solar System

Planet	Average Distance from the Sun (miles)	Closest Distance from Earth (miles)	Farthest Distance from Earth (miles)
Mercury	36,000,000	50,000,000	136,000,000
Venus	67,200,000	25,000,000	161,000,000
Earth	92,900,000	—	—
Mars	142,000,000	35,000,000	248,000,000
Jupiter	484,000,000	368,000,000	600,000,000
Saturn	887,000,000	745,000,000	1,031,000,000
Uranus	1,780,000,000	1,606,000,000	1,953,000,000
Neptune	2,800,000,000	2,667,000,000	2,915,000,000
Pluto	3,670,000,000	2,663,000,000	4,644,000,000

Challenge question: How is it possible for Pluto sometimes to be farther from Earth than Neptune and at other times be closer to Earth than Neptune?

Our nearest star, other than the sun, is Proxima Centauri, which is just over 25,000,000,000,000 (25×10^{12}) miles away.

◆ **LESSON 41 Writing Powers of 10**

THINKING STORY

Efficiency Experts

Part 3

A fter the Efficiency Experts helped Mr. Schnitzel, they had a visit from Ms. Hafiz. "I have a shop next door to Mr. Schnitzel's butcher shop," she said. "I hope you can save me steps the way you did for him. I brought you a map of my shop."

Ms. Hafiz's Shop

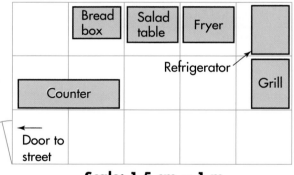

Scale: 1.5 cm = 1 m

"From this map I'd say you run a restaurant," Portia said.

"A take-out restaurant," explained Ms. Hafiz. "I make hamburgers and falafels that people pick up."

"What are falafels?" Manolita asked.

"They are like meatballs, but they are made from ground-up chickpeas," Ms. Hafiz said. "People in the Middle East put them in sandwiches. Americans call the sandwiches falafels. If you come to my shop, I'll give you one. They're very good!"

"But now I'll tell you how I make one. Suppose I am standing here at the counter," she said, pointing to the map.

"A customer orders a falafel. First I go to the fryer and put in three scoops of falafel dough. Then I go to the bread box and take out a piece of pita bread. It's round and hollow, so you can stuff things inside it. Then I go back to the fryer, take out the three falafels when they are done, and put them inside the pita bread. Next I go to the salad table. There I put salad and a special sauce into the pita bread. Then I go back to the counter. I put the whole thing inside a bag and give it to the customer."

"Falafels sound good," said Manolita. "Do you sell many?"

"Quite a few," said Ms. Hafiz. "But I sell twice as many hamburgers. I have to walk around even more to make a hamburger. First I am at the counter. Then I go to the refrigerator and take out a hamburger patty. Then I go to the grill and put it on. Then I go to the bread box and take out a bun. Then I go back to the grill, warm the bun, and put the hamburger on it. Next I go to the salad table and add lettuce, pickle, tomato, onion—whatever the customer wants. Finally I take it to the counter, put it in a bag, and give it to the customer."

"Your problem is more complicated than Mr. Schnitzel's," Manolita said. "But I'm sure we can solve it for you. In fact, I think I can see a way to save you a lot of steps. We need to switch around just three things in your shop."

. . . the end

Work in groups. Discuss how you figured out your answers. Compare your answers with those of other groups.

1 How could you tell from the map that Ms. Hafiz does not run a sit-down restaurant?

2 About how far does Ms. Hafiz have to walk while making and serving a falafel? How far for a hamburger? Now figure the average distance she has to walk while serving a customer.

3 By moving only three things in Ms. Hafiz's shop, save her as many steps as possible. Draw a map to show your plan. On the average how many meters will your plan save her?

4 By moving anything you want (except the door), design the best room plan you can for Ms. Hafiz.

LESSON 42

Multiplying and Dividing Using Exponents

$10^5 \times 10^2 = (10 \times 10 \times 10 \times 10 \times 10) \times (10 \times 10)$

◆   How many factors of 10 are in the product? Could you have gotten the answer by simply adding the original exponents?

Whenever we multiply two numbers written in exponential notation with the same base, the answer can be written with that base. To find the exponent of the answer, add the exponents of the factors.
So, $10^5 \times 10^2 = 10^{(5 + 2)} = 10^7$

$$10^7 \div 10^5 = \frac{(10 \times 10 \times 10 \times 10 \times 10 \times 10 \times 10)}{(10 \times 10 \times 10 \times 10 \times 10)}$$

◆   How many factors of 10 will be in the answer?

Whenever we divide two numbers written in exponential notation with the same base, the answer can be written with that base. To find the exponent of the answer, take the exponent of the dividend (first number) minus the exponent of the divisor (second number).
So $10^7 \div 10^5 = 10^{(7 - 5)} = 10^2$

Use the chart you prepared on page 149. How long would it take a spaceship traveling at an average speed of 1000 miles per hour to travel from Earth to Jupiter? Assume that the spaceship travels the shortest possible distance.

We know that Jupiter's closest distance to Earth is 368×10^6 miles. The speed of the spaceship is 1×10^3 miles per hour.

Therefore, it will take at least $\frac{368 \times 10^6 \text{ miles}}{1 \times 10^3 \text{ miles per hour}} = 368 \times 10^3$ hours.

It will take the spaceship at least 368,000 hours to reach Jupiter.

Use a calculator to solve these problems.

1   Convert 368,000 hours into weeks, into months, and into years.

2   Suppose the spaceship was traveling at an average speed of 2000 miles per hour. How many years would it take?

Use a computer or other means to draw and complete the chart to show how many years it would take a spaceship to reach the planets under the conditions shown. The answers for Jupiter are already shown.

Number of Years for a Spaceship to Travel from Earth

Planet	Closest Distance from Earth (miles)	at 500 miles per hour	at 1000 miles per hour	at 10,000 miles per hour
Mercury				
Venus				
Earth				
Mars				
Jupiter	368×10^6	84.0	42.0	4.20
Saturn				
Uranus				
Neptune				
Pluto				

Multiply or divide. Watch the signs. Leave answers in exponential form.

3. $10^3 \times 10^6$

4. $10^8 \div 10^5$

5. $10^6 \div 10^2$

6. $10^5 \times 10^3$

7. $(4 \times 10^5) \times (3 \times 10^8)$

8. $10^5 \times 10^4$

9. $(15 \times 10^9) \div (5 \times 10^6)$

10. $10^{12} \div 10^5$

11. $(2 \times 10^4) \times (3 \times 10^3)$

12. $10^{15} \div 10^{12}$

13. $(12 \times 10^6) \div (3 \times 10)$

14. $10^3 \times 10^8$

LESSON
43

Approximation with Exponents

Sometimes you need to approximate multidigit numbers. You can use exponential notation to help you approximate.

Example: 3748 × 72,654 is about $(4 \times 10^3) \times (7 \times 10^4)$
or about 28×10^7.

If you want, you can write this as 280,000,000. The precise answer is 272,307,192, so 280,000,000 is a good approximation.

Remember:

A. Round each number to a number with only one nonzero digit.

B. Think in exponential notation.

C. Multiply.

With a little practice you should be able to do this kind of problem without pencil and paper.

Approximate. Use exponential notation.

1 348 × 657

2 26,437 × 841

3 5103 × 89,248

4 7499 × 8478

5 643,871 × 869

6 65,024 × 76,503

7 382 × 512

8 21,503 × 498

9 7047 × 6894

10 250 × 750

11 921 × 584

12 312 × 6928

Notice that for problems 4, 6, and 10, you probably rounded both numbers the same direction, even though both were about halfway between the two numbers with one nonzero digit. In such cases you will get more accurate answers if you round the two numbers in opposite directions.

Midori lives in a city of 150,000 people. One day she wondered roughly how much time she would need to shake hands with everyone in her city.

Midori decided to find the answer to her question. She found that it took about 8 seconds to shake hands with ten people. She did this calculation:

$150,000 = 15 \times 10^4$ people

If it takes 8 seconds to shake hands with ten people, then it takes $8 \div 10$, or 0.8, second to shake hands with one person.

$0.8 \times 15 \times 10^4 = 12 \times 10^4$, or 120,000

So it would take about 12×10^4 seconds for Midori to shake hands with everyone in her city.

◆   How many minutes is that?

◆   How many hours is that?

◆   How many days is that?

Solve these problems.

⑬   Find out how many students there are at your school. How long would it take you to shake hands with all of them? (Hint: How long does it take you to shake hands with ten people?)

⑭   Find out about how many people live in your city, town, or village. How long would it take you to shake hands with all these people? (Hint: How long does it take you to shake hands with ten people?)

⑮   Find out about how many people live in your state. How long would it take you to shake their hands?

⑯   Find out about how many people live in the United States of America. How long would it take you to shake their hands?

⑰   Find out about how many people live in the world. How long would it take you to shake their hands?

◆ **LESSON 43** Approximation with Exponents

Multiply or divide. Watch the signs.

18 $10^4 \times 10^3$

19 $(2 \times 10^4) \times (4 \times 10^3)$

20 $(8 \times 10^6) \times (5 \times 10^4)$

21 $10^8 \div 10^5$

22 $10^7 \div 10^4$

23 $(6 \times 10^5) \div (3 \times 10^3)$

24 $(9 \times 10^9) \times (8 \times 10^8)$

25 $(4 \times 10^4) \times (4 \times 10^4)$

26 $(16 \times 10^8) \div (4 \times 10^4)$

27 $(3 \times 10^5) \times 10^4$

28 $(2 \times 10^8) \div 10^6$

29 $(2 \times 10^3) \times 10^3$

30 $(10 \times 52) \times 10^2$

31 $(20 \times 10^4) \div 10^3$

32 $(2 \times 10^5) \div 10^3$

33 $(24 \times 10^8) \div (8 \times 10^5)$

34 $(48 \times 10^7) \div (6 \times 10^3)$

35 $(18 \times 10^6) \times (2 \times 10^4)$

36 $(20 \times 10^6) \times (2 \times 10^4)$

37 $(30 \times 10^6) \times (2 \times 10^4)$

38 $(40 \times 10^6) \times (2 \times 10^4)$

39 $(40 \times 10^6) \div (2 \times 10^4)$

40 $(4 \times 10^7) \div (2 \times 10^4)$

41 $(28 \times 10^7) \div (4 \times 10^4)$

42 $(63 \times 10^{11}) \div (7 \times 10^5)$

43 $10^8 \times 10^4$

44 $10^{12} \div 10^8$

45 $(7 \times 10^{12}) \div 10^8$

46 $(40 \times 10^6) \div (8 \times 10^4)$

47 $(4 \times 10^3) \times (6 \times 10^2)$

Add or subtract. Watch the signs.

48 605 + 359

49 605 − 359

50 7005 − 2168

51 7099 + 1011

52 250 145 + 205

53 14 28 + 95

54 368 420 + 502

55 132 407 + 59

56 $(-10) + 5$

57 $(-10) - 5$

58 $5 - 10$

59 $(-5) + 10$

Solve these problems.

60 Sara used a calculator to add the following numbers: 345.60, 273.43, and 751.29. The answer the calculator showed was 75,748.03. What error did Sara most likely make?

61 When Sara asked for change for $1.00, she received 15 coins. Some were nickels and the rest were dimes. How many nickels and how many dimes did she receive?

62 Each year Earth travels about 2.92×10^8 miles as it revolves around the sun.
  a. About how many miles does it travel each day? (Assume that there are 365 days in one year.)

  b. Calculate the approximate average speed (in miles per hour) of Earth as it travels around the sun.

63 An apartment rents for $634 per month. How much is that per year?

64 The New City School System has 649 students in kindergarten through eighth grade. It is planning to spend $4,575,322 to operate this year.
  a. About how many students would you expect to find in each grade?

  b. About how much money will New City spend for each student this year?

  c. If ten students transfer out of the district, by how much do you think the operating expenses will change? Why?

  d. There is a rule in New City that says a class can never have more than 25 students. About how many regular classroom teachers do you think there are in this school system? Explain your answers and tell your assumptions.

65 A parking garage charges $3.00 for the first hour and $1.50 for each additional hour or part of an hour. How much will it cost to park there for 3 hours and 25 minutes?

66 Mrs. Moynihan's car gets about 24 miles to the gallon of gasoline. How many miles can she expect to go with 12.5 gallons of gasoline?

Interpreting Multidigit Numbers

SOCIAL STUDIES
CONNECTION

In 1960 the United States government had a total income of about $92,492,000,000. In that same year the government spent about $92,223,000,000. The population of the United States in 1960 was about 179,323,000 people.

◆ How does the government get income?

◆ For what purposes does the government spend money?

When the government spends less money than it receives, we say it has a *surplus* for that period. When it spends more than it receives, we say it has a *deficit* for that period.

◆ In 1960 did the United States government have a surplus or a deficit?

◆ How much was the surplus or deficit?

◆ If the surplus or deficit had been divided equally among all the people of the United States, estimate what each person's share would have been. Each person's share of the surplus or deficit is called the *per capita share*.

Information about United States income, spending, and population for selected years is given in the chart below.

Use a calculator to complete the last two columns. Work out ways for doing the calculations even if your calculators can show only eight digits.

United States Income, Spending, and Population 1910–1994

Year	Income (dollars)	Spending (dollars)	Population	Surplus (+) or Deficit (−)	Per Capita Surplus (+) or Deficit (−)
1910	676,000,000	694,000,000	91,972,000	−18,000,000	−$0.19
1915	683,000,000	746,000,000	100,546,000	−63,000,000	−$0.63
1920	6,649,000,000	6,358,000,000	105,710,000	+291,000,000	+$2.75
1925	3,641,000,000	2,924,000,000	115,829,000	▦	▦
1930	4,058,000,000	3,320,000,000	122,775,000	▦	▦
1935	3,706,000,000	6,497,000,000	127,250,000	▦	▦
1940	6,361,000,000	9,456,000,000	131,669,000	▦	▦
1945	45,216,000,000	92,690,000,000	139,928,000	▦	▦
1950	39,485,000,000	42,597,000,000	151,325,000	▦	▦
1955	65,469,000,000	68,509,000,000	165,275,000	▦	▦
1960	92,492,000,000	92,223,000,000	179,323,000	▦	▦
1965	116,833,000,000	118,430,000,000	194,303,000	▦	▦
1970	193,743,000,000	196,588,000,000	203,302,000	▦	▦
1975	280,997,000,000	326,105,000,000	213,600,000	▦	▦
1980	520,050,000,000	579,011,000,000	226,545,805	▦	▦
1985	733,996,000,000	936,809,000,000	237,924,000	▦	▦
1990	1,031,462,000,000	1,251,850,000,000	248,709,873	▦	▦
1991	1,054,265,000,000	1,323,757,000,000	252,131,000	▦	▦
1992	1,090,453,000,000	1,380,794,000,000	255,028,000	▦	▦
1993	1,153,226,000,000	1,408,532,000,000	257,783,000	▦	▦
1994	1,257,187,000,000	1,460,557,000,000	260,341,000	▦	▦

◆ LESSON 44 Interpreting Multidigit Numbers

Check to be sure your answers make sense. Let's consider the year 1920 to see how you can easily check your answers.

In that year, income was about 6 billion 650 million dollars. Spending was about 6 billion 360 million dollars.

$$650 - 360 = 290$$

So the surplus should be about 290 million dollars. The answer 291 million dollars makes sense.

The surplus was about 3×10^8 dollars. The population was about 1×10^8.

$$\frac{3 \times 10^8}{1 \times 10^8} = \frac{3}{1} = 3$$

So the per capita surplus of $2.75 makes sense.

Discuss answers to these questions. You may need calculators for some of the questions.

1 In general, did the income of the United States government increase over the years shown in the chart?

2 Did spending increase?

3 Which increased more, income or spending?

4 Are there years that did not follow the general trend?

In 1960 the total deficit of the United States that had accumulated over the years was $290,862,000,000.

5 What was the per capita share of the deficit in 1960?

6 What was the share of the deficit for a family of four people? For a class the size of yours? For a school the size of yours?

In 1965 a newspaper reported that the accumulated deficit was about 323 million dollars when the real deficit was about 323 billion dollars.

7 What was the per capita share that year?

8 What would it have been had the deficit really been 323 million dollars? How great a difference is that?

Research: Find out what the current accumulated deficit or surplus is. Your librarian should be able to help. What is the per capita share? The share for a family of four? The share for your class? The share for your school?

Work in small groups of three or four. You may use a calculator.
Give your best estimate of the answer. Then estimate the amount
of error there is likely to be in your answer.

(9) How many times will your heart beat in your lifetime?

(10) Using $1 bills, how many dollars are in a stack that is 1 cm tall?

(11) How many dollars could be stacked
in a pile that started on Earth and
went to the moon? (Hint: The moon
is about 384,400 kilometers from
Earth. There are 1000 meters in a
kilometer, and 100 centimeters in
a meter.)

(12) How many dollars would be needed to reach the moon if they could be
placed end to end?

(13) If you spent one dollar each minute, how many years would it take
you to spend one million dollars?

(14) If you spent one dollar each minute, how many years would it take
you to spend one billion dollars?

(15) If you counted 100 dollars every minute and kept counting without
stopping, how many years would it take to count to one billion dollars?

**In your Math Journal record how you were able to solve problems
in this lesson that used numbers with too many digits to display on
your calculator.**

Scientific Notation

You've learned the procedure for using exponents to express multidigit numbers. This procedure is often called **scientific notation,** since scientists often use multidigit numbers.

In scientific notation we place a decimal point after the first digit in a number. Then we show what power of 10 we would multiply by to move the decimal point to the "right place."

Examples:

$35 = 3.5 \times 10$ $35{,}897 = 3.5897 \times 10^4$

$400 = 4.00 \times 10^2 = 4 \times 10^2$ $30{,}000 = 3.0000 \times 10^4 = 3 \times 10^4$

Write these numbers using scientific notation.

1 2000   **2** 25,000   **3** 1,570,000

4 26,987   **5** 293,000   **6** 10,900,000

Scientific notation is also helpful in using a calculator. With scientific notation you can work with numbers that have a great many digits, even though most calculators show only eight-digit numbers. Use your calculator to multiply 35,897 by 42,683.

◆   What happened?

Now use scientific notation and your calculator to multiply 35,897 by 42,683. We do it this way:

$(3.5897 \times 10^4) \times (4.2683 \times 10^4) = (3.5897 \times 4.2683) \times 10^8$

The answer is about 15.321916×10^8. We could now move the decimal point eight places to the right and find that the answer is about 1,532,191,600.

In doing any calculation, a calculator drops digits that don't fit, so the correct or complete answer is usually greater than the calculator display. (In this case the complete answer is 1,532,191,651.)

Work in groups on these problems. Use a calculator and scientific notation. Find approximate answers to the following. Leave your answers in scientific notation.

7 7342 × 59,684

8 1440 × 365,000

9 87,596 × 4832

10 86,400 × 36,500

11 94,000 × 83,000

12 200,792.5 × 499.02

13 How many minutes are there in a day? How many minutes are there in 1000 years if you assume each year has 365 days and ignore leap years?

14 How many seconds are there in a day? How many seconds are there in 70 years (ignore leap years)?

15 Light travels about 2.997925×10^5 km per second. Light from the sun takes about 499.02 seconds to reach Earth. About how many kilometers apart are the sun and Earth? (Note: At different times of the year, Earth is closer to or farther from the sun, so the above are average figures.)

We can divide numbers with many digits by using scientific notation and subtracting exponents. For example:

536,498,327 ÷ 59,348 is

$(5.36498327 \times 10^8) \div (5.9348 \times 10^4)$, or 0.9039871×10^4, or 9.039871×10^3, or 9039.871.

Work in groups. Use a calculator and scientific notation to get approximate answers to the following.

16 835,492,643 ÷ 52,474

17 270,000,000 ÷ 500

18 67,000,000,000 ÷ 2,000,000

19 5,000,000,000 ÷ 250,000,000

20 540,000,000,000 ÷ 225,000,000

21 490,000,000 ÷ 56,000,000

22 280,000,000 ÷ 3500

23 490,000,000 ÷ 56,000

Light from Proxima Centauri, the nearest star to Earth other than the sun, takes $4\frac{1}{4}$ years to reach Earth.

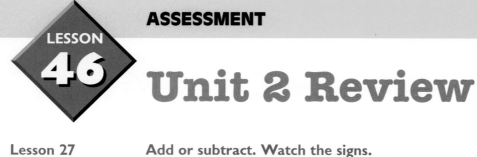

ASSESSMENT

Unit 2 Review

Lesson 27

Add or subtract. Watch the signs.

1 2.34 + 5.18   **2** 2.04 − 1.74   **3** 29.6 + 53.8

4 51.8 − 2.34   **5** 2.04 − 1.75   **6** 1.07 + 6.35

Lesson 29

Multiply or divide. Watch the signs.

7 0.932 × 100   **8** 93.2 ÷ 10   **9** 64.72 × 100

10 64.72 ÷ 100   **11** 9.36 ÷ 1000   **12** 9.36 × 1000

Lesson 29

Solve these problems. You may use the table of metric units on page 588 if necessary.

13 33 mg = ■ g   **14** 0.3 m = ■ cm   **15** 7 L = ■ mL

16 750 mL = ■ L   **17** 450 g = ■ kg   **18** 250 m = ■ km

Lessons 30 and 31

Multiply.

19 22 × 1.23   **20** 2.2 × 12.3   **21** 37 × 0.09

22 0.37 × 0.09   **23** 32 × 2.02   **24** 0.032 × 20.2

Lessons 34 and 35

Divide.

25 $0.2\overline{)642}$ **26** $0.07\overline{)4.963}$ **27** $0.12\overline{)2.448}$

Lessons 39 and 41

Write in standard form.

28 4×10^7 **29** 9×10^3 **30** 5×10^6

Lessons 39 and 41

Write in exponential form.

31 7,000,000   **32** 4000   **33** 80,000,000

Lesson 42

Do the calculations and write your answers in exponential form.

34 $(9 \times 10^8) \times (8 \times 10^9)$ **35** $(30 \times 10^5) \div (6 \times 10^3)$

36 $(3 \times 10^4) \times (3 \times 10^4)$ **37** $(20 \times 10^7) \div (5 \times 10^3)$

164 • Decimals and Exponents

PROBLEM SOLVING

Lessons 27, 28, 34, 36, 37, 40, and 44

Solve these problems.

38 Leote is a costume maker. She has 15 meters of fabric. She is cutting pieces 0.75 meter long to make vests for a play. How many vests will she be able to make?

39 Matt usually earns $5.20 an hour. If he works on Saturday, he gets time and a half. That means he gets paid at 1.5 times the usual rate. How much does Matt earn per hour when he works on Saturday?

40 A stack of 100 sheets of notepaper is 1.05 centimeters thick. How thick is each sheet?

41 There are about 500,000 oil wells in the United States. These oil wells produce about 3,000,000,000 barrels of oil each year. On the average, how many barrels of oil does each oil well produce in a year?

42 Mrs. Azim's lawn is 20.2 meters wide and 30.5 meters long. She is buying fertilizer. Each bag will cover 400 square meters. How many bags does she need to buy?

43 One Sunday Mr. Gartner's odometer read 64,287.3 miles. The following Sunday it read 64,542.8 miles. How far did Mr. Gartner drive during the preceding week?

44 Anna bought a carton of juice for $1.89, a loaf of bread for $1.59, and a can of soup for $0.99. How much change should she receive from a $5 bill?

45 Kevin is making campaign signs for the student council election. He has four colors of markers and four colors of paper. How many different color combinations could he use if he uses one marker on each sign?

LESSON 47

Unit 2 Practice

Lesson 27

Add or subtract. Watch the signs.

① 2.5 + 1.5   ② 2.5 − 1.5   ③ 4.0 − 1.5

④ 17.3 + 4.6   ⑤ 1.73 + 0.46   ⑥ 6.21 − 1.04

⑦ 3.05 − 1.7   ⑧ 1.05 + 0.05   ⑨ 4.75 + 3.25

⑩ 9 − 3.7   ⑪ 9.6 − 3.85   ⑫ 8 − 0.5

⑬ 8 + 0.5   ⑭ 2.05 + 6.5   ⑮ 10.0 − 7.5

Lesson 29

Multiply or divide. Watch the signs.

⑯ 18.3 × 10   ⑰ 18.3 ÷ 10   ⑱ 1.83 × 1000

⑲ 183 ÷ 1000   ⑳ 18.3 × 100   ㉑ 3.04 ÷ 10

㉒ 30.4 × 10   ㉓ 30.4 ÷ 1000   ㉔ 0.304 ÷ 10

㉕ 0.304 × 100   ㉖ 32.97 ÷ 100   ㉗ 329.7 ÷ 10,000

㉘ 3.297 × 100   ㉙ 3.297 × 10,000   ㉚ 329.7 ÷ 100

Lesson 29

Solve these problems. You may use the table of metric units on page 588 if necessary.

㉛ 600 mg = ■ g   ㉜ 36 cm = ■ m   ㉝ 50 mL = ■ L

㉞ 2 g = ■ mg   ㉟ 0.5 m = ■ cm   ㊱ 2 L = ■ mL

㊲ 3.5 kg = ■ g   ㊳ 500 m = ■ km   ㊴ 1.2 L = ■ mL

㊵ 5000 mg = ■ g   ㊶ 50 cm = ■ m   ㊷ 50 dm = ■ m

㊸ 50 m = ■ km   ㊹ 50 cm = ■ dm   ㊺ 50 km = ■ m

Lessons 30 and 31

Multiply.

㊻ 2.34 × 518   ㊼ 2.34 × 5.18   ㊽ 23.4 × 51.8

㊾ 1.2 × 12   ㊿ 1.2 × 1.2   51 55 × 0.22

52 55 × 0.222   53 5.5 × 0.22   54 5.5 × 0.222

55 5.5 × 0.2222   56 6.35 × 1.07   57 635 × 10.7

58 6.35 × 10.7   59 6.3 × 11   60 6.3 × 0.11

Lessons 34 and 35

Divide.

61. $1.6\overline{)0.48}$ 62. $0.33\overline{)1.089}$ 63. $0.33\overline{)184.8}$

64. $0.7\overline{)5.6}$ 65. $2.1\overline{)9.45}$ 66. $5.5\overline{)3.355}$

67. $0.24\overline{)4.8}$ 68. $0.11\overline{)63.8}$ 69. $3.2\overline{)1.408}$

70. $0.12\overline{)72}$ 71. $0.33\overline{)1.023}$ 72. $0.66\overline{)5.082}$

73. $0.09\overline{)8.19}$ 74. $0.21\overline{)0.441}$ 75. $2.2\overline{)12.10}$

Lessons 39 and 41

Write each in standard form.

76. 7×10^2 77. 10^3 78. 2×10^1

79. 7×10^3 80. 6×10^4 81. 5×10^3

82. 8×10^5 83. 3×10^6 84. 8×10^2

85. 4×10^8 86. 8×10^1 87. 3×10^3

Lessons 39 and 41

Write each in exponential form.

88. 5000 89. 3,000,000 90. 1300

91. 2,000,000 92. 16,000 93. 400,000

94. 10,000 95. 45,000,000 96. 20,000

97. 600 98. 2,000,000,000 99. 7,000,000

Lesson 42

Do the following calculations. Write your answers using exponents.

100. $10^3 \times 10^5$ 101. $10^8 \div 10^3$

102. $(5 \times 10^4) \times (4 \times 10^3)$ 103. $(5 \times 10^4) \times (7 \times 10^3)$

104. $(12 \times 10^4) \div (3 \times 10^2)$ 105. $(3 \times 10^3) \times (4 \times 10^9)$

106. $(40 \times 10^4) \div (8 \times 10^3)$ 107. $(4 \times 10^5) \div (8 \times 10^3)$

108. $(3 \times 10^4) \div (5 \times 10^2)$ 109. $(24 \times 10^3) \div (6 \times 10^2)$

110. $(24 \times 10^6) \div (8 \times 10^3)$ 111. $(6 \times 10^6) \times (5 \times 10^5)$

◆ **LESSON 47   Unit 2 Practice**

**Lessons
27–29, 36,
37, and 40**

Solve these problems.

112 Jing-wei's total bill at the grocery store was $14.32. She gave the clerk a $20 bill. What was her change?

113 Ray bought an old encyclopedia at an auction for $7.75. He gave the seller a $10 bill. What was his change?

114 The price of Elena's new desk was $148.98. The tax was $8.94. What was the total cost?

115 The total cost of Elsie's new computer was $910.54. The price tag said $859.00. How much tax did Elsie pay?

116 A stack of 100 sheets of paper has a thickness of 1.2 centimeters. How thick is each sheet?

117 One hundred paper clips weigh about 55 grams. About how much does one paper clip weigh?

118 Leonard weighed ten 0–5 cubes. They weighed 49 grams. He said that each one weighed 49 centigrams. Was he right?

119 Patricia is choosing an outfit to wear to school. She is considering five sweaters and three skirts, all of which match each other. How many different outfits could she make from these clothes?

120 Sonia ran 2200 meters.
   a. How many kilometers was that?
   b. How many millimeters was that?

121 Mr. Jones has five liters of cider. He is going to use glasses that hold about 450 milliliters. Does he have enough cider to serve eight people one glass of cider each?

122 Tamara had 750 centimeters of model railroad track before her birthday. She got another 250 centimeters of track for her birthday. How much track does she have now?

123 Postcards cost $0.27 each, including tax. How many postcards can Gary buy if he has $2.50?

Lessons 31, 34–36

Solve these problems.

124 Dennis bought a ham for $17.71. The ham weighed 2.3 kilograms. What was the price per kilogram?

125 Enrique will make eight birdhouses. It takes 0.75 meter of lumber for each birdhouse. How many meters of lumber does Enrique need to buy?

126 Valerie plans to make ten loaves of bread. Each loaf requires 0.55 kilogram of flour. How many 2.0-kilogram bags of flour does Valerie need to buy?

127 Mr. and Mrs. Newman want to buy carpet for their family room. The room is 5.5 meters long and 4.0 meters wide. The carpet they like is 4.0 meters wide and costs $26.50 per running meter. How much will it cost them to buy that carpet for the family room?

128 Marco and some friends are going to make aprons from 20 meters of fabric. Each apron requires 1.5 meters of fabric. How many aprons can they make?

129 Jeff wants to make curtains for the four windows in his room. He needs 2.15 meters of fabric for each curtain. How many meters of fabric does he need to buy? (Remember: one window needs two curtains.)

130 Jenna earns $5.75 an hour at her part-time job. Last week she worked 15 hours. How much did she earn?

131 The total amount of money paid for tickets to a circus was $62,155. The cost of one ticket was $15.50. How many people bought tickets to the circus?

132 One concession stand at the circus was selling popcorn for $2.25 per tub. The stand sold 247 tubs of popcorn, its only product. How much money did the stand take in?

UNIT 2

Unit Test

Add or subtract. Watch the signs.

1 $3.45 + 23.8$ **2** $7.09 - 3.24$ **3** $7.09 - 3.25$

4 $23.8 - 3.45$ **5** $31.7 + 42.8$ **6** $2.08 + 7.21$

Multiply or divide. Watch the signs.

7 0.679×10 **8** $6.79 \div 100$ **9** 34.92×1000

10 $34.92 \div 1000$ **11** $88.6 \div 100$ **12** 88.6×100

Solve these problems. You may use the table of metric units on page 588 if necessary.

13 $123 \text{ mg} = \blacksquare \text{ g}$ **14** $0.7 \text{ m} = \blacksquare \text{ cm}$ **15** $9 \text{ L} = \blacksquare \text{ mL}$

16 $350 \text{ mL} = \blacksquare \text{ L}$ **17** $335 \text{ g} = \blacksquare \text{ kg}$ **18** $150 \text{ m} = \blacksquare \text{ km}$

Multiply.

19 33×1.71 **20** 3.3×17.1 **21** 43×0.03

22 4.3×0.003 **23** 0.042×30.1 **24** 0.042×301

Divide.

25 $0.03\overline{)696}$ **26** $0.8\overline{)48.64}$ **27** $0.15\overline{)0.3075}$ **28** $0.19\overline{)6.27}$

Write in standard form.

29 10^6 **30** 6×10^4 **31** 3×10^5 **32** 5×10^3

Write in exponential form.

33 500 **34** 6000 **35** $800,000$ **36** $90,000$

Write answers in exponential form.

37 $(8 \times 10^8) \times (3 \times 10^3)$ **38** $(2 \times 10^5) \times (2 \times 10^5)$

39 $(6 \times 10^4) \div (2 \times 10^3)$ **40** $(28 \times 10^3) \div (7 \times 10^3)$

Solve these problems.

41 At the beginning of the day the odometer on the schoolbus showed 5016.3 kilometers. At the end of the day the odometer showed 5255.9 kilometers. How many kilometers did the bus go that day?

42 Mr. Hughes has a 60-meter length of rope. He wants to cut it into pieces that are 3.5 meters long. How many 3.5-meter pieces can he make?

43 Mrs. Rosen earns $10.40 an hour. How much does she earn for working eight hours?

44 A stack of 1000 sheets of paper is 11.0 centimeters thick. How thick is each sheet?

45 Shelly is buying lunch at school. She could get cheese, pepperoni, or mushroom pizza, and milk, orange juice, or apple juice. How many different combinations of pizza and drink could she get?

46 Diego is training for a race. He knows the end of his street is about 150 meters from his house. If he runs to the end of his street and back twice a day for a week, how many meters will he have run?

47 If Diego runs 150 meters from his house to the end of his street and then back twice a day for a week, how many kilometers will he have run?

48 Sandra bought a necklace that was on sale for $21.99. She paid $23.31. How much tax did she pay?

49 The Environmental Club was selling buttons for 75¢ each. They raised $82.50. How many buttons did they sell?

50 Mr. Jackson's lawn is 15.3 meters wide and 24.2 meters long. He is buying grass seed. Each bag covers 400 square meters. How many bags does he need?

Planning a Trip

The 15 boys and the 14 girls in the sixth grade class at Washington Street School were invited to attend the opening of a museum in our nation's capital, Washington, D.C.

Their community was an eight-hour drive from Washington. The museum opening was scheduled for Saturday morning at 9 A.M. Although the ceremony was expected to be over by noon, they wanted to spend the rest of Saturday visiting the White House, the Capitol, and other points of interest. They had to return home by 8 P.M. on Sunday.

Since they had to pay their own way, they investigated the cost of the trip. Then they had to decide how to get the needed money. Here's what they found.

A charter bus costs $400 per day, including 200 free miles. Each additional mile costs 85 cents.

A comfortable hotel, walking distance from the museum, was willing to give the class a special room rate of $50.00 per night. The rooms could hold four students or two adults comfortably.

The cost for meals was estimated to be $4.00 for breakfast, $7.00 for lunch, and $8.00 for dinner.

Besides the 29 children, their teacher, Ms. Jones, and three additional teacher's aides would make the trip.

The children decided that they would raise enough money to pay for transportation, room, and food for each child, for the teacher, and for the three aides. Other costs, such as souvenirs and snacks, would be paid by each individual person.

◆ Work in groups to estimate how much money needs to be raised.

◆ How much is the cost for each student?

◆ If one boy in the class cannot make the trip, will the trip cost less? How much less? Will the cost per student be more or less?

The class decided that it needed to raise $3400 for the trip.

◆ What is a fair way to raise money?

Plan a trip for your class. Find out how much the trip would cost and develop plans to raise the needed money.

Percents and Number Theory

REAL-LIFE APPLICATIONS

- calculating percents

- discounts and taxes

- compound interest

- divisibility rules

- prime factorization

Bankers use math . . .

Investors put money into stocks and bonds. Companies use the money from stock sales to improve and grow. Bonds are sold by companies or government agencies to raise money. The bond sellers promise to pay interest to the buyers. All of these investments use percents to determine how much money the investors will receive.

LESSON 48

Percents

You've probably seen **percents** in numbers you've read in newspapers and magazines and in signs. Percents are used to express store sales, tax rates, poll results, sports data, and other kinds of data.

Remember that percent (%) means "per hundred." So 5% means five per hundred or $\frac{5}{100}$. A 5% sales tax means you pay $5 of tax for every $100 worth of things you buy, or 5¢ per $1.00.

When you work with percents, it is sometimes useful to write them in decimal form. To change a percent to a decimal, you have to divide by 100. So you start with the percent and move the decimal point two places to the left.

Examples: Change 5% to a decimal.

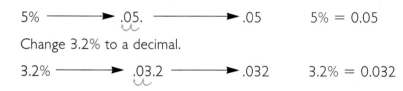

5% ⟶ .05. ⟶ .05   5% = 0.05

Change 3.2% to a decimal.

3.2% ⟶ .03.2 ⟶ .032   3.2% = 0.032

To change a decimal to a percent, move the decimal point two places to the right.

Examples: Change 0.06 to a percent.

0.06 ⟶ 0.06. ⟶ 6%

Change 0.2 to a percent.

0.2 ⟶ 0.20. ⟶ 20%

Change each percent to a decimal.

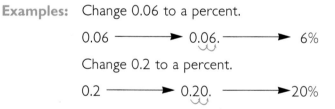

1 3%   **2** 8%   **3** 7.2%   **4** 1%   **5** 10%

6 100%   **7** 50%   **8** 25%   **9** 0.1%   **10** 20%

Change each decimal to a percent.

11 0.25   **12** 0.20   **13** 0.4   **14** 0.9   **15** 1

16 0.05   **17** 0.01   **18** 0.333   **19** 0.014   **20** 0.75

We can find a percent of any number. For example, find 8% of 70.

One way to do this problem is to think "8% of $70 would be 8¢ per $1.00 or 8¢ for every $1.00. So 8% of $70 is 8¢ × 70, or 560¢, which is $5.60." So 8% of 70 is 5.6. Here is another way to do this.

Change the percent to a decimal.   8% = 0.08
                    Multiply.   0.08 × 70 = 5.6
                                  8% of 70 = 5.6

Find each amount.

21 5% of 100   **22** 7% of 100   **23** 25% of 100

24 5% of 8   **25** 7% of 63   **26** 12% of 4

27 25% of 4   **28** 12.5% of 80   **29** 7% of 21

30 Kaya wants to buy a calculator. Its price is $19.99. If there is a 5% sales tax, how much will Kaya have to pay for the calculator (including the tax)?

31 How could you solve problem 30 without using pencil and paper or a calculator?

Suppose the sales tax is 5%. Figure out the total cost of these items. Try to do these in your head.

	Item	Price	Cost
32	Jeans	$29.99	■
33	T-shirt	$8.99	■
34	Calculator	$24.99	■
35	Calendar	$1.99	■
36	Notebook	$0.99	■

◆ **LESSON 48 Percents**

Working with percents often involves multiplying decimals. A common mistake people make when multiplying decimals is placing the decimal point in the wrong position. Avoid this error by thinking about whether the answer is reasonable.

In each problem two of the answers are clearly wrong and one is correct. Choose the correct answer.

㊲	4.02 × 22	**a.** 0.8844	**b.** 8.844	**c.** 88.44
㊳	33 × 0.07	**a.** 0.0231	**b.** 0.231	**c.** 2.31
㊴	0.63 × 2.1	**a.** 1.323	**b.** 13.23	**c.** 132.3
㊵	409 × 0.12	**a.** 4.908	**b.** 49.08	**c.** 490.8
㊶	7.11 × 1.13	**a.** 803.43	**b.** 80.343	**c.** 8.0343
㊷	32.2 × 10.9	**a.** 3520.7	**b.** 350.98	**c.** 35.207
㊸	2.11 × 8.6	**a.** 1814.6	**b.** 181.46	**c.** 18.146
㊹	2.9 × 2.9	**a.** 8.41	**b.** 84.1	**c.** 841
㊺	4.3 × 3.4	**a.** 0.1462	**b.** 1.462	**c.** 14.62
㊻	37 × 0.08	**a.** 296	**b.** 2.96	**c.** 29.6
㊼	25 × 1.04	**a.** 2.6	**b.** 26	**c.** 260
㊽	1.5 × 4.2	**a.** 630	**b.** 0.63	**c.** 6.3
㊾	12 × 4.8	**a.** 57.6	**b.** 5.76	**c.** 0.576
㊿	5.6 × 3.1	**a.** 17.36	**b.** 173.6	**c.** 1736
51	2.3 × 5.6	**a.** 0.1288	**b.** 1.288	**c.** 12.88
52	4.7 × 5.8	**a.** 272.6	**b.** 27.26	**c.** 2.726
53	4.8 × 6.7	**a.** 3216	**b.** 321.6	**c.** 32.16
54	4.56 × 2.3	**a.** 10.488	**b.** 104.88	**c.** 1048.8
55	3.16 × 3.3	**a.** 1.0428	**b.** 10.428	**c.** 104.28

Solve this problem.

56 Ruth saw a sign that said, "Ice Show Tickets: $15.50." She said, "Oh, it will cost $3720 for the 24 students in our class to go to the ice show." Was Ruth right?

COOPERATIVE LEARNING

Tips Game

Players:	**Two or more**
Materials:	**Two 0–5 cubes, two 5–10 cubes**
Object:	**To make the most money on tips**
Math Focus:	**Calculating percents, adding amounts of money, place value, and mathematical reasoning**

GAME

RULES

1. Each player is waiting on customers in a restaurant and will get five tips. One tip will be 10%; three tips will be 15%; and one tip will be 20%.

2. Roll all four cubes. Find the bill for a customer by making an amount in dollars and cents. A 10 can be used anywhere in the amount, but it will have to be regrouped if it is not in the place for tens of dollars. For example, if you roll 10, 9, 5, and 5, you could make $109.55 (10, 9, 5, 5), $100.55 (9, 10, 5, 5), or $96.05 (9, 5, 10, 5), or other amounts of money.

3. Decide which tip you'll get from this customer. Then calculate the tip. Keep a record of your tips.

4. After five rounds, add the tips. The player with the most money wins.

SAMPLE GAME

	Round 1	Round 2	Round 3	Round 4	Round 5
Ty rolled:	8 3 7 3	1 5 5 6	1 6 4 10	4 5 5 8	10 0 8 2
Ty made:	$87.33	$65.51	$106.41	$85.54	$108.20
Ty chose:	15%	15%	20%	10%	15%
Ty's tip:	$13.10	$9.83	$21.28	$8.55	$16.23
Isra rolled:	3 5 0 10	8 5 8 4	3 9 6 2	8 10 1 5	9 0 5 2
Isra made:	$105.30	$88.54	$96.32	$108.51	$95.20
Isra chose:	20%	15%	15%	15%	10%
Isra's tip:	$21.06	$13.28	$14.45	$16.28	$9.52

Ty's total was $68.99; Isra's total was $74.59. Isra was the winner.

LESSON 49

Computing Percent Discounts

Sometimes stores give discounts. This means they reduce the price by some amount. Often the discount is stated as a percent.

The Bantam Department Store is having a sale. Athletic shoes are on sale for 20% off the regular price. Pat wants to buy a pair that usually costs $93.98. How much will the shoes cost?

We know that 20% of $93.98 is $18.796. The store rounds this to the next higher cent: $18.80.

$93.98	regular price
− $18.80	20% discount
$75.18	sale price

The tags on each item show the regular price and the discount. Give the sale price of each item.

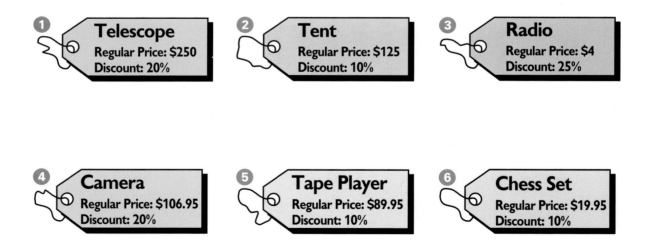

1 **Telescope**
Regular Price: $250
Discount: 20%

2 **Tent**
Regular Price: $125
Discount: 10%

3 **Radio**
Regular Price: $4
Discount: 25%

4 **Camera**
Regular Price: $106.95
Discount: 20%

5 **Tape Player**
Regular Price: $89.95
Discount: 10%

6 **Chess Set**
Regular Price: $19.95
Discount: 10%

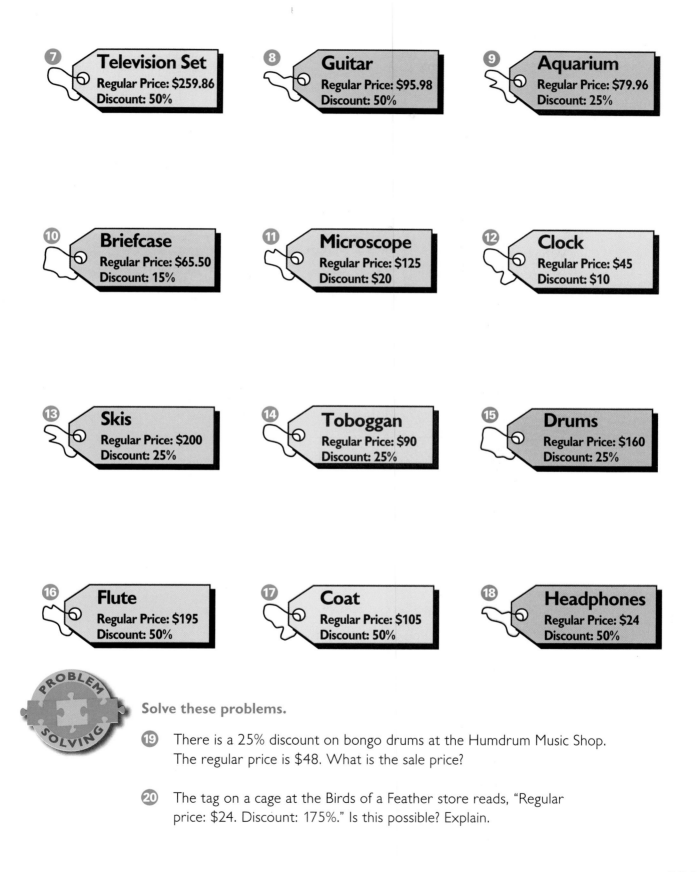

7 **Television Set**
Regular Price: $259.86
Discount: 50%

8 **Guitar**
Regular Price: $95.98
Discount: 50%

9 **Aquarium**
Regular Price: $79.96
Discount: 25%

10 **Briefcase**
Regular Price: $65.50
Discount: 15%

11 **Microscope**
Regular Price: $125
Discount: $20

12 **Clock**
Regular Price: $45
Discount: $10

13 **Skis**
Regular Price: $200
Discount: 25%

14 **Toboggan**
Regular Price: $90
Discount: 25%

15 **Drums**
Regular Price: $160
Discount: 25%

16 **Flute**
Regular Price: $195
Discount: 50%

17 **Coat**
Regular Price: $105
Discount: 50%

18 **Headphones**
Regular Price: $24
Discount: 50%

PROBLEM SOLVING

Solve these problems.

19 There is a 25% discount on bongo drums at the Humdrum Music Shop. The regular price is $48. What is the sale price?

20 The tag on a cage at the Birds of a Feather store reads, "Regular price: $24. Discount: 175%." Is this possible? Explain.

Percents on a Calculator

Using a calculator can save you time when solving percent problems. You can do these problems on a calculator using a percent key, **%**, if your calculator has one. You use it like this, though your calculator may work slightly differently from the one in the examples.

Find the cost of a $56 item with a 4% sales tax.

What to Do:	**What the Display Shows:**
Clear the calculator. ⟶	0
Push **5** **6**. ⟶	56
Push **+**. ⟶	56
Push **4**. ⟶	4
Push **%**. ⟶	2.24

(The display now shows 4% of 56, which is 2.24. If you needed to know this number, you would write it down before going on to the next step.)

Push **=**. ⟶ 58.24

The cost of the item, with tax, is $58.24.

◆ What answer do you get if you do the problems as 4% + 56?

◆ What answer do you get if you find 56 × 4%?

◆ What answer do you get if you find 4% × 56?

◆ How can you find the cost of the item if your calculator doesn't have a percent key?

◆ Think of a percent problem for which using mental arithmetic would be quicker than using a calculator.

Calculators can also be used to find percent discounts. Find the price of a $7.43 item with a 15% discount.

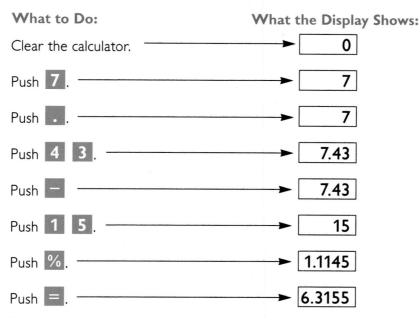

What to Do:	What the Display Shows:
Clear the calculator.	0
Push **7**.	7
Push **.**.	7
Push **4** **3**.	7.43
Push **−**	7.43
Push **1** **5**.	15
Push **%**.	1.1145
Push **=**.	6.3155

The discounted price is $6.32. (You get that by rounding $6.3155 up to the next cent. The amount of the discount, $1.1145, is rounded down to $1.11.)

Use a calculator to solve these problems.

1. 5% of 100
2. 7% of 100
3. 25% of 100
4. 5% of 8
5. 7% of 63
6. 12% of 4
7. 25% of 4
8. 12.5% of 80
9. 7% of 21

Solve these problems.

10. Irma wants to buy a video game for $24.99. If there is a 5% sales tax, how much will she have to pay for the game, including the tax?
11. Bob bought a $142 camera with a 10% discount. How much did he pay?
12. Marta will buy a printer for $395. If there is an 8% sales tax, how much will she pay, including tax?
13. A speaker system is discounted 20%. The regular price is $200. If the sales tax is 5%, what is the total cost of the system?
14. Mr. Montovano installed a new furnace that should reduce his monthly gas bill by 15%. If the bill was $70, what should it be now?
15. Use a calculator to solve problems 1–19 on pages 180 and 181.

◆ LESSON 50   Percents on a Calculator

 **Work in groups and use a calculator to solve these problems.**

16 A $56 jacket is on sale at a 20% discount. The sales tax is 4%.

a. With the discount and tax, what is the cost of the jacket?

b. Does it make a difference whether you add the tax first and then take the discount or take the discount first and then add the tax?

17 A $129.98 bicycle is on sale at a 30% discount. The sales tax is 5%. How much will the bicycle cost with the discount and tax?

18 A $300 stereo is on sale at a 5% discount. The sales tax is 5%.

a. What is the cost of the stereo?

b. Since you subtract 5% and then add 5%, why isn't the answer $300?

19 A $600 stove is on sale at a 7% discount. The sales tax is 7%. How much will the stove cost?

20 A sign in Woolly's Clothing Store reads, "40% off the marked price of every item." Lisa buys four pairs of socks priced at $1.98 a pair, a shirt priced at $15.50, and another shirt priced at $19.98. She also buys two pairs of jeans priced at $16.50 and $24.98. If the sales tax is 5%, how much will Lisa's total be?

21 Malcolm's total bill for a set of three new CDs was $38.52. A 7% sales tax was included in the bill. How much of the $38.52 was for the CDs, and how much was for the tax?

22 Fiona paid $20.98 for a double CD, including the 5% sales tax. What was the price of the CD without tax? (Hint: The tax was rounded to the nearest cent.)

$50 Price Game

Players:	**Two or more**
Materials:	**Two 0–5 cubes, two 5–10 cubes, a calculator for each player**
Object:	**To make the sale price closest to $50**
Math Focus:	**Mental arithmetic**

RULES

1 Roll any cube and multiply the number rolled by 10 to find the percent discount. For example, if you roll a 2, the discount is 20%.

2 Roll the other three cubes and use two of the numbers rolled to make the regular price. (Try to get a sale price close to $50.)

3 Write the sale price. For example, if you roll 6, 9, and 4, you could make the regular price $64. The sale price would be 20% off $64. Another way to think of it is $64 – (20% of $64).

4 The player whose sale price is closest to $50 wins. Don't calculate the precise sale price unless you can't otherwise tell who wins.

SAMPLE GAME

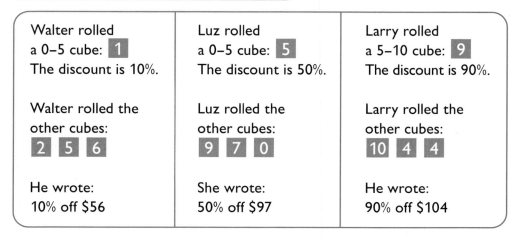

Walter rolled a 0–5 cube: **1** The discount is 10%.	Luz rolled a 0–5 cube: **5** The discount is 50%.	Larry rolled a 5–10 cube: **9** The discount is 90%.
Walter rolled the other cubes: **2** **5** **6**	Luz rolled the other cubes: **9** **7** **0**	Larry rolled the other cubes: **10** **4** **4**
He wrote: 10% off $56	She wrote: 50% off $97	He wrote: 90% off $104

They knew that Larry's sale price wasn't at all close to $50, but they weren't sure whether Walter or Luz was closer to $50. They calculated the two sale prices. Walter's sale price was $50.40, and Luz's was $48.50. Walter was the winner.

Sales Tax and Discounts

For each of the following problems, first estimate the total cost, and then do the calculation to see how close your estimate was.

1 Adam wants to buy a jacket that usually sells for $50. The store is having a 20% off sale on everything in the store. Sales tax is 5%. Adam has $43. Will he be able to buy the jacket? If not, how much more money does he need? If so, how much change will he receive?

2 Matthew wants to buy some shoes that usually cost $49.98. They are on sale for 20% off. Sales tax is 5%. He has $41. Will he be able to buy the shoes? If not, how much more money does he need? If so, how much change will he receive?

3 Rajiv is ordering a model kit from a catalogue. The regular price is $34.95, but he has a coupon for 10% off. Shipping costs $3.95, and there is no sales tax. Rajiv has $35.00 to spend on the order. Can he afford the model kit? If not, how much more money does he need? If so, how much money will he have left?

4 Alan plans to buy a football that has a list price of $29.99. Today it is on sale for 25% off. Sales tax is 4%. He has $23.50. Will he be able to buy the football? If not, how much more money does he need? If so, how much change will he receive?

5 Albert plans to buy a computer monitor for $500. He discovers that it is on sale this week for 20% off. He knows he will have to pay 7% sales tax. He has saved $400 to buy the monitor. How much more money will he need if he is going to buy the monitor this week?

6 Albert couldn't manage to buy the monitor when it was on sale for 20% off, but the next week the sale changed to a 25% off sale. Could he afford to buy it then? The sales tax is still 7%.

7 Joan wants to buy a dress that usually sells for $30. Today the dress is on sale for 25% off. Sales tax is 4%. She has $25. Will she be able to buy the dress? If not, how much more money does she need? If so, how much change will she receive?

When Adam went to the store to buy the $50 jacket that was on sale for 20% off, the sales clerk added the 5% tax first, and then deducted the 20% discount. Adam objected and said he would pay less sales tax if the discount were calculated first, and then the tax were added. The clerk said it would be cheaper the way he did it because Adam could get a bigger discount, since the discount was calculated on both the original price AND the tax. What do you think? Discuss this with your classmates and then calculate the final price both ways.

For the following exercises the original price, the discount rate, and the sales tax rate are given.

Determine the final price for each item if you add the tax first, and then deduct the discount. Figure out what the final price will be if you deduct the discount first and then add the tax.

	Original Price of Item	Discount Rate	Tax Rate
8	$100.00	40%	4%
9	$99.99	40%	4%
10	$200.00	20%	2%
11	$200.00	80%	4%
12	$200.00	80%	8%
13	$50.00	10%	4%
14	$150.00	50%	5%
15	$150.00	25%	10%

Solve these problems.

16 Two furniture stores in a state with 5% sales tax are selling the same sofa with a regular price of $500. The first store is having a "5% off" sale, in which they reduce the price of all items by 5%, and customers pay tax on the discounted price. The second store is having a sale in which customers pay the regular price, but the store pays the sales tax for the customer.

a. In which store would the sofa cost less? How much less?

b. In which store would a $600 sofa cost less? How much less?

c. Is there a rule you can use to tell in advance which store would charge less for a sofa with a given price?

◆ **LESSON 51 Sales Tax and Discounts**

THINKING STORY

Competition

Part 1

" I don't know what's gone wrong with my store," said Mr. Muddle. "I used to sell about 150 T-shirts a week. But for the past few weeks I've been lucky to sell 100 a week."

"Have you raised your prices?" Portia asked.

"No," said Mr. Muddle. "I still charge just $9.00 for a T-shirt. That makes it hard to earn a living. I used to get T-shirts from the factory for $3.33 each. My other costs were about $800 a month. Now the T-shirts cost me $4.00 each, and my other costs are about $1000 a month."

"Maybe you don't advertise enough," said Manolita.

"I advertise as much as ever," Mr. Muddle said. "I don't think that's it. I think people just aren't buying T-shirts the way they used to. My friend Mr. Sneaky has started a T-shirt store right next to mine. He isn't doing very well either. In fact, he sells only about half as many T-shirts as I'm selling now."

. . . to be continued

Work in groups. Discuss your answers and how you figured them out. Then compare your answers with those of other groups.

1 About how much profit per week did Mr. Muddle make in the past? About how much profit is he making now? What percent decline is that?

2 Is Mr. Muddle right that people aren't buying as many T-shirts as they used to? Explain.

3 Why do you think Mr. Muddle is selling fewer T-shirts?

4 Would you expect business to get better or worse for Mr. Muddle in the next few months? Why?

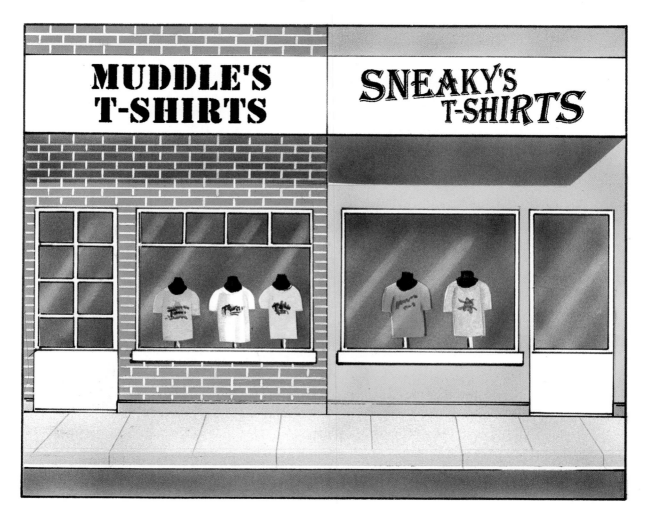

Calculating Interest

If you deposit money in a savings bank, the bank pays you for the use of your money. This payment is called *interest*. The money you deposit is called the *principal*. If the bank pays 5% interest per year, after one year you will have the amount of money you put in plus 5% more.

Example:

You deposit $70 in a bank that pays 6% interest. How much will you have after one year?

Find 6% of 70: $0.06 \times 70 = 4.2$
$70 + 4.2 = 74.20$
You will have $74.20 after one year.

How much will you have after five years?

Start with $70.00.

Time	Calculation	Amount
After one year	$0.06 \times 70 = 4.2$ $70 + 4.2 = 74.20$	$74.20
After two years	$0.06 \times 74.20 = 4.452$ $74.20 + 4.45 = 78.65$	$78.65
After three years	$0.06 \times 78.65 = 4.719$ $78.65 + 4.72 = 83.37$	$83.37
After four years	$0.06 \times 83.37 = 5.0022$ $83.37 + 5.00 = 88.37$	$88.37
After five years	$0.06 \times 88.37 = 5.3022$ $88.37 + 5.30 = 93.67$	$93.67

After five years if you haven't taken any money out of your account, you'll have $93.67.

Notice that the bank gives you interest on all the money you have in the bank, including last year's interest. This is called *compound interest* because you get interest on previous interest as well as on the money you deposited.

When a bank credits interest to your account only once a year, we say that the bank "compounds annually."

In each case calculate the amount of money you would have if interest is compounded annually.

	Principal	Rate of Interest	Number of Years	Amount
1	$100	6%	1	■
2	$100	8%	2	■
3	$100	5%	5	■
4	$200	7%	1	■
5	$200	7%	5	■
6	$ 50	6%	5	■
7	$100	4%	5	■
8	$100	3%	10	■
9	$100	8%	10	■
10	$100	7%	5	■

11. Which would earn more interest, $1000 deposited for one year at 6% interest or $1000 deposited for two years at 3% interest? How much more?

12. Which would earn more interest, $2000 deposited for three years at 2% interest or $2000 deposited for two years at 3% interest? How much more?

13. Which would earn more interest, $100 deposited for two years at 10% interest or $200 deposited for one year at 5% interest? How much more?

14. Which would earn more interest, $100 deposited for two years at 5% interest or $200 deposited for one year at 10% interest? How much more?

LESSON 53

Compound Interest

Finding compound interest the way you did in Lesson 52 is straightforward but can take a long time. There is a quicker way.

Remember: 7% is the same as 0.07.
1 + 0.07 is the same as 1.07.

Multiplying a number by 1.07 is the same as taking the number once and adding 7% to it.

Example:
How much money will you have after one year if you deposit $200 in the bank at 7% interest?

Multiply 200 × 1.07.

```
    2 00
  × 1.07
  14 00
 200
 2 14.00
```

After one year, you would have $214.00.

Example:
How much money would you have if you left $200 in the bank for five years at 7% interest?

Multiply 200 by 1.07 five times.

$$200 \times 1.07 \times 1.07 \times 1.07 \times 1.07 \times 1.07$$

To multiply this on a calculator, follow these steps (remember, your calculator may work slightly differently):

Push `on/c`, `2` `0` `0`, `×`, `1` `.` `0` `7`, `=`, `=`, `=`, `=`, `=`.

After five years you would have $280.51.

Is this the same answer you got for problem 5 on page 191?

(Your answer may differ by 1¢ if you rounded after each year.)

Challenge: In your Math Journal describe how to calculate compound interest using exponents.

You can also do this problem on a calculator by adding 7% each year:

Push , **2 0 0**, **+**, **7**, **%**, **=**

+, **7**, **%**, **=**

+, **7**, **%**, **=**

+, **7**, **%**, **=**

+, **7**, **%**, **=**

Again, the answer is $280.51.

Use a calculator to solve these problems.

1 Ms. Morgan deposited $250 in the Last National Bank at 7% interest.

    a. How much money will she have after ten years?

    b. How long must Ms. Morgan leave her money in the bank to double the amount she deposited?

2 Jake deposited $1000 in the Last National Bank at 4.5% interest for 12 years. How much money did he have in the bank at the end of 12 years?

3 Mr. Pacheco's bank is now paying 5.1% interest per year.

    a. How long will it take him to double his money?

    b. If Mr. Pacheco deposits $1000, how much will he have after nine years?

4 Mr. Nicolai put $80 in a bank at 4% interest for ten years. Mrs. Finnegan put $60 in a bank at 6% interest for ten years.

    a. At the end of ten years, who will have more money?

    b. Who will have earned more interest?

◆ LESSON 53   Compound Interest

Some banks pay interest four times a year instead of just once a year. Interest paid in this way is "compounded quarterly." For example, if a bank pays 8% annually, it might pay 2% every quarter.

◆ If a bank compounds the interest quarterly, how many times a year will the bank add interest to an account?

Use a calculator, when it's helpful, to solve these problems.

5 The Trust-Us Bank advertises "6% interest compounded quarterly."

a. What is $\frac{1}{4}$ of 6%?

b. If you deposit $1000, how much will you have after one-quarter of a year?

c. How many quarters are in one year?

d. If you deposit $1000, how much will you have after one year (four quarters)?

e. If you deposit $1000 in the Safe-Here Bank (which pays 6% interest once a year), how much will you have after one year?

f. Compare your answers to d and e. How much more money do you get from the bank that compounds quarterly?

6 If two banks pay the same rate of interest, why does the bank that compounds quarterly pay more interest than the bank that compounds annually?

7 If a bank compounded interest semiannually (twice a year), would it pay more or less interest than a bank paying the same interest rate compounded quarterly?

Some banks pay interest every month instead of just once a year or once a quarter. Interest paid in this way is "compounded monthly."

◆ If a bank compounds the interest monthly, how many times a year will the bank add interest to an account?

◆ If a bank pays 3% annual interest compounded monthly, what percent of the money deposited will be paid in interest each month?

Use a calculator, when it's helpful, to solve these problems.

8 The Lock-Up Bank pays 6% interest compounded monthly.

    a. If you have money in the Lock-Up Bank, what percent of that money will you earn in interest each month?

    b. If you deposit $1000, how much will you have after one month?

    c. If you deposit $1000, how much will you have after one-quarter of a year (three months)?

    d. If you deposit $1000, how much will you have after one year (12 months)?

    e. Compare your answer for d with your answer for d in problem 5 on page 194. How much more money do you get in the bank that compounds monthly?

◆ Why does a bank that compounds monthly pay more interest than one that compounds quarterly?

◆ Would a bank that compounds interest daily pay more interest on the same principal than one that compounds monthly?

Reversing Percent Problems

You have learned how to find a fraction of a number when expressed as a percent. In this lesson you'll learn a way to find a number when you know a percent of it.

To do so, you'll "undo" a procedure that has taken place.

Examples:

Kimiko bought a golf club for $53.50, which included a 7% sales tax. What was the price of the club without the tax?

To do this, first look at how the cost with tax could have been calculated—by multiplying the price by 1.07.

price $\longrightarrow$ $\times 1.07$ $\longrightarrow$ cost with tax

To get the price from the cost with tax, you should be able to do the opposite (divide by 1.07).

price $\longleftarrow$ $\div 1.07$ $\longleftarrow$ cost with tax

(Notice that if you got the cost simply by adding on 7%, you wouldn't have known how to do the opposite.)

Divide 53.50 by 1.07. What is your answer for the price of the club?

Check to see if the answer is right.

What is 7% of 50?

If the price was $50, the tax would be $3.50, and the cost with tax would be $53.50. So the answer is right.

Mr. Wilcox bought a book during a sale at Medium-Rare Books. The book was on sale for 35% off its regular price. He paid $12.34 for it before tax. What was the original price of the book (the price before the discount)? Again, first look at how the discount price could have been calculated. It could have been done by multiplying the original price by (1 − 0.35), which is 0.65. This is similar to finding the cost of something with a 7% sales tax by multiplying by (1 + 0.07), or 1.07. You can also think of the discount price as paying $0.65 for each dollar of the original price.

original price ————×0.65———▶ discount price

You can reverse this by dividing by 0.65.

original price ◀————÷0.65———— discount price

Divide 12.34 by 0.65. Use a calculator.

What is your answer for the original price of the book?

Check to see that the answer makes sense:

What is 65% of 18.98? 12.337, or 12.34

So the answer makes sense.

Note that 18.99 × 0.65 = 12.3435 and 18.98 × 0.65 = 12.337. (Since both round to $12.34, the original price could have been $18.98 or $18.99.)

Another book was on sale for 20% off and cost $4.76 before tax. To find the original cost, find 1 − 0.20, which is 0.80, and divide 4.76 by 0.80.

The original price was $5.95.

◆ LESSON 54 Reversing Percent Problems

Use a calculator, if necessary, to solve these problems.

1 The sales tax in Stan's city is 4%. Suppose he paid $15.34 for a package of greeting cards, including tax. What was the price without tax?

2 Mr. Silvanos bought a sofa on sale for $520. That was 35% off the regular price. What was the regular price of the sofa?

3 Hannah wants to buy a pair of boots. The regular price of the boots is $125. The store is having a 20% discount sale, and the sales tax is 7%. How much will Hannah have to pay for the boots?

4 The Save-a-Lot Discount Store is having a 20% discount sale. In that city the sales tax is 7%. What was the original price of a camera for which a customer paid $64.20? Hint: Here is how the cost with tax could have been calculated:

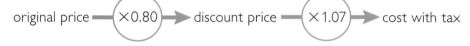

original price ──▶ ⟨×0.80⟩ ──▶ discount price ──▶ ⟨×1.07⟩ ──▶ cost with tax

(Work backward to calculate the original price.)

5 Edward bought a sweater that was on sale for 30% off its regular price. With 6% sales tax, he paid $22.25. What was the original price of the sweater?

6 Tips at restaurants are usually calculated based on the total check, not including the tax. A check including 7% tax came to $25.68.

a. What was the total before the tax?

b. What would be a 15% tip on that total?

7 Lara bought a book marked $5.95 from a store that sells all books at 20% off. Tax was 6%. How much did she pay for the book?

8 Which costs less, a $200 stereo at 20% off or at $20 off?

9 Sook has $162.00 in the bank. His bank pays 5% interest, compounded annually. He has not deposited any money during the past year. How much money did he have in the bank one year ago?

10 Ted bought a wallet priced at $34.85 and a briefcase priced at $89.98. He had to pay a 6% sales tax. How much did he have to pay all together?

11 Marta wants to buy a shirt that is marked $24.98. The sales tax is 5%. Marta has $30.00. Does she have enough money to buy the shirt?

12 Anoki was buying a radio with a price tag that was unclear.

The clerk could not tell if it was supposed to be $10 off or 10% off, so she gave Anoki a choice.

a. Which should Anoki choose?

b. Why?

13 Miriam wants to buy some apples. She can buy 50 kilograms of apples at the Farmer's Market for $0.70 a kilogram. She can buy 2.5 kilograms of apples at the City Market for $0.90 a kilogram. Where should she buy the apples?

14 Mr. and Mrs. Kramer have budgeted $800 for a new refrigerator. They have seen advertisements at the following prices and discounts: $899 and 10% off, $950 and 20% off, $999 and 25% off, and $1095 and 30% off. Which of these could fall within their budget?

UNIT 3

Mid-Unit Review

Change each percent to a decimal.

1 2%   **2** 64%   **3** 5.5%   **4** 0.3%   **5** 90%

Change each decimal to a percent.

6 0.35   **7** 0.5   **8** 0.006   **9** 0.425   **10** 0.60

Find each amount.

11 8% of 100   **12** 8% of 50   **13** 12.5% of 40   **14** 25% of 200

Choose the correct answer. Watch the signs.

15 2.4 × 5	**16** 0.41 × 3.8	**17** 3.2 × 6.5	**18** 1.56 × 7.3
a. 12	**a.** 0.1558	**a.** 0.208	**a.** 1.1388
b. 1.2	**b.** 1.558	**b.** 2.08	**b.** 11.388
c. 0.12	**c.** 15.58	**c.** 20.8	**c.** 113.88

Determine the final price for each item.

	Original Price of Item	Discount Rate	Tax Rate	Final Price
19	$100	20%	4%	▪
20	$100	30%	5%	▪
21	$200	25%	10%	▪
22	$300	50%	4%	▪

In each case calculate the amount of money you would have.

	Principal	Rate of Interest	Number of Years	Amount
23	$100	5%	1	▪
24	$100	7%	2	▪
25	$200	4%	5	▪
26	$200	6%	10	▪

Solve these problems.

27 There is a 25% discount on small trees at the Green Thumb nursery. The regular price is $96. What is the sale price?

28 Lorenzo wants to buy a personal stereo that lists for $120. If the sales tax is 6%, how much will he have to pay for it?

29 An $80 dictionary is on sale at a 10% discount. The sales tax is 7%. With the discount and the tax, what is the cost of the dictionary?

30 Erin wants to buy some CDs that regularly sell for $18 but now are on sale for 25% off. Sales tax is 5%. If Erin has $100 to spend, how many of the CDs can she afford to buy?

31 Mr. Wang put $200 in a bank at 5% interest. How much money will he have after ten years?

32 Ms. Goldstein put $600 in the bank at 6% interest. How long must she leave the money in the account to double the amount she deposited?

33 Jim wants to buy a jacket that usually sells for $175. Today the jacket is on sale for 20% off. Sales tax is 5%. He has $150. Will he be able to buy the jacket? If so, how much change will he get? If not, how much more money will he need?

34 The Safe Bank pays 5% interest compounded monthly. If you were to deposit $1000, how much money would you have after one month? After one year?

35 The sales tax in Sam's city is 6%. Suppose he paid $79.50 for a baseball glove, including the tax. What is the price of the glove without the tax?

Applying Percents

Sometimes using the percent key or doing other computations on a calculator can speed up the problem-solving process, but sometimes it is quicker to solve problems mentally.

Use a calculator only if necessary to help you solve these problems.

1 Toni wants to buy a backpack that is priced at $40. The sales tax is 5%. What will the total cost be?

2 Which costs less, a $50 jacket at 10% off or at $10 off?

3 A $100 chair is on sale at 15% off. The sales tax is 5%. Including the tax, will the chair cost more than $100?

4 A dealer is offering a 10% discount on all used cars in stock. Will a car with a price of $5136 be on sale for less than $5000?

5 Bill wants to buy a shirt that is on sale at 20% off the regular price of $30. There is a 5% sales tax. How much will Bill pay for the shirt, including tax?

6 Eva's new suit is 35% wool. Is the suit more than one-half wool?

7 A weather report said there was a 20% chance of rain on Tuesday. According to the report, was there a greater chance of rain than of no rain?

8 Kristina's basketball team played ten games. The team won seven games and lost three. What percent of the games did the team win?

9 Which would cost less, an item on sale at half price or at 20% off?

10 A board game that normally sells for $20 is on sale at 25% off with 6% tax. What will the total cost of the game be?

11 Which would cost more, a $10 cassette tape at regular price, or a $15 CD that is on sale at 30% off?

12 The sale price of a hair dryer is $19.95. The regular price is $25.00. Is the discount more than 10%?

13 Renee made 23 out of 25 free throw attempts in basketball. What percent of her shots did she make?

14 Calvin got two hits out of ten times at bat. What percent of his times at bat did he get a hit?

15 Which costs more, a $200 coat that is on sale for 25% off or a $200 coat that is on sale for $40 off?

16 Which costs more, a $40 book with a discount of $10 or a $40 book with a discount of 10%?

17 Which costs more, a $150 oven with a discount of $10 or a $150 oven with a discount of 10%?

18 Richard's salary is $200 per week. He is going to get a 5% raise. How much will his salary be then?

19 Ms. Morales's salary is $500 per week, but her employer takes out 20% for federal tax and 4% for state tax. How much will her take-home pay be if these are the only two deductions?

20 Mr. Patel has calculated that about 30% of his monthly pay is deducted for various taxes. His salary is $4000 per month. About how much money does he actually receive each month?

21 A survey of 50 students found that 30 of those surveyed would like a greater variety of foods in the school cafeteria. What percent of the students want a greater variety?

22 Which costs less, a $50 painting with a discount of $15 or a $50 painting with a discount of 15%?

How do you decide whether to use a calculator to help you solve problems using percents? Record your ideas in your Math Journal.

Keeping Sharp

LESSON 56

Keep in shape by practicing your mental math skills and your basic computation facts. Look for shortcuts.

Solve these problems. Use paper and pencil only if necessary.

1. 9 ÷ 3
2. 90 ÷ 30
3. 900 ÷ 300
4. 900 ÷ 3
5. 35 + 35
6. 35 + 70
7. 105 + 35
8. 380 − 375
9. 12 × 12
10. 9 × 7
11. 4.98 + 3.02
12. 12.75 + 1.25
13. 135.2 − 1.2
14. 12 + 3
15. 12 − 3
16. 12 × 3
17. 12 ÷ 3
18. 120 × 30
19. 1200 ÷ 40
20. 1.97 × 10
21. 175 ÷ 25
22. 150 ÷ 75
23. 1500 ÷ 75
24. 9 × 8
25. 9 × 9
26. 9 × 10
27. 9 × 11
28. 9 × 12
29. 9 × 13
30. 9 × 14

Solve for _n_. Use paper and pencil only if necessary.

31. 20 × n = 60
32. 200 × n = 600
33. 90 × n = 8100
34. 900 × n = 8100
35. 750 × n = 1500
36. 75 × n = 1500
37. 33 × n = 990
38. 30 × n = 990
39. 14 × n = 280
40. 140 × n = 28,000
41. 60 × n = 120
42. 6 × n = 1200

Solve these problems. Use paper and pencil only if necessary.

43. 350,000 + 349,999
44. 75 75 75 + 75
45. 42 × 15
46. 100,000 − 55,000

47. 325 + 399
48. 105 195 + 200
49. 420 × 15
50. 25)1000

A bolt of lightning is as bright as one million 100-watt lightbulbs.

ALGEBRA READINESS

Solve for _n_. Use paper and pencil only if necessary.

(51) $n = 50\%$ of 200   (52) $200 = n\%$ of 100   (53) $175 = n\%$ of 175

(54) $200 = 50\%$ of n (55) $150 = n\%$ of 75   (56) $15 = 300\%$ of n

(57) $100 = n\%$ of 400   (58) $4 = n\%$ of 1   (59) $n = 25\%$ of 800

Solve these problems. Use pencil and paper when necessary.

(60) $100 \times 86 = ?$ (61) $2 \times 86 = ?$

(62) $200 \times 86 = ?$ (63) $478{,}629 - 1 = ?$

(64) $478{,}629 - 478{,}628 = ?$ (65) $235{,}780 - 235{,}779 = ?$

(66) $25 + 25 + 25 + 25 = ?$ (67) $4 \times 25 = ?$

(68) $100 \div 4 = ?$ (69) $25 \times 8 = ?$

(70) $200 \div 25 = ?$ (71) $25 \times 400 =$

Solve for _n_.

(72) $n + n + n + n = 100$ (73) $4 \times n = 100$ (74) $4 \times n = 400$

(75) $n \times 4 = 400$ (76) $8 \times n = 800$ (77) $800 \div n = 8$

(78) $16 \div n = 8$ (79) $n - n = 1$ (80) $n - n = 0$

(81) $40 \div 8 = n$ (82) $8 \times n = 40$ (83) $7 \times n = 14$

(84) $n = 14 \div 7$ (85) $n \times 0 = 12$ (86) $12 \div 0 = n$

(87) $0 \times n = 0$ (88) $0 \div 0 = n$ (89) $7 \div 0 = n$

(90) $n \div 7 = 0$ (91) $n \times 7 = 0$ (92) $0 \div 8 = n$

In each problem two of the answers are clearly wrong and one is correct. Choose the correct answer.

(93) $574 + 2651$ **a.** 835   **b.** 3225   **c.** 2123

(94) $19{,}680 \div 492$ **a.** 40   **b.** 400   **c.** 4000

(95) 72×53 **a.** 3426   **b.** 3816   **c.** 4936

(96) $24{,}386 - 17{,}591$ **a.** 9765   **b.** 7695   **c.** 6795

(97) 807×93 **a.** 751   **b.** 7551   **c.** 75,051

(98) $43{,}380 \div 60$ **a.** 72   **b.** 723   **c.** 7284

◆ **LESSON 56** Keeping Sharp

THINKING STORY Competition

Part 2

THIS WEEK ONLY.
Every T-shirt
20% TO 70% OFF!

You may want to refer to the first part of this Thinking Story on pages 188-189.

One day Mr. Muddle was walking past a clothing store. A big sign in front said, "This week only. Everything 20% to 70% off!" The store was crowded with customers "There's an idea," said Mr. Muddle. "Maybe if I have a sale like that, more people will buy my T-shirts."

So Mr. Muddle made up a bunch of stickers and put one on each T-shirt. Some said "20% off;" some said "50% off;" and some said "70% off." Since he sold only 1 kind of T-shirt, he just mixed the stickers up and put one on each T-shirt. Then he put a sign in his window. "This week only. Every T-shirt 20% to 70% off!" As he had hoped, crowds flocked to his store to buy T-shirts.

"How is your sale going?" asked Mr. Sneaky. He was standing outside his own T-shirt store, unhappy because no one was in his store buying anything.

"The sale is going great," said Mr. Muddle. "I sold all the T-shirts that were 70% off in the first two hours. So I've had to keep changing the stickers on the other T-shirts to make more of them 70% off."

A week later a sign went up in the window of Mr. Sneaky's T-shirt store. It said, "This week only. 20% off on all one-star T-shirts. 50% off on all two-star T-shirts. 70% off on all three-star T-shirts."

Mr. Muddle went next door to see how his neighbor's sale was going. "I'm curious," said Mr. Muddle. "I have only one kind of T-shirt in my store, but you seem to have three. What's the difference between a one-star, a two-star, and a three-star T-shirt?"

"It's simple," said Mr. Sneaky. "They're all the same kind of shirt, but a one-star is the regular price with 20% taken off. A two-star is double the price with 50% taken off. For a three-star shirt I triple the price and then take 70% off."

. . . to be continued

Work in groups. Discuss your answers and how you figured them out. Then compare your answers with those of other groups.

1 Remember that Mr. Muddle buys T-shirts for $4 each and usually sells them for $9 each. How much money does he gain or lose on each T-shirt in his special sale?

2 Which is the best buy at Mr. Sneaky's sale, a one-star, a two-star, or a three-star T-shirt? Why?

3 Whose sale is likely to attract more customers, Mr. Muddle's or Mr. Sneaky's? Why?

LESSON 57

ACT IT OUT

Multiples of 9

Tricky Nines

Try this activity with your friends.

Manolo said to Ken, "Choose any whole number from 1 to 10. Then multiply it by 9. Add the digits of your answer. The sum of the digits will be 9."

Ken chose the number 7. He multiplied it by 9, getting 63. He added 6 and 3 and got 9 as the sum, just as Manolo had said he would. "That's very good," said Ken, "but I bet you can't do it again."

Manolo thought he could. He repeated the instructions and again said that the sum of the digits would be 9.

◆ Was he right? Try all the numbers that Ken might have started with.

"That's not fair," said Ken. "The sum is always 9."

◆ Is Ken right?

"In fact," said Ken, "every multiple of 9 has a sum of digits equal to 9."

◆ Is he right?

"I don't think that's true," Manolo argued. "What about 9 × 11?"

"Well," said Ken, "that's 99. And 9 + 9 = 18. If you add the digits of 18 you get 9. That's what I really meant."

◆ Is Ken right now?

For each problem multiply and then add the digits of the answer.
If the sum is not a single-digit number, keep adding the digits
until you get a single-digit number.

1 11 × 9   **2** 17 × 9   **3** 21 × 9

4 22 × 9   **5** 129 × 9   **6** 131 × 9

7 Is the final sum always 9?

8 Choose at least five different numbers and multiply each by 9. Try to
find one for which Ken's rule doesn't work.

Manolo thinks that Ken's rule (page 208) also works backward. He says,
"Suppose you keep adding the digits of a number until you have a one-
digit sum. If that sum is 9, then your number is divisible by 9. If that
sum is not 9, then your number is not divisible by 9."

**Use a computer or other means to draw a chart, and complete the
chart to see if Manolo's rule works.**

Number	Final Sum of Digits	Remainder When Divided by 9	Does Rule Work?
351	9	0	yes
4122	■	■	■
551	■	■	■
2637	■	■	■
442	■	■	■

9 Choose at least five different numbers for which the final sum of digits
is 9. Divide each by 9. Try to find a number for which Manolo's rule
doesn't work.

10 Choose at least five different numbers for which the final sum of digits
is not 9. Divide each by 9. Try to find a number for which Manolo's rule
doesn't work.

LESSON 58

Finding Divisibility Rules

Can 74 students in the sixth grade be divided equally into groups of three? Sometimes it's useful to check for divisibility without actually dividing.

1 Which of these numbers are divisible by 2?

a. 6	**b.** 7	**c.** 12	**d.** 15
e. 50	**f.** 53	**g.** 97	**h.** 100
i. 105	**j.** 1000	**k.** 10,467	**l.** 10,472

In your Math Journal, try to state a rule that will tell you whether a number is divisible by 2. (Hint: Does the last digit help?)

2 Which of these numbers are divisible by 5?

a. 10	**b.** 15	**c.** 18	**d.** 45
e. 145	**f.** 1000	**g.** 1013	**h.** 1035

Record each of these in your Math Journal.

◆ Write a rule that will tell you whether a number is divisible by 5.

◆ State a rule for deciding whether a number is divisible by 10.

◆ Find a rule for deciding whether a number is divisible by 3. (Hint: Think about the rule for 9. Try several numbers to see if your rule works.)

3 Try your rule for deciding whether a number is divisible by 3 on each of these numbers. (In each case use the rule to see if the number is divisible by 3, and then divide to check.)

a. 12	**b.** 93	**c.** 126	**d.** 15	**e.** 24
f. 13	**g.** 23	**h.** 43	**i.** 26	**j.** 36
k. 46	**l.** 35,166	**m.** 8247	**n.** 8248	**o.** 8249

Record each of these in your Math Journal.

◆ Find a rule for deciding whether a number is divisible by 4. (Hint: Look at the last two digits.)

◆ Find a rule for deciding whether a number is divisible by 8. (Hint: Look at the last three digits.)

4 Can 74 students be divided equally into groups of 3?

5 On your paper draw two large circles that overlap like the ones shown here. Label one "Divisible by 2" and one "Divisible by 3." Then, decide whether each of the numbers shown below is divisible by 2, by 3, by both 2 and 3, or by neither 2 nor 3. If a number is divisible by 2 but not by 3, write it inside the "2" circle but *not* inside the "3" circle. If the number is divisible by 3 but not by 2, write it inside the "3" circle but *not* the "2" circle. If a number is divisible by both 2 and 3, write the number inside both circles where 12 has been written. If a number is not divisible by either 2 or 3, write the number outside the circles. The first five numbers have been written in the correct places.

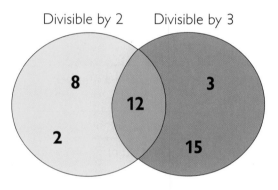

Numbers to be checked for divisibility by 2 and by 3:

2	8	12	3	15	6	9	35	30	20
18	55	81	45	16	24	14	21	10	17

6 You have now placed all the numbers into one of the three sections made by the two circles or outside the circles. Are there any numbers inside only the "divisible by 2" section that are divisible by 6?

7 Are there any numbers inside only the "divisible by 3" section that are divisible by 6?

8 Where are all the numbers that are divisible by 6? Check to be sure you are correct.

Record in your Math Journal a rule for deciding whether a number is divisible by 6.

◆ **LESSON 58 Finding Divisibility Rules**

Here are some rules for divisibility.

Divisor	Divisibility Rule
2	If a whole number ends with an **even** digit, it is divisible by 2.
3	If the sum of the digits is divisible by 3, the number is divisible by 3.
4	If the last two digits make a number divisible by 4, the number is divisible by 4.
5	If the number ends with 0 or 5, it is divisible by 5.
6	If the number is divisible by both 2 and 3, it is divisible by 6.
7	There are rules for divisibility by 7. But the simplest way to find out is simply to divide.
8	If the last three digits make a number divisible by 8, the number is divisible by 8.
9	If the sum of the digits is divisible by 9, the number is divisible by 9.
10	If the last digit is 0, the number is divisible by 10.

For each rule it is also true that if the condition does not hold, then the number is not divisible by that divisor. This is important, too.

Use the chart to help you solve the following problems.

9 Consider the number 7140.

   a. Is 7140 divisible by 7? How can you check without dividing?

   b. Is 7140 divisible by 8? How can you check without dividing?

   c. Is 7140 divisible by 9? How can you check without dividing?

   d. Is 7140 divisible by 10? How can you check without dividing?

   e. How can the work you've done in checking for divisibility by 7, 8, 9, and 10 help you tell quickly whether 7140 is divisible by 2, 3, 5, and 6?

10 What is the least number greater than 0 that is divisible by
   a. 2, 3, 6, and 7?   **b.** 3, 6, 8, and 9?   **c.** 4, 5, 8, and 10?

11 In problem 10, did you need to use four division rules to check the answer? Explain.

Use a computer or other means to draw this chart. Then complete it by using a ✔ to tell whether each of the following numbers is divisible by 2, 3, 4, 5, 6, 7, 8, 9, and 10.

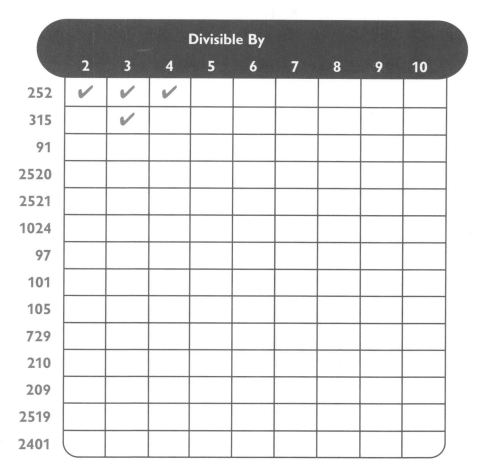

	Divisible By								
	2	**3**	**4**	**5**	**6**	**7**	**8**	**9**	**10**
252	✔	✔	✔						
315		✔							
91									
2520									
2521									
1024									
97									
101									
105									
729									
210									
209									
2519									
2401									

◆ Did you find that 2520 is divisible by all the numbers—2, 3, 4, 5, 6, 7, 8, 9, and 10?

◆ Since 2520 is divisible by 7, could 2521 also be divisible by 7?

◆ What would the remainder be if 2521 were divided by 7? Divide to see if you're right.

◆ Since 2520 is divisible by 2, 3, 4, 5, 6, 7, 8, 9, and 10, could 2521 be divisible by any of them?

Record in your Math Journal the strategies you used for completing the chart. Did you need to use every divisibility rule for checking every number?

Using Divisibility Rules

Emily is packing small boxes of raisins in cartons. The top of each box is 3 centimeters wide and 5 centimeters long. She wants to pack the boxes so they stand up straight in the carton. She has cartons of several sizes from which to choose. She wants to choose a carton so that there won't be space on the sides and the boxes will fit nicely. All the cartons are the same height as the boxes of raisins. But the lengths and widths of the cartons are different. These are the sizes of the cartons:

10 centimeters by 10 centimeters   12 centimeters by 12 centimeters

15 centimeters by 15 centimeters   20 centimeters by 20 centimeters

Emily tried the smallest carton first.

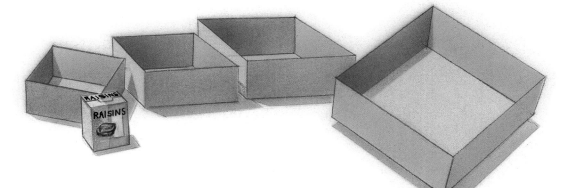

"These don't fit evenly," Emily said.

Pablo was watching and decided to help. "You don't have to try every carton," he said. "Just think a little."

◆ Can you tell how Emily can figure out whether a certain carton will work?

"I could have told you the 10-centimeter by 10-centimeter carton wouldn't work," said Pablo. "Since 10 is divisible by 5, you can put some boxes across the carton without leaving any space. But 10 is not divisible by 3, so you cannot fit all the rows of boxes without leaving space at the end."

"I see," said Emily. "Then the 12-centimeter carton won't work either."

◆ Is Emily right? How do you know?

◆ Which size carton should she use?

◆ Draw a picture to show how the boxes will fit in the carton you will use. Use graph paper if necessary.

◆ How many cartons would she need in order to pack 150 boxes?

A week later Pablo was again watching Emily packing cartons. "You know," Emily said, "the boxes of raisins are bigger now. They are 4 centimeters by 6 centimeters instead of 3 centimeters by 5 centimeters."

◆ Which size carton should Emily use now? Draw a picture to show that you are right.

◆ How many cartons would she need in order to pack 150 boxes?

◆ Suppose the boxes were each 4 centimeters by 5 centimeters. Which size carton would Emily use? Draw a picture to show that you are right.

◆ Could Emily pack these 4-centimeter by 5-centimeter boxes into a carton that was 12 centimeters by 15 centimeters? Draw a picture to show whether it would work.

Emily bought a new batch of cartons in four different sizes:

12 centimeters by 12 centimeters

12 centimeters by 15 centimeters

12 centimeters by 20 centimeters

15 centimeters by 20 centimeters

For each size box, tell which of the new cartons Emily could use to pack the boxes exactly.

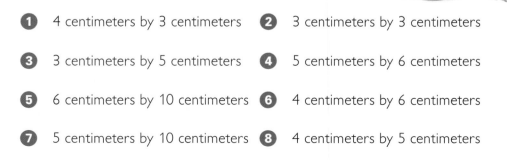

1 4 centimeters by 3 centimeters **2** 3 centimeters by 3 centimeters

3 3 centimeters by 5 centimeters **4** 5 centimeters by 6 centimeters

5 6 centimeters by 10 centimeters **6** 4 centimeters by 6 centimeters

7 5 centimeters by 10 centimeters **8** 4 centimeters by 5 centimeters

◆ LESSON 59 Using Divisibility Rules

Imagine that you want to cover a floor with square tiles. You want to use the largest tiles possible. They can be any size, but they must be square.

9 A floor is 40 decimeters by 30 decimeters.

a. What is the largest square tile you could use to cover the floor?

b. How many of those tiles will fit on the floor?

10 A floor is 45 decimeters by 30 decimeters.

a. What is the largest square tile you could use to cover the floor?

b. How many of those tiles will fit on the floor?

11 A floor is 64 decimeters by 48 decimeters.

a. What is the largest square tile you could use to cover the floor?

b. How many of those tiles will fit on the floor?

12 A floor is 28 decimeters by 50 decimeters.

a. What is the largest square tile you could use to cover the floor?

b. How many of those tiles will fit on the floor?

13 A floor is 35 decimeters by 50 decimeters.

a. What is the largest square tile you could use to cover the floor?

b. How many of those tiles will fit on the floor?

14 A floor is 25 decimeters by 45 decimeters.

a. What is the largest square tile you could use to cover the floor?

b. How many of those tiles will fit on the floor?

15 A floor is 24 decimeters by 48 decimeters.

a. What is the largest square tile you could use to cover the floor?

b. How many of those tiles will fit on the floor?

16 A floor is 24 decimeters by 28 decimeters.

a. What is the largest square tile you could use to cover the floor?

b. How many of those tiles will fit on the floor?

17 A floor is 16 decimeters by 27 decimeters.

a. What is the largest square tile you could use to cover the floor?

b. How many of those tiles will fit on the floor?

Watch the signs.

18 6×7 **19** 8×6 **20** $42 \div 6$ **21** $49 \div 7$

22 $6 + 7$ **23** $6 + 9$ **24** 6×9 **25** $36 \div 6$

26 $19 - 9$ **27** $24 \div 4$ **28** 9×7 **29** 9×9

30 $54 \div 9$ **31** $45 \div 5$ **32** $13 - 8$ **33** $18 - 9$

34 $18 \div 9$ **35** $81 \div 9$ **36** 8×5 **37** $40 \div 4$

38 $15 - 7$ **39** 7×5 **40** $36 \div 9$ **41** 8×3

42 $21 \div 3$ **43** $27 \div 3$ **44** $32 \div 4$ **45** 8×8

Add or subtract. Use shortcuts when you can.

46
$$16,000 - 10,999$$

47
$$2987 + 1013$$

48
$$992 + 992$$

49
$$15,399 + 701$$

50
$$79,801 - 15,999$$

51
$$9876 - 4321$$

52
$$1215 + 1812$$

53
$$17,890 - 599$$

Multiply. Use shortcuts when you can.

54
$$37,037 \times 3$$

55
$$37,037 \times 27$$

56
$$598 \times 50$$

57
$$598 \times 51$$

58
$$101 \times 66$$

59
$$10,101 \times 66$$

60
$$4444 \times 500$$

61
$$673 \times 123$$

Divide.

62 $12\overline{)1440}$ **63** $33\overline{)2541}$ **64** $56\overline{)13,104}$ **65** $28\overline{)19,740}$

66 $42\overline{)6762}$ **67** $37\overline{)49,284}$ **68** $24\overline{)720}$ **69** $16\overline{)4096}$

LESSON 60

Factors

You've learned divisibility rules for several numbers. In this lesson you'll learn about **factors** of a given number, those whole numbers that can be multiplied by a whole number to equal the given number.

We say that 6 is *divisible* by 2 because there is no remainder when we divide 6 by 2.

We also say:

> 2 is a *divisor* of 6.
>
> 2 is a *factor* of 6.
>
> 6 is a *multiple* of 2.

We say that 72 is divisible by 12 because there is no remainder when we divide 72 by 12.

We also say:

> 12 is a divisor of 72.
>
> 12 is a factor of 72.
>
> 72 is a multiple of 12.

Suppose we want to find all the factors of 72. We can simply test each number, starting with 1, to see if it is a factor of 72.

> 1 is a factor (72 ÷ 1 = 72, so 1 × 72 = 72)
>
> 2 is a factor (72 ÷ 2 = 36, so 2 × 36 = 72)
>
> 3 is a factor (72 ÷ 3 = 24, so 3 × 24 = 72)
>
> 4 is a factor (72 ÷ 4 = 18, so 4 × 18 = 72)
>
> 5 is not a factor (72 ÷ 5 has remainder 2)
>
> 6 is a factor (72 ÷ 6 = 12, so 6 × 12 = 72)
>
> 7 is not a factor (72 ÷ 7 has remainder 2)
>
> 8 is a factor (72 ÷ 8 = 9, so 8 × 9 = 72)
>
> 9 is a factor (72 ÷ 9 = 8, so 9 × 8 = 72)
>
> 10 is not a factor (72 ÷ 10 has remainder 2)
>
> 11 is not a factor (72 ÷ 11 has remainder 6)
>
> 12 is a factor (72 ÷ 12 = 6, so 12 × 6 = 72)

The next number we test that is a factor of 72 will be 18. Since we already know that $4 \times 18 = 72$, 18×4 must be 72. Similarly, since $3 \times 24 = 72$, $24 \times 3 = 72$, and 24 is a factor of 72.

Notice that the factors come naturally in pairs; 8 is paired with 9 because $8 \times 9 = 72$, 1 is paired with 72, 2 is paired with 36, 3 with 24, and so on. As soon as you start repeating pairs, you know that you have all the possible factors and you don't have to continue.

Another way to think about the factors of 72 is to picture all of the rectangles with side lengths in whole units that could be made within an **area** of 72 square units.

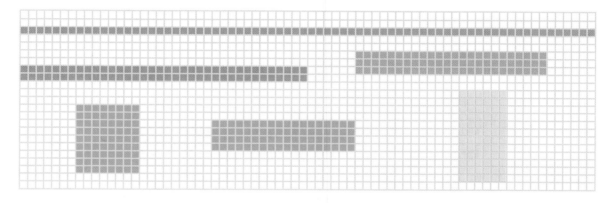

Any number that is the length of a side of one of these rectangles is a factor of 72. The factors of 72 are 1, 2, 3, 4, 6, 8, 9, 12, 18, 24, 36, and 72.

For each number list all the factors.

1 12	**2** 36	**3** 2	**4** 93
5 1	**6** 91	**7** 20	**8** 14
9 24	**10** 9	**11** 13	**12** 16
13 100	**14** 31	**15** 28	**16** 45
17 23	**18** 39	**19** 50	**20** 42
21 35	**22** 26	**23** 18	**24** 56
25 37	**26** 51	**27** 81	**28** 40

◆ **LESSON 60** Factors

THINKING STORY

Competition

Part 3

You may want to refer to the earlier parts of this Thinking Story on pages 188-189 and 206-207.

M r. Muddle was still looking for ways to sell more T-shirts. "You need to advertise," Mr. Breezy told him. "Then more people will know about your store and come buy from you. That's how people learn about my dog training school."

"Do you advertise on television?" Mr. Muddle asked.

"No, that costs too much for a small business like mine," said Mr. Breezy. "Here's how I advertise and it costs practically nothing." He pointed to a sign on the wall of his office.

"But that's an ad for Raul's Garage," said Mr. Muddle.

"Exactly. And Raul has an ad in his garage for my dog training school."

"And here's an ad on your wall for Spiffy Dry Cleaners. I'll bet they have an ad on their wall. . . ."

"For Breezy's College of Canine Knowledge. Right. Now you get the idea."

Mr. Muddle thanked Mr. Breezy for the idea. Then he went back to his store and made a poster that looked like this:

He took the sign with him and went next door to Sneaky's T-Shirts. "I've got a wonderful deal for you, Mr. Sneaky," he said. "You'll be able to advertise for free, I'll be able to advertise for free, and we'll both make more money."

. . . to be continued

Work in groups. Discuss your answers and how you figured them out. Then compare your answers with those of other groups.

❶ Explain how Mr. Breezy's way of advertising works. Why do the other merchants agree to it?

❷ Mr. Breezy said his way of advertising costs "practically nothing." What costs would you count?

❸ Does it make sense for Mr. Muddle to trade ads with Mr. Sneaky? What is it that Mr. Muddle has failed to understand about Mr. Breezy's way of advertising?

Prime and Composite Numbers

You may have noticed in the previous lesson that some numbers have many factors and some have only two. We can classify whole numbers according to how many factors they have.

A **prime number** has exactly two factors, 1 and itself.

A **composite number** has more than two factors.

The number 1 is neither prime nor composite since it has only one factor. It is the only whole number that is neither prime nor composite.

For each number write *P* on your paper if the number is prime, *C* if it is composite, or *N* if it is neither.

1 1	**2** 2	**3** 3
4 4	**5** 5	**6** 6
7 7	**8** 8	**9** 9
10 10	**11** 11	**12** 12
13 13	**14** 14	**15** 15
16 18	**17** 19	**18** 20
19 22	**20** 28	**21** 29
22 30	**23** 99	**24** 101
25 105	**26** 1001	**27** 89
28 124	**29** 252	**30** 2520

31 What are the prime numbers that are less than 20?

Every whole number except 1 can be factored into prime numbers in exactly one way (except for the order of the factors). We call this prime factorization. For example, $28 = 2 \times 2 \times 7$. Of course, $28 = 7 \times 2 \times 2$ and $28 = 2 \times 7 \times 2$, but we do not consider these different prime factorizations of 28, because all that is changed is the order of the factors. Usually, we write factors in increasing order and use exponents if we can.

$$28 = 2^2 \times 7$$

To find the prime factors of a number, factor it into any two factors and continue factoring until all factors are prime.

Example:

Show the prime factorization of 2156.

Find any factor of 2156. Since 56 is divisible by 4, 2156 is divisible by 4.

$$2156 = 4 \times 539$$

Next, find factors of 4 and 539. Continue finding factors until all factors left are prime.

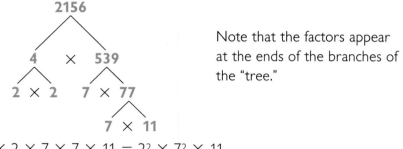

Note that the factors appear at the ends of the branches of the "tree."

$$2156 = 2 \times 2 \times 7 \times 7 \times 11 = 2^2 \times 7^2 \times 11$$

We can use these steps for any number.

Show the prime factorization of 672.

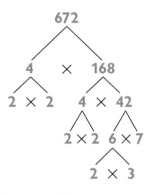

Of course, different trees can be drawn, but the prime factors will be the same in any case.

$$672 = 2^5 \times 3 \times 7$$

32 Try to draw different trees for these examples.

33 Show the prime factorization of 53.

34 Show the prime factorization for each of the numbers in problems 2–30 on page 222.

The largest living thing on Earth is believed to be the "General Sherman" sequoia tree located in Sequoia National Park, California. It is 275 feet tall and weighs over 1400 tons (as much as the weight of nine blue whales or 360 elephants).

◆ **LESSON 61 Prime and Composite Numbers**

THINKING STORY

Competition

Part 4

You may want to refer to the earlier parts of this Thinking Story on pages 188–189, 206–207, and 220–221.

Mr. Muddle tried still another way to sell more T-shirts. He tried keeping his store open all night. But that didn't work. He had to pay a helper because he couldn't stay awake all night to look after the store. Soon Mr. Sneaky started keeping his T-shirt store open all night too. Neither of them sold any more T-shirts because nobody came to buy T-shirts in the middle of the night. It cost so much to stay open all night that they both had to raise the prices of their T-shirts.

"I give up," Mr. Muddle said. "No matter what I do to sell more T-shirts, Mr. Sneaky does it too. Things always end up as bad as before."

"Why don't you buy out Mr. Sneaky's business?" Loretta the Letter Carrier asked. "Then you would be the only person left selling T-shirts. You would be sure to get more business."

Mr. Muddle thought that was a brilliant idea. He called in his friends Ferdie, Portia, Manolita, Marcus, and Willy. He told them of his plan. "I'll give you money. I want you to go next door to Mr. Sneaky's store. Keep buying T-shirts until his T-shirts are all gone. Then I'll be the only person in town selling T-shirts."

"I'm sorry, Mr. Muddle," said Willy. "Your plan won't work."

"Nothing works," Mr. Muddle said sadly. "Mr. Sneaky is sure to win, no matter what I do. He copies all my ideas. He has a bigger store, a newer store. He has more T-shirts, brighter lights, and an expensive sign in front. I guess I'll just do the best I can and be poor."

So Mr. Muddle quit having sales. He quit staying open all night. He charged $9 for each T-shirt, the same as before. He sold only 70 or 80 of them a week. He was so poor that he started buttering his bread on the edge because it took less butter than on the flat side. But suddenly, after a few months, he started selling more and more T-shirts. He went next door to see if Mr. Sneaky was also doing better. But the sign above Mr. Sneaky's store no longer said, "Sneaky's T-shirts." It said, "Sneaky's Discount CDs. 20% off on all one-star CDs. 50% off on all two-star CDs. 70% off on all three-star CDs."

. . . the end

Work in groups. Discuss your answers and how you figured them out. Then compare your answers with those of other groups.

❶ Who gained and who lost from having the T-shirt stores open all night? Explain.

❷ Why wouldn't Mr. Muddle's plan for buying out Mr. Sneaky's business work?

❸ What would you need to do in order to buy out the business of someone like Mr. Sneaky?

❹ Why did business suddenly get much better for Mr. Muddle?

❺ Why do you think Mr. Sneaky changed businesses?

LESSON
62

Checking Products

In this unit you have learned some rules for divisibility. These rules tell you whether a number is divisible by any of the numbers from 1 to 10 and can help you check your answers to some problems.

There is a method for checking multiplication in which you add digits.

First add the digits of each factor. Multiply the sums. Then add the digits of the product. That sum should be the same as the sum of the digits of the product of the two factors. When we say add the digits, we mean to go on adding until we arrive at a one-digit number.

Examples:

$314 \times 256 = ?$ Check the multiplication with the rule.

```
      2 5 6      Add the digits of the factors.
    × 3 1 4      2 + 5 + 6 = 13     1 + 3 = 4
    1 0 2 4      3 + 1 + 4 = 8
      2 5 6      Multiply the sums.   8 × 4 = 32
    7 6 8        Add the digits.      3 + 2 = 5
  8 0,3 8 4      Add the digits of the product of the multiplication.
                 8 + 0 + 3 + 8 + 4 = 23     2 + 3 = 5
```

Both numbers are the same. We can be pretty sure the answer is correct.

$654 \times 9876 = ?$

```
      9 8 7 6      9 + 8 + 7 + 6 = 30     3 + 0 = 3
    ×   6 5 4      6 + 5 + 4 = 15         1 + 5 = 6
    3 9 5 0 4      6 × 3 = 18             1 + 8 = 9
    4 9 3 8 0
    5 9 2 5 6
  6,4 5 8,9 0 4    6 + 4 + 5 + 8 + 9 + 0 + 4 = 36     3 + 6 = 9
```

Both numbers are the same. We can be pretty sure the answer is correct.

Joanna calculated 213×65 as 14,845. She wanted to check her answer.

$213 \times 65 = 14,845$
$2 + 1 + 3 = 6$
$6 + 5 = 11$ $1 + 1 = 2$
$6 \times 2 = 12$ $1 + 2 = 3$
$1 + 4 + 8 + 4 + 5 = 22$ $2 + 2 = 4$

The two numbers are not the same. Joanna must have made a mistake in her calculation.

Use the rule to see which of these answers are wrong.

1. 317 × 714 = 226,338
2. 87 × 65 = 5565
3. 518 × 273 = 141,414
4. 145 × 325 = 47,125
5. 87 × 56 = 4972
6. 92 × 29 = 2668
7. 23 × 578 = 13,294
8. 69 × 57 = 3933
9. 519 × 127 = 65,713
10. 73 × 84 = 6432
11. 258 × 963 = 248,854
12. 518 × 309 = 160,062
13. 951 × 753 = 716,103
14. 48 × 307 = 14,736

If you don't get the same sums, you know the answer is wrong. Sometimes, however, the sums will be the same even though the answer is wrong.

Example: 73 × 84 = 6123

To check this problem, you would do these calculations:

7 + 3 = 10   1 + 0 = 1

8 + 4 = 12   1 + 2 = 3

3 × 1 = **3**

6 + 1 + 2 + 3 = 12   1 + 2 = **3**

It seems that the answer is correct, but it isn't. The correct answer is 6132.

Example: 564 × 88 = 48,732

To check, you would do this:

5 + 6 + 4 = 15   1 + 5 = 6

8 + 8 = 16   1 + 6 = 7

6 × 7 = 42   4 + 2 = **6**

4 + 8 + 7 + 3 + 2 = 24   2 + 4 = **6**

It seems that the answer is correct, but it isn't. The correct answer is 49,632.

Remember: **If the rule says the answer is wrong, then the answer is wrong; if the rule doesn't say the answer is wrong, it may be right or wrong.**

Unit 3 Review

Lessons 48 and 56

Solve these problems. Watch the signs.

1 234 + 518

2 2.34 × 51.8

3 48.23 − 17.005

4 2.96 + 53.8

5 4.8 − 1.6

6 48 ÷ 1.6

Lesson 48

Give the decimal equivalent.

7 53%

8 6%

9 101%

10 53.7%

11 61%

12 6.1%

13 200%

14 0.9%

Lessons 48

Write each of these as a percent.

15 0.27

16 0.86

17 0.04

18 0.925

19 2.34

20 0.003

21 0.815

22 10.3

Lessons 48

Find each amount.

23 5% of 100

24 20% of 60

25 12.5% of 30

26 10% of 80

27 25% of 200

28 5% of 9

Solve these problems.

29 The tax in Lester's city is 7%. With tax, how much will he pay for a television set that is marked $200.00?

Lessons 49 and 55

30 Armando wants to buy a CD cabinet that is marked $120. The sales tax is 6%. How much will the cabinet cost?

31 Grace is buying ice skates on sale. The original price was $110.00. There is a 20% discount. What is the sale price?

32 Which costs more, a $150 VCR on sale at 20% off or on sale for $20 off?

33 Reggie is buying a desk chair on sale. The original price was $300. The discount is 30%. How many dollars will the discount be?

Lessons 60 and 61

Show the prime factorization of each of these numbers. If the number is prime, just write the number with a *P* next to it. Use exponents if you wish.

34 4 **35** 252 **36** 2500 **37** 300

38 5 **39** 1260 **40** 1024 **41** 240

Solve these problems.

Lessons 49, 52–54, and 59

42 A comic book set priced at $15 is on sale at a 40% discount. What is the sale price of the comics?

43 Which is a better buy, a $79.98 bicycle on sale at 50% off or on sale at half price?

44 Ingrid deposited $70 in the bank at 4% interest per year. How much money will she have after one year?

45 Curtis deposited some money in the bank last year at 5% interest. After one year the bank said he had $147. How much did he deposit last year?

46 What is the largest size square tile you can use to cover the floor in a room that is 48 decimeters long and 36 decimeters wide?

47 Mario bought a sweatshirt at a 20% discount. The sales tax was 5%. How much did Mario pay?

48 Fran has $25 to spend on a computer game. The game she wants costs $28.95 but is on sale at 20% off. Can she afford that game?

49 Which will earn more interest in three years, $500 invested at 5% compounded quarterly or $500 invested at 5% compounded monthly?

50 With 6% tax, a pair of shoes costs $42.35. What was the price before tax?

LESSON 64

Unit 3 Practice

Lessons 48 and 56

Watch the signs.

① 0.2 + 0.143   ② 0.2 − 0.143   ③ 0.2 × 0.143

④ 0.6 + 0.571   ⑤ 0.6 − 0.571   ⑥ 0.6 × 0.571

⑦ 0.375 + 0.25   ⑧ 0.375 − 0.25   ⑨ 0.375 × 0.25

⑩ 0.5 × 0.3   ⑪ 0.5 + 0.3   ⑫ 0.5 − 0.3

⑬ 0.625 − 0.333   ⑭ 0.625 × 0.333   ⑮ 0.625 + 0.333

⑯ 0.333 × 9   ⑰ 9 × 0.667   ⑱ 0.286 × 21

⑲ 21 × 0.571   ⑳ 21 × 0.714   ㉑ 6 × 0.667

Lesson 48

Write each of these as a decimal.

㉒ 1%   ㉓ 5%   ㉔ 10%   ㉕ 75%

㉖ 2.5%   ㉗ 6.2%   ㉘ 1.1%   ㉙ 35%

㉚ 0.6%   ㉛ 0.02%   ㉜ 0.12%   ㉝ 12%

㉞ 42%   ㉟ 8.5%   ㊱ 28.7%   ㊲ 0.9%

Lesson 48

Write each of these as a percent.

㊳ 0.1   ㊴ 0.15   ㊵ 0.0045   ㊶ 0.09

㊷ 0.01   ㊸ 0.35   ㊹ 1.0   ㊺ 0.086

㊻ 0.05   ㊼ 0.005   ㊽ 0.65   ㊾ 2.4

㊿ 0.07   51 0.025   52 0.605   53 0.75

Lesson 48

Find each amount.

54 5% of 100   55 5% of 500   56 12% of 100

57 12% of 60   58 3% of 200   59 3% of 20

60 12.5% of 100   61 12.5% of 50   62 60% of 80

63 60% of 40   64 75% of 100   65 75% of 200

Solve this problem.

66 Mr. Archer invests $3000 at 4% interest compounded annually. Mrs. Butler invests $3000 at 4% interest compounded quarterly. At the end of one year, how much more interest will Mrs. Butler have earned than Mr. Archer?

Lesson 53

Lessons 60 and 61

Show the prime factorization of each number. If the number is prime, write the number with a *P* next to it. Use exponents if you wish.

67 3   **68** 6   **69** 9   **70** 16   **71** 24

72 36   **73** 72   **74** 12   **75** 18   **76** 22

77 25   **78** 125   **79** 625   **80** 198   **81** 378

82 31   **83** 729   **84** 61   **85** 549   **86** 250

87 144   **88** 156   **89** 42   **90** 420   **91** 700

Lesson 49

Find the cost, with tax, of each item.

92 $30 clock with 5% sales tax

93 $400 television with 7% sales tax

94 $750 sofa with 6% sales tax

95 $10 football with 6% sales tax

96 $15 mouse pad with 5% sales tax

97 $25 video game with 7% sales tax

98 $5.50 book with 5% sales tax

99 $77.98 bicycle with 6% sales tax

Lesson 49

Find the discount price of each item.

	Item	Regular Price	Discount
100	basketball	$10.00	10%
101	notebook	$1.25	20%
102	guitar	$96.00	25%
103	CD player	$124.50	$30
104	book	$4.75	30%

Lessons 52 and 53

105 Mr. Redwing put $500 in the bank at 7% interest, compounded annually. Use a calculator. How much will he have at the end of

a. one year?   **b.** three years?   **c.** five years?

Unit Test

Solve these problems. Watch the signs.

1 4.87 + 3.19   **2** 612 − 351   **3** 2.4 × 1.8

4 64.8 ÷ 0.48   **5** 5.19 + 43.8   **6** 12.7 − 4.65

Give the decimal equivalent.

7 35%   **8** 9%   **9** 125%   **10** 28.3%

11 16%   **12** 9.3%   **13** 300%   **14** 0.6%

Write each of these as a percent.

15 0.19   **16** 0.37   **17** 0.06   **18** 0.741

19 2.79   **20** 0.005   **21** 0.732   **22** 6.5

Find each amount.

23 5% of 200   **24** 20% of 40   **25** 12.5% of 40

26 10% of 60   **27** 25% of 100   **28** 5% of 6

Solve these problems.

29 The tax in Mrs. Turner's city is 6%. With tax, how much will she pay for a dryer that is marked $400.00?

30 Alfred wants to buy a fax machine that is on sale for $150. The tax is 5%. How much will the fax machine cost?

31 Mr. Becker is buying a boat on sale. The original price was $3400.00. There is a 10% discount. What is the sale price?

32 Rudy is buying a CD player on sale. The original price was $130. The discount is 20%. How much less will he pay?

33 Which costs more, a $40 jacket on sale at 10% off or on sale at $10 off?

34 With 5% tax, a picture frame costs $7.88. What was the cost before tax?

Show the prime factorization of each of these numbers. If the number is prime, just write the number with a *P* next to it. Use exponents if you wish.

35 6   **36** 101   **37** 243   **38** 160

39 7   **40** 120   **41** 900   **42** 1000

Solve these problems.

43 A $50 sweatshirt was on sale at 20% off. The tax was 5%. Bridget paid for the sweatshirt. How much change did she receive?

44 Jacob has $12. He finds a baseball cap regularly $16.50 on sale for 20% off. Can he afford the cap?

45 Which earns more interest over two years, $300 invested at 4% compounded monthly or $300 invested at 4% compounded quarterly?

46 A book priced at $12 is on sale at a 50% discount. How much will the book cost on sale?

47 Which is a better buy, a $150.00 bicycle on sale at 50% off or on sale at $50 off?

48 Belva deposited $70 in the bank at 4% interest per year. How much money will she have after one year?

49 Mrs. Kito deposited some money in the bank last year at 6% interest. After one year the bank said she had $212. How much did she deposit last year?

50 What is the largest size square tile you can use to cover the floor in a room that is 36 decimeters long and 24 decimeters wide?

A Birthday Present

Suppose you received a birthday present of $100.

What are some things you could do with that amount of money?

◆ If you placed the money in a bank account at 5% annual interest, how much would your investment be worth in one year?

◆ If you asked the bank to send you the interest at the end of the year, how much will be sent to you? How much will still be in your bank account?

◆ Suppose you kept the $100 in the bank. How much money will be sent to you at the end of the second year? How much will still be in your bank account?

Think about it. If you have $100, you can spend it on something you want, or if you invest it at 5%, you can get $5 a year for the rest of your life and still have the $100.

◆ What are some reasons for saving your money instead of spending it?

◆ What are some reasons for spending your money instead of saving it?

A Savings Plan

Suppose you decided to put your $100 in the bank or in another investment for a long time and let the money grow. At 5% annual interest, how much will your investment be worth at the end of each year? At 10% annual interest, how much will it be worth?

To find out, use a calculator or computer to extend this chart for at least ten years.

$100 Initial Investment
Value at End of Each Year (Dollars)

Years	5%	10%
1	$105.00	$110.00
2	$110.25	$121.00

Study the completed chart. You may need to extend the chart to answer some questions.

How long would it take to double your original investment if you earn 5% per year?

How long will it take to double your original investment if you earn 10% per year?

If you let the initial $100 grow, how much will you have after 40 years? First estimate; then calculate the amounts.

Get information from banks in your neighborhood. How much interest does each pay on savings accounts? What fees, if any, does each charge? Organize your information so that it is easy to compare banks. Are you able to find a bank that offers a good savings program for sixth graders?

UNIT 4

Fractions and Mixed Numbers

UNDERSTANDING PARTS AND PROPORTIONS

- **operations with fractions**
- **decimal equivalents**
- **probability**
- **improper fractions and mixed numbers**
- **ratios, rates, and averages**

SCHOOL TO WORK CONNECTION

Firefighters use math . . .

Firefighters learn how to read their instruments so they can make necessary adjustments. These instruments tell things like how much water is in the truck and what is the water pressure. The instruments use measures that are in both whole numbers and fractions.

Fractions of Whole Numbers

We can use fractions to describe how much of something we are taking.

To take $\frac{3}{5}$ of a pizza, we divide the pizza into 5 equal parts and take 3 of them.

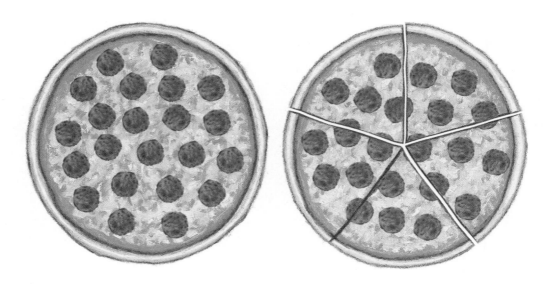

Remember: **The denominator (bottom number) of a fraction tells how many equal parts there are.**

$$\frac{3}{5} \quad \text{---- numerator} \quad \text{---- denominator}$$

The numerator (top number) tells how many of these parts to take.

To find a fraction of a number, you can divide the number into as many equal parts as the denominator tells you, and then take as many as the numerator says.

For example, to find $\frac{3}{5}$ of 60, divide 60 into 5 equal parts.

Since 60 ÷ 5 = 12, each part will be 12.

Then take 3 of those parts.

3 × 12 = 36

So $\frac{3}{5}$ of 60 = 36.

One way to find $\frac{3}{5}$ of 60 is to divide 60 by 5 and then multiply by 3. What would happen if you multiplied by 3 and then divided by 5?

$$60 \times 3 = 180 \qquad\qquad 180 \div 5 = 36$$

◆   Is this the same answer as before?

◆   Try this method with other problems. Do you get the same answer, whether you divide first then multiply, or multiply first then divide?

Notice that in order to find $\frac{3}{5}$ of a number, you always multiply by 3 at some time. Because taking a fraction of a number always involves multiplying, we call the "of" operation "multiplication." So $\frac{2}{3}$ of 60 and $\frac{2}{3} \times 60$ mean the same thing.

With multiplication of whole numbers, as you know, the order in which you multiply doesn't change the product. The same thing is true for fractions and whole numbers.

$$\frac{3}{4} \text{ of } 60 = \frac{3}{4} \times 60 = 60 \times \frac{3}{4}$$

Solve for *n* in the following.

1. $\frac{2}{5}$ of 60 = n

2. $\frac{2}{5} \times 60 = n$

3. $60 \times \frac{2}{5} = n$

4. $n = \frac{3}{4}$ of 60

5. $n = \frac{3}{4} \times 60$

6. $n = 60 \times \frac{3}{4}$

7. $\frac{1}{2}$ of n = 60

8. $\frac{1}{2}$ of 30 = n

9. $\frac{2}{3} \times 90 = n$

10. $120 \times \frac{4}{5} = n$

11. $360 \times \frac{1}{12} = n$

12. $\frac{0}{3}$ of 30 = n

13. $\frac{n}{4} \times 20 = 5$

14. $\frac{n}{4}$ of 20 = 10

15. $20 \times \frac{n}{4} = 15$

16. $\frac{2}{3} \times 6 = n$

17. $\frac{2}{3} \times 12 = n$

18. $\frac{2}{3} \times n = 12$

19. $\frac{1}{4} \times 8 = n$

20. $\frac{n}{4} \times 8 = 8$

21. $\frac{1}{2} \times 50 = n$

22. $\frac{1}{5} \times 50 = n$

23. $\frac{2}{5} \times 50 = n$

24. $\frac{n}{5} \times 50 = 40$

Solve these problems.

25. A pair of jeans is on sale for $\frac{2}{3}$ of the regular price. If the regular price is \$36, what is the sale price?

26. A newspaper reported that $\frac{3}{4}$ of the town's residents who were surveyed approved of the mayor's job performance. If 200 residents were surveyed, how many approved of the mayor's job performance?

27. A math teacher announced that $\frac{3}{5}$ of the class earned an "A" or a "B" on the last math test. If the class has 25 students, how many had an A or a B?

◆ LESSON 65 Fractions of Whole Numbers

SOCIAL STUDIES CONNECTION

Solve these problems.

28 In order to win an election with two candidates, one must win a majority of the votes cast. A majority is any number greater than $\frac{1}{2}$ of those voting. If 200 votes are cast in an election with two candidates, what is the fewest number of votes a candidate can receive to win the election?

29 Why do we not agree that a candidate will win if she or he receives exactly half of the votes cast?

30 If there are more than two candidates, we sometimes declare the winner to be the candidate who received the most votes, even if that is not a majority. We say such a candidate received a plurality of the votes.

a. If there are 300 votes cast and there are three candidates, what is the fewest number of votes a candidate might receive and still win?

b. Would a candidate who won 101 votes in such an election necessarily win? Explain.

31 The President of the United States is chosen by the Electoral College, which has 538 members. How many votes must a candidate get in the Electoral College to have a majority?

32 If a candidate fails to get a majority in the Electoral College, the outcome is decided in the House of Representatives, but each of the 50 states gets only one vote and the candidate must get a majority to win. If no candidate wins in the Electoral College, how many votes are required in order to win in the House of Representatives?

33 In order to pass in Congress, a bill must receive a majority vote in the House of Representatives and in the Senate.

a. How many of the 435 votes in the House of Representatives must a bill receive in order to pass?

b. How many of the 100 votes in the Senate must a bill receive in order to pass?

34 In order to override a veto (or rejection) by the President, a bill must receive a $\frac{2}{3}$ vote in the House and in the Senate.

a. How many votes are needed in the House of Representatives to override a veto?

b. How many votes are needed in the Senate to override a veto?

Fractions of 60 Game

Players:	Two or more
Materials:	Two 0–5 cubes
Object:	To score a total of 150 or more
Math Focus:	Finding fractions of numbers and adding

RULES

1. Take turns rolling both cubes. Combine the numbers rolled to make a fraction no greater than 1.

2. Find that fraction of 60 and write the answer.

If you rolled:	You would take:	Your answer would be:
2 3	$\frac{2}{3}$ of 60	40
0 4	$\frac{0}{4}$ of 60	0
2 2	$\frac{2}{2}$ of 60	60

3. Add the answer to your last score.

4. If you roll a 0, your score for that turn is 0.

5. If you roll 0 and 0, roll both cubes again.

6. The first player whose score totals 150 or more is the winner.

OTHER WAYS TO PLAY THIS GAME

1. Try to score a different total.

2. Change the game to "Fractions of 120."

Suppose this game were played with a 5–10 cube. Which rolls would give answers that are not whole numbers? Record your answers in your Math Journal.

LESSON
66

Multiplying Fractions

Sometimes we need to find a fraction of a fraction. This example helps show how we can do that. Using a piece of paper as a pizza, act out this story.

Find $\frac{2}{3}$ of $\frac{4}{7}$ of a pizza.

Divide the pizza into 7 equal pieces and separate 4 of them. That is $\frac{4}{7}$ of the pizza.

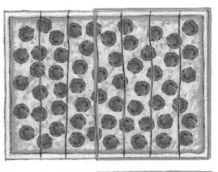

To take $\frac{2}{3}$ of that, cut each of the 7 pieces into 3 equal pieces. Then from each of the $\frac{4}{7}$ that we separated, take 2 of these smaller pieces. So all together we take 8 of the smaller pieces.

In effect, we have cut the pizza into 3 × 7, or 21, equal pieces. Then we took 2 × 4, or 8, of those pieces.

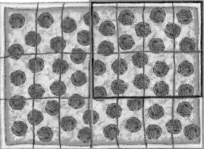

$$\frac{2}{3} \text{ of } \frac{4}{7} = \frac{2 \times 4}{3 \times 7} = \frac{8}{21}$$

Notice that $\frac{2}{3}$ of $\frac{4}{7} = \frac{2 \times 4}{3 \times 7}$. So it is reasonable to write $\frac{2}{3} \times \frac{4}{7}$ for $\frac{2}{3}$ of $\frac{4}{7}$. We can use this rule for multiplying fractions: To multiply two fractions, multiply their numerators to get the numerator of the answer and multiply denominators to get the denominator of the answer.

Solve these problems. Be careful.

1 $\frac{1}{2}$ of $\frac{1}{4}$ **2** $\frac{1}{2}$ of $\frac{1}{3}$ **3** $\frac{1}{3}$ of $\frac{1}{2}$ **4** $\frac{1}{2}$ of $\frac{2}{3}$

5 $\frac{1}{2}$ of $\frac{3}{5}$ **6** $\frac{2}{5}$ of $\frac{3}{4}$ **7** $\frac{3}{7} \times \frac{3}{4}$ **8** $\frac{4}{5} \times \frac{2}{3}$

9 $\frac{5}{6} \times \frac{5}{9}$ **10** $\frac{2}{3} \times \frac{1}{5}$ **11** $\frac{3}{8} \times \frac{1}{2}$ **12** $\frac{2}{5} \times \frac{1}{7}$

Solve.

13 $\frac{1}{3}$ of 30   14 $\frac{1}{4}$ of 60   15 $\frac{1}{2}$ of 100   16 $\frac{1}{5}$ of 100

17 $\frac{2}{3}$ of 75   18 $\frac{3}{4}$ of 80   19 $\frac{2}{5}$ of 40   20 $\frac{4}{5}$ of 40

21 $\frac{1}{3}$ of 24   22 $\frac{2}{3}$ of 24   23 $\frac{1}{7}$ of 35   24 $\frac{1}{8}$ of 40

25 $\frac{4}{5}$ of 30   26 $\frac{3}{5}$ of 80   27 $\frac{1}{2}$ of 36   28 $\frac{2}{3}$ of 120

Solve these problems.

29 If you roll a 0–5 cube many times, about what fraction of the time would you expect to roll a 0?

30 If you roll a 0–5 cube many times, about what fraction of the time would you expect to roll a 3?

31 If you roll a 0–5 cube 60 times, about how many times would you expect a 0 to come up? Try it to see if you get about the number of 0s you expected.

32 If you roll a 0–5 cube many times, about what fraction of the time would you expect to roll an odd number (1, 3, or 5)?

33 If you roll a 0–5 cube 60 times, about how many times would you expect to roll an odd number? Try it to see.

34 If you roll a 0–5 cube many times, about what fraction of the time would you expect to roll a number less than 5?

35 Two-thirds of the 600 students at Ford High School play some kind of team sport. Of those who do, $\frac{1}{10}$ play football.

  a. What fraction of the students at Ford High School play football?

  b. How many students at Ford play football?

36 A grove in Florida has 400 trees. Of those trees, $\frac{1}{4}$ are grapefruit trees and $\frac{3}{4}$ are orange trees. A recent frost damaged $\frac{1}{2}$ of the orange trees but no grapefruit trees.

  a. What fraction of the total trees did the frost damage?

  b. How many trees were damaged?

A banyan tree in India has the widest spread of any plant on Earth. Its branches cover an area as large as four football fields.

Decimal Equivalents of Fractions

We can find $\frac{3}{100}$ of a meter by dividing a meter into 100 parts and taking 3 of them. We also know that this is 0.03 meter. So $\frac{3}{100}$ or 0.03 is the number that we get when we divide 3 by 100.

We know that $\frac{3}{8}$ can mean to divide something into 8 equal parts and take 3 of those parts.

The fraction $\frac{3}{8}$ can also represent a number.

Think of the bar of a fraction as meaning "divided by." To write a fraction as a decimal, find the numerator divided by the denominator.

If we want to write the number $\frac{3}{8}$ as a decimal, we can divide 3 by 8.

$$\begin{array}{r} 0.\ 3\ 7\ 5 \\ 8\overline{)3.^30^60^40} \end{array}$$

We can write: $\frac{3}{8} = 3 \div 8 = 0.375$.

We call 0.375 the **decimal equivalent** of $\frac{3}{8}$.

Try to find a decimal equivalent of $\frac{2}{11}$ (divide 2 by 11).

$$\begin{array}{r} 0.1\ 8\ 1\ 8 \\ 11\overline{)2.0^90^20^90} \end{array}$$

We can carry this division on and on. So we can approximate $\frac{2}{11}$ with a decimal to as many places as we wish, but it has no decimal equivalent. For example, we would say that to the nearest thousandth, $\frac{2}{11}$ is about 0.182. Notice that to round to the nearest thousandth, we must carry the division out to the ten thousandths place.

For each fraction write the decimal equivalent or an approximation rounded to the nearest thousandth.

1. $\frac{1}{2}$ 2. $\frac{1}{4}$ 3. $\frac{3}{4}$ 4. $\frac{1}{3}$ 5. $\frac{2}{3}$

6. $\frac{1}{5}$ 7. $\frac{2}{5}$ 8. $\frac{3}{5}$ 9. $\frac{4}{5}$ 10. $\frac{1}{6}$

11. $\frac{2}{6}$ 12. $\frac{1}{7}$ 13. $\frac{1}{8}$ 14. $\frac{2}{8}$ 15. $\frac{3}{8}$

Up to 1 Game

Players:	Two or more
Materials:	Four 0–5 cubes
Object:	To be the last player to get to 1
Math Focus:	Comparing and ordering fractions and decimals, finding decimal equivalents of common fractions, and mathematical reasoning

RULES

1. Take turns rolling all four cubes.

2. On your turn use any two of the numbers you roll to make a fraction or a decimal less than 1. (For example, if you roll 2, 3, 2 and 1, you could make $\frac{1}{3}$, $\frac{2}{3}$, $\frac{1}{2}$, or any of these decimals: .12, .21, .22, .23, .32, .13, and .31.)

3. Keep a record of the amount you make on each turn. If you make a fraction, write the decimal equivalent or an approximation.

4. On each turn you must write an amount greater than the amount you made on your previous turn.

5. On any turn if you cannot write an amount less than 1 but greater than your previous turn, then you are out. The last player to go out wins.

SAMPLE GAME

	Hilda's Record		Ben's Record	
Turns	Numbers Rolled	Amount Made	Numbers Rolled	Amount Made
1	2 3 3 4	0.23	3 2 5 2	0.22
2	1 2 0 5	0.25	1 3 0 5	0.333 $\left(\frac{1}{3}\right)$
3	1 2 2 5	0.40 $\left(\frac{2}{5}\right)$	1 0 4 5	0.41
4	2 2 0 3	0.667 $\left(\frac{2}{3}\right)$	3 0 3 5	0.50
5	2 2 0 5	can't go	5 5 2 3	0.52

Ben won.

◆ **LESSON 67** Decimal Equivalents of Fractions

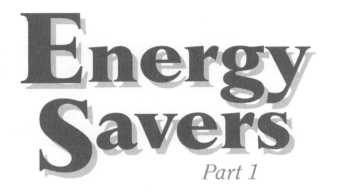

Energy Savers

Part 1

"For an Energy Savers Club project we're trying to get people to save energy," Manolita said. "Will you help us, Mr. Muddle?"

"I'm always glad to do my part," said Mr. Muddle. "Last year you had me save empty bottles. Then no one ever came to pick them up. If I save energy for you this year, I hope someone will come around to collect it."

"That's not how it works," Marcus said.

"I was just joking," Mr. Muddle said. "I know you save energy by using less electricity or heating fuel or gas."

"We'd like you to save gas by starting a car pool," Willy said.

"I like that idea," said Mr. Muddle. "I'll get to ride to work with my neighbors. And we'll save money as well as energy. Each day one person drives all the others to work. That way only one car is being driven instead of three or four or five."

Mr. Muddle said that he would start a car pool right away. The next day the Energy Savers checked back to see how it was working. "I enjoyed driving Ms. Eng and Mr. Breezy and Loretta the Letter Carrier to work," said Mr. Muddle.

"But it was a lot of driving. I drove about 50 kilometers, and it took almost two hours. I'll have to close my store early in order to drive each person home from work."

"Let's draw a map of your route," said Marcus. "Maybe we can find a way to make the drive shorter."

. . . to be continued

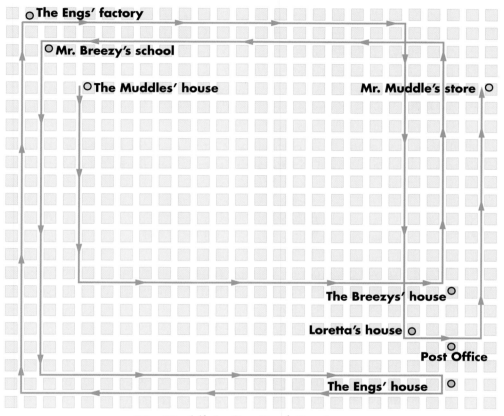

Mr. Muddle's Car Pool Route

5 blocks = 1 kilometer

Work in groups. Discuss your answers and how you figured them out. Compare your answers with other groups.

1. The map shows the route that Mr. Muddle took. Plan the shortest route you can for Mr. Muddle that will get everyone to work. List the stops in order and the distances between stops. What is the total distance?

2. Suppose each person drives to work by the shortest route. What is the total number of kilometers that everyone would drive? Compare this distance with your answer for problem 1.

3. What is wrong with the car pool Mr. Muddle set up? What would be a better kind of car pool for people who want to save gas?

Equivalent Fractions

A given number can be written as a fraction in many different ways.

◆   Find the decimal equivalent of $\frac{1}{2}$.

◆   Find the decimal equivalent of $\frac{2}{4}$.

◆   What do you notice?

We call two different ways of writing a number as a fraction **equivalent fractions.**

Examples:

Change $\frac{2}{3}$ to an equivalent fraction that has a denominator of 18.

Divide each of the three original parts into six equal parts. Now we have 18 equal parts. We must take 12 of those to be equivalent to the original two parts.

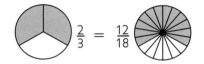

$$\frac{2}{3} = \frac{12}{18}$$

Notice that we could have found the same result by multiplying the numerator and the denominator by 6, which is equivalent to multiplying the fraction by $\frac{6}{6}$, or 1.

Change $\frac{4}{5}$ to an equivalent fraction that has a numerator of 8.

In order to get 8 equal blue pieces, we must divide each of the blue pieces into two equal parts. We must also divide the remaining piece into two equal parts so that all parts are equal. This gives us 10 equal parts.

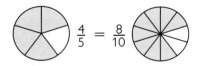

$$\frac{4}{5} = \frac{8}{10}$$

We could also multiply $\frac{4}{5}$ by $\frac{2}{2}$. We get $\frac{4}{5} \times \frac{2}{2} = \frac{8}{10}$

Multiplying or dividing the numerator and denominator of a fraction by the same amount produces an equivalent fraction.

Complete to write an equivalent fraction.

1 $\frac{2}{3} = \frac{?}{12}$ **2** $\frac{3}{4} = \frac{?}{12}$ **3** $\frac{1}{6} = \frac{2}{?}$ **4** $\frac{5}{6} = \frac{?}{12}$

5 $\frac{1}{4} = \frac{5}{?}$ **6** $\frac{3}{4} = \frac{?}{20}$ **7** $\frac{1}{2} = \frac{?}{20}$ **8** $\frac{1}{5} = \frac{?}{20}$

9 $\frac{2}{5} = \frac{?}{20}$ **10** $\frac{3}{5} = \frac{12}{?}$ **11** $\frac{4}{5} = \frac{16}{?}$ **12** $\frac{3}{10} = \frac{?}{20}$

13 $\frac{3}{4} = \frac{12}{?}$ **14** $\frac{2}{5} = \frac{6}{?}$ **15** $\frac{1}{3} = \frac{?}{18}$ **16** $\frac{3}{10} = \frac{?}{100}$

To produce an equivalent fraction with a denominator less than the original denominator, we can divide the numerator and denominator by the same number. We call this *reducing the fraction*. A fraction is in reduced form if it cannot be further reduced.

Example: Change $\frac{15}{18}$ to an equivalent fraction with a denominator of 6.

$$\frac{15}{18} = \frac{?}{6}$$ We divide 18 by 3 to get 6, so we divide 15 by 3 to get 5.

$$\frac{15}{18} = \frac{3 \times 5}{3 \times 6} = \frac{3}{3} \times \frac{5}{6}$$

Since $\frac{3}{3} = 1$, we can say $\frac{15}{18} = \frac{5}{6}$.

To reduce a fraction, find a number that is a factor of both the numerator and denominator.

Example: Reduce $\frac{8}{12}$.

Since we can multiply the numerator and denominator by the same number, we can also divide the numerator and denominator by the same number without changing the fraction's numerical value. $\frac{8}{12} = \frac{8 \div 4}{12 \div 4} = \frac{2}{3}$.

Complete to write an equivalent reduced fraction.

17 $\frac{12}{16} = \frac{?}{4}$ **18** $\frac{12}{18} = \frac{2}{?}$ **19** $\frac{6}{10} = \frac{?}{5}$ **20** $\frac{5}{15} = \frac{?}{3}$

21 $\frac{16}{20} = \frac{?}{10}$ **22** $\frac{10}{12} = \frac{5}{?}$ **23** $\frac{15}{25} = \frac{?}{5}$ **24** $\frac{16}{24} = \frac{4}{?}$

25 $\frac{12}{20} = \frac{?}{?}$ **26** $\frac{6}{14} = \frac{?}{?}$ **27** $\frac{8}{18} = \frac{?}{?}$ **28** $\frac{4}{20} = \frac{?}{?}$

29 $\frac{18}{24} = \frac{?}{?}$ **30** $\frac{8}{20} = \frac{?}{?}$ **31** $\frac{6}{15} = \frac{?}{?}$ **32** $\frac{10}{20} = \frac{?}{?}$

Reducing Fractions

Alexis needs to divide 126 by 189. "That looks hard," she says. "There must be something I can do to make this easier."

She decides to write the problem as a fraction:

$$\frac{126}{189}$$

She notices that the sum of the digits of 126 is 9 and the sum of the digits of 189 is 18. That tells her that 126 and 189 are both divisible by 9. So she rewrites the fraction.

$$\frac{126}{189} = \frac{9 \times 14}{9 \times 21}$$

Then she rewrites it again:

$$\frac{9}{9} \times \frac{14}{21}$$

"I see," says Alexis. "That's the same as $\frac{9}{9}$ of $\frac{14}{21}$, or just $\frac{14}{21}$. So:

$$\frac{126}{189} = \frac{9}{9} \times \frac{14}{21} = \frac{14}{21}$$

"I wonder if there's a way to make this fraction even simpler."

◆ Do you see a way to make the problem still easier? Is there some number that is a factor of both 14 and 21?

This fraction reduces to $\frac{2}{3}$. Divide 2 by 3. Find the answer to at least seven decimal places. Now divide 126 by 189.

◆ Are both answers the same?

In most cases it is easier to work with $\frac{2}{3}$ than $\frac{126}{189}$.

Factoring numbers is useful when rewriting fractions as equivalent fractions in reduced form.

◆ Why might this process be called "reducing fractions"?

When we have reduced a fraction as much as we can, we say we have completely reduced it. Remember, the reduced fraction still stands for the same number as the original fraction.

To reduce a fraction completely, decide what factors the numerator and denominator have in common and divide the numerator and denominator by those factors. Here are two ways you might keep your records for reducing $\frac{336}{840}$.

A. $\frac{336}{840} = \frac{4 \times 84}{4 \times 210} = \frac{2 \times 42}{2 \times 105} = \frac{3 \times 14}{3 \times 35} = \frac{7 \times 2}{7 \times 5} = \frac{2}{5}$

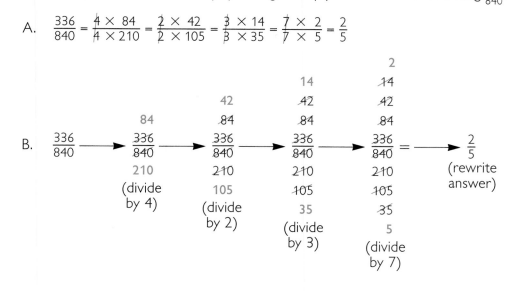

B.

The second method is messier, but it does not require rewriting the problem each time. You may use either method, or a different one if you prefer.

The order in which you find the factors is not important.

◆ Is there a way to reduce $\frac{336}{840}$ using fewer steps? If so, how?

Reduce each fraction completely.

1. $\frac{6}{9}$
2. $\frac{3}{12}$
3. $\frac{8}{12}$
4. $\frac{2}{6}$
5. $\frac{2}{4}$

6. $\frac{3}{9}$
7. $\frac{4}{10}$
8. $\frac{6}{8}$
9. $\frac{6}{15}$
10. $\frac{14}{21}$

11. $\frac{135}{225}$
12. $\frac{252}{315}$
13. $\frac{504}{648}$
14. $\frac{91}{273}$
15. $\frac{30}{210}$

16. $\frac{210}{525}$
17. $\frac{378}{756}$
18. $\frac{126}{162}$
19. $\frac{28}{126}$
20. $\frac{126}{252}$

21. $\frac{120}{180}$
22. $\frac{75}{125}$
23. $\frac{135}{243}$
24. $\frac{96}{168}$
25. $\frac{48}{96}$

26. $\frac{60}{75}$
27. $\frac{23}{92}$
28. $\frac{64}{192}$
29. $\frac{171}{207}$
30. $\frac{39}{52}$

◆ LESSON 69   Reducing Fractions

When reducing fractions, the greater the factor we start with, the fewer steps it takes. For example, we can reduce $\frac{16}{24}$ as follows:

A. $\frac{16}{24} = \frac{\not{2} \times 8}{\not{2} \times 12} = \frac{\not{2} \times 4}{\not{2} \times 6} = \frac{\not{2} \times 2}{\not{2} \times 3} = \frac{2}{3}$

Or we could reduce it like this:

B. $\frac{16}{24} = \frac{\not{8} \times 2}{\not{8} \times 3} = \frac{2}{3}$

Instead of just finding a common factor of two numbers, we often want to find the **greatest common factor.** If you know the greatest common factor of the numerator and denominator of a fraction, you can completely reduce it by just dividing by that one number.

To find the greatest common factor of two numbers, you can simply look at all the factors and choose the greatest one they have in common.

Example: Find the greatest common factor of 60 and 84.

A.   List all the factors of each number.

B.   Then look for the greatest factor they have in common.

60	84
1 × 60	1 × 84
2 × 30	2 × 42
3 × 20	3 × 28
4 × 15	4 × 21
5 × ⑫	6 × 14
6 × 10	7 × ⑫

The greatest common factor of 60 and 84 is 12.

Another way to find the greatest common factor is to completely factor each number. Let's try this with the same problem. Find the greatest common factor of 60 and 84.

Write $60 = 2^2 \times 3 \times 5$

And $84 = 2^2 \times 3 \times 7$

So the greatest common factor is $2^2 \times 3$, or 12.

Find the greatest common factor of each pair of numbers.

31   12 and 18   **32**   72 and 120   **33**   126 and 162

34   9 and 24   **35**   252 and 315   **36**   14 and 42

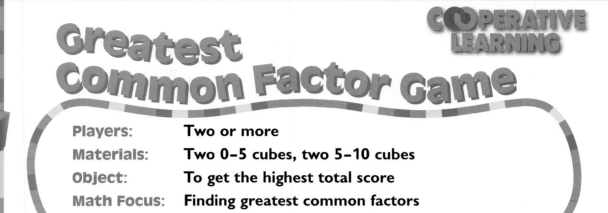

Greatest Common Factor Game

Players:	Two or more
Materials:	Two 0–5 cubes, two 5–10 cubes
Object:	To get the highest total score
Math Focus:	Finding greatest common factors

RULES

1. Decide in advance how many turns each player will take (usually from five to ten turns).

2. Take turns rolling all four cubes and use them to form two two-digit numbers. If you roll a 10, one of the numbers will have three digits. For example, a 10 and a 4 might be used to form 104 and 410. If you roll 10 and 10, you could form one four-digit number, 1010, or two three-digit numbers. If you roll 0 and 0, roll again.

3. Find the greatest common factor of the two numbers, and add that to your score.

4. Continue until each player has taken the agreed-upon number of turns.

5. The player with the greatest total wins.

SAMPLE GAME

	Round	Numbers Rolled	Numbers Made	Greatest Common Factor	Score
Hasin's Record	1	1 5 5 8	51, 85	17	17
	2	3 4 7 9	34, 79	1	18
	3	2 4 8 9	42, 98	14	32
Lisa's Record	1	7 7 2 4	42, 77	7	7
	2	2 2 5 8	28, 52	4	11
	3	3 3 5 5	53, 53	53	64

Lisa won because her total score (64) was higher.

Multiplying and Reducing Fractions

When multiplying fractions, you can sometimes use common factors to help simplify the computations. For example: If you are multiplying $\frac{16}{24}$ by $\frac{9}{10}$, you could start by multiplying the numerators, getting 144. Then multiply the denominators to get 240. The answer is $\frac{144}{240}$. The numbers 144 and 240 both have a factor of 48, so this is equal to

$$\frac{144}{240} = \frac{48 \times 3}{48 \times 5} = \frac{3}{5}$$

However, you could have started with the original problem and found common factors in the numerators and denominators. You can divide by the common factors before you multiply. To multiply $\frac{16}{24} \times \frac{9}{10}$, you might start by noticing there is a factor of 8 in both 16 and 24:

A. $\ \frac{2\ \cancel{16}}{3\ \cancel{24}} \times \frac{9}{10}$

Next, you might see that there is a factor of 3 in both 9 and 3:

B. $\ \frac{2\ \cancel{16}}{1\ \mathbf{3}\cancel{24}} \times \frac{\cancel{9}\ 3}{10}$

Finally, there is a factor of 2 in both 2 and 10:

C. $\ \frac{1\ \cancel{2}\cancel{16}}{1\ \mathbf{3}\cancel{24}} \times \frac{\cancel{9}\ 3}{\cancel{10}\ 5}$

Now, since $1 \times 3 = 3$, and $1 \times 5 = 5$, the final answer is $\frac{3}{5}$. Notice that this was easier than multiplying all the numbers together and then looking for common factors in the numerator and denominator at the end.

Solve the following multiplication problems. Reduce answers completely.

1. $\frac{2}{3} \times \frac{6}{11} = ?$ 　　2. $\frac{8}{18} \times \frac{3}{8} = ?$ 　　3. $\frac{5}{6} \times \frac{9}{10} = ?$

4. $\frac{9}{16} \times \frac{12}{27} = ?$ 　　5. $\frac{4}{14} \times \frac{21}{24} = ?$ 　　6. $\frac{3}{4} \times \frac{6}{7} = ?$

7. $\frac{8}{25} \times \frac{35}{48} = ?$ 　　8. $\frac{5}{27} \times \frac{36}{50} = ?$ 　　9. $\frac{7}{12} \times \frac{18}{25} = ?$

10. $\frac{12}{75} \times \frac{15}{64} = ?$ 　　11. $\frac{3}{7} \times \frac{5}{11} = ?$ 　　12. $\frac{4}{9} \times \frac{6}{16} = ?$

13. $\frac{120}{225} \times \frac{105}{112} = ?$ 　　14. $\frac{3}{7} \times \frac{35}{45} = ?$ 　　15. $\frac{6}{11} \times \frac{3}{5} = ?$

16. $\frac{2}{3} \times \frac{3}{4} = ?$ 　　17. $\frac{3}{7} \times \frac{4}{9} = ?$ 　　18. $\frac{20}{33} \times \frac{12}{25} = ?$

Watch the signs.

19 72 + 9 = ■   **20** 72 ÷ 9 = ■   **21** 72 − 9 = ■

22 72 × 9 = ■   **23** 8 × 7 = ■   **24** 54 ÷ 6 = ■

25 17 − 8 = ■   **26** 9 × 4 = ■   **27** 8 + 8 = ■

28 8 × 8 = ■   **29** 0 × 7 = ■   **30** 7 + 0 = ■

31 43 − 9 = ■   **32** 43 + 9 = ■   **33** 52 ÷ 4 = ■

34   437   **35**   437   **36**   649   **37**   173
       − 286   + 286   × 100   × 200

38 9)3213   **39** 6)5034   **40** 5)4315   **41** 7)861

Solve these problems.

42 At the beginning of the week the odometer on Maureen's bicycle showed 9743.2 kilometers. At the end of the week the odometer showed 0027.5 kilometers.

   a. What do you think happened?

   b. How far do you think the bicycle went that week?

43 A theater group is presenting four shows this season. Tickets cost $16.50 each. A season ticket good for all four shows costs $55. How much would you save on each show by buying a season ticket?

44 A taxi in the Take-You Taxi Company can carry four passengers plus the driver. How many Take-You taxis will be needed to take 15 people from the PTA meeting to the football game?

◆ **LESSON 70** Multiplying and Reducing Fractions

THINKING STORY

Energy Savers

Part 2

You may want to refer to the first part of this Thinking Story on pages 246–247.

Marcus told the Energy Savers about his idea for a new way to save energy. "Get rid of stop signs. I heard on the radio that every time a car stops and starts up again, it uses $\frac{1}{100}$ of a tank of gas."

"Great idea!" said Ferdie. "Let's take down all the stop signs in town. That way we'll save more energy than any other group. There must be 1000 stop signs. That's ten tanks of gas. And there must be about 3000 cars. By taking down the stop signs we'll save 30,000 tanks of gas a day!"

The club adviser, Mr. Harper, said, "You'd better figure in the extra gas that ambulances and tow trucks will use. After all, won't they be on the road more often if we follow your plan?"

"Wait a minute," said Portia. "I think Marcus has his facts wrong. Some cars are little and have little tiny gas tanks. Some cars are big and have great big gas tanks. How can you say every car uses up $\frac{1}{100}$ of a tank of gas when it stops and starts? It doesn't make any sense. That's like saying you use $\frac{1}{100}$ of a tube of toothpaste each time you brush your teeth, when toothpaste tubes are all different sizes."

. . . to be continued

Work in groups. Discuss your answers and how you figured them out. Then compare your answers with those of other groups.

1 Suppose there are 1000 stop signs and 3000 cars in town. Is Ferdie right that stopping at stop signs uses up 30,000 tanks of gas a day? What would drivers have to do in order for that to be true?

2 What do you think Mr. Harper was trying to get the club members to see about their plan?

3 How could it be possible that cars with different-sized gas tanks all use about $\frac{1}{100}$ tank of gas when they stop and start? Hint: Big cars and small cars are all built so that they can go about the same distance on a tank of gas.

4 Why does it make sense to give the amount of gas used as a fraction of a tank rather than as a number of gallons?

Comparing Fractions

There are several ways to compare two fractions with different denominators to see which is greater.

One method is to use a calculator, convert each fraction to an equivalent or approximate decimal, and compare the decimals. For example, to decide which is greater, $\frac{3}{7}$ or $\frac{4}{9}$, you can find a decimal approximation of each.

$$\frac{3}{7} = 3 \div 7, \text{ which is about } 0.4285714$$

$$\frac{4}{9} = 4 \div 9, \text{ which is about } 0.4444444$$

The greater decimal is 0.4444444, so $\frac{4}{9}$ must be the greater fraction.

A second method of comparing $\frac{3}{7}$ and $\frac{4}{9}$ is to rewrite both fractions as equivalent fractions with the same denominator. We say that a number that is a multiple of both original denominators is a **common denominator.** The product of the two original denominators will always be a common denominator.

We can use a common denominator of 63 to compare $\frac{3}{7}$ with $\frac{4}{9}$.

$$\frac{3}{7} \times \frac{9}{9} = \frac{27}{63}$$
$$\frac{4}{9} \times \frac{7}{7} = \frac{28}{63}$$

◆ Which is greater, $\frac{27}{63}$ or $\frac{28}{63}$?

Notice that if you use the product of the denominators as the common denominator, each new fraction will have the product of its numerator and the other fraction's denominator as its new numerator. In this example the numerator of the first fraction is 3×9, and the numerator of the second fraction is 4×7. Since the denominators are the same, this product tells which fraction is greater.

So, a third way to decide which is greater, $\frac{3}{7}$ or $\frac{4}{9}$, is to find the two products, 3×9 and 4×7. Whichever numerator appears in the greater product is the numerator of the greater fraction.

Sometimes you can compare fractions in other ways as well.

Example: Compare $\frac{7}{12}$ and $\frac{13}{30}$.

Notice that $\frac{7}{12}$ is slightly greater than $\frac{1}{2}$, since $\frac{1}{2} = \frac{6}{12}$ and $\frac{7}{12}$ is greater than $\frac{6}{12}$.

Also notice that $\frac{13}{30}$ is slightly less than $\frac{1}{2}$, since $\frac{1}{2} = \frac{15}{30}$ and $\frac{13}{30}$ is less than $\frac{15}{30}$.

◆ Which is greater, $\frac{7}{12}$ or $\frac{13}{30}$?

258 • Fractions and Mixed Numbers

Once we know which fraction is greater, we can write the fractions with a <, >, or = symbol between them to show whether the first fraction is less than, greater than, or equal to the second. Remember, the point of the symbol points towards the lesser number.

So, for our example, you would write $\frac{3}{7} < \frac{4}{9}$, since $\frac{3}{7}$ is less than $\frac{4}{9}$.

Write each of the following fraction pairs with a <, >, or = symbol between them.

1. $\frac{1}{3} \blacksquare \frac{1}{2}$ 2. $\frac{4}{7} \blacksquare \frac{5}{9}$ 3. $\frac{1}{6} \blacksquare \frac{2}{11}$ 4. $\frac{7}{13} \blacksquare \frac{8}{13}$

5. $\frac{73}{87} \blacksquare \frac{74}{87}$ 6. $\frac{1}{2} \blacksquare \frac{1}{3}$ 7. $\frac{5}{7} \blacksquare \frac{5}{8}$ 8. $\frac{12}{17} \blacksquare \frac{12}{18}$

9. $\frac{13}{27} \blacksquare \frac{1}{2}$ 10. $\frac{14}{27} \blacksquare \frac{1}{2}$ 11. $\frac{17}{36} \blacksquare \frac{1}{2}$ 12. $\frac{18}{36} \blacksquare \frac{1}{2}$

13. $\frac{19}{36} \blacksquare \frac{1}{2}$ 14. $\frac{5}{9} \blacksquare \frac{7}{12}$ 15. $\frac{21}{36} \blacksquare \frac{7}{12}$ 16. $\frac{4}{7} \blacksquare \frac{1}{2}$

17. $\frac{5}{11} \blacksquare \frac{1}{2}$ 18. $\frac{4}{7} \blacksquare \frac{5}{11}$ 19. $\frac{10}{19} \blacksquare \frac{9}{20}$ 20. $\frac{11}{12} \blacksquare \frac{13}{14}$

21. Arrange the following fractions in order from least to greatest:

$$\frac{1}{8}, \frac{3}{5}, \frac{4}{10}, \frac{5}{6}, \frac{2}{3}, \frac{17}{20}$$

22. There is a puzzle about a man with three sons. He died and left $\frac{1}{2}$ of what he owned to his eldest son, $\frac{1}{4}$ of what he owned to the middle son, and $\frac{1}{6}$ of what he owned to the youngest son. But the man owned only 11 cows. He had no other property. How could the sons divide the cows without killing them?

A wise man with a cow came along. He added his cow to the herd. Then he gave the eldest son $\frac{1}{2}$ of the 12 cows. To the middle son he gave $\frac{1}{4}$ of the 12 cows. And he gave the youngest son $\frac{1}{6}$ of the 12 cows. Then he went away with his own cow.

a. Why did this work?

b. Did the wise man carry out the dead father's instructions?

◆ LESSON 71 Comparing Fractions

When fractions have different denominators, we can compare them by rewriting each as an equivalent fraction with a common denominator. Then we compare the numerators.

To compare $\frac{5}{12}$ and $\frac{7}{18}$ you could use 12×18, which is 216, as a common denominator:

$$\frac{5}{12} = \frac{5 \times 18}{12 \times 18} = \frac{90}{216}$$

$$\frac{7}{18} = \frac{7 \times 12}{18 \times 12} = \frac{84}{216}$$

Since $\frac{90}{216} > \frac{84}{216}$, then $\frac{5}{12} > \frac{7}{18}$.

However, there are lesser denominators that could have been used. For example, 36 is a multiple of both 12 and 18. We could have written:

$$\frac{5}{12} = \frac{5 \times 3}{12 \times 3} = \frac{15}{36}$$

$$\frac{7}{18} = \frac{7 \times 2}{18 \times 2} = \frac{14}{36}$$

Again, since $\frac{15}{36} > \frac{14}{36}$, then $\frac{5}{12} > \frac{7}{18}$.

The number 216 is one common multiple of 12 and 18 (216 is a multiple of 12, since $216 = 18 \times 12$ and a multiple of 18, since $216 = 12 \times 18$). Here are some other common multiples of 12 and 18:

    108   ($108 = 9 \times 12$ and $108 = 6 \times 18$)

    72   ($72 = 6 \times 12$ and $72 = 4 \times 18$)

    36   ($36 = 3 \times 12$ and $36 = 2 \times 18$)

◆ Can you find a common multiple of 12 and 18 that is greater than 216? Name one.

◆ Can you find a common multiple of 12 and 18 that is between 36 and 216 other than those listed? Name two.

◆ Can you find a common multiple of 12 and 18 that is less than 36?

The **least common multiple** of two numbers is the lowest number (except 0) that is a multiple of both numbers.

Here are two methods for finding the least common multiple of two numbers. The examples show how to find the least common multiple of 6 and 8.

Method 1

List the multiples of each number and choose the lowest common multiple. You don't need to go beyond the product of the two numbers. List a few multiples of one number and then a few of the other number until you find the least common multiple.

Multiples of 8: 8, 16, 24, 32, 40, 48

Multiples of 6: 6, 12, 18, 24

Method 2

List the prime factors of each number. The least common multiple must have each of these factors used as many times as it appears in the number in which it occurs most often.

$$6 = 2 \times 3 \qquad 8 = 2 \times 2 \times 2$$

$$2 \times 2 \times 2 \times 3 = 8 \times 3 = 24$$

Using either method, we find the least common multiple of 6 and 8 is 24.

Find the least common multiple of each pair of numbers.

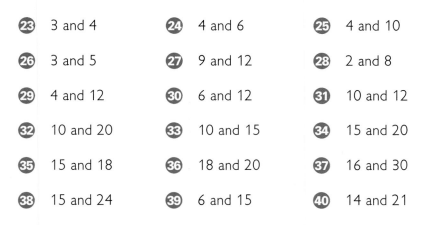

23 3 and 4   24 4 and 6   25 4 and 10

26 3 and 5   27 9 and 12   28 2 and 8

29 4 and 12   30 6 and 12   31 10 and 12

32 10 and 20   33 10 and 15   34 15 and 20

35 15 and 18   36 18 and 20   37 16 and 30

38 15 and 24   39 6 and 15   40 14 and 21

LESSON 72

Adding and Subtracting Fractions

A clothing pattern calls for $\frac{1}{3}$ of a yard of cloth. A second pattern calls for $\frac{3}{5}$ of a yard of the same cloth.

◆ Will 1 yard of cloth be enough for both patterns?

To find out, add $\frac{1}{3}$ and $\frac{3}{5}$.

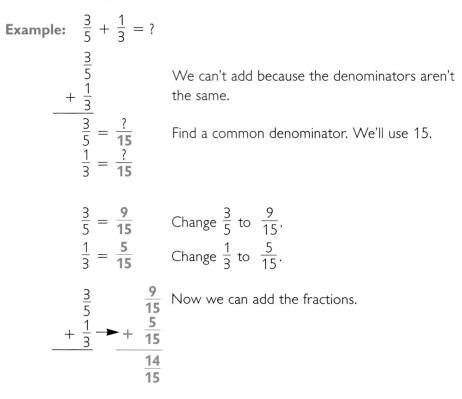

Example: $\frac{3}{5} + \frac{1}{3} = ?$

$$\begin{array}{r} \frac{3}{5} \\ + \frac{1}{3} \\ \hline \end{array}$$
We can't add because the denominators aren't the same.

$\frac{3}{5} = \frac{?}{15}$ Find a common denominator. We'll use 15.
$\frac{1}{3} = \frac{?}{15}$

$\frac{3}{5} = \frac{9}{15}$ Change $\frac{3}{5}$ to $\frac{9}{15}$.
$\frac{1}{3} = \frac{5}{15}$ Change $\frac{1}{3}$ to $\frac{5}{15}$.

$$\begin{array}{r} \frac{3}{5} \\ + \frac{1}{3} \end{array} \rightarrow \begin{array}{r} \frac{9}{15} \\ + \frac{5}{15} \\ \hline \frac{14}{15} \end{array}$$
Now we can add the fractions.

Since $\frac{14}{15}$ of a yard is less than 1 yard, 1 yard of cloth is enough.

Add.

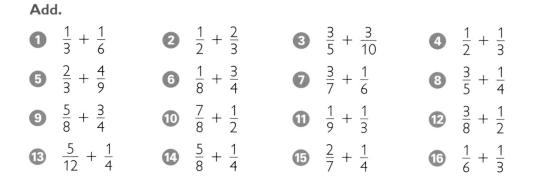

1. $\frac{1}{3} + \frac{1}{6}$ 2. $\frac{1}{2} + \frac{2}{3}$ 3. $\frac{3}{5} + \frac{3}{10}$ 4. $\frac{1}{2} + \frac{1}{3}$

5. $\frac{2}{3} + \frac{4}{9}$ 6. $\frac{1}{8} + \frac{3}{4}$ 7. $\frac{3}{7} + \frac{1}{6}$ 8. $\frac{3}{5} + \frac{1}{4}$

9. $\frac{5}{8} + \frac{3}{4}$ 10. $\frac{7}{8} + \frac{1}{2}$ 11. $\frac{1}{9} + \frac{1}{3}$ 12. $\frac{3}{8} + \frac{1}{2}$

13. $\frac{5}{12} + \frac{1}{4}$ 14. $\frac{5}{8} + \frac{1}{4}$ 15. $\frac{2}{7} + \frac{1}{4}$ 16. $\frac{1}{6} + \frac{1}{3}$

When you subtract fractions, many of the steps are the same as when you add fractions.

Example: $\dfrac{3}{5} - \dfrac{1}{3} = ?$

$$\begin{array}{r} \dfrac{3}{5} \\[4pt] -\ \dfrac{1}{3} \\ \hline \end{array}$$

We can't subtract because the denominators aren't the same.

$\dfrac{3}{5} = \dfrac{?}{15}$

$\dfrac{1}{3} = \dfrac{?}{15}$

Find a common denominator. We'll use 15.

$\dfrac{3}{5} = \dfrac{9}{15}$ Change $\dfrac{3}{5}$ to $\dfrac{9}{15}$.

$\dfrac{1}{3} = \dfrac{5}{15}$ Change $\dfrac{1}{3}$ to $\dfrac{5}{15}$.

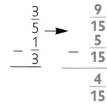

Now we can subtract the fractions.

$$\begin{array}{r} \dfrac{9}{15} \\[4pt] -\ \dfrac{5}{15} \\ \hline \dfrac{4}{15} \end{array}$$

Subtract.

17 $\dfrac{1}{3} - \dfrac{1}{6}$ **18** $\dfrac{2}{3} - \dfrac{1}{2}$ **19** $\dfrac{3}{5} - \dfrac{3}{10}$ **20** $\dfrac{5}{6} - \dfrac{7}{12}$

21 $\dfrac{2}{3} - \dfrac{4}{9}$ **22** $\dfrac{3}{4} - \dfrac{1}{8}$ **23** $\dfrac{3}{7} - \dfrac{1}{6}$ **24** $\dfrac{3}{4} - \dfrac{3}{8}$

25 $\dfrac{3}{4} - \dfrac{5}{8}$ **26** $\dfrac{7}{8} - \dfrac{1}{2}$ **27** $\dfrac{1}{3} - \dfrac{1}{9}$ **28** $\dfrac{3}{7} - \dfrac{2}{7}$

Add or subtract. Watch the signs.

29 $\dfrac{2}{3} + \dfrac{7}{9}$ **30** $\dfrac{2}{5} + \dfrac{1}{10}$ **31** $\dfrac{7}{8} - \dfrac{3}{4}$ **32** $\dfrac{3}{5} + \dfrac{1}{4}$

33 $\dfrac{7}{9} - \dfrac{2}{3}$ **34** $\dfrac{5}{6} - \dfrac{1}{2}$ **35** $\dfrac{3}{7} + \dfrac{1}{3}$ **36** $\dfrac{1}{4} + \dfrac{1}{8}$

37 $\dfrac{5}{6} + \dfrac{1}{2}$ **38** $\dfrac{2}{5} - \dfrac{1}{10}$ **39** $\dfrac{5}{9} - \dfrac{1}{3}$ **40** $\dfrac{1}{3} - \dfrac{1}{9}$

Adding and Subtracting Special Fractions

When you add or subtract fractions, quite often the denominator of one fraction will be a factor of the denominator of the other. In these cases you can use the greater denominator as a common denominator. You will save work by doing that.

Example: $\dfrac{2}{3} + \dfrac{1}{6} = ?$

Since 3 is a factor of 6, you can use 6 as a common denominator.

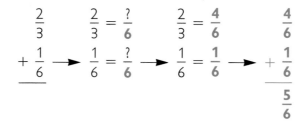

$$\dfrac{2}{3} \qquad \dfrac{2}{3} = \dfrac{?}{6} \qquad \dfrac{2}{3} = \dfrac{4}{6} \qquad \dfrac{4}{6}$$

$$+\dfrac{1}{6} \longrightarrow \dfrac{1}{6} = \dfrac{?}{6} \longrightarrow \dfrac{1}{6} = \dfrac{1}{6} \longrightarrow +\dfrac{1}{6}$$

$$\dfrac{5}{6}$$

Add or subtract. For many of these, the denominator of one of the fractions can be used as a common denominator. Reduce answers if possible.

1. $\dfrac{2}{3} - \dfrac{1}{6}$

2. $\dfrac{2}{3} - \dfrac{4}{7}$

3. $\dfrac{1}{2} - \dfrac{1}{3}$

4. $\dfrac{1}{2} - \dfrac{1}{6}$

5. $\dfrac{1}{4} + \dfrac{1}{2}$

6. $\dfrac{1}{6} + \dfrac{1}{3}$

7. $\dfrac{1}{7} + \dfrac{3}{14}$

8. $\dfrac{1}{2} - \dfrac{3}{8}$

9. $\dfrac{1}{2} - \dfrac{1}{4}$

10. $\dfrac{1}{2} + \dfrac{1}{3}$

11. $\dfrac{3}{8} - \dfrac{1}{4}$

12. $\dfrac{3}{4} - \dfrac{3}{8}$

Solve this problem.

13. Leona baked a cheesecake and cut it into twelfths. She, Henry, and Nita each ate one piece. Then five more pieces were eaten at supper.

   a. How much of the cheesecake did Leona, Henry, and Nita eat?

   b. How much of the cheesecake was eaten at supper?

   c. How much of the cheesecake was left after supper?

GAME

Circo 11 Game

Players:	**Two**
Materials:	**Two 0–5 cubes, paper, two pencils or pens of different colors**
Object:	**To win more circles**
Math Focus:	**Mental addition of common fractions, using fractions, and mathematical reasoning**

RULES

1. Make one game board for both players by drawing 11 circles on a sheet of paper. Put a dot at about the center of each circle. (The circles don't need to be perfectly drawn.) Each player uses a different color pencil or pen.

2. Take turns rolling both cubes and making a fraction equal to 1 or less. (If you roll a 0, roll that cube again.) For example, if you roll a 2 and a 3, you make the fraction $\frac{2}{3}$. Then capture that fraction of a circle by using your pen or pencil to mark off a pie-shaped part of any circle and write the fraction in that part. (The part does not have to be drawn to the exact size, but the closer the better.)

3. On a turn you may capture parts in more than one circle. The fractions for the parts you capture must all have the same denominator. For example, if you make the fraction $\frac{3}{5}$, you may take $\frac{1}{5}$ of one circle and $\frac{2}{5}$ of another or $\frac{1}{5}$ of each of three circles. But you may not take $\frac{1}{2}$ of one circle and $\frac{1}{10}$ of another.

4. Whenever you think you have captured more than $\frac{1}{2}$ of a circle, you may win the circle by proving that your parts make up more than $\frac{1}{2}$ of the circle. This may be done by approximation or by finding an exact sum (mentally, with paper and pencil, or with a calculator).

5. If $\frac{1}{2}$ of a circle is captured by one player and the other $\frac{1}{2}$ is captured by the other player, neither player wins the circle.

6. The player who has captured more circles is the winner.

LESSON 74

Least Common Multiples of Three or More Numbers

A band director wants the band to be able to march in rows of 6, 8, or 9, with no one left over. What's the least number of band members she'll need? To find out, find the least common multiple.

The least common multiple of three or more numbers can be found in the same ways it is found for two numbers.

Example: Find the least common multiple of 6, 8, and 9.

Method 1

List the multiples of each number and choose the least common multiple. Again, list a few multiples of each number at a time. Stop when you find the least common multiple.

Multiples of 9: 9, 18, 27, 36, 45, 54, 63, 72, 81, 90
Multiples of 8: 8, 16, 24, 32, 40, 48, 56, 64, 72, 80, 88
Multiples of 6: 6, 12, 18, 24, 30, 36, 42, 48, 54, 60, 66, 72

The band leader will need 72 members.

Method 2

List the prime factors of each number and find the product of the greatest power of each prime factor.

$$6 = 2 \times 3 \qquad 8 = 2^3 \qquad 9 = 3^2$$

The least common multiple of 6, 8, and 9 is $2^3 \times 3^2$, or 72.

The band must have at least 72 members.

Notice that the second method is much easier for finding the least common multiple of three or more numbers.

Find the least common multiple of each set of numbers.

1 3, 6, and 9   **2** 7, 14, and 21   **3** 4, 6, 9, and 12

4 4, 8, and 16   **5** 3, 5, and 7   **6** 1, 2, 3, and 4

7 2, 3, and 5   **8** 8, 12, and 24   **9** 2, 3, 4, and 6

10 6, 5, and 10   **11** 4, 12, and 5   **12** 3, 5, 6, and 15

Finding the least common multiple can be helpful if you ever need to add three or more fractions with different denominators.

Example: $\frac{2}{5} + \frac{1}{4} + \frac{3}{10} = ?$

The least common multiple of 5, 4, and 10 is 20.

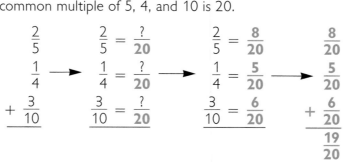

$$\frac{2}{5} \qquad \frac{2}{5} = \frac{?}{20} \qquad \frac{2}{5} = \frac{8}{20} \qquad \frac{8}{20}$$
$$\frac{1}{4} \rightarrow \frac{1}{4} = \frac{?}{20} \rightarrow \frac{1}{4} = \frac{5}{20} \rightarrow \frac{5}{20}$$
$$+\frac{3}{10} \qquad \frac{3}{10} = \frac{?}{20} \qquad \frac{3}{10} = \frac{6}{20} \qquad +\frac{6}{20}$$
$$\frac{19}{20}$$

Now try these. Use your answers to problems 1–12 on page 266.

13. $\frac{1}{3} + \frac{1}{6} + \frac{1}{9}$ 14. $\frac{1}{6} + \frac{1}{5} + \frac{3}{10}$ 15. $\frac{1}{4} + \frac{5}{12} + \frac{1}{5}$

16. $\frac{3}{16} + \frac{1}{4} + \frac{3}{8}$ 17. $\frac{1}{3} + \frac{1}{5} + \frac{1}{7}$ 18. $\frac{7}{24} + \frac{1}{12} + \frac{1}{8}$

Compare. Write >, <, or =.

19. $\frac{3}{5} \blacksquare \frac{5}{8}$ 20. $\frac{2}{3} \blacksquare \frac{4}{7}$ 21. $\frac{5}{6} \blacksquare \frac{7}{8}$

22. $\frac{1}{3} \blacksquare \frac{10}{18}$ 23. $\frac{3}{8} \blacksquare \frac{5}{12}$ 24. $\frac{3}{4} \blacksquare \frac{18}{24}$

Solve these problems.

25. A band director wants his band to march in rows of 4, 5, or 6. What's the least number of members needed?

26. A band director with fewer than 50 band members finds that if she arranges her band in rows of 2, 3, or 4, there is one person left over, but if she arranges her band in rows of 5, there is no one left over. How many people are in the band?

27. The band in problem 26 grows to between 50 and 100 members, and the director finds that she has the same problem as before. If she arranges the band in rows of 2, 3, or 4, one person is left over, but if she puts members in rows of 5, no one is left over. How many people are in the band now?

◆ **LESSON 74** **Least Common Multiples of Three or More Numbers**

Energy Savers

Part 3

You may want to refer to the earlier parts of this Thinking Story on pages 246–247 and 256–257.

The Energy Savers had another meeting. "I have important news," Manolita said. "Mr. Dill wants to have a stop sign put up by his house on Pickle Street. He says it's for safety. But everyone knows it's just to keep people from driving past his house. Just think how much gas will be wasted if people have to stop every time they pass his house."

"Right," said Ferdie. "Every car that stops will use up $\frac{1}{100}$ of a tank of gas. We can count the number of cars that go past Mr. Dill's house and multiply by 100. Then we'll know how many tanks of gas that stop sign will waste."

"We must be sure we have our facts right," Mr. Harper warned. "Marcus says that a car uses $\frac{1}{100}$ of a tank of gas when it stops and starts. He says he heard it on the radio. But he can't remember who said it or what the proof was."

Marcus's mother said she would help him get some proof. One day she had to drive along a highway where there were no stop signs. To make a good test she drove slowly, the same speed that she would have driven in town. Her trip was 126 kilometers. She used 11 liters of gas. For the next few days she did all her driving in town. She counted the number of times she had to stop and start. As soon as she had driven 126 kilometers, she stopped to get gas. She found it had taken 21 liters of gas to drive 126 kilometers in town. In that distance she had made 200 stops.

When Marcus's mother reported these facts to Marcus, he did some figuring. "I hope the gas tank of your car holds about 5 liters," he said.

"Oh, no," she said. "It holds 50 liters. I don't know of any car that holds only 5 liters."

"Then either the person on the radio said the wrong thing or I heard it wrong," Marcus said sadly.

. . . to be continued

Work in groups. Discuss your answers and how you figured them out. Then compare your answers with those of other groups.

1 What's wrong with Ferdie's way of figuring out how many tanks of gas the stop sign will waste?

2 While driving 126 kilometers around town, how much gas did Marcus's mother use stopping and starting? (Hint: How much gas did she use to go the same distance without any stops?)

3 From problem 2 you should know how much gas Marcus's mother used in making about 200 stops and starts. About how much of a tank of gas was used for each stop and start, $\frac{1}{10}$, $\frac{1}{100}$, $\frac{1}{1000}$ or even less?

4 Marcus's mother has to drive past Mr. Dill's house twice a day. About how much extra gas would she use in a year to stop at his stop sign?

Probability

In this lesson you'll learn about the concept of probability, or chance, and how to find the probabilities of simple events.

◆ If you were to roll a 0–5 cube a great many times, about what fraction of the time would you expect to roll a 0?

◆ What fraction of the time would you expect to roll a 3?

◆ What fraction of the time would you expect to roll a 5?

If, in the long run, we expect something to happen $\frac{1}{6}$ of the time, we say that the **probability** of that event happening is $\frac{1}{6}$. When we roll a fair 0–5 cube, any one of the six numbers is equally likely to come up. We think of these numbers as six equally likely events, and we say that the probability of each is $\frac{1}{6}$.

Answer the following questions.

1 If you roll a 0–5 cube, what is the probability of getting a 5?

2 If you roll a 0–5 cube, what is the probability of getting a 2?

3 If you roll a 0–5 cube, what is the probability of getting a 2 or a 5?

4 If you roll a 0–5 cube, what is the probability of getting a 0, 2, or 4?

5 If you roll a 0–5 cube, what is the probability of getting a 1, 3, or 5?

6 If you roll a 0–5 cube, what is the probability of getting a 0, 1, 2, 3, 4, or 5?

7 If you roll a 0–5 cube, what is the probability of getting a 4 or less?

8 If you roll a 0–5 cube, what is the probability of getting a 5 or greater?

9 If you roll a 0–5 cube, what is the probability of getting a 6?

10 If something is sure to happen (as in problem 6), what is its probability?

11 If something cannot happen (such as getting a 6 when you roll a 0–5 cube), what is its probability?

If you know the probability of an event, then you can estimate how many times that event will occur in 10 tries, 20 tries, 30 tries, and so on. Your estimate should be reasonably close to the actual results.

Answer the following questions.

12 If you flip a coin, what is the probability of it landing on heads?

13 If you flip a coin ten times, about how many times would you expect it to land on heads?

14 If you flip a coin 50 times, about how many times would you expect it to land on heads?

15 If you roll a 0–5 cube 120 times, about how many times would you expect to roll

    a. a 5?   **b.** a 6?   **c.** a 0?

16 Sheila rolls a 0–5 cube 90 times. About how many times would you expect her to roll a 3 or a 5?

17 If you roll a 0–5 cube many times, about what fraction of the time would you expect not to roll a 3? (Hint: It is the same fraction of the time that you would expect to roll a 0, 1, 2, 4, or 5.)

18 Austin rolls a 0–5 cube 120 times. About how many times would you expect that he will roll a number other than 3?

19 If you roll a 5–10 cube many times, about what fraction of the time would you expect to roll something other than 5 or 10?

20 Jessica rolls a 5–10 cube 90 times. About how many times would you expect her to roll 6, 7, 8, or 9?

More than 5,000,000 students participate in high school sports. However, only one in 50 makes a college team, and one in 1000 makes it to the pros. There are fewer than 3500 people in the United States who play professional sports for a living.

◆ **LESSON 75   Probability**

C◯◯PERATIVE LEARNING

Roll a 15 Game

Players:	**Two**
Materials:	**Two 0–5 cubes, two 5–10 cubes**
Object:	**To get the sum closer to 15**
Math Focus:	**Addition and subtraction, mathematical reasoning**

RULES

1. Roll the cubes one at a time.

2. Add the numbers as you roll. The sum of all the cubes you roll should be as close to 15 as possible.

3. You may stop after two, three, or four rolls.

4. The player with the sum closer to 15 wins the round. (The best score is 15; the next best scores are 14 and 16; and so on.)

Answer these questions about the "Roll a 15" game.

21 Kevin went first. He rolled a 10 and then a 4. What should Kevin do now?

22 Sara went first. She rolled a 9 and a 3. What should Sara do now?

23 Lauren went first. Her score was 16. Kevin went second. First he rolled an 8. Then he rolled a 6. What should Kevin do now?

24 Lauren went first. Her score was 17. Kevin went second. First he rolled a 9. Then he rolled a 4. What should Kevin do now?

Answer these questions about the "Roll a 15" game.

25 Olga is the first player in the game. She has already rolled a 6 and 7, so her score is 13 so far. If she now rolls a 0–5 cube, what is the probability that her score will

    a. get closer to 15?

    b. get further from 15?

    c. stay the same distance from 15?

26 What would the three probabilities (a, b, and c in problem 25) be if her score was 12 after rolling two 5–10 cubes?

27 What would the three probabilities (a, b, and c in problem 25) be if her score was 14 after rolling two 5–10 cubes?

28 Find the sum of the three probabilities in problems 24, 25, and 26.

    a. Is the sum the same for each problem?

    b. Will the sum be the same for every possible score?

29 Pierre is the second player. Olga, the first player, has a score of 15. Pierre's first roll was 7 and his second roll is 4. What is the probability that he will win?

30 Pierre is the second player again. This time Lori is the first player. She stops with a score of 13. Pierre's first roll is 5 (on the 5–10 cube), and his second roll is 7. On his next roll he rolls a 0. On his last roll what is the probability that his score will

    a. win?

    b. tie?

    c. lose?

    d. remain the same?

Analyzing Probability
Anything but 10 Game

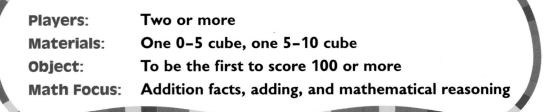

COOPERATIVE LEARNING

Players:	Two or more
Materials:	One 0–5 cube, one 5–10 cube
Object:	To be the first to score 100 or more
Math Focus:	Addition facts, adding, and mathematical reasoning

RULES

1. Roll both cubes. Find the sum of the two numbers you rolled.

2. If the sum is not 10, you get the number of points you rolled. You may roll again, or you may stop and add those points to your score. Continue rolling until you roll a sum of 10 or choose to stop.

3. When you roll a sum of 10, you lose your turn, and you lose any points you may have earned on that turn.

4. The first player to score 100 or over is the winner.

SAMPLE GAME

Turn	Ernie's Roll	Sum	Score	Pearl's Roll	Sum	Score
1	7, 5	12		9, 4	13	
	5, 4	9		6, 2	8	21
	10, 5	15	36	Pearl stopped.		
	Ernie stopped.					
2	8, 3	11		10, 4	14	
	6, 4	10	36	7, 1	8	43
	Ernie lost his turn.			Pearl stopped.		

After two turns Pearl was ahead.

For the "Anything But 10 Game," you want to know the probability of getting a 10 when you roll both cubes.

When you roll the two cubes, there are 11 possible sums: 5, 6, 7, 8, 9, 10, 11, 12, 13, 14, and 15. You may have noticed that you get a sum of 10 more often than some other sums, such as 5 or 15.

Think of it this way: The 0–5 cube can land 0, 1, 2, 3, 4, or 5. If the cube is fair, each of these numbers is equally likely to come up.

The 5–10 cube can land 5, 6, 7, 8, 9, or 10, and each of these numbers is equally likely.

Since neither cube knows what the other is doing, the results of one cube will not affect the other.

If the 0–5 cube lands 0, the 5–10 cube is equally likely to land 5, 6, 7, 8, 9, or 10. If the 0–5 cube lands 1, the 5–10 cube is equally likely to land 5, 6, 7, 8, 9, or 10. The same is true if the 0–5 cube lands 2, or 3, and so on.

Solve the following problems.

1 There are 36 equally likely cases that can come up when you roll a 0–5 cube and a 5–10 cube. One case would be (0, 5); another would be (0, 6); and so on. See if you can list them all. Hint: Make an addition table for addends 0−5 and 5−10.

2 How many cases in problem 1 had a sum of 10?

3 What is the probability of getting a sum of 10 if you roll a 0–5 and a 5–10 cube?

4 What percent of the time would you expect to roll a sum of 10 if you rolled a 0–5 cube and 5–10 cube many times?

5 How many cases in problem 1 had a sum of

    a. 9?   **b.** 11?   **c.** 8?   **d.** 12?   **e.** 7?

    f. 13?   **g.** 6?   **h.** 14?   **i.** 5?   **j.** 15?

6 Are the probabilities of the 11 events (sums) equal?

◆ **LESSON 76** Analyzing Probability

7 Work in pairs or in groups of three. Use a computer or other means to make a chart like the one shown, but fill in only the Sum column (at the left). One person rolls a 0–5 cube and a 5–10 cube and calls out the sum. Another person keeps a tally to see how many times each sum is rolled. Roll the cubes exactly 100 times. (When you think you're getting close to 100 times, stop and count.) Write the total number of times you rolled each sum. Are your results similar to those shown in the Tally column on this chart?

Sum	Tally of How Many Times the Sum Was Rolled	Number of Times Sum Was Rolled	Percent of Times Sum Was Rolled	Probability of Rolling That Sum	Expected Percent of Times the Sum Would Be Rolled
5	|||	3	3%	$\frac{1}{36}$	2.778
6	++++		6			
7	++++ |||	8			
8	++++ ++++ ||||	14			
9	++++ ++++		11			
10	++++ ++++ ||||	14			
11	++++ ++++ ||	12			
12	++++ ++++ ||	12			
13	++++ ++++	10			
14	++++		6			
15						4			
Total		100			

8 Remember that *percent* means "per hundred." If you rolled a 5 three times in 100 tries, those three rolls represent 3% of the tries.

a. What percent of the times was each sum rolled in the experiment shown above?

b. In your experiment what percent of the time was each sum rolled? (Fill in the Percent column on your chart.)

9 In problem 1 on page 275 you listed all of the 36 equally likely results of rolling a 0–5 and 5–10 cube. From that list or table, find the probability of each sum. Record your answers in the column of your chart labelled "Probability of Rolling That Sum."

Example: Your list should show that you can get a sum of 8 in four ways: (0, 8), (1, 7), (2, 6), and (3, 5). The probability of getting an 8 is $\frac{4}{36}$, or $\frac{1}{9}$.

10 Change each probability to a decimal (rounded to the nearest hundred thousandth). For example, $\frac{1}{9}$ would be 0.11111. Then change each decimal to a percent. For example, 0.11111 becomes 11.111%. Write these percents in the Expected Percent column of the chart you made.

11 What is the sum of the numbers in the Probability column of the chart you made?

Compare these expected percents with the percents you got when you did the experiment.

12 What is the sum of the numbers in the Expected Percent column of the chart you made? Convert the percent to a number.

13 Why might your answers to problems 11 and 12 be different?

14 Combine everyone's results for the experiment.

a. Find the total number of times each sum was rolled (for the whole class).

b. Calculate the percent of times each sum was rolled.

c. Compare these percents with the expected percents.

d. Are the class percents closer to the expected percents than yours were?

15 Suppose a class of 24 students did this experiment: Each group of two students rolled the cube 1000 times.

a. How many total rolls would the class have?

b. How many times would you expect a 7 to be rolled?

c. How many times would you expect a 10 to be rolled?

d. How many times would you expect a 15 to be rolled?

LESSON
77

Practice with Fractions and Decimals

Keep in shape by practicing adding, subtracting, and multiplying fractions and decimals and by practicing expressing fractions as decimals.

Solve these problems. Watch the signs. Reduce your answers.

1. $\frac{1}{4} + \frac{1}{2}$

2. $\frac{2}{7} + \frac{3}{7}$

3. $\frac{3}{5} + \frac{2}{5}$

4. $\frac{1}{2} - \frac{1}{4}$

5. $\frac{3}{7} - \frac{2}{7}$

6. $\frac{3}{5} - \frac{2}{5}$

7. $\frac{1}{2} \times \frac{1}{4}$

8. $\frac{3}{5} \times \frac{2}{5}$

9. $\frac{1}{4} + \frac{1}{6}$

10. $\frac{1}{4} - \frac{1}{6}$

11. $\frac{3}{4} - \frac{2}{3}$

12. $\frac{3}{4} \times \frac{2}{3}$

13. $\frac{1}{3} - \frac{2}{9}$

14. $\frac{1}{3} + \frac{2}{9}$

15. $\frac{1}{2} \times \frac{2}{3}$

Solve these problems. Watch the signs.

16. $0.25 + 0.5$

17. $0.29 + 0.43$

18. $0.60 + 0.40$

19. $0.5 - 0.25$

20. $0.43 - 0.29$

21. $0.60 - 0.40$

22. 0.5×0.25

23. 0.6×0.4

24. $0.25 + 0.17$

25. $0.25 - 0.17$

26. $0.75 - 0.67$

27. 0.75×0.67

28. $0.33 - 0.22$

29. $0.33 + 0.22$

30. 0.5×0.67

31. Write the decimal equivalent, or a decimal approximation to the nearest hundredth, for each of your answers in problems 1–15.

32. Compare your decimal answers to problem 31 with the decimal answers to problems 16–30. Are the answers equal or approximately equal?

33. Compare problems 1–15 with problems 16–30. Are the decimals in problems 16–30 equivalent to or approximations of the fractions in problems 1–15?

$\frac{1}{2} + \frac{1}{2} = 1$ $0.5 + 0.5 = 1.0$

$0.5 \times 0.5 = 0.25$

$\frac{1}{2} \times \frac{1}{2} = \frac{1}{4}$

Find the missing digits.

34
```
        2 4 . 6
2 ■ ) 5 6 8 . 0
      4 6
      1 0 8
        9 2
        1 6 0
        1 3 8
```

35
```
        ■ 0 . 4 1
1 7 ) 6 8 7 . 0 0
      6 8
        7 0
        6 8
          2 0
          1 7
            3
```

36
```
        3 7 . 1 6
2 4 ) 8 9 2 . 0 0
      7 2
      1 7 2
      1 ■ 8
          4 0
          2 4
          1 6 0
          1 4 4
            1 6
```

37
```
        1 ■ 3
4 5 ) 5 5 3 5
      4 5
      1 0 3
        9 0
        1 3 5
        1 3 5
```

38
```
        2 ■ . 7 8
4 1 ) 8 5 2 . 0 0
      8 2
        3 2 0
        2 8 7
          3 3 0
          3 2 8
              2
```

39
```
        3 1 . 0 6
■ 1 ) 9 6 3 . 0 0
      9 3
        3 3
        3 1
          2 0 0
          1 8 6
            1 4
```

40
```
        1 1 . 7 6
6 3 ) 7 4 1 . 0 0
      6 3
      1 1 1
        6 3
        4 8 0
        4 4 1
          3 9 0
          3 7 8
            ■ 2
```

41
```
        ■ 9
2 2 ) 2 1 7 8
      1 9 8
      1 9 8
      1 9 8
```

42
```
        6 5 . 7 ■
1 2 ) 7 8 9 . 0 0
      7 2
      6 9
      6 0
        9 0
        8 4
          6 0
          6 0
```

43
```
        3 ■
2 4 ) 7 9 2
      7 2
      7 2
      7 2
```

44
```
        5 ■
3 4 ) 2 0 0 6
      1 7 0
      3 0 6
      3 0 6
```

45
```
        1 0 3
1 2 ) 1 2 3 6
      1 2
        ■ 6
        3 6
```

Improper Fractions and Mixed Numbers

Some fractions have numerators that are greater than or equal to the denominators, such as $\frac{7}{3}$, $\frac{5}{2}$, $\frac{9}{7}$, and $\frac{6}{6}$. A fraction like this is called an **improper fraction.** Sometimes it is convenient to work with improper fractions. And sometimes we change them to mixed numbers or whole numbers by dividing.

Example:

$\frac{7}{3} = ?$ To evaluate $\frac{7}{3}$, we divide 7 by 3. $3\overline{)7}$ 2 R1

$\frac{7}{3} = 2$ wholes and a remaining $\frac{1}{3}$

$\frac{7}{3} = 2\frac{1}{3}$

We write $2\frac{1}{3}$ and say "two and a third" or "two and one-third."

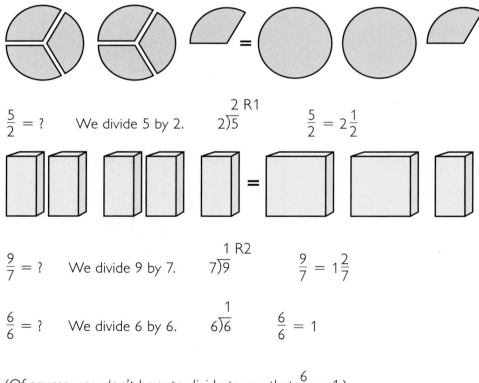

$\frac{5}{2} = ?$ We divide 5 by 2. $2\overline{)5}$ 2 R1 $\frac{5}{2} = 2\frac{1}{2}$

$\frac{9}{7} = ?$ We divide 9 by 7. $7\overline{)9}$ 1 R2 $\frac{9}{7} = 1\frac{2}{7}$

$\frac{6}{6} = ?$ We divide 6 by 6. $6\overline{)6}$ 1 $\frac{6}{6} = 1$

(Of course, you don't have to divide to see that $\frac{6}{6} = 1$.)

To find the decimal equivalent or a decimal approximation of an improper fraction, we carry the division beyond the decimal point.

Examples: $\frac{5}{2}$ $2\overline{)5.0}$ = 2.5

$\frac{5}{2}$ = 2.5

$\frac{7}{3}$ $3\overline{)7.000}$ = 2.333

$\frac{7}{3}$ is equal to 2.33, to the nearest hundredth.

You can convert a mixed number to a decimal by converting the fractional part.

Examples: $2\frac{1}{2}$ $\frac{1}{2}$ = 0.5

$2\frac{1}{2}$ = 2.5

$2\frac{1}{3}$ $\frac{1}{3}$ is about 0.33.

$2\frac{1}{3}$ is about 2.33.

Change each improper fraction to a mixed or whole number.

1. $\frac{4}{3}$　2. $\frac{7}{5}$　3. $\frac{10}{8}$　4. $\frac{25}{5}$　5. $\frac{10}{10}$

6. $\frac{7}{2}$　7. $\frac{24}{7}$　8. $\frac{9}{4}$　9. $\frac{26}{5}$　10. $\frac{10}{6}$

11. $\frac{8}{5}$　12. $\frac{10}{3}$　13. $\frac{6}{2}$　14. $\frac{8}{3}$　15. $\frac{5}{4}$

Find the decimal equivalent or an approximation to the nearest hundredth.

16. $1\frac{1}{2}$　17. $6\frac{1}{5}$　18. $\frac{9}{10}$　19. $\frac{11}{9}$　20. $\frac{8}{5}$

21. $\frac{5}{2}$　22. $\frac{10}{8}$　23. $\frac{10}{9}$　24. $1\frac{1}{9}$　25. $\frac{8}{6}$

26. $\frac{4}{3}$　27. $\frac{8}{9}$　28. $\frac{1}{9}$　29. $1\frac{2}{9}$　30. $\frac{1}{7}$

31. $1\frac{2}{3}$　32. $\frac{9}{8}$　33. $\frac{2}{9}$　34. $\frac{8}{4}$　35. $1\frac{1}{7}$

LESSON 79

GAME

Practice with Decimal Equivalents

COOPERATIVE LEARNING

Up to 2 Game

Players:	**Two or more**
Materials:	**Two 0–5 cubes, two 5–10 cubes**
Object:	**To make a greater number on each turn, but to be the last player to go past 2**
Math Focus:	**Comparing and ordering fractions, finding decimal equivalents of proper and improper fractions, and mathematical reasoning**

RULES

1. Take turns rolling all four cubes.

2. Use any two of the numbers you roll to make a fraction or a decimal of 2 or less than 2. (For example, if you roll 3, 3, 5, and 10, you could make $\frac{3}{3}, \frac{3}{5}, \frac{3}{10}, \frac{5}{3}, \frac{5}{10}, \frac{10}{5}$, or any of these decimals: .103, .105, .310, .33, .35, .510, .53, 1.03, 1.05. Notice that you may place the point between the 1 and the 0 if you roll a 10.)

3. Keep a record of the number you make on each turn. Write the number as a decimal. If you make a fraction, write the decimal equivalent or an approximation. You may round approximations to the nearest thousandth. (For example, if you make $\frac{2}{3}$, you may write 0.667.) Use the chart on page 283.

4. On each turn you must write a number greater than the number you made on your previous turn, but you cannot make a number greater than 2.

5. On any turn if you cannot write 2 or a number less than 2 but greater than your previous turn, then you are out.

6. The last player to go out wins.

Table of Decimal Approximations or Equivalents of Fractions

Numerator

	1	2	3	4	5	6	7	8	9	10
1	1	2	3	4	5	6	7	8	9	10
2	0.5	1	1.5	2	2.5	3	3.5	4	4.5	5
3	0.333	0.667	1	1.333	1.667	2	2.333	2.667	3	3.333
4	0.25	0.5	0.75	1	1.25	1.5	1.75	2	2.25	2.5
5	0.2	0.4	0.6	0.8	1	1.2	1.4	1.6	1.8	2
6	0.167	0.333	0.5	0.667	0.833	1	1.167	1.333	1.5	1.667
7	0.143	0.286	0.429	0.571	0.714	0.857	1	1.143	1.286	1.429
8	0.125	0.25	0.375	0.5	0.625	0.75	0.875	1	1.125	1.25
9	0.111	0.222	0.333	0.444	0.556	0.667	0.778	0.889	1	1.111
10	0.1	0.2	0.3	0.4	0.5	0.6	0.7	0.8	0.9	1

Denominator (left vertical label)

for reference when playing the "Up to 2" Game

In your Math Journal write about the strategies you used in playing this game.

Answer the following questions about the "Up to 2" Game.

1. Is it always possible to make a number less than or equal to 2?

2. Is it always possible to make a number greater than 1 but not greater than 2?

3. If this game were played with four 0–5 cubes, instead of two of each kind, would you be more or less likely to get a roll that you could use to make a number between 1 and 2?

4. If this game were played with four 5–10 cubes instead of two of each kind, would you be more or less likely to get a roll that you could use to make a number between 1 and 2?

5. Give an example of a roll of four 0–5 cubes that you could not use to make a number greater than 1 but not greater than 2.

Part 4

You may want to refer to earlier parts of this Thinking Story on pages 246–247, 256–257, and 268–269.

" Help me think of new ways to save energy," Manolita told her parents.

"You could ask people to insulate their houses," her mother said.

"Someone has already thought of that," Manolita said.

"Then you could ask people to keep their houses cooler in winter," her father said. "That can save a lot of energy."

"Someone has already thought of that too," Manolita said.

"Speaking of cooler houses," said her mother, "does anyone feel a cold draft in here?"

They all felt the draft. Manolita looked around to find where it was coming from. She found that the cold air was coming in through the mail slot. It was being held open by an ad someone had stuck in it.

"That happens almost every day," Manolita's mother said. "There ought to be a law. It would be easy enough for people to push the ads all the way through the slot. Then it wouldn't stay open."

Manolita's parents got out some books on heating. They did some figuring. They showed that an open mail slot could increase heating costs by five to ten percent.

"I wish you'd stop thinking about that old mail slot and help me think of ways to save energy," Manolita said.

the end

Work in groups. Discuss how you figured your answers and compare them with those of other groups.

1 The average heating bill in Manolita's town is $500 a year. If her parents figured correctly, how much extra would it cost if a mail slot were open all the time?

2 Where Manolita lives, people use their furnaces about 150 days a year. Of course, no one's mail slot is likely to be open all that time. Estimate how much time during those 150 days a mail slot might be open. Figure that ads are placed in it almost every day.

3 Using what you know from questions 1 and 2, estimate how much it costs people to have ads stuck in their mail slots. Be prepared to explain your estimate.

4 When Ferdie heard about this he said, "I think open mail slots should save energy. After all, they make the house cooler. Everybody says that keeping your house cooler in winter saves energy." Do you agree? Why or why not?

LESSON
80

Adding and Subtracting Mixed Numbers

Ms. Owens is planning to drive from Miller's Creek to Rattlesnake Bluff by way of Green Valley. She knows it will take about $2\frac{3}{4}$ hours to drive from Miller's Creek to Green Valley and about $3\frac{1}{2}$ hours to drive from Green Valley to Rattlesnake Bluff. About how long will the entire trip from Miller's Creek to Rattlesnake Bluff take?

To find the answer, add $2\frac{3}{4}$ and $3\frac{1}{2}$. Here's how.

First estimate the answer. Since the sum of the two fractions is a little more than 1, the answer will be a little more than 6.

$$2\frac{3}{4}$$
$$+ 3\frac{1}{2}$$

Add the fraction parts. We can't add because the denominators are different.

$$2\frac{3}{4} = 2\frac{?}{4} = 2\frac{3}{4}$$

Find a common denominator.

$$3\frac{1}{2} = 3\frac{?}{4} = 3\frac{2}{4}$$

We'll use 4. The fraction $\frac{1}{2} = \frac{2}{4}$.

$$2\frac{3}{4} \qquad\qquad 2\frac{3}{4}$$
$$+ 3\frac{1}{2} \rightarrow + 3\frac{2}{4}$$
$$\overline{\qquad} \qquad \overline{5\frac{5}{4}}$$

Add the fraction parts. Add the whole numbers. $\frac{5}{4}$ is an improper fraction.

$\frac{5}{4} = 1\frac{1}{4}$ so $5\frac{5}{4} = 5 + 1\frac{1}{4}$

$$5\frac{5}{4} = 6\frac{1}{4}$$

Rewrite the answer.

Check: $6\frac{1}{4}$ is a little more than 6, so it checks with our estimate.

It will take about $6\frac{1}{4}$ hours to drive from Miller's Creek to Rattlesnake Bluff by way of Green Valley.

Dan drove from Miller's Creek to Rattlesnake Bluff on the interstate highway in $4\frac{1}{2}$ hours. How much less than $6\frac{1}{4}$ hours was that?

To find out, subtract $4\frac{1}{2}$ from $6\frac{1}{4}$. Here's how.

First estimate the answer. Since $\frac{1}{2}$ is more than $\frac{1}{4}$, the answer should be a little less than 2.

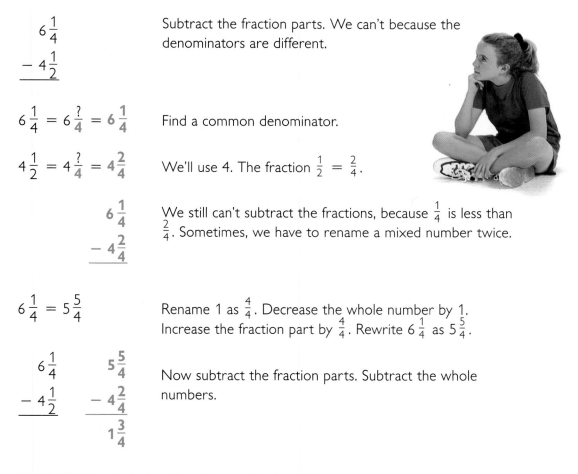

$$6\frac{1}{4}$$
$$-\ 4\frac{1}{2}$$

Subtract the fraction parts. We can't because the denominators are different.

$$6\frac{1}{4} = 6\frac{?}{4} = 6\frac{1}{4}$$

Find a common denominator.

$$4\frac{1}{2} = 4\frac{?}{4} = 4\frac{2}{4}$$

We'll use 4. The fraction $\frac{1}{2} = \frac{2}{4}$.

$$6\frac{1}{4}$$
$$-\ 4\frac{2}{4}$$

We still can't subtract the fractions, because $\frac{1}{4}$ is less than $\frac{2}{4}$. Sometimes, we have to rename a mixed number twice.

$$6\frac{1}{4} = 5\frac{5}{4}$$

Rename 1 as $\frac{4}{4}$. Decrease the whole number by 1. Increase the fraction part by $\frac{4}{4}$. Rewrite $6\frac{1}{4}$ as $5\frac{5}{4}$.

$$6\frac{1}{4} \qquad 5\frac{5}{4}$$
$$-\ 4\frac{1}{2} \qquad -\ 4\frac{2}{4}$$
$$\overline{\qquad\qquad 1\frac{3}{4}}$$

Now subtract the fraction parts. Subtract the whole numbers.

Check: This is a little less than 2, so it checks with our estimate.

It took about $1\frac{3}{4}$ hours less to drive from Miller's Creek to Rattlesnake Bluff on the interstate than it did by way of Green Valley.

◆ **LESSON 80 Adding and Subtracting Mixed Numbers**

Change each improper fraction to a mixed number with a proper
fraction or a whole number.

1 $\dfrac{6}{5}$ **2** $\dfrac{9}{7}$ **3** $1\dfrac{4}{3}$ **4** $2\dfrac{3}{2}$ **5** $\dfrac{10}{5}$

6 $1\dfrac{5}{4}$ **7** $3\dfrac{6}{6}$ **8** $2\dfrac{7}{5}$ **9** $5\dfrac{4}{3}$ **10** $2\dfrac{9}{4}$

11 $3\dfrac{5}{2}$ **12** $2\dfrac{9}{2}$ **13** $\dfrac{10}{2}$ **14** $1\dfrac{10}{9}$ **15** $4\dfrac{4}{3}$

16 $4\dfrac{5}{3}$ **17** $2\dfrac{10}{7}$ **18** $5\dfrac{11}{8}$ **19** $6\dfrac{6}{6}$ **20** $7\dfrac{10}{10}$

Rewrite each mixed number as an improper fraction.

21 $3\dfrac{1}{2}$ **22** $4\dfrac{3}{8}$ **23** $2\dfrac{2}{3}$ **24** $2\dfrac{1}{2}$ **25** $4\dfrac{1}{3}$

26 $2\dfrac{7}{8}$ **27** $3\dfrac{4}{7}$ **28** $2\dfrac{1}{5}$ **29** $4\dfrac{7}{10}$ **30** $3\dfrac{7}{12}$

31 $5\dfrac{3}{10}$ **32** $2\dfrac{1}{8}$ **33** $4\dfrac{1}{12}$ **34** $3\dfrac{8}{9}$ **35** $6\dfrac{1}{4}$

36 $4\dfrac{2}{5}$ **37** $5\dfrac{1}{3}$ **38** $3\dfrac{3}{8}$ **39** $6\dfrac{2}{7}$ **40** $2\dfrac{1}{6}$

Add or subtract.

41 $2\dfrac{5}{8} + 3\dfrac{4}{8}$ **42** $3\dfrac{2}{7} - 1\dfrac{4}{7}$ **43** $5\dfrac{3}{5} - 2\dfrac{2}{5}$ **44** $5\dfrac{3}{5} + 2\dfrac{2}{5}$

45 $8\dfrac{1}{3} + 4\dfrac{1}{2}$ **46** $8\dfrac{1}{3} - 4\dfrac{1}{2}$ **47** $3\dfrac{1}{2} + 2\dfrac{3}{4}$ **48** $3\dfrac{1}{2} - \dfrac{3}{4}$

49 $5\dfrac{1}{3} - 1\dfrac{1}{2}$ **50** $12\dfrac{1}{3} - 5\dfrac{1}{2}$ **51** $4\dfrac{2}{3} - 1\dfrac{3}{4}$ **52** $14\dfrac{2}{3} - 11\dfrac{3}{4}$

Solve this problem.

53 Ms. Owens discovered another route from Miller's Creek to
Rattlesnake Bluff. This route goes through Orange Park. It took her
$2\dfrac{1}{2}$ hours to drive from Miller's Creek to Orange Park and $3\dfrac{1}{4}$ hours
to drive from Orange Park to Rattlesnake Bluff.

   a. How long did it take Ms. Owens to go from Miller's Creek to
Rattlesnake Bluff on this route?

   b. How much less time would it take to go from Miller's Creek to
Rattlesnake Bluff through Orange Park than through Green Valley?

Make 1 Game

Players:	**Two or more**
Materials:	**Two 0–5 cubes, two 5–10 cubes**
Object:	**To make a problem with the answer closest to 1**
Math Focus:	**Mental arithmetic and addition and subtraction of fractions**

RULES

1. Take turns rolling all four cubes.

2. Make two fractions. The fractions can be proper, improper, or both.

3. Make an addition or subtraction problem with the fractions that gives an answer close to 1. Don't calculate the answer yet.

4. The player whose problem has an answer closest to 1 wins the round. You don't need to calculate the answers unless you can't tell by looking.

SAMPLE GAME

Tomás rolled:

Jackie rolled:

Tomás made:

$\frac{5}{5} - \frac{0}{9}$

Jackie made:

$\frac{6}{5} - \frac{1}{8}$

(Tomás knew that he couldn't use 0 in the denominator of a fraction.)

Tomás won this round. Both players knew that Tomás had 1 exactly and that Jackie had more than 1.

Describe in your Math Journal your strategies for playing this game.

LESSON 81

Using Mixed Numbers

There are times in real life that you'll need to apply what you've learned about computing with fractions and mixed numbers. Following recipes is one common application.

Solve these problems.

1 Cesar wants to make about 200 cookies. The recipe will make about 100 cookies, so he decides to double it. The recipe calls for these ingredients:

$1\frac{1}{2}$ cups of butter	$\frac{3}{4}$ teaspoon of grated orange rind
1 cup of sugar	$\frac{3}{8}$ teaspoon of nutmeg
$\frac{3}{4}$ teaspoon of salt	3 cups of flour
2 teaspoons of vanilla extract	

The recipe says to bake the cookies in a preheated oven for 12 minutes at 375°.

  a. How much of each ingredient should Cesar use in the doubled recipe?

  b. About how long should he bake the cookies?

  c. At what temperature should he bake the cookies?

2 Ruth was making a cake that called for $2\frac{1}{4}$ cups of flour and $1\frac{1}{3}$ cups of sugar. She confused the two amounts. By mistake she poured $1\frac{1}{3}$ cups of flour into a bowl and began to mix in the sugar. After mixing in 1 cup of sugar she thought, "My, this is going to be a sweet cake." Then she realized what she had done.

  a. How much more flour should she add?

  b. How much more sugar should she add?

  c. Suppose she had put in $1\frac{1}{3}$ cups of flour and $2\frac{1}{4}$ cups of sugar and had decided that she had to double the recipe to make it work out. Then, how much more sugar and how much more flour would she add?

  d. How could Ruth measure about $\frac{1}{6}$ cup if she has measuring cups marked $\frac{1}{2}$ cup, $\frac{1}{3}$ cup, and $\frac{1}{4}$ cup?

Solve these problems.

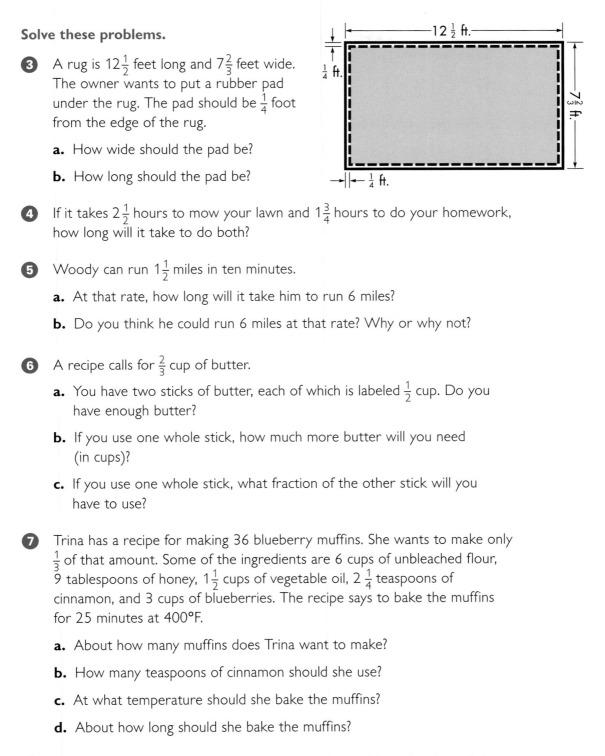

12 ½ ft.

¼ ft.

7 ⅔ ft.

→‖← ¼ ft.

3 A rug is $12\frac{1}{2}$ feet long and $7\frac{2}{3}$ feet wide. The owner wants to put a rubber pad under the rug. The pad should be $\frac{1}{4}$ foot from the edge of the rug.

   a. How wide should the pad be?

   b. How long should the pad be?

4 If it takes $2\frac{1}{2}$ hours to mow your lawn and $1\frac{3}{4}$ hours to do your homework, how long will it take to do both?

5 Woody can run $1\frac{1}{2}$ miles in ten minutes.

   a. At that rate, how long will it take him to run 6 miles?

   b. Do you think he could run 6 miles at that rate? Why or why not?

6 A recipe calls for $\frac{2}{3}$ cup of butter.

   a. You have two sticks of butter, each of which is labeled $\frac{1}{2}$ cup. Do you have enough butter?

   b. If you use one whole stick, how much more butter will you need (in cups)?

   c. If you use one whole stick, what fraction of the other stick will you have to use?

7 Trina has a recipe for making 36 blueberry muffins. She wants to make only $\frac{1}{3}$ of that amount. Some of the ingredients are 6 cups of unbleached flour, 9 tablespoons of honey, $1\frac{1}{2}$ cups of vegetable oil, $2\frac{1}{4}$ teaspoons of cinnamon, and 3 cups of blueberries. The recipe says to bake the muffins for 25 minutes at 400°F.

   a. About how many muffins does Trina want to make?

   b. How many teaspoons of cinnamon should she use?

   c. At what temperature should she bake the muffins?

   d. About how long should she bake the muffins?

7 Kevin is making waffles. His recipe calls for 4 cups of flour, but he only has 3 cups, so he is adjusting the recipe. If the original recipe made two dozen waffles, how many waffles can Kevin make?

Mid-Unit Review

Solve for *n* in the following.

1 $\frac{1}{2}$ of 18 = n

2 $\frac{2}{3}$ of 24 = n

3 n = $\frac{2}{5}$ of 40

Solve these problems.

4 $\frac{1}{3}$ of 42

5 $\frac{2}{3}$ of 60

6 $\frac{1}{4}$ of 80

7 $\frac{2}{3} \times \frac{4}{11}$

8 $\frac{2}{9} \times \frac{7}{8}$

9 $\frac{21}{44} \times \frac{3}{7}$

For each fraction find the decimal equivalent or an approximation rounded to the nearest thousandth.

10 $\frac{1}{4}$

11 $\frac{5}{6}$

12 $\frac{5}{8}$

13 $\frac{4}{5}$

14 $\frac{2}{7}$

15 $\frac{10}{6}$

16 $\frac{4}{9}$

17 $1\frac{1}{3}$

18 $1\frac{3}{5}$

19 $\frac{10}{8}$

Complete to write an equivalent fraction in simpler form.

20 $\frac{10}{14} = \frac{?}{7}$

21 $\frac{12}{18} = \frac{?}{3}$

22 $\frac{8}{10} = \frac{4}{?}$

23 $\frac{8}{20} = \frac{2}{?}$

Reduce each fraction completely.

24 $\frac{2}{6}$

25 $\frac{9}{12}$

26 $\frac{50}{175}$

27 $\frac{20}{80}$

28 $\frac{9}{45}$

Find the greatest common factor of each pair of numbers.

29 12 and 20

30 9 and 15

31 24 and 132

Copy each pair of fractions but insert <, >, or =.

32 $\frac{1}{3}$ ■ $\frac{2}{5}$

33 $\frac{5}{6}$ ■ $\frac{7}{8}$

34 $\frac{5}{12}$ ■ $\frac{9}{24}$

Find the least common multiple of each set of numbers.

35 2 and 5

36 4 and 16

37 5 and 10

38 6 and 15

39 2, 4, and 8

40 3, 5, and 9

41 3, 4, and 14

42 6, 4, and 9

Add or subtract. Reduce answers if possible.

43 $\frac{2}{3} + \frac{5}{9}$

44 $\frac{1}{5} + \frac{3}{4}$

45 $\frac{9}{10} - \frac{3}{5}$

46 $\frac{1}{4} - \frac{1}{8}$

47 $\frac{2}{3} - \frac{1}{2}$

48 $\frac{3}{4} - \frac{3}{8}$

49 $\frac{2}{7} + \frac{5}{14}$

50 $\frac{4}{5} + \frac{1}{10}$

51 $2\frac{1}{3} + \frac{3}{4}$

52 $4\frac{1}{4} - 2\frac{7}{8}$

53 $10\frac{1}{5} - 1\frac{1}{2}$

54 $2\frac{2}{3} + 5\frac{2}{3}$

Change each improper fraction to a mixed or whole number.

55 $\frac{5}{4}$

56 $\frac{27}{5}$

57 $\frac{15}{2}$

58 $\frac{10}{3}$

59 $\frac{12}{6}$

Change each mixed number to an improper fraction.

60 $2\frac{1}{3}$

61 $3\frac{2}{7}$

62 $1\frac{4}{5}$

63 $4\frac{3}{4}$

64 $3\frac{1}{8}$

Solve these problems.

65 If you roll a 0–5 cube many times, about what fraction of the time would you expect to roll a 4?

66 If you roll a 0–5 cube, what is the probability of getting an even number?

67 If you roll a 0–5 cube, what is the probability of getting a 1 or a 5?

68 If you roll a 0–5 cube 150 times, about how many times would you expect to roll a 0?

69 If you roll a 0–5 cube many times, about what fraction of the time would you expect to roll either a 2 or a 4? About what fraction of the time would you expect not to roll a 0 or a 5?

70 If it takes $\frac{3}{4}$ of an hour to write an essay and $\frac{1}{2}$ an hour to edit it, how long will it take to write and edit the essay? At those rates of writing and editing, how long would it take to write and edit three essays?

Keeping Sharp

Mrs. Norton needs to rent a car. She will use it for two days and will drive between 100 and 200 miles. She has a choice of three companies.

Small Car Special

SURE THING
AUTO RENTAL

$18.95 per day
15¢ per mile

Small Car Special **Cheap** AUTO RENTAL CO.

$23.95 per day
12¢ per mile

Small Car Special

Comfo-Car
RENTAL COMPANY

$34.95 per day
200 free miles

12¢ per mile over 200

Sure Thing Auto Rental charges $18.95 per day plus 15¢ per mile. Cheap Auto Rental Company charges $23.95 per day plus 12¢ per mile. Comfo-Car Rental Company charges $34.95 per day with 200 free miles plus 12¢ per mile over 200.

Solve these problems.

1 Which automobile company will be least expensive?

2 If Mrs. Norton drives less than 100 miles, which company will be least expensive?

3 If Mrs. Norton drives 300 miles, which company will be least expensive?

While planning to open a checking account, Joshua learned the rates charged by two local banks. The 8th National Bank charged $3.00 per month plus 10¢ for each check written. The 9th National Bank charged 25¢ for each check but did not have a monthly charge. Joshua plans to write between five and ten checks each month.

4 Which bank is likely to be less expensive for Joshua?

5 If Joshua really does write between five and ten checks per month, can he be sure that the bank you answered in problem 4 will always be less expensive?

6 How many checks would Joshua have to write for the other bank to be less expensive?

Joshua's older sister Andrea lives in another city. She knows she wants to open a checking account with 10th Federal Bank because it has branches near her home and office, but she is choosing between three kinds of accounts.

The Basic account costs $4.00 per month with five free checks and costs 50¢ for each additional check.

The Standard account has no fees per check and no monthly charge, as long as the balance in the account is at least $750; if the balance is less than $750, there is an $8.50 charge that month.

The Super account has no fees per check and no monthly charge, as long as the balance in the account is at least $2000; if the balance is less than $2000, there is a $12.50 charge that month. The Super account pays 2% annual interest. (The Basic and Standard accounts do not pay interest.)

Andrea writes 25 to 30 checks per month.

7 How much will the Basic account cost her per month if she continues to write 25 to 30 checks?

8 If Andrea cannot be sure of keeping more than $500 in her account, which account would be least expensive?

9 If Andrea keeps about $2500 in her account for a year, how much interest would she earn with a Super account?

10 Suppose Andrea plans to keep over $2000 in her account but knows there will be one or two months when her balance falls to around $1500. Which account would have the lowest net cost?

◆ **LESSON 82** Keeping Sharp

Make 2 Game

COPERATIVE
LEARNING

Players:	**Two**
Materials:	**Two 0–5 cubes, two 5–10 cubes**
Object:	**To get closer to 2 without going over**
Math Focus:	**Finding decimal equivalents of common fractions, adding common fractions and decimal equivalents, and mathematical reasoning**

RULES

1. The first player chooses a starting number in decimal form between 0.50 and 1.50.

2. The second player rolls all four cubes, uses any two of the numbers rolled to make a fraction or a decimal, and adds this amount to the first player's starting number. The second player gets the score.

3. The players reverse roles and repeat steps 1 and 2.

4. The player who makes an amount closer to 2 without going over is the winner of the round.

SAMPLE GAME

Eduardo and Polly were playing.

Round 1:	Eduardo chose 1.47.	Polly rolled 2, 4, 5, and 10. She made 0.52.
	Polly chose 1.25.	Eduardo rolled 2, 3, 8, and 10. He made $\frac{2}{3}$, which is about 0.67.

Polly won this round because 1.47 + 0.52 is closer to 2 than 1.25 + 0.67.

MATH JOURNAL

In your Math Journal explain the strategies you used when playing the game. Did it make a difference what number the first player chose?

Work in groups and use a calculator to solve the following problems. Discuss in your group whether your solutions make sense.

⓫ There are 307 sixth-grade students in the South Prauline School. By contract no more than 25 students can be put in one classroom with one teacher. How many teachers and classrooms will be needed for the sixth grade? If students are divided as equally as possible among the teachers, how many students will each teacher have?

⓬ There are 2056 students who attend the South Prauline School. A total of 1239 students walk to school or are brought by public transportation or by their parents. The others must be brought to school by school buses. If each school bus is allowed to carry no more than 40 students, what is the minimum number of bus trips necessary? Is it possible that more bus trips will be necessary?

⓭ The North Prauline School has only 79 sixth-grade students. By contract only 25 students can be assigned to one classroom with one teacher, as in the South Prauline School. How many teachers and classrooms are needed for the North Prauline sixth grade? If students are divided as equally as possible, how many students will each teacher have?

⓮ Of the 517 students who attend the North Prauline School, 284 are brought on school buses. If school buses are allowed to transport no more than 40 students, what is the minimum number of bus trips needed?

⓯ All of the sixth-grade students from both North Prauline School and South Prauline School are going on a field trip, along with their teachers and four parents per class. No more than 40 people can ride each bus.

   a. How many buses are needed to transport everyone going on the field trip from North Prauline School?

   b. How many buses are needed to transport everyone going on the trip from South Prauline School?

   c. If buses can carry some people from each school, how many buses are needed to transport everyone going on the field trip?

ACT IT OUT

Division by Fractions

A Material Problem with Fractions

Mr. Alekos has $32\frac{1}{2}$ yards of material from which to make suits. Each suit requires $1\frac{2}{3}$ yards of material. How many suits can Mr. Alekos make from $32\frac{1}{2}$ yards of material?

◆ Estimate an answer to this problem. Can you narrow the range of possible answers?

Work in groups. Find at least three different ways to solve this problem.

◆ Does each way of solving the problem give you the same answer? How can you check to be sure your answer is right?

There are many ways to find out how many suits Mr. Alekos can make. Here are five different ways.

A. By multiplying

$1\frac{2}{3}$ yards for one suit

5 yards for three suits (we multiplied by 3)

30 yards for 18 suits (we multiplied by 6)

$31\frac{2}{3}$ yards for 19 suits (we added 1 suit)

This leaves $\frac{1}{3} + \frac{1}{2}$, or $\frac{5}{6}$, of a yard of material. It is not enough for another suit.

Mr. Alekos can make 19 suits.

B. By adding

$1\frac{2}{3} + 1\frac{2}{3} + 1\frac{2}{3}$ and so on until the total passes $32\frac{1}{2}$. Then count how many times you wrote $1\frac{2}{3}$ before the total passed $32\frac{1}{2}$.

The answer is 19.

Mr. Alekos can make 19 suits.

C. By changing the numbers to decimals and dividing

$1\frac{2}{3}$ is about 1.667.

$32\frac{1}{2}$ is the same as 32.5.

$$1.667) \overline{32.500}$$

$$
\begin{array}{r}
19 \\
1667) \overline{32500} \\
\underline{1667} \\
15830 \\
\underline{15003} \\
827
\end{array}
$$

Mr. Alekos can make 19 suits.

(If you used a calculator, you could divide 32.5 by 1.6666667. You would get 19.499999, which would tell you that Mr. Alekos can make 19 suits.)

◆ **LESSON 83** Division by Fractions

D. By intelligent guessing and multiplying

$$1\tfrac{2}{3} \times n = 32\tfrac{1}{2}$$

Let's change $1\tfrac{2}{3}$ and $32\tfrac{1}{2}$ to improper fractions.

$$\tfrac{5}{3} \times n = \tfrac{65}{2}$$

$13 \times 5 = 65$ What can you multiply 3 by to get 2?

This is hard. Maybe you could multiply by an extra 3 in the numerator to get rid of the 3 in the $\tfrac{5}{3}$.

$$\tfrac{5}{3} \times \tfrac{13 \times 3}{?} = \tfrac{65 \times 3}{3 \times ?} = \tfrac{65}{2}$$

What number would you like the ? to stand for? You might choose 2 because $\tfrac{65 \times 3}{3 \times 2}$ is equivalent to $\tfrac{65}{2}$.

Try $\tfrac{13 \times 3}{2}$ for n.

$$\tfrac{5}{3} \times \tfrac{13 \times 3}{2} = \tfrac{65 \times 3}{3 \times 2} = \tfrac{65}{2}$$

$\tfrac{13 \times 3}{2}$ was the right number for n, but that was hard.

$$\tfrac{13 \times 3}{2} = \tfrac{39}{2} = 19\tfrac{1}{2}$$

So Mr. Alekos can make 19 suits (and have material left over for $\tfrac{1}{2}$ suit).

E. By dividing the fractions (after converting to mixed numbers)

$$\tfrac{65}{2} \div \tfrac{5}{3}$$

How can you do this? Find a common denominator. Since 6 is a multiple of both 2 and 3, rewrite the fractions as $\tfrac{195}{6} \div \tfrac{10}{6}$. Now both fractions have the same denominator.

You can think of the problem as 195 of something (sixths) divided by 10 of the same thing (sixths).

$195 \div 10 = 19.5$, or $19\tfrac{1}{2}$

So Mr. Alekos can make 19 suits (with material left over for $\tfrac{1}{2}$ suit).

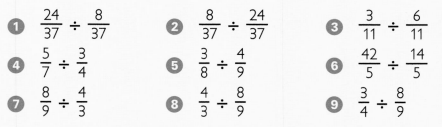

Divide the following fractions. Give your answer as a fraction or whole number.

1 $\dfrac{24}{37} \div \dfrac{8}{37}$

2 $\dfrac{8}{37} \div \dfrac{24}{37}$

3 $\dfrac{3}{11} \div \dfrac{6}{11}$

4 $\dfrac{5}{7} \div \dfrac{3}{4}$

5 $\dfrac{3}{8} \div \dfrac{4}{9}$

6 $\dfrac{42}{5} \div \dfrac{14}{5}$

7 $\dfrac{8}{9} \div \dfrac{4}{3}$

8 $\dfrac{4}{3} \div \dfrac{8}{9}$

9 $\dfrac{3}{4} \div \dfrac{8}{9}$

Solve the following problems.

10 Ms. Wilkins needs $4\frac{2}{3}$ yards of material to make one pair of curtains. She has $43\frac{1}{6}$ yards of material. How many pairs of curtains can she make? Will she have any material left over? How much?

11 Two schools are going to have a long-distance relay race. Each team must run $16\frac{1}{2}$ miles. Each runner will run only $\frac{3}{4}$ of a mile before handing off the baton to the next runner. How many runners will each school need on its relay team?

12 Jeremy was serving pizzas at the school picnic. Each student was supposed to get $\frac{3}{8}$ of a pizza. Jeremy had $5\frac{1}{2}$ pizzas to serve. How many students did he serve? Was there any pizza left over? How much?

13 Giorgio ran $14\frac{1}{2}$ laps around the track. His younger brother, Sam, ran $5\frac{1}{4}$ laps. "I ran three times as far as you," said Giorgio. "No, you didn't," said Sam, "$5\frac{1}{4} \times 3$ is $15\frac{3}{4}$ laps. You only ran $14\frac{1}{2}$ laps." Who's right? Exactly how many times Sam's distance did Giorgio run?

14 Donna knows it takes her about $\frac{1}{4}$ hour to walk a mile.

   a. How many hours will it take her to walk $1\frac{1}{2}$ miles?

   b. About how many minutes is that?

LESSON 84

Functions

ALGEBRA READINESS

In each case tell what number *n* stands for or what number the ? stands for. Watch which way each arrow goes.

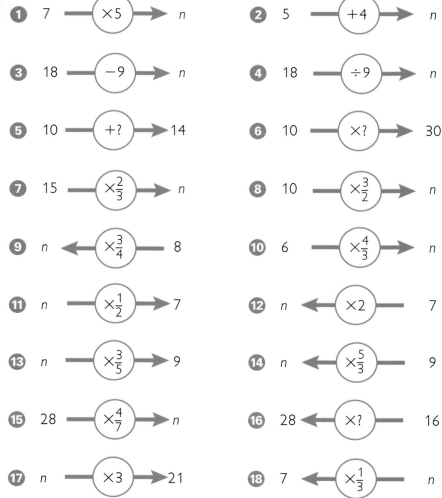

① 7 —(×5)→ *n*

② 5 —(+4)→ *n*

③ 18 —(−9)→ *n*

④ 18 —(÷9)→ *n*

⑤ 10 —(+?)→ 14

⑥ 10 —(×?)→ 30

⑦ 15 —(×$\frac{2}{3}$)→ *n*

⑧ 10 —(×$\frac{3}{2}$)→ *n*

⑨ *n* ←(×$\frac{3}{4}$)— 8

⑩ 6 —(×$\frac{4}{3}$)→ *n*

⑪ *n* —(×$\frac{1}{2}$)→ 7

⑫ *n* ←(×2)— 7

⑬ *n* —(×$\frac{3}{5}$)→ 9

⑭ *n* ←(×$\frac{5}{3}$)— 9

⑮ 28 —(×$\frac{4}{7}$)→ *n*

⑯ 28 ←(×?)— 16

⑰ *n* —(×3)→ 21

⑱ 7 ←(×$\frac{1}{3}$)— *n*

If you multiply 15 by $\frac{2}{3}$, you will get 10. What can you multiply 10 by to get 15?

Do you see a relationship between $\frac{2}{3}$ and $\frac{3}{2}$?

We can show this with arrows:

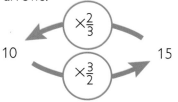

10 (×$\frac{2}{3}$) 15
    (×$\frac{3}{2}$)

302 • Fractions and Mixed Numbers

What number does the ? stand for? What number does *n* stand for? Find ? and *n*.

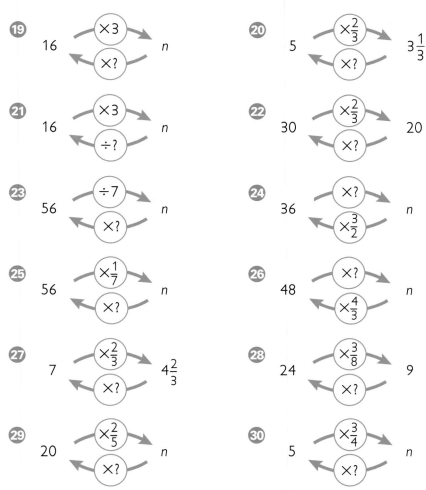

19 16 ×3 ↔ ×? → *n*

20 5 ×⅔ ↔ ×? → 3⅓

21 16 ×3 ↔ ÷? → *n*

22 30 ×⅔ ↔ ×? → 20

23 56 ÷7 ↔ ×? → *n*

24 36 ×? ↔ ×³⁄₂ → *n*

25 56 ×⅐ ↔ ×? → *n*

26 48 ×? ↔ ×⁴⁄₃ → *n*

27 7 ×⅔ ↔ ×? → 4⅔

28 24 ×⅜ ↔ ×? → 9

29 20 ×⅖ ↔ ×? → *n*

30 5 ×¾ ↔ ×? → *n*

For problems 35–38, solve for ? only.

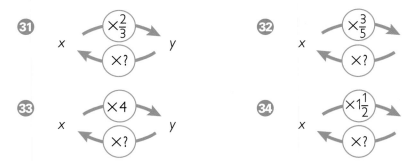

31 *x* ×⅔ ↔ ×? → *y*

32 *x* ×⅗ ↔ ×? → *y*

33 *x* ×4 ↔ ×? → *y*

34 *x* ×1½ ↔ ×? → *y*

LESSON 85

Dividing Fractions

You found this pattern in problem 31 of the previous lesson.

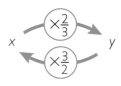

If you multiply any number by $\frac{2}{3}$ and then multiply the product by $\frac{3}{2}$, you get back the number with which you started. Try it with a few numbers.

The fraction $\frac{3}{2}$ is called the **reciprocal** or **multiplicative inverse** of $\frac{2}{3}$.

And $\frac{2}{3}$ is the reciprocal of $\frac{3}{2}$.

When a fraction and its reciprocal are multiplied, their product is 1.

We find the reciprocal by switching the numerator and the denominator.

Multiplying by the reciprocal of a number does the opposite of multiplying by the number.

Dividing by a number also does the opposite of multiplying by the number.

◆   Why might the reciprocal be called the multiplicative inverse?

To divide by a number, you can multiply by its reciprocal.

Example: $24 \div \frac{2}{3} = ?$

Instead of dividing by $\frac{2}{3}$, multiply by $\frac{3}{2}$.

$24 \times \frac{3}{2} = 36$

36 should be the answer to $24 \div \frac{2}{3}$.

Since multiplication and division are inverse operations, you can check that answer by multiplying $\frac{2}{3} \times 36$ to see if you get 24.

Example: Kurt used $1\frac{1}{2}$ cups of sugar to make a pitcher of lemonade. The pitcher holds $8\frac{1}{3}$ glasses of lemonade. How much sugar is there in each glass (if the sugar is evenly distributed)?

$$1\frac{1}{2} \div 8\frac{1}{3} = ?$$

First estimate the answer. If we had 1 cup of sugar and 9 glasses, it would be about $\frac{1}{9}$ cup per glass. If there had been 2 cups of sugar and 8 glasses, it would be about $\frac{1}{4}$ cup per glass. The answer should be between these numbers.

We can find the precise answer by changing to improper fractions and dividing:

$$\frac{3}{2} \div \frac{25}{3} = \frac{3}{2} \times \frac{3}{25} = \frac{9}{50}$$

Each glass contains $\frac{9}{50}$ of a cup of sugar. You can see that this answer makes sense by converting it and the estimate to decimals and comparing them.

Example: Kurt is sharing the lemonade with 4 of his friends. If they all share the lemonade equally, how many glasses will each person receive?

$$8\frac{1}{3} \div 5 = ?$$

First, estimate the answer. If the pitcher held only 5 glasses, each person would get 1 glass, and if it held 10 glasses, each person would get 2 glasses. The answer must be between 1 and 2.

To find the exact amount, change to improper fractions and divide:

$$8\frac{1}{3} \div 5 = \frac{25}{3} \div \frac{5}{1} = \overset{5}{\cancel{\frac{25}{3}}} \times \frac{1}{\cancel{5}_{1}} = \frac{5}{3}$$

The answer is $\frac{5}{3}$ or $1\frac{2}{3}$. Each person can have $1\frac{2}{3}$ glasses of lemonade.

This agrees with our estimate.

◆ LESSON 85   Dividing Fractions

Remember: To divide by a number you can multiply by its reciprocal.

Examples:

$$\frac{3}{7} \div \frac{5}{9} = \frac{3}{7} \times \frac{9}{5} = \frac{27}{35}$$

$$32\frac{1}{2} \div 1\frac{2}{3} = \frac{65}{2} \div \frac{5}{3} = \frac{65}{2} \times \frac{3}{5}$$

$$= \frac{13}{2} \times \frac{3}{1} = \frac{39}{2} = 19\frac{1}{2}$$

Divide. Reduce when possible.

1 $12 \div \frac{2}{3}$ **2** $16 \div \frac{4}{5}$ **3** $\frac{3}{7} \div \frac{3}{7}$ **4** $\frac{6}{7} \div \frac{3}{7}$

5 $\frac{5}{12} \div \frac{10}{3}$ **6** $100 \div 25$ **7** $12 \div 25$ **8** $\frac{3}{5} \div 7$

9 $\frac{1}{4} \div \frac{1}{2}$ **10** $\frac{1}{2} \div \frac{1}{4}$ **11** $\frac{3}{8} \div \frac{1}{3}$ **12** $\frac{3}{8} \div 3$

13 $\frac{1}{2} \div \frac{1}{3}$ **14** $\frac{2}{5} \div \frac{3}{7}$ **15** $\frac{5}{8} \div \frac{5}{4}$ **16** $\frac{9}{4} \div \frac{3}{2}$

17 $\frac{12}{5} \div \frac{3}{5}$ **18** $\frac{4}{7} \div \frac{2}{7}$ **19** $\frac{5}{6} \div \frac{1}{3}$ **20** $\frac{1}{3} \div \frac{5}{6}$

21 $2\frac{1}{2} \div 4$ **22** $4 \div 2\frac{1}{2}$ **23** $\frac{5}{6} \div 2$ **24** $\frac{3}{5} \div \frac{2}{3}$

25 Use a calculator to solve problems 8, 9, 10, 12, 15, and 16 again. Compare your calculator answers with your fraction answers by changing the fraction answers to decimals.

For example, here's how you would solve problem 8.

$$\frac{3}{5} \div 7 = 0.6 \div 7$$

Push **.** **6**, **÷**, **7**, **=** ⟶ 0.0857142

Let's say your answer to $\frac{3}{5} \div 7$ was $\frac{3}{35}$ when you solved it with paper and pencil.

Find a decimal approximation for $\frac{3}{35}$ by dividing: $3 \div 35$.

Push **3**, **÷**, **3 5**, **=** ⟶ 0.0857142

Both methods give the same answer.

How much is one dollar worth?

In the United States our basic unit of money, or currency, is the dollar. Other countries have different units of currency. Some of these units are shown in the chart.

Country	Currency
Mexico	peso
China	yuan
Japan	yen
Ecuador	sucre
Canada	dollar
India	rupee
United Kingdom	pound
Zambia	kwacha

The value of each currency changes as a result of changes in the economies of the different countries. For example, on April 30, 1970 the value of the British pound was 2.39 U.S. dollars. Twenty-four years later, on April 30, 1994, its value was 1.53 U.S. dollars.

26 Using the business section of a newspaper, find the value of each of these currencies today.

At currency exchange locations, people can change one currency for another of the same value.

Suppose you are calculating currency values for Ropponia, Tropponia, and Dopponia. The units of currency in these imaginary countries are the ropple, the tropple, and the dopple.

One ropple is worth $\frac{5}{8}$ of one tropple.

One tropple is worth $\frac{4}{10}$ of one dopple.

One dopple is worth $2\frac{1}{2}$ tropples.

Answer these questions. Be sure your answers make sense.

27 How many ropples can you get for one dopple?

28 How many dopples can you get for one ropple?

29 Did you need all of the information you were given?

LESSON 86

Using Maps and Charts

The Rough-Ride Railroad Company runs a train line between East Village and West Village. Look at this map. It shows the stations on the line and the distances, in kilometers, between some of them.

How many kilometers is it from

1 East Village to Granitetown?

2 East Village to Junction City?

3 Granitetown to Middledorf?

4 Middledorf to Princeton?

5 Burgerville to Junction City?

6 Princeton to West Village?

7 Princeton to Princeton?

13

East Village

Granitetown

4

Junction City

11

Use a computer or other means to draw a chart, and complete the chart to make a record of the distances between all the stations.

	East Village	Granitetown	Junction City	Middledorf	Burgerville	Princeton	West Village
East Village	0					43	
Granitetown		0					
Junction City			0				
Middledorf				0			
Burgerville				3	0		
Princeton						0	
West Village							0

Save your chart. You will need it for an upcoming lesson.

Answer the following questions.

8 What do the 0s mean in the chart?

9 Do you need to calculate every distance in the chart?

10 What shortcuts did you use in completing the chart?

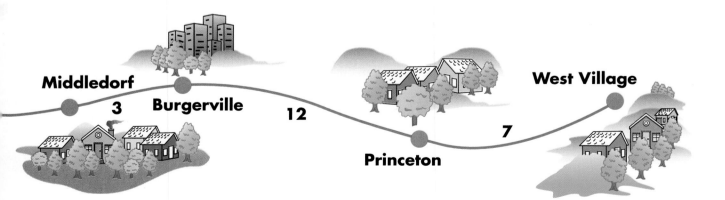

Ratios

We usually compare numbers in one of these ways:

    A. We find the difference between the numbers.

    B. We find the quotient (or **ratio**) of the numbers.

    C. We simply report the numbers.

Suppose Penny rode 9 kilometers and Ross rode 6 kilometers.

A.   To find the difference, subtract 6 from 9. Using the difference we could say:

    "Penny rode 3 kilometers farther than Ross," or "Ross rode 3 kilometers less than Penny."

◆   Based on these statements alone, can you tell how far Ross and Penny rode?

B.   To find the ratio, express the distances as a fraction. The ratio of Penny's distance to Ross's distance is $\frac{9}{6}$, which reduces to $\frac{3}{2}$, or $1\frac{1}{2}$. The ratio of Ross's distance to Penny's distance is $\frac{6}{9}$, which reduces to $\frac{2}{3}$. Using the ratio, we could say:

    "Penny rode $1\frac{1}{2}$ times as far as Ross," or "Ross rode $\frac{2}{3}$ as far as Penny."

◆   Based on these statements alone, can you tell how far Ross and Penny rode?

C.   We may simply report the numbers and not find the difference or ratio. Then we would simply say:

    "Penny rode 9 kilometers, and Ross rode 6 kilometers."

◆   Based on this statement alone, can you tell how far Ross and Penny rode?

Notice that in the last statement we do not lose information. But the other two statements organize the information to emphasize certain points and may be more useful for some purposes.

How we choose to compare numbers depends on the kind of information we are trying to stress and how the information will be used. But just giving a number or numbers is not enough. You must use a sentence or phrase to show the meaning.

 Work in groups to consider the following statements. Think of ways in which you could report the information. Discuss which ways would be most useful.

1 Emma bought a stamp for 25¢ and sold it for 50¢.

2 Jan bought a lot of stamps for 25¢ each and sold them for 50¢ each.

3 It costs Mr. McLaren 20¢ per kilometer to drive his small car and 40¢ per kilometer to drive his van.

4 Hal is 150 centimeters tall, and Lena is 143 centimeters tall.

Read each of the following. Think of ways to report the information. Give the advantages of reporting it as a difference, as a ratio, or simply as numbers:

5 Mary is 7 years old. Her sister is 14 years old. Mary was born in 1992. She'd like to know what year her sister was born.

6 A small container of milk holds one quart. A large container holds 4 quarts. We know that one quart will serve four people.

7 José walked 6 miles in two hours.

8 Abigail walked 10 miles and Sam walked 7 miles.

9 Rachel made a shade of orange by mixing $\frac{1}{2}$ can of yellow paint with $\frac{1}{4}$ can of red paint. She wants to keep track of how much she used of each color so that she can make the shade again.

10 Tickets to a Saturday evening performance of a play cost $22.50. Tickets to a Sunday afternoon performance cost $19.00.

◆ LESSON 87   Ratios

The Rough-Ride Railroad Company runs two trains a day from East Village to West Village. Here is the timetable for the two trains.

Rough-Ride Railroad Company Timetable

Station		Chug-Chug Local	East-West Express
East Village	*Departs*	8:00 A.M.	1:00 P.M.
Granitetown	*Departs*	8:21 A.M.	–
Junction City	*Departs*	8:27 A.M.	–
Middledorf	*Departs*	8:48 A.M.	–
Burgerville	*Departs*	9:04 A.M.	–
Princeton	*Departs*	9:16 A.M.	–
West Village	*Arrives*	9:30 A.M.	2:00 P.M.

11 About how many minutes does it take the Chug-Chug Local to go from
  a. East Village to Granitetown?
  b. East Village to Middledorf?
  c. East Village to Princeton?
  d. Junction City to Middledorf?
  e. Middledorf to West Village?
  f. Princeton to West Village?

12 About how many hours does it take to go from East Village to West Village on
  a. the Chug-Chug Local?
  b. the East-West Express?

13 Why do you think the East-West Express is quicker?

14 It is 50 kilometers from East Village to West Village. Between those two stations what is the average speed
  a. of the East-West Express?
  b. of the Chug-Chug Local?

Here are some of the fares that the Rough-Ride Railroad Company charged last year:

East Village to Middledorf........ $4.20

East Village to Princeton........... $6.45

Middledorf to Burgerville $0.45

Granitetown to Junction City .. $0.60

15 How do you think the fares were calculated? (Hint: Look at the chart of distances you made when you worked on page 309.)

This year the Rough-Ride Railroad Company is charging $0.24 per kilometer. A worker at the company began to make a chart showing the fare between any two stations.

16 Why are some of the boxes on the chart crossed out?

17 Use a computer or other means to draw the chart below, and complete the chart.

Rough-Ride Railroad Company Schedule of Fares	East Village	Granitetown	Junction City	Middledorf	Burgerville	Princeton	West Village
East Village	✕						
Granitetown		✕					
Junction City			✕		$3.36		
Middledorf				✕			
Burgerville					✕		
Princeton						✕	
West Village	$12.00						✕

LESSON 88

Averages and Rates

Sometimes when we describe numerical data, it is useful to use one number, called the average, to describe the data. Finding averages helps us to understand the data and to make predictions based on the data.

People talk about and use averages often.

◆ What do you think **average** means?

The following example shows one way to calculate an average.

Example: Find the average of 21, 23, 27, 29, and 26.

Add the numbers: $21 + 23 + 27 + 29 + 26 = 126$

Divide by how many numbers there were: $126 \div 5 = 25.2$

25.2 is the average of 21, 23, 27, 29, and 26.

This average is called the **mean.**

Sometimes an average gives useful information, but sometimes it doesn't. Sometimes an average is useful for one application but not for another.

Since an average is a ratio, an average of whole numbers is not necessarily a whole number.

Find the averages.

1 13, 15, 16, 18

2 13, 14, 14, 14, 15

3 13, 15, 17, 19, 21

4 13, 17, 19, 15, 14

5 13, 13, 14, 14

6 13, 13, 13, 13, 13

7 5, 5, 5, 10, 10, 15, 15, 15

8 5, 10, 10, 10, 10, 10, 10, 15

Solve these problems.

9 Sasha is measuring the heights of two groups of plants. The five plants in one group have heights of 6.2 cm, 5.7 cm, 6.2 cm, 5.3 cm, and 5.6 cm. What is the average height of the plants in this group?

10 The five plants in Sasha's other group have heights of 5.2 cm, 5.8 cm, 5.3 cm, 5.3 cm, and 5.4 cm. What is the average height of the plants in this group?

Rates are special kinds of ratios that are used to report certain kinds of information. So we often talk about average rates.

Example: Leroy rode his bicycle 24 kilometers in two hours. On the average how fast did he ride?

We can set up a ratio to compare the distance Leroy rode and the time it took.

$$\frac{24 \text{ kilometers}}{2 \text{ hours}}$$

Since $\frac{24}{2} = 12$, we can say that Leroy's average speed was 12 kilometers per hour.

We can check this by asking ourselves, "If Leroy rode steadily at 12 kilometers per hour for two hours, how far would he go?"

$$12 \times 2 = 24$$

Leroy would go 24 kilometers in two hours. This checks with the original information.

Use a calculator and work in groups. Check your answers to see that they make sense.

11 A 7.5-kilogram bag of flour costs $3.78, and a 5.0-kilogram bag of the same flour costs $3.02.

  a. How much does the flour cost per kilogram in a 7.5-kilogram bag?

  b. How much does the flour cost per kilogram in a 5.0-kilogram bag?

  c. Which bag costs less per kilogram?

12 Brittany can run 100 meters in 14.6 seconds. Do you think she can run 10,000 meters in 1460 seconds?

13 Mrs. Flores paddled a canoe 32 kilometers in about four hours. About what was her average speed?

14 Matthew read a 100-page book in 40 minutes. About how many pages did he read per minute?

15 An airplane flight between two cities covers about 1400 miles and takes about three hours.

  a. What is the airplane's average speed in miles per hour?

  b. What is the airplane's average speed in miles per minute?

◆ LESSON 88 Averages and Rates

Solve these problems.

16 Mrs. Collins drove about 500 kilometers in eight hours and used 54 liters of gasoline.

  a. About what was her average speed?

  b. On the average about how many kilometers did Mrs. Collins drive for each liter of gasoline?

  c. If she continued at that average speed, how far could she have gone in 12 hours?

  d. About how much gasoline would she use to drive 800 kilometers if she was using gasoline at the same rate?

17 A 5-kilogram bag of Fancy Feline cat food costs $6.98 at one store. At another store a 6-kilogram bag of the same cat food costs $5.98. Which store has the better buy?

18 Liza played three games of miniature golf. Her scores were 78, 82, and 74. What was her average score for the three games?

19 Sidney keeps a record of the time he spends doing homework. Last week he spent two hours on Monday, $1\frac{1}{2}$ hours on Tuesday, two hours on Wednesday, one hour on Thursday, and one hour on Friday. What was the average time per day he spent on homework for that five-day period?

20 Sidney has a math test on Friday. He wants to study a total of at least two hours spread evenly over the next four nights.

  a. How many hours should he study each night?

  b. How many minutes is that?

21 Sidney has been helping his younger brother practice basic math facts using flashcards. He can correctly answer 15 questions in 60 seconds. On the average how many seconds does it take him to answer each question?

22 A loaf of Farmer Brown whole grain bread costs $0.85, and a loaf of Super A bread costs $0.83. Farmer Brown bread weighs 500 grams, and Super A bread weighs 300 grams.

a. How much does Farmer Brown bread cost per gram?

b. How much does Super A bread cost per gram?

23 Mr. Mikami is driving from Southville to Northfield, a distance of 540 kilometers. He wants to make the trip in ten hours.

a. About how many kilometers per hour must he average?

b. After four hours of driving, Mr. Mikami had traveled 200 kilometers. What was his average speed for the first four hours?

c. He still wants to make the trip last ten hours. About what speed should he average for the rest of the trip?

24 Jennifer took five spelling tests and got these scores: 80, 86, 88, 82, 80.

a. What was her average score for the five tests?

b. Jennifer then got 100s on three tests. What was her average after the eight tests?

c. Does the average fairly represent Jennifer's performance in spelling?

25 On the last spelling test, the class average for 24 students was 78.

a. If someone who was absent takes the spelling test and gets a score of 80, will the class average go up or down?

b. By how much will the class average change? (Hint: Find the total number of points scored by the 24 students who first took the test.)

c. By how much would it have changed the average if the absent student had a score of 100?

Mean, Median, and Mode

In the previous lesson we defined the average as the number you get when you add together a bunch of numbers and divide by the number of numbers. So the average of 3, 4, and 5 would be (3 + 4 + 5) divided by 3, which is 4. This is usually called the **mean.**

Two other numbers that are sometimes called averages are the **median** and the **mode.**

The **median** of a set of numbers is the middle number when the numbers are put in order from least to greatest.

For example, in the set 3, 3, 4, 6, 6, 7, 8, 8, 9, 10, and 17, the number 7 is the median because it is in the middle (there are five numbers on either side of it) when the numbers are put in order.

Notice that the mean of the numbers is $7\frac{4}{11}$, a number fairly close to the median. Often the mean and median are equal or close to being equal.

If there is an even number of numbers, the median is the mean of the two middle numbers.

For example, in the set 4, 4, 5, 7, 7, and 8, the two numbers in the middle are 5 and 7. The median is $\frac{5+7}{2} = \frac{12}{2} = 6$.

Median

The **mode** is the number that appears most often in a set of numbers. If more than one number ties for "the most often," all of them are modes. So, in the last set of data above, 4 and 7 are both modes.

Find the mean, median, and mode of each of the following sets of numbers.

1   1, 2, 2, 3, 3, 4, 5, 5, 5, 5, 5, 6, 7, 7, 8, 8, 9

2   6, 7, 7, 8, 8, 9, 10, 10, 10, 10, 10, 11, 12, 12, 13, 13, 14

3   2, 4, 4, 6, 6, 8, 10, 10, 10, 10, 10, 12, 14, 14, 16, 16, 18

4   Compare the sets of numbers in problems 1, 2, and 3. Is there something you could do to the numbers in problem 1 to get those in problem 2? In problem 3? What?

5   What is the relationship of the mean, the median, and the mode in problem 2 to the corresponding averages in problem 1? How do those averages in problem 3 compare with the ones in problem 1?

Find the mean, median, and mode of the following sets of numbers.

6   201, 202, 202, 203, 203, 204, 205, 205, 205, 205, 205, 206, 207, 207, 208, 208, 209

7   100, 200, 200, 300, 300, 400, 500, 500, 500, 500, 500, 600, 700, 700, 800, 800, 900

8   103, 104, 104, 105, 105, 106, 107, 107, 107, 107, 107, 108, 109, 109, 110, 110, 111

9   10, 10, 10, 10, 14, 15, 15, 19, 50

Solve this problem.

10   A small business was having a labor dispute. The union members claimed that the average wage was $10,000. The owner claimed that the average wage was $17,000. A mediator was hired who examined the records and said the average was really $14,000. How could all three be correct? Write a set of wages for which all three of these numbers could be called the average. Which salary do you think is the owner's? (Hint: review your results for problem 9.)

◆ **LESSON 89   Mean, Median, and Mode**

Solve these problems.

11   Ashley, Heather, and Charlene were having a long jump contest. They decided that each person would get to jump five times, and the person with the greatest average for the five jumps would win. After they finished, they each examined the results, and each one declared herself the winner. The lengths of each of their jumps in centimeters are reported below. Explain what happened, and why each claimed she was the winner.

Long Jump Distances					
	Jump 1	Jump 2	Jump 3	Jump 4	Jump 5
Ashley	173	173	180	181	183
Heather	164	174	174	179	184
Charlene	162	162	175	209	212

12   The high temperatures (in degrees Fahrenheit) for Tucson, Arizona for each day of one week were

Monday, 98; Tuesday, 104; Wednesday, 110; Thursday, 112; Friday, 114; Saturday, 113; and Sunday, 109.

What was the average high temperature in Tucson for that week?

13   The low temperatures in Madison, Wisconsin for one week were

Monday, 7; Tuesday, 4; Wednesday, 2; Thursday, 0; Friday, 6; Saturday, 8; Sunday, 12.

What was the average low temperature in Madison for that week?

14   One week in Madison the low temperatures were all negative. They were

Monday, –7; Tuesday, –8; Wednesday, –12; Thursday, –14; Friday, –15; Saturday, –18; and Sunday, –20.

What was the average low temperature in Madison that week?

15   One week in Minneapolis some low temperatures were negative and some were positive. They were

Monday, 2; Tuesday, 3; Wednesday, 0; Thursday, –4; Friday, –3; Saturday, –1; and Sunday, 3.

What was the average low temperature in Minneapolis that week?

16 Dirk sells pennants and pins at local weekend football games. His profit has been an average of $12 per game for the past four games. There will be a total of 16 weekends during the football season. If he continues to average $12 per game, how much money will he make all together?

17 Ms. Evander drove 17 miles on Monday, 23 miles on Tuesday, 0 miles on Wednesday, 53 miles on Thursday, 53 miles on Friday, 87 miles on Saturday, and 0 miles on Sunday. What was her average miles driven per day?

18 Mr. Mahaffey drives an average of 273 miles per week. Assuming he does that all year, how many miles will he drive in a year?

19 Ms. Gerber filled her car with gas on Monday morning. She then drove 56 miles on Monday, 43 miles on Tuesday, 76 miles on Wednesday, 68 miles on Thursday, and 58 miles on Friday. Then she filled the tank with 16.2 gallons of gas. What was the average number of miles she drove on a gallon of gas during that week?

20 Mr. Lewis announced that the average number of children in a family in the country of Fractonia is 2.3. Do you think this is a mean, a median, or a mode? Why?

21 Deanna ran a lawn-mowing business one summer. For the first four weeks her earnings were $10, $30, $50, and $50.

a. What were her average earnings per week?

b. Do you think she will have the same average after the next four weeks?

Choosing an Appropriate Average

Whether the mean, the median, or the mode is the best average to use depends on the situation and the information you are describing.

For each of the following situations, decide whether the mean, median, or mode is appropriate and explain why. Calculate the appropriate average in each case if the necessary information is given in the problem.

1 What is the average number of days in a month?

2 What is the average number of days in a week?

3 What is the average number of minutes you are in school each day?

4 What is the average number of students in each sixth-grade class at your school?

5 What is the average age of everyone in your classroom, including your teacher?

6 What is the average height of students in your class?

7 What is the average salary of the governors of the 50 states?

8 What is the average number of people who have voted in your town in the last five elections?

For each situation tell whether the mean, median, or mode is appropriate and explain why.

9 I own a small business and wish to find out how much I spend on salaries each month, so I want to know the average salary that is paid to my 20 employees.

10 I am considering accepting a job in a small company, so I ask what the average salary is for their employees.

11 What is my average grade on mathematics tests taken so far this term?

12 I get paid once a month. I want to calculate my average pay per week, after taxes.

13 I am trying to convince my parents to give me a greater allowance than the $7 a week I receive now. I find out the allowances my friends receive. Two of them get $6 a week, one gets $7, one gets $10, and one gets $20.

    a. What kind of average should I use to show that I should receive a greater allowance?

    b. What kind of average might my parents use to justify my current allowance?

14 I am conducting a telephone survey for the school newspaper on the average number of hours of sleep students report they get each night.

The United States is the country with the greatest number of telephones, about 143,325,000. The country with the greatest ratio of telephones to population is Sweden, with an average of 68.43 telephones for every 100 people. The United States ranks fifth, with 56.12 telephones for every 100 people.

Solving Proportions

Jing-Mei, Alex, Sam, Abby, and Sara started a lawn mowing business during summer vacation. They put their income into a special bank account and kept a record of the number of hours they worked. At the end of the summer they decided to divide the money in proportion to the number of hours each worked. They earned a total of $1230.

The table on page 325 shows how many hours each person worked:

◆   How many hours did they work all together?

To divide the money proportionally, the business partners could write equal ratios:

$$\frac{\text{hours worked}}{\text{total hours worked}} = \frac{\text{money earned}}{\text{total money earned}}$$

Two equal ratios are called a proportion. Solving a proportion means finding the missing number.

By writing and solving this proportion, each partner can compute his or her share of the money.

For instance, since Sara worked 12 out of the 100 total hours, to find Sara's share of the money, we can solve the proportion $\frac{12}{100} = \frac{n}{1230}$, where n is her share.

One way to solve for a missing term in a proportion is to find a common denominator for the two ratios. Once the denominators are the same, if the ratios are equal, the numerators must also be equal.

Example: To solve this problem we can write the fractions with a common denominator of 12,300.

◆   What should we multiply the numerator and denominator of $\frac{12}{100}$ by to get a denominator of 12,300?

◆   What should we multiply the numerator and denominator of $\frac{n}{1230}$ by to get a denominator of 12,300?

$\frac{12}{100} = \frac{1476}{12,300}$, and $\frac{n}{1230}$ means the same as $\frac{10 \times n}{12,300}$, so we say $\frac{1476}{12,300} = \frac{10 \times n}{12,300}$.

Since the fractions have the same denominator, they must also have the same numerator.

$1476 = 10 \times n$, so n must be $1476 \div 10$, which is 147.6. Sara has earned $147.60.

1. From the information in the chart calculate each person's share of the $1230.00 they accumulated in the bank account. Using a computer or other means, draw the chart and complete it.

Name	Hours Worked	Fraction of Money Earned	Dollars Earned
Jing-Mei	30		
Alex	15		
Sam	25		
Abby	18		
Sara	12		
Total			$1230.00

Solve these problems. Check that your answers make sense.

2. Was this a fair way to divide the income? Why or why not?

3. What other ways could they have used?

4. What other methods besides equal ratios could they have used to divide the money proportionally?

◆ LESSON 91 Solving Proportions

You can use proportions to solve problems involving scale drawings.
Map scales can be written as ratios.

The Amazon River in South America is about 3900 miles long. If a
drawing uses the scale 1 inch = 300 miles, how long should the drawing
of the Amazon River be?

To solve this problem we can write a proportion like this:

$$\frac{1 \text{ inch}}{300 \text{ miles}} = \frac{n}{3900 \text{ miles}}, \text{ or just } \frac{1}{300} = \frac{n}{3900}$$

◆ What is the least common multiple of 300 and 3900?

◆ By what should we multiply the numerator and denominator of $\frac{1}{300}$?

We can rewrite the proportion as $\frac{13}{3900} = \frac{n}{3900}$. Since the denominators
are equal, the numerators must be equal, so $n = 13$.
The drawing should be 13 inches long.

**How long will a diagram of the river
be if drawn to the following scales?**

⑤ 10 miles = 1 inch

⑥ 100 miles = 10 inches

⑦ 100 miles = $\frac{1}{8}$ inch

**What scale should be used to draw the
Amazon River with the following lengths?**

⑧ 6 inches

⑨ 12 inches

⑩ 15 inches

⑪ If you were drawing a map of the Amazon
River to include in a geography textbook,
what scale would you use? The page size is
$8\frac{1}{2}$ inches by 11 inches. Explain your answer.

326 • Fractions and Mixed Numbers

GEOGRAPHY CONNECTION

Do research to find the five longest rivers in the world in addition to the Amazon. Using a computer or other means, draw a chart like this one, and complete the information in the chart for each river.

Longest Rivers of the World

River	Approximate Length (miles)	Country of Source	Country of Outflow	Scale to Fit in a Standard Geography Textbook
Amazon	3900	Peru	Brazil	500 miles = 1 inch

FANTASTIC FACT

The world's highest waterfall is Angel Falls on the Carrao River in Venezuela. It has a drop of 3212 feet.

Similar Figures

Grant wants to know how tall the flag pole is. He can't climb the pole to measure it, so he decides to use the shadow of the pole to help him. He puts a small pole in the ground as vertically (or straight up) as he can. He measures the small pole from the ground to the top. It is 2 meters tall. He measures the shadow of the small pole. It is 3 meters long. Then he measures the shadow of the flag pole. It is 27 meters long. From this information he thinks he can figure out how tall the pole is.

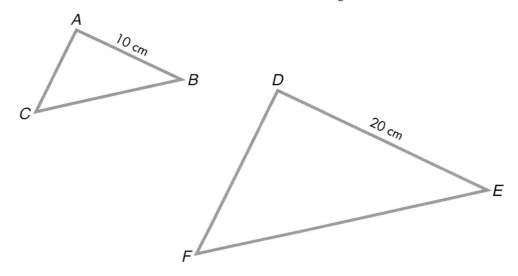

Answer these questions.

1 Can you see how he will do that? What is the height of the flag pole?

In general, if two figures are similar, the corresponding sides are in proportion.

2 The triangles shown below are similar with corresponding sides *AB* measuring 10 cm and *DE* measuring 20 cm. The measures of *AC* and *CB* are 8 cm and 13 cm. Find the lengths of *DF* and *FE*.

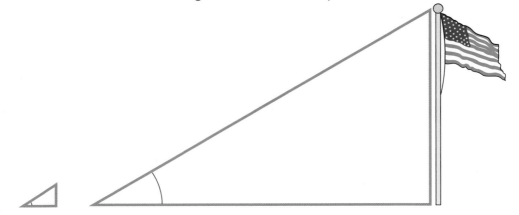

Solve these problems.

3 The three figures shown below are similar. The lengths of the sides of *ABCDE* are given in the figure as are the lengths of *GH* and *LM*. What are the lengths of the other four sides of *GHIJK* and *LMNOP*?

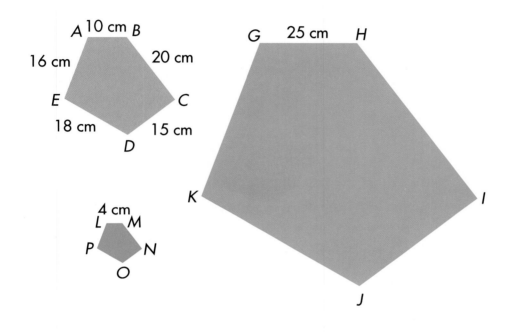

4 Alexa wants to find out how tall a certain spruce tree is. She measures the shadow of the tree. It is 60 feet. She knows that she is 5 feet tall. She measures her shadow, and it is 12 feet long. How tall is the spruce tree?

LESSON 93 Unit 4 Review

Lesson 65 Solve.

① $\frac{1}{2}$ of 30   ② $\frac{1}{4}$ of 24   ③ $\frac{1}{6}$ of 18   ④ $\frac{1}{5}$ of 20

Lesson 65 Multiply.

⑤ $\frac{1}{3} \times 24$ ⑥ $\frac{1}{6} \times 66$ ⑦ $\frac{1}{7} \times 21$ ⑧ $\frac{1}{4} \times 40$

Lesson 66 Solve these problems.

⑨ $\frac{1}{2}$ of $\frac{1}{4}$ ⑩ $\frac{3}{4}$ of $\frac{4}{15}$ ⑪ $\frac{2}{3}$ of $\frac{6}{7}$ ⑫ $\frac{3}{5}$ of $\frac{4}{5}$

Lessons 66 and 67 Multiply.

⑬ $\frac{1}{4} \times \frac{2}{9}$ ⑭ $\frac{1}{3} \times \frac{7}{11}$ ⑮ $\frac{1}{6} \times \frac{4}{5}$ ⑯ $\frac{2}{3} \times \frac{5}{7}$

Lesson 67 For each fraction write the decimal equivalent or an approximation rounded to the nearest thousandth.

⑰ $\frac{3}{8}$ ⑱ $\frac{3}{4}$ ⑲ $\frac{4}{3}$ ⑳ $1\frac{1}{9}$ ㉑ $2\frac{1}{5}$

Lessons 72 and 73 Add or subtract.

㉒ $\frac{4}{7} + \frac{2}{7}$ ㉓ $\frac{4}{7} - \frac{2}{7}$ ㉔ $\frac{2}{3} - \frac{1}{6}$ ㉕ $\frac{2}{3} + \frac{1}{6}$

㉖ $\frac{3}{8} - \frac{1}{4}$ ㉗ $\frac{3}{8} + \frac{3}{4}$ ㉘ $\frac{4}{5} - \frac{1}{2}$ ㉙ $\frac{4}{5} + \frac{1}{2}$

Lessons 79 and 80 Add or subtract. Check your answers to be sure they make sense.

㉚ $3\frac{1}{2} - 1\frac{1}{3}$ ㉛ $3\frac{1}{2} + \frac{1}{3}$ ㉜ $4\frac{1}{4} + 1\frac{2}{3}$ ㉝ $4\frac{1}{4} - 1\frac{2}{3}$

㉞ $3\frac{1}{8} + \frac{5}{8}$ ㉟ $3\frac{1}{8} - \frac{5}{8}$ ㊱ $2\frac{3}{5} + 2\frac{1}{10}$ ㊲ $2\frac{3}{5} - 2\frac{1}{10}$

Divide.

Lessons 83 and 85 ㊳ $\frac{3}{4} \div \frac{1}{3}$ ㊴ $\frac{2}{9} \div \frac{3}{5}$ ㊵ $2\frac{1}{4} \div \frac{2}{3}$ ㊶ $\frac{3}{4} \div \frac{1}{2}$

㊷ $3\frac{1}{2} \div \frac{2}{3}$ ㊸ $\frac{4}{5} \div \frac{1}{5}$ ㊹ $1\frac{3}{4} \div \frac{7}{8}$ ㊺ $5\frac{1}{3} \div 8$

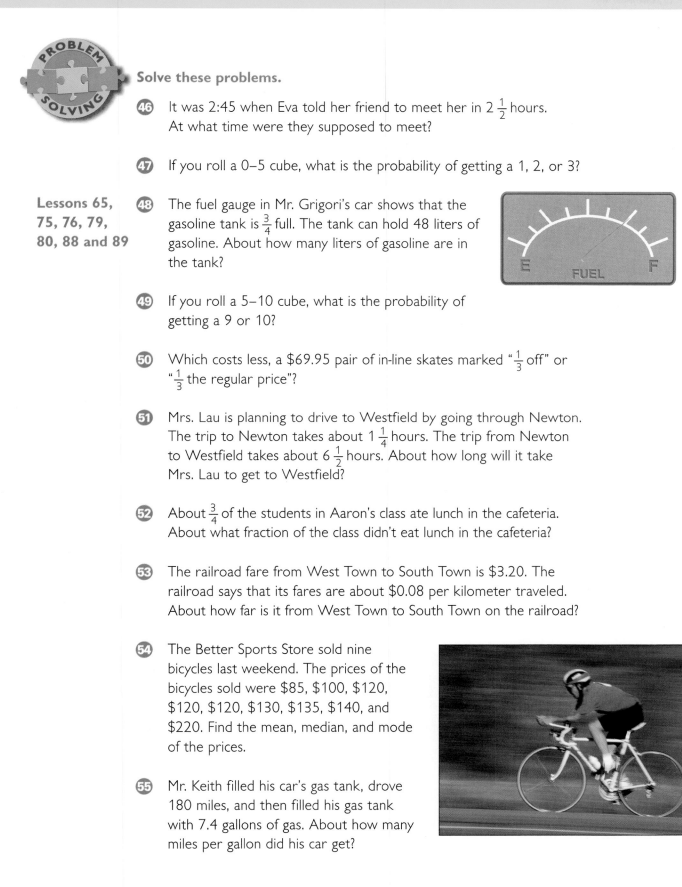

Solve these problems.

46 It was 2:45 when Eva told her friend to meet her in $2\frac{1}{2}$ hours. At what time were they supposed to meet?

47 If you roll a 0–5 cube, what is the probability of getting a 1, 2, or 3?

Lessons 65, 75, 76, 79, 80, 88 and 89

48 The fuel gauge in Mr. Grigori's car shows that the gasoline tank is $\frac{3}{4}$ full. The tank can hold 48 liters of gasoline. About how many liters of gasoline are in the tank?

E   FUEL   F

49 If you roll a 5–10 cube, what is the probability of getting a 9 or 10?

50 Which costs less, a $69.95 pair of in-line skates marked "$\frac{1}{3}$ off" or "$\frac{1}{3}$ the regular price"?

51 Mrs. Lau is planning to drive to Westfield by going through Newton. The trip to Newton takes about $1\frac{1}{4}$ hours. The trip from Newton to Westfield takes about $6\frac{1}{2}$ hours. About how long will it take Mrs. Lau to get to Westfield?

52 About $\frac{3}{4}$ of the students in Aaron's class ate lunch in the cafeteria. About what fraction of the class didn't eat lunch in the cafeteria?

53 The railroad fare from West Town to South Town is $3.20. The railroad says that its fares are about $0.08 per kilometer traveled. About how far is it from West Town to South Town on the railroad?

54 The Better Sports Store sold nine bicycles last weekend. The prices of the bicycles sold were $85, $100, $120, $120, $120, $130, $135, $140, and $220. Find the mean, median, and mode of the prices.

55 Mr. Keith filled his car's gas tank, drove 180 miles, and then filled his gas tank with 7.4 gallons of gas. About how many miles per gallon did his car get?

LESSON 94

Unit 4 Practice

Lesson 65

Solve.

1. $\frac{1}{3}$ of 12
2. $\frac{2}{3}$ of 12
3. $\frac{1}{4}$ of 12
4. $\frac{3}{4}$ of 12

5. $\frac{1}{7}$ of 28
6. $\frac{1}{8}$ of 72
7. $\frac{3}{8}$ of 72
8. $\frac{2}{8}$ of 72

9. $\frac{1}{4}$ of 72
10. $\frac{1}{5}$ of 60
11. $\frac{3}{4}$ of 60
12. $\frac{4}{4}$ of 60

13. $\frac{1}{2}$ of 60
14. $\frac{2}{2}$ of 60
15. $\frac{1}{9}$ of 72
16. $\frac{3}{4}$ of 100

17. $\frac{1}{5}$ of 100
18. $\frac{3}{5}$ of 100
19. $\frac{1}{10}$ of 100
20. $\frac{3}{10}$ of 100

Lesson 65

Multiply.

21. $\frac{3}{7} \times 28$
22. $\frac{6}{7} \times 28$
23. $\frac{1}{5} \times 35$
24. $\frac{2}{5} \times 35$

25. $\frac{4}{5} \times 35$
26. $\frac{3}{5} \times 60$
27. $\frac{1}{3} \times 60$
28. $\frac{2}{3} \times 60$

29. $\frac{1}{4} \times 60$
30. $\frac{2}{4} \times 60$
31. $\frac{2}{9} \times 72$
32. $\frac{5}{9} \times 72$

33. $\frac{8}{9} \times 72$
34. $\frac{9}{9} \times 72$
35. $\frac{1}{4} \times 100$
36. $\frac{7}{10} \times 100$

37. $\frac{9}{10} \times 100$
38. $\frac{1}{2} \times 100$
39. $\frac{2}{2} \times 100$
40. $\frac{10}{10} \times 100$

Lesson 65

Solve.

41. $\frac{1}{2}$ of 10
42. $\frac{1}{4}$ of 12
43. $\frac{3}{4}$ of 16
44. $\frac{1}{3}$ of 30

45. $\frac{2}{3}$ of 30
46. $\frac{3}{5}$ of 50
47. $\frac{7}{10}$ of 100
48. $\frac{1}{8}$ of 80

49. $\frac{3}{8}$ of 24
50. $\frac{1}{7}$ of 14
51. $\frac{1}{6}$ of 36
52. $\frac{1}{9}$ of 72

53. $\frac{2}{9}$ of 72
54. $\frac{3}{9}$ of 72
55. $\frac{4}{9}$ of 72
56. $\frac{2}{3}$ of 45

Lessons 66 and 70

Multiply.

57. $\frac{3}{7} \times \frac{1}{3}$
58. $\frac{1}{3} \times \frac{2}{5}$
59. $\frac{1}{2} \times \frac{3}{4}$
60. $\frac{1}{3} \times \frac{2}{9}$

61. $\frac{1}{6} \times \frac{1}{3}$
62. $\frac{1}{7} \times \frac{1}{2}$
63. $\frac{2}{7} \times \frac{1}{2}$
64. $\frac{3}{5} \times \frac{1}{4}$

65. $\frac{4}{5} \times \frac{1}{4}$
66. $\frac{5}{9} \times \frac{3}{10}$
67. $\frac{2}{3} \times \frac{5}{7}$
68. $\frac{1}{2} \times \frac{3}{8}$

Lesson 67

Write the decimal equivalent or an approximation to the nearest thousandth.

69 $\frac{1}{5}$ **70** $\frac{2}{5}$ **71** $\frac{4}{5}$ **72** $\frac{1}{2}$ **73** $\frac{1}{4}$

74 $\frac{1}{3}$ **75** $\frac{3}{6}$ **76** $\frac{4}{6}$ **77** $\frac{2}{3}$ **78** $\frac{5}{6}$

79 $\frac{3}{8}$ **80** $\frac{4}{8}$ **81** $\frac{5}{8}$ **82** $\frac{7}{8}$ **83** $\frac{7}{9}$

84 $\frac{1}{9}$ **85** $\frac{2}{9}$ **86** $\frac{3}{9}$ **87** $\frac{4}{9}$ **88** $\frac{5}{9}$

Lessons 72, 73, 79, and 80

Add or subtract.

89 $\frac{3}{5} + \frac{1}{5}$ **90** $\frac{3}{5} - \frac{1}{5}$ **91** $\frac{5}{7} + \frac{3}{7}$ **92** $\frac{5}{7} - \frac{3}{7}$

93 $\frac{4}{9} + \frac{7}{9}$ **94** $\frac{11}{12} - \frac{5}{12}$ **95** $\frac{1}{4} + \frac{1}{3}$ **96** $1\frac{1}{4} + 2\frac{1}{3}$

97 $\frac{3}{5} - \frac{1}{2}$ **98** $3\frac{3}{5} - 2\frac{1}{2}$ **99** $2\frac{2}{3} + 1\frac{1}{6}$ **100** $1\frac{1}{4} + 2\frac{3}{8}$

101 $3\frac{3}{4} - 1\frac{2}{3}$ **102** $10\frac{1}{2} + 5\frac{3}{4}$ **103** $11\frac{2}{5} - 9\frac{5}{6}$ **104** $6\frac{1}{4} - 3\frac{7}{8}$

Lessons 66, 69, 79, 80, 83, and 85

Multiply or divide. Give answers in the form of proper fractions or mixed numbers. Reduce if possible.

105 $\frac{1}{6} \times \frac{1}{5}$ **106** $\frac{1}{3} \times \frac{1}{2}$ **107** $\frac{1}{6} \div \frac{1}{2}$ **108** $\frac{3}{4} \times \frac{2}{3}$

109 $\frac{2}{3} \times \frac{3}{4}$ **110** $\frac{5}{6} \div \frac{1}{6}$ **111** $1\frac{5}{6} \div \frac{1}{6}$ **112** $1\frac{1}{2} \div \frac{1}{2}$

113 $1\frac{1}{2} \div \frac{2}{3}$ **114** $2\frac{3}{4} \times \frac{4}{5}$ **115** $1\frac{1}{3} \times 1\frac{1}{3}$ **116** $2\frac{7}{8} \div 1\frac{1}{4}$

117 $\frac{3}{7} \div 2\frac{1}{3}$ **118** $2\frac{1}{2} \times 2\frac{1}{2}$ **119** $3\frac{1}{3} \div 3\frac{1}{3}$ **120** $2\frac{1}{4} \div 3$

◆ **LESSON 94** **Unit 4 Practice**

Lessons 65, 75, 76, 79, 80, 88 and 89

Solve these problems.

121 Bob's Bargain Store is having a sale in which every item in the store is $\frac{1}{3}$ off the regular price. What is the sale price of each of these items?

    a. Radio—regular price $18

    b. Coat—regular price $66

    c. Baseball cap—regular price $9.99

122 Nina's club has a rule that at least $\frac{2}{3}$ of the members must be present for a vote. Of the 24 members, 20 of them were present.

    a. Is that enough for a vote?

    b. What is the fewest number of members that can be there for a vote?

123 Brian's scores on his last ten spelling tests were 90, 90, 90, 95, 90, 80, 90, 90, 100, and 90.

    a. Find the mean, median, and mode of his scores.

    b. What type of average best reflects Brian's performance in spelling?

124 Ms. Sloan is driving from Arkville to Zooport, a distance of 260 kilometers. When she starts, the odometer in her car shows 35,640.4 kilometers.

    a. About what will the odometer show when Ms. Sloan is about halfway there?

    b. About what will the odometer show when she returns to Arkville (she takes a direct route each way)?

    c. When Ms. Sloan left Arkville, the fuel gauge showed that her gasoline tank was $\frac{3}{4}$ full. When she arrived at Zooport, the tank was $\frac{1}{4}$ full. Does she have enough gasoline to get back to Arkville?

125 If you roll a 5–10 cube, what is the probability of rolling a

    a. 7?   **b.** 5?

    c. 7 or a 5?   **d.** one-digit number?

    e. two-digit number?   **f.** number greater than 6?

    g. number less than 7?   **h.** 7 or less?

Inverso Game

Players: One or more
Materials: One calculator for each player
Object: To get as close to the goal of 1 as you can
Math Focus: Using a calculator and approximating the reciprocal of numbers

RULES

1. Enter any multidigit number on the calculator.

2. Push ×.

3. Enter a decimal number less than 1 (you are trying to get a product close to 1).

4. Push =. How close to 1 did you get?

SAMPLE GAME

Renata entered 56,234 by pushing 5 6 2 3 4. Then she pushed ×.

She thought, "What number times 56,234 will be about 1?"

She entered 0.00002 by pushing . 0 0 0 0 2.
Then she pushed =, and the display showed 1.12468.
"That's not bad for a first try," she said.

OTHER WAYS TO PLAY THIS GAME

1. Start over. Enter 0.00002 × 56,234. After pushing =, push ×, enter another number (trying to get even closer to 1), and push =. Keep doing this to see if you can get 1 exactly or get very close.

2. Play "Inverso" with a partner. You enter a number, and then your partner tries to get as close to 1 as possible with one multiplication. Then reverse roles. Whoever gets closer to 1 wins that round.

3. Choose other goals instead of 1.

Unit Test

Solve.

1 $\frac{1}{2}$ of 24   **2** $\frac{1}{4}$ of 20   **3** $\frac{1}{6}$ of 24   **4** $\frac{1}{3}$ of 12

Multiply.

5 $\frac{1}{9} \times 27$ **6** $\frac{1}{3} \times 18$ **7** $\frac{1}{4} \times 12$ **8** $\frac{1}{5} \times 25$

Solve.

9 $\frac{1}{3}$ of $\frac{3}{7}$ **10** $\frac{1}{6}$ of $\frac{5}{6}$ **11** $\frac{1}{7}$ of $\frac{3}{4}$ **12** $\frac{2}{3}$ of $\frac{2}{3}$

Multiply.

13 $\frac{1}{4} \times \frac{2}{7}$ **14** $\frac{1}{3} \times \frac{2}{3}$ **15** $\frac{1}{5} \times \frac{3}{4}$ **16** $\frac{3}{5} \times \frac{1}{3}$

For each fraction write the decimal equivalent or an approximation rounded to the nearest thousandth.

17 $\frac{1}{7}$ **18** $\frac{5}{8}$ **19** $1\frac{1}{4}$ **20** $\frac{5}{3}$ **21** $2\frac{4}{9}$

Add or subtract.

22 $\frac{3}{5} + \frac{1}{5}$ **23** $\frac{3}{5} - \frac{1}{5}$ **24** $\frac{3}{4} - \frac{3}{8}$ **25** $\frac{3}{4} + \frac{3}{8}$

26 $\frac{5}{6} - \frac{1}{3}$ **27** $\frac{5}{6} + \frac{2}{3}$ **28** $\frac{9}{10} + \frac{4}{5}$ **29** $\frac{9}{10} - \frac{4}{5}$

Add or subtract. Check your answers to be sure they make sense.

30 $2\frac{1}{4} - 1\frac{1}{8}$ **31** $2\frac{1}{4} + 1\frac{1}{8}$ **32** $3\frac{1}{3} - 1\frac{5}{6}$ **33** $4\frac{1}{3} + 1\frac{5}{6}$

34 $3\frac{1}{5} + \frac{3}{10}$ **35** $3\frac{1}{5} - \frac{3}{10}$ **36** $2\frac{3}{4} + 4\frac{1}{3}$ **37** $5\frac{1}{2} - 2\frac{5}{8}$

Divide.

38 $\frac{2}{3} \div \frac{5}{6}$ **39** $\frac{1}{3} \div \frac{2}{3}$ **40** $2\frac{2}{9} \div \frac{1}{6}$ **41** $4\frac{1}{2} \div \frac{3}{4}$

42 $3\frac{3}{8} \div 2\frac{1}{4}$ **43** $3 \div \frac{4}{7}$ **44** $\frac{1}{35} \div \frac{1}{5}$ **45** $1\frac{1}{5} \div 1\frac{1}{2}$

ASSESSMENT

Solve these problems.

46 The fuel gauge in Mrs. Miller's car shows that the gasoline tank is $\frac{1}{4}$ full. The tank can hold 72 liters of gasoline. About how many liters of gasoline are in the tank?

47 It was 1:30 when Elia told his friend to meet him in $3\frac{1}{4}$ hours. At what time were they supposed to meet?

48 If you roll a 0–5 cube, what is the probability of getting a 2 or a 3?

49 If you roll a 5–10 cube, what is the probability of getting a 9?

50 The railroad fare from Northfield to Eastland is $5.40. The railroad says its fares are about $0.09 per kilometer traveled. About how far is it from Northfield to Eastland on the railroad?

51 Which costs less, a $25.00 basketball marked "$\frac{2}{3}$ off" or "$\frac{2}{3}$ the regular price"?

52 Mr. Waneta is planning to drive from Blueville to Greenfield by going through Endtown. The trip to Endtown takes about $11\frac{1}{4}$ hours. The trip from Endtown to Greenfield takes about $2\frac{1}{2}$ hours. About how long will it take Mr. Waneta to get to Greenfield?

53 About $\frac{7}{8}$ of the students in Bill's class walk to school. About what fraction of the class doesn't walk to school?

54 The high temperatures in Tepidtown last week were 18°C, 15°C, 17°C, 18°C, 17°C, 16°C, and 18°C. Find the mean, median, and mode of these temperatures.

55 In four hours of fishing Wyn caught six fish. How many fish did she average per hour?

Unit 4 Test • **337**

FAIR ADVERTISING

Work in groups to study and discuss these advertisements.
Write what is fair about them. Write what is unfair about them.

BUY SUPER DUPER POTATO CHIPS

WE GUARANTEE THAT THEY WILL STAY CRISP FOR UP TO 5 YEARS.

6 OUNCE BAG . . . .
ONLY! **50¢**

BUY SUPER COLA

REGULAR PRICE IS $1.29.

NOW FOR
A LIMITED TIME!

ONE LITER BOTTLE . . . **89¢**

ONLY ONE BOTTLE PER CUSTOMER. OFFER GOOD IF YOU PURCHASE $50.00 WORTH OF GROCERIES.
OFFER GOOD ON SATURDAY ONLY.

Find advertisements in the newspaper. Work in cooperative groups to decide which are fair and which are not fair.

Make three scrap albums: one for the fair advertisements, one for those that are not fair, and one for those of which you are not sure.

UNIT 5

Algebra Readiness

UNDERSTANDING VARIABLES

- graphs—double bar, multiple line, and circle

- graphing ordered pairs and function rules

- graphing negative numbers

- graphing linear and nonlinear functions

Government workers use math . . .

Government workers use graphs all the time. Part of their job is to gather information about the national population. This information includes the number of people per household, how many are employed, how many are looking for work, how many are homeless, and so on. Information is sorted, graphed, and analyzed.

LESSON 95

Creating a Graph

Ethan was doing seed germination experiments. This table shows the data he recorded for one of his experiments.

SCIENCE CONNECTION

Day	Percent Germination
1	0
2	4
3	24
4	40
5	10
6	2
7	0
8	0

To show the results of his work, Ethan decided to make a graph.

◆ Which of these graphs better shows the results of Ethan's experiment? Explain your answer.

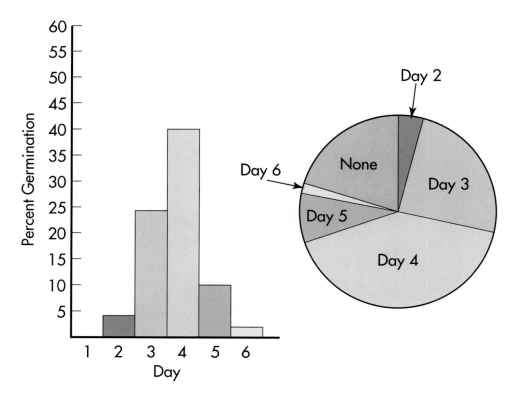

A group of students decided to study the Scrumptious Ice Cream Parlor to see which of the five flavors of ice cream the store offered sold the best. The students spent all day in the store and recorded their results in the chart.

Flavor	Percent of Ice Cream Sold
Vanilla	50
Chocolate	30
Strawberry	13
Raspberry	5
Pistachio	2

To show their results, the students decided to make a graph.

◆ Which of these graphs better shows the results of the survey? Explain your answer.

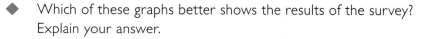

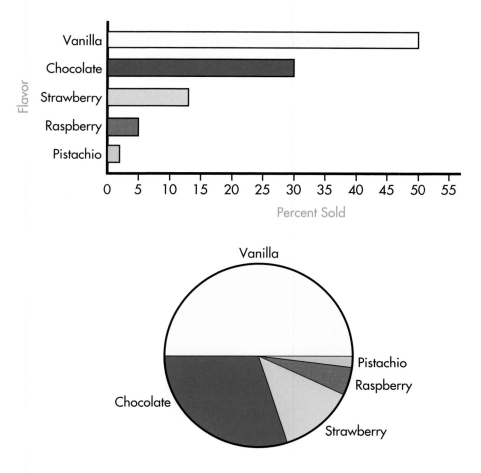

◆ LESSON 95   Creating a Graph

How much time do students in your school watch television each week? Take a survey.

Before beginning the survey, think about the following questions. Be prepared to explain your choices.

1 About how many students are in your school?

2 About how many students must you ask to be reasonably certain that your data is meaningful?

3 About how many students must be asked from each grade?

4 Should you do a separate survey for each grade?

5 Should you ask questions orally, or should you prepare a written survey?

6 What results do you expect to find?

7 Conduct a survey keeping in mind the decisions you made in the above problems. Copy and complete the chart on page 345.

8 Decide which kind of graph is most meaningful for your data.

9 Graph your results. Consider using graphing software.

10 Are you surprised at the results of your survey? Why or why not?

11 Do you think the results would be similar if you asked how much time students spent reading? Why or why not?

The first U.S. President to appear on television was Franklin Roosevelt, who was seen opening the New York World's Fair on April 30, 1939.

Use a computer or other means to draw and complete a chart from the information you collected.

Hours each week watching television	Number of students	Percentage of students
between 0 and 4		
between 4 and 8		
between 8 and 12		
between 12 and 16		
between 16 and 20		
between 20 and 24		
between 24 and 28		
more than 28		

One way to find the percentage of students in each category is to express the number of students out of the total number as a fraction, and then convert the fraction to a decimal and the decimal to a percent.

For example, suppose five of the 45 sixth graders you surveyed say they watch between 12 and 16 hours of television each week.

Write the fraction $\frac{5}{45}$.

Convert the fraction to a decimal. 5 ÷ 45 is about 0.111.

To change the decimal to a percent, multiply by 100.

0.111 × 100 = 11.1

So about 11.1% of the students surveyed said they watch between 12 and 16 hours of television each week.

Interpreting a Graph

Long-playing record albums were first successfully introduced in 1948 and dominated music sales for several decades. Compact disc players were introduced in 1983.

This graph shows the sales of record albums and compact discs each year from 1984 through 1994.

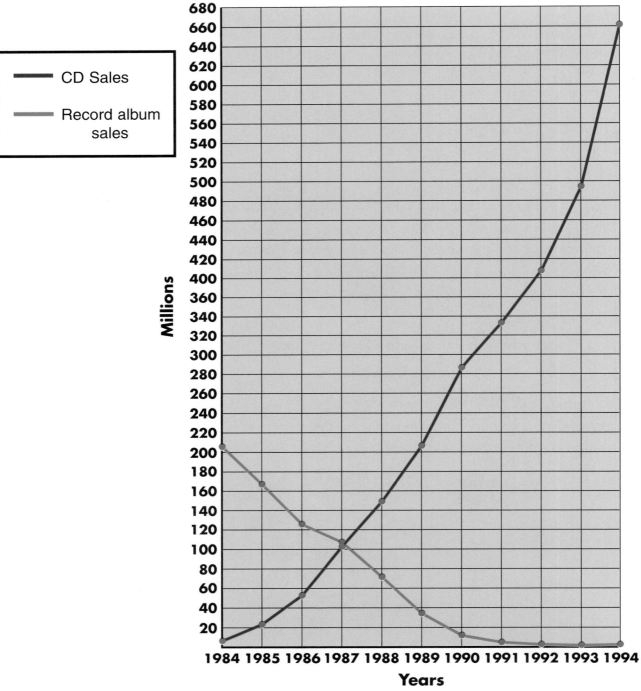

Answer the following questions about the graph.

1 About how many more record albums than CDs were sold in 1984?

2 About how many more CDs than record albums were sold in 1994?

3 In what year did CD sales first exceed record album sales?

4 How do you account for the shapes of the two graphs?

5 What would you predict about the difference in record album and CD sales in 2004?

6 Do you think CD sales will ever decline like record album sales did? Why or why not?

7 If a line for cassette sales was added to this graph, what do you think it would look like?

8 In what other ways could this data have been presented?

9 Do you think this kind of graph was the best way to present this data? Why or why not?

10 Think of two other measures that would be interesting to compare over a period of years. Collect data and display it in an appropriate graph.

Misleading Graphs

Aaron took over his father's company in 1993. In 1995 he published the graph shown below to show how the profits had increased over the years he had been running the company.

1 Approximately what were the profits for each of the years 1993, 1994, and 1995?

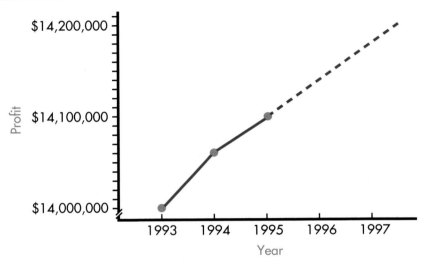

In the year 1997 Aaron published the graph shown below to show there had been very little change in the profits of the company since he took over.

2 Approximately what were the profits for each of the years 1993 through 1997?

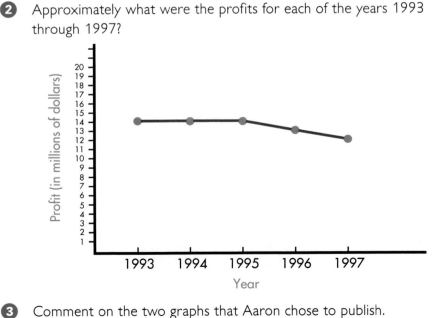

3 Comment on the two graphs that Aaron chose to publish. Which one do you think is more honest? Why?

4 In the first graph above, what do you think the dotted line indicates?

The Serious Cereal Company hired new management in 1993. In 1997 the management published the following picture graph to show how much sales had increased.

5 What, approximately, was the total number of boxes sold in 1993 and 1997?

6 With just a quick look, does it seem to you that the sales had more than doubled? Why do you suppose that is?

Think about two boxes. One is twice as long in each dimension as the other.

7 How many of the small boxes would fit in the big one? Discuss this with your classmates. Could you fit four of the small boxes in a front layer inside the larger box? Could you also fit four boxes in a back layer?

8 Picture graphs can be misleading. What do you think might be a clearer way for the Serious Cereal Company to use picture graphs without making people think that the sales had been multiplied by 8 instead of 2?

LESSON

98

ACT IT OUT

Organizing Data

Is Business Booming?

Jeremy dropped a handful of small pieces of paper on the table.

"What are you doing?" Lydia asked.

"I want to see how my dog-walking business is doing," Jeremy said. "Each week since I started my business, I have written down on a slip of paper how much money I made that week. These are my business records."

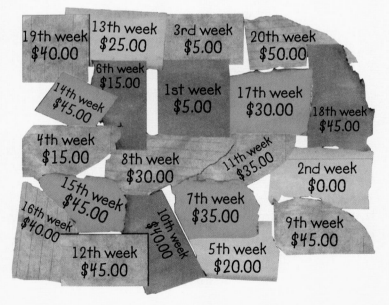

◆ Can you tell from Jeremy's records how well his business is doing?

"All these slips of paper are confusing," said Lydia. "I think you ought to put your records in order. I'll help you if you like."

"Sure," Jeremy said. "Let's get started."

They put the slips in order, with the first week first, the second week second, and so on. Then they made a chart for all the information.

Week	Profit	Week	Profit
1	$5.00	11	35.00
2	0.00	12	45.00
3	5.00	13	25.00
4	15.00	14	45.00
5	20.00	15	45.00
6	15.00	16	40.00
7	35.00	17	30.00
8	30.00	18	45.00
9	45.00	19	40.00
10	40.00	20	50.00

"Look!" said Jeremy. "On the 20th week I hit an all-time high profit of $50.00. That's $10.00 better than the week before—a 25% increase in one week. My business is booming!"

◆ Is this chart a better way to keep records than the slips of paper Jeremy was using?

Do you agree with Jeremy that his business is booming? Why or why not? Explain your answer in your Math Journal.

◆ LESSON 98 Organizing Data

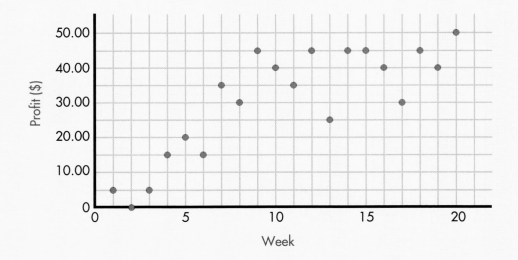

"I'm not so sure that your business is booming," Lydia told Jeremy. "It may not even be growing anymore."

"I don't understand," said Jeremy. "What's wrong with my figures?"

"Nothing," said Lydia. "But let's make a picture of the information. Maybe a graph will help us see more clearly how your business is doing."

"OK," said Jeremy. Then he and Lydia made a graph like this one.

◆ Does the graph make it easier to see how Jeremy's business is doing?

◆ How do you think Jeremy's business is doing?

We use graphs to help organize, understand, and interpret information.

To locate (or plot) a **point** corresponding to a pair of numbers on a graph, we start at the origin and go right as many steps as the first number shows, and then up as many steps as the second number shows.

Example   Plot the point (2, 5). Start at the origin (0, 0).

Go two steps to the right.   Go five steps up.

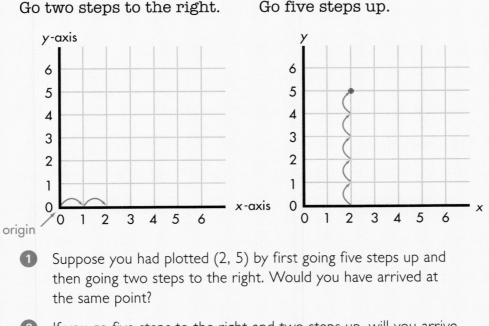

1. Suppose you had plotted (2, 5) by first going five steps up and then going two steps to the right. Would you have arrived at the same point?

2. If you go five steps to the right and two steps up, will you arrive at the same point?

3. Are the points (2, 5) and (5, 2) the same?

4. On a sheet of graph paper draw coordinate **axes** (an x-axis and a y-axis). Plot and label the points (2, 5) and (5, 2).

Ordered Pairs and Function Rules

ALGEBRA READINESS

An **ordered pair** of numbers is a pair of numbers in which order is important. Ordered pairs can occur in many ways.

Dates, for example, are often given by listing the number of the month and then the day of the month. The two numbers are usually separated with a slash mark. So 3/25 would mean March 25. Many people do this in reverse. To them, 25/3 would mean the 25th of March.

1 Tell what date each of these might mean.

    a. 3/20   **b.** 15/6   **c.** 13/12   **d.** 12/13

    e. 12/12   **f.** 11/12   **g.** 6/10   **h.** 26/5

The pair of numbers that tells the location of a point on a graph is an ordered pair, because order is important in graphing. For example, (2, 5) and (5, 2) are ordered pairs for different points. We call the pair of numbers that tells the location of a point on a graph the **coordinates** of that point.

2 Write the coordinates for each of these points: O, A, B, C, D, E, and F.

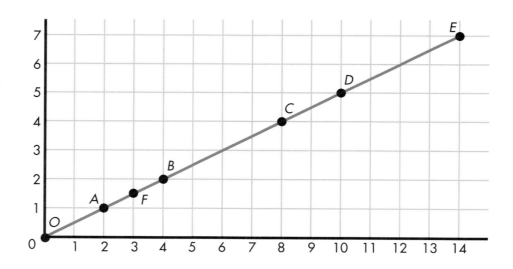

A **function rule** can be used to generate ordered pairs. For example, the rule x —⊗3⟶ y can be used to generate ordered pairs in this way:

A. Choose a number. For example, 2.

B. Multiply it by 3. $2 \times 3 = 6$

C. Write the ordered pair. The first number, or input, is the number chosen; the second number, or output, is three times that number: (2, 6).

3 Choose four more numbers. Use each number to make an ordered pair from the rule x —⊗3⟶ y. (Use x as the first number and y as the second.)

4 Can you think of a function rule that could be used to generate the ordered pairs for the points O, A, B, C, D, E, and F on page 354?

For each of the function rules in problems 5–10, make a set of five ordered pairs of numbers. (Use the number you choose for x as the input and the corresponding value of y as the output.)

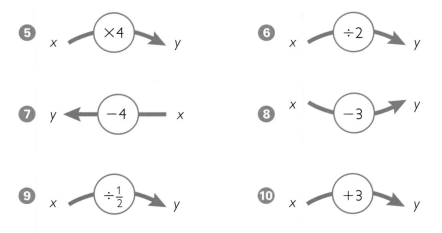

11 Graph each set of ordered pairs that you made for problems 5–10. Compare your graph with those made by others in the class.

◆ Did you all plot the same points?

◆ In what way are your graphs similar?

Translation, Rotation, Reflection, and Symmetry

Two figures are **congruent** if we can fit one exactly on top of the other, or if we can imagine doing so. We can show that two figures are congruent by describing what we would have to do to fit them on top of each other.

One method of moving a figure to see if it fits on top of another is called **translation.** In a translation we simply move one figure in a straight line until it fits exactly on the other one.

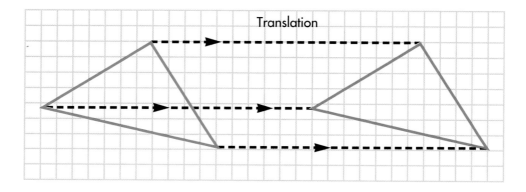

Another method of moving a figure to see if it fits on top of another is to turn the figure in a circle around a point. In the **rotation** shown here, what is the point around which the figure is being rotated?

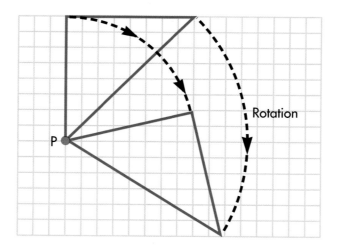

Sometimes figures look exactly alike, but one is a mirror image of the other. In this case we would have to flip one of the images over to make them fit. You can imagine cutting a triangle out of a sheet of paper and flipping it in order to make it fit on another. We can also show that two images would fit on each other by using a mirror and showing that one looks just like the other when it is reflected in a mirror. In the figure below the two triangles are mirror images of each other.

◆ Where would you put the mirror to show this?

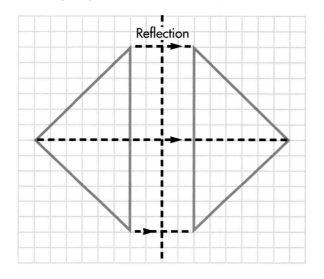

We say that a figure has a **line of symmetry** if there is a line that could be drawn so the figure looks the same on one side as on the other. Or we could place a mirror on the line and the figure looks the same with the mirror as without it.

◆ **LESSON 100** Translation, Rotation, Reflection, and Symmetry

Answer these questions.

1 Which of the motions described in the previous two pages reminds you of a sled ride?

2 Which of the motions reminds you of a merry-go-round ride?

3 Which reminds you of folding a sheet of paper to make a paper airplane?

4 When you see a photograph of yourself, do you look different from the way you look in the mirror? Why do you suppose that is?

5 Think about the world around you. Describe five actions that might reasonably remind somebody of a translation.

6 Describe five actions or activities that might reasonably remind somebody of a rotation.

7 Describe five objects or actions that might reasonably remind somebody of a reflection.

8 List five objects in your classroom that have lines of symmetry.

For each of the following figures, tell how many lines of symmetry the figure has.

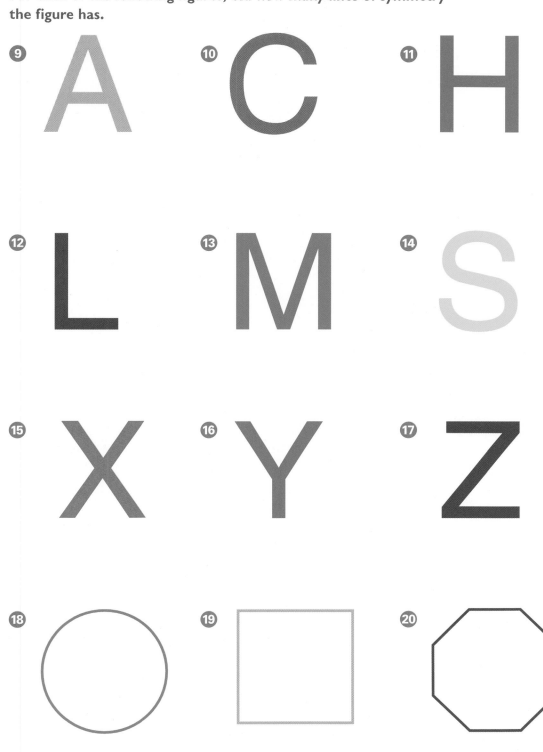

9. A

10. C

11. H

12. L

13. M

14. S

15. X

16. Y

17. Z

18. (circle)

19. (square)

20. (octagon)

◆ **LESSON 100 Translation, Rotation, Reflection, and Symmetry**

It is always possible to move one figure to another congruent figure in the same plane by translations, rotations, and reflections. For example, we can move triangle *ABC* so it is on top of triangle *DEF* by translating the figure so that *A* fits on top of *D*. Then rotate the translated triangle around point *D* until *B* fits on top of *E* and *C* fits on top of *F*.

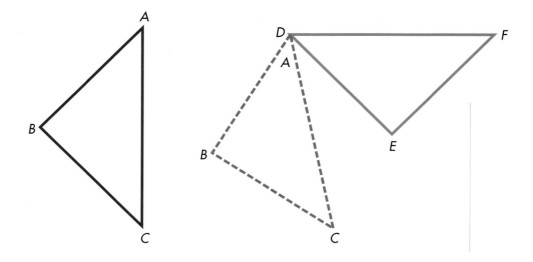

In the example below, we must first reflect trapezoid *GHIJ*. We can then move the reflected trapezoid *GHIJ* so it is on top of trapezoid *KLMN*. Reflect the figure so that *I* fits on top of *L*. Then rotate the trapezoid around point *L* until *H* is on top of *M*, *G* is on top of *N*, and *J* is on top of *K*.

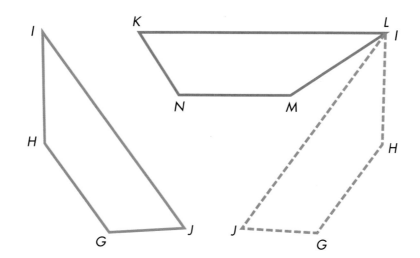

Describe how you could use translations, rotations, and reflections to move one of the figures in each problem to be on top of the other.

㉑

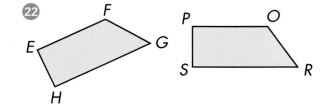

㉒

㉓

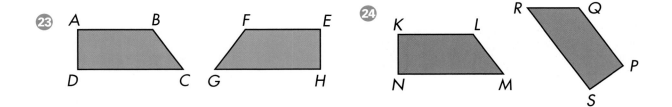

㉔

㉕

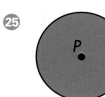

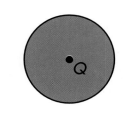

㉖

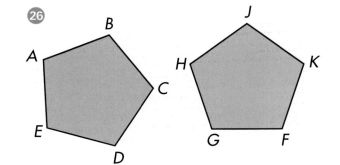

Graphing Functions

A function expresses a relationship between two numbers. We often call these numbers x and y.

If we can use the first number in an ordered pair as x in a function rule and get the second number as y, then we say the ordered pair (x, y) satisfies the function rule.

ALGEBRA READINESS

Examples: Does the ordered pair (2, 6) satisfy the function rule

x —$\boxed{\times 3}$→ y?

Use the first number as x. 2 —$\boxed{\times 3}$→ y

Do you get the second number for y? 2 —$\boxed{\times 3}$→ 6

Yes. So (2, 6) satisfies the function rule
x —$\boxed{\times 3}$→ y.

Does the ordered pair (4, 8) satisfy the function rule

x —$\boxed{\times 3}$→ y? 4 —$\boxed{\times 3}$→ 12

No, (4, 8) does not satisfy the function
rule x —$\boxed{\times 3}$→ y.

1 Which of these ordered pairs will satisfy the function rule x —$\boxed{\times 3}$→y?

    a. (8, 24)   **b.** (1.5, 4.5)   **c.** (7, 20)   **d.** $(2\frac{1}{2}, 6\frac{1}{2})$

2 Which of these ordered pairs will satisfy the function rule x —$\boxed{-7}$→y?

    a. (10, 7)   **b.** (20, 13)   **c.** (9.3, 2.3)   **d.** $(8\frac{1}{4}, 1\frac{3}{4})$

Copy each ordered pair. Replace x or y with the correct number so that the pair satisfies the rule x —$\boxed{\times 3}$→ y.

3 (3, y)   **4** (1, y)   **5** (0, y)   **6** (2, y)

7 (2.4, y)   **8** (0.1, y)   **9** (0.6, y)   **10** (3.5, y)

11 (1.4, y)   **12** (1.7, y)   **13** (0.4, y)   **14** (0.8, y)

15 (1.1, y)   **16** (2.7, y)   **17** (3.2, y)   **18** (x, 9)

19 (x, 11.1)   **20** (x, 12)   **21** (x, 13.2)   **22** (x, 15)

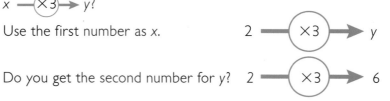

We often graph functions to help us see and understand some of their characteristics.

To graph the function that has the rule

x —(×3)→ y, we could find all

ordered pairs that satisfy this rule and then graph them. Of course, we can't find all the ordered pairs. But we should be able to decide where they would be by plotting a few of them and thinking about the pattern.

On a sheet of graph paper, draw coordinate axes like the ones shown here. Graph the 20 ordered pairs you found for

x —(×3)→ y when you did

problems 3–22 on page 362. We have plotted (2.4, 7.2) for you to show you how to plot ordered pairs with decimals.

To plot (2.4, 7.2), start at the origin, move 2.4 steps to the right and 7.2 steps up. (Estimate the tenths as best you can. Use a millimeter ruler if it helps.)

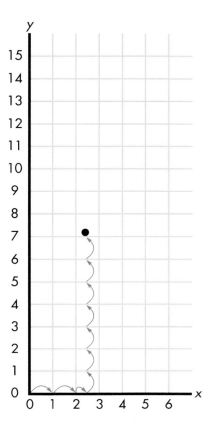

◆ How can you estimate 2.4 steps?

◆ Do you notice anything interesting about the points you graphed?

◆ If you graphed the point (107, 321), do you think it would be on the same **line** as the other points?

◆ Can you think of a point that satisfies the rule x —(×3)→ y that wouldn't be on the line?

◆ How many points of a line do you need to know to decide where the line goes?

Graph these functions.

23 x —(÷2)→ y 24 x —(−3)→ y

25 x —(×2)→ y 26 x —(+7)→ y

Graphing Data

Often it is difficult to tell whether information that is collected or presented in no particular order fits into any pattern. As we saw in Lesson 98, it is usually helpful to organize data in order to draw conclusions.

Captain Sanchez of Allaway Airlines likes to keep records of how much weight was on board his airplane and how many passengers he had for each trip. The passengers and their luggage and all other freight are weighed before each flight. He calls this the "carried weight." After 12 flights Captain Sanchez had these records:

Flight Number	1	2	3	4	5	6
Number of Passengers	9	22	4	11	15	17
Carried Weight (pounds)	1569	3826	739	1936	2631	2994

Flight Number	7	8	9	10	11	12
Number of Passengers	11	5	14	2	9	24
Carried Weight (pounds)	1923	917	2468	385	1597	4198

On the 13th flight somebody forgot to weigh the passengers, luggage, and other freight. Captain Sanchez knew there were 20 passengers. He wanted to know the approximate weight of passengers, luggage, and freight.

◆ How could he estimate the weight?

Captain Sanchez knew that his plane should not have more than 5500 pounds in carried weight.

◆ How could he estimate how many passengers could be carried without going above the 5500-pound limit?

364 • Algebra Readiness

Solve these problems.

1 Draw a graph of the information from Captain Sanchez's records. Use a full sheet of graph paper. Draw and label your axes as shown here. The point for the first flight (9, 1569) is already plotted.

◆ How can you use your graph to help answer the questions on page 364?

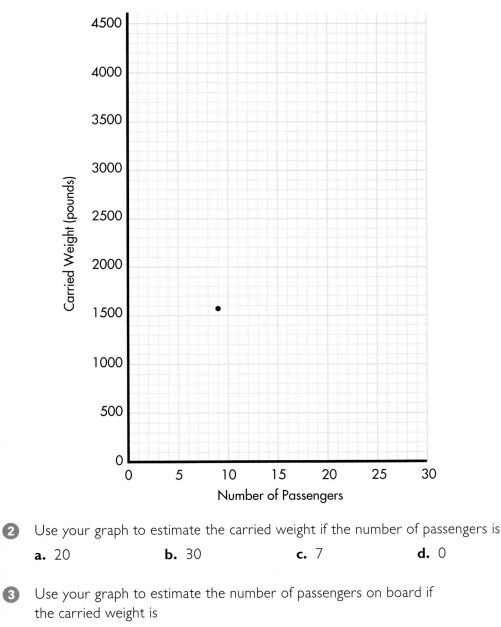

2 Use your graph to estimate the carried weight if the number of passengers is

a. 20 **b.** 30 **c.** 7 **d.** 0

3 Use your graph to estimate the number of passengers on board if the carried weight is

a. 4400 lb **b.** 1775 lb **c.** 26 lb

d. 220 lb **e.** 2300 lb **f.** 3000 lb

◆ LESSON 102 Graphing Data

Captain Fligh of Wing-It Airlines kept records just like the ones Captain Sanchez kept. When Captain Fligh graphed the data for her first ten flights, her graph looked like this:

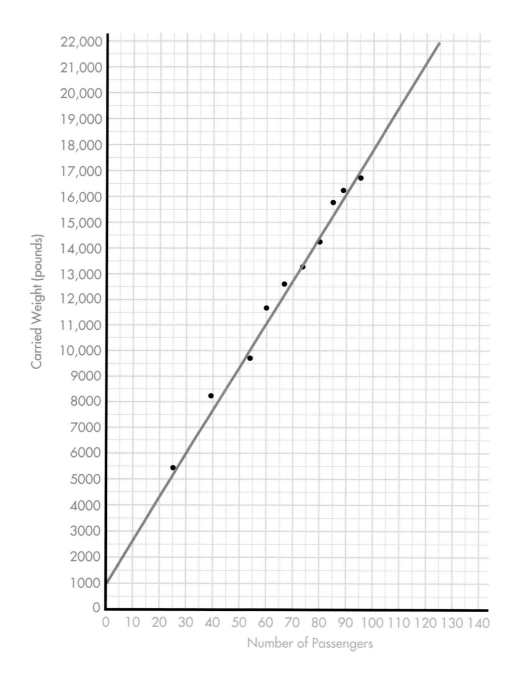

Solve these problems.

④ Captain Fligh's airplane can have no more than 22,000 pounds in carried weight. About how many passengers can be carried without going over the limit?

⑤ About how much carried weight would there be if the number of passengers were

   a. 50?   **b.** 100?   **c.** 0?   **d.** 45?

⑥ About how many passengers would there be if the carried weight were

   a. 15,500 lb?   **b.** 11,000 lb?   **c.** 2000 lb?   **d.** 1000 lb?

⑦ On the average, about how much does a passenger and his or her luggage on Captain Fligh's flights weigh?

⑧ Suppose an average passenger weighs about 140 pounds. On the average, about how much luggage does a passenger take on board one of Captain Fligh's flights?

⑨ On the average, about how much luggage does a passenger take on board one of Captain Sanchez's flights?

⑩ Why do you think there is a difference?

LESSON 103

Making and Interpreting Line Graphs

SCIENCE CONNECTION

Ms. Cruz's sixth-grade class kept a record of the outdoor temperature at 10:00 A.M. each day for a month. The first three days the temperatures were 3°C, 5°C, and 4°C. The class made a table to keep track of the temperatures.

Day	1	2	3	4	5	6	7	8	9	10	11	12	13	14
Temperature (°C)	3°	5°	4°											

Day	15	16	17	18	19	20	21	22	23	24	25	26	27	28
Temperature (°C)														

On the fourth day the thermometer looked like this one.

°Celsius

◆ What temperature should the class write for the fourth day?

◆ What month do you think it was when the class kept these records? Why?

Day	1	2	3	4	5	6	7	8	9	10	11	12	13	14
Temperature (°C)	3°	5°	4°	−2°	−4°	0°	1°	6°	9°	10°	7°	1°	0°	0°

Day	15	16	17	18	19	20	21	22	23	24	25	26	27	28
Temperature (°C)	1°	−3°	−6°	−8°	−4°	−1°	3°	2°	1°			−1°	2°	4°

No temperature was recorded for the 24th and 25th. Those days were on a weekend, and the students who were supposed to record the temperature forgot to do it.

Use a computer or other means to create a graph of the temperatures in the chart. Draw and label the axes like this:

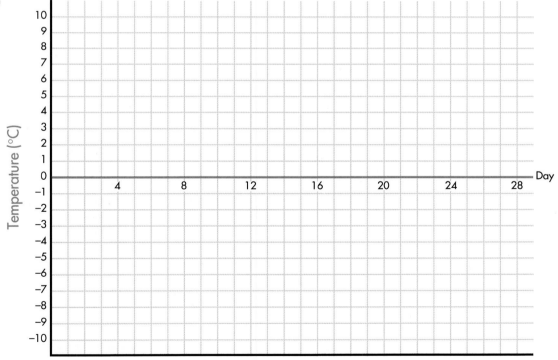

◆   How will you plot the point (4, −2)?

◆   About what do you think the temperatures were on the 24th and 25th?

LESSON 104

Graphing Functions: Negative Values

You have learned that with a function rule, you can choose values for x and find values for y, and then graph the ordered pairs. In this lesson you'll learn about graphing functions that involve negative numbers.

Do you remember the graph of the function with the rule $x \longrightarrow \boxed{\times 3} \longrightarrow y$? It looked like a straight line. To graph that function, you used only 0 and positive numbers (numbers greater than 0) for x and y. What happens if you also use negative numbers (numbers less than 0) for x and y?

1 Use a computer or other means to create a table, and complete the table so that each ordered pair satisfies the rule $x \longrightarrow \boxed{\times 3} \longrightarrow y$.

x	5	1	0	−2	−1	−5	−3	−4	−1.5	−2.5
y	15	■	■	■	■	■	■	■	■	■

Hint for multiplying $3 \times (-2)$: Think of -2 as losing $2. If you lose $2 each day for three days, what will your financial condition be? Then what is $3 \times (-2)$?

2 Graph the ten ordered pairs you found in problem 1. Draw the axes. Draw your x-axis so it goes from -5 to 5 and your y-axis so it goes from -15 to 15. Are all the points on one straight line?

3 Find a function rule for which some positive values for x result in negative values for y.

4 Find a function rule for which some negative values of x result in positive values for y.

Use a computer or other means to draw the tables below, and complete each table so that each ordered pair satisfies the given rule. Then graph each set of ordered pairs.

$x \xrightarrow{\times 2} y$

5

x	0	4	−3	1.4	−2.5	0.7
y	▣	▣	▣	▣	▣	▣

$x \xrightarrow{-4} y$

6

x	10	5	4	2	0	−2
y	▣	▣	▣	▣	▣	▣

$x \xrightarrow{+2} y$

7

x	0	5	−5	−2.5	−0.5	−1
y	▣	▣	▣	▣	▣	▣

8 Look at your graphs for problems 2, 5, 6, and 7.

   a. Do the points in each graph fall on a straight line?

   b. In each case, do you think that other points that satisfy the rule would fall on the line you graphed?

   c. In every case, do you think that the coordinates of every point on the line satisfy the function rule?

9 If you were sure a graph would be a straight line, how many points would you need to plot to draw the line?

◆ LESSON 104 Graphing Functions: Negative Values

Mrs. Brooks decided to open a restaurant. She started a corporation six months before the restaurant opened and deposited $50,000 in the corporation's bank account. She kept records of the amount of cash the corporation had for $1\frac{1}{2}$ years. In her records she called the month the restaurant opened "0 month" and gave earlier months negative numbers. Study her records and then answer the questions on the next page.

Mrs. Brooks's Restaurant, Inc.

Month	Available Cash ($)
−6	50,000
−5	50,200
−4	50,400
−3	50,600
−2	45,700
−1	21,300
0	−15,000
+1	−35,000
+2	−33,700
+3	−29,100
+4	−25,600
+5	−20,100
+6	−12,500
+7	−6,700
+8	−1,500
+9	+4,100
+10	+8,800

The chart above shows the available cash at the beginning of each month in Mrs. Brooks's corporation. (All figures are rounded to the nearest hundred dollars.)

Use the chart to answer these questions.

10 At the beginning of which month did the restaurant have the least cash?

11 In which month did the available cash drop the most? Why do you think this might have happened?

12 In which month did the available cash increase the most?

13 What does it mean for a business to have a negative amount of available cash?

14 How could the business have earned money before the restaurant opened?

15 Mrs. Brooks wanted to take $1000 per month profit from her corporation.

a. Could she do so without endangering her business?

b. Could she take $2000 per month?

16 What is the greatest amount Mrs. Brooks could take out in profit each month?

17 Do you think the restaurant will be a successful business? Why?

Graph the data. Then use the graph to answer the next question.

18 If profit is not removed and the pattern continues, how much available cash do you think there is likely to be on the first of the 19th month? on the first of the 24th month? Why?

LESSON
105

GAME

Practice with Graphing

COOPERATIVE LEARNING

Get the Point Game

Players:	**Two**
Materials:	**Graph paper, crayons or markers (four colors), a black pen or pencil**
Object:	**To find the coordinates of the secret point**
Math Focus:	**Locating and plotting coordinates on a graph, intuitive geometry, and mathematical reasoning**

RULES

1. Decide what size "playing field" will be used. Each player makes a playing field by drawing coordinate axes on a sheet of graph paper.

2. The first player chooses a secret point with integer coordinates and draws two straight lines through the point, cutting in half each square through which they pass. (See the Sample Game.) This separates the playing field into four parts. The first player then colors each of the four parts a different color.

3. Without seeing what the first player has done, the second player guesses a point by calling out its coordinates. Then the first player tells the color of that point. A point on one of the two dividing lines is described as black.

4. The second player keeps guessing points until he or she gets the secret point.

5. Players switch roles.

374 • Algebra Readiness

SAMPLE GAME

Lynn and Keith decided on a playing field that goes from −5 to 5 on each axis. Lynn was the first player. She chose (3, −2) as the secret point, drew two lines, and colored the sections as shown.

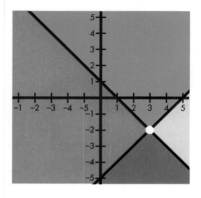

Keith made a playing field just like Lynn's but without the lines and colors. On his field Keith kept a record of each move.

1. Keith said, "(0, 0)." Lynn said, "Red." Keith circled the point (0, 0) in red.

2. Keith said, "(1, 1)." Lynn said, "Green." Keith circled the point (1, 1) in green. He knew there was a line between (0, 0) and (1, 1).

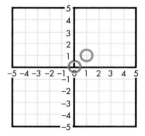

3. Keith said, "(4, −2)." Lynn said, "Yellow." Keith circled that point in yellow. Now Keith knows that the line lies between (1, 1) and (4, −2).

4. Keith said, "(2, 0)." Lynn said, "Green." Keith circled that point in green. Now Keith knows that the line is between (2, 0) and (4, −2).

5. Keith said, "(4, −1)." Lynn said, "Black." Keith circled that point in black. Now Keith knows where the line is. He draws it to find the point where the two lines intersect.

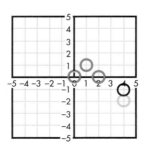

6. Keith said, "(3, −2)." Lynn said, "That's the point I chose. You got it in six moves."

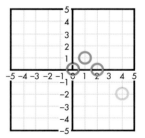
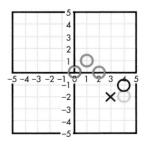

◆ **LESSON 105 Practice with Graphing**

THINKING STORY

Diet for a Small Terrier

Part 1

The telephone rang at Breezy's training school for dogs. "Mr. Breezy," said the caller. "I have a toy terrier named Tiny. I'd like to send him to you."

"Sorry," said Mr. Breezy. "We have a hard enough time training real dogs. I don't think we could train a toy."

"Tiny is a very real dog—toy terrier is his breed," said the caller. "Besides, I don't want you to teach Tiny anything. Tiny used to be a trim little dog who weighed 5 kilograms. Now he has grown lazy and fat. I'd like to send him to you for exercise and diet. I want him to get back his youthful figure."

"Dog reducing isn't exactly my line," said Mr. Breezy. "But I'll give it a try. Bring Tiny over."

When Tiny came, the first thing Mr. Breezy did was weigh him. Tiny weighed almost exactly 7 kilograms "It shouldn't be too hard to get a dog to lose 2 kilograms," said Mr. Breezy. "Portia, your job will be to see that Tiny gets plenty of exercise every day. Marcus, your job will be to see that Tiny gets just the right amount to eat each day."

"How much is that?" Marcus asked.

"You'll have to look that up in a book," said Mr. Breezy. "Since we want Tiny to weigh 5 kilograms, we should feed him the right number of calories for a 5-kilogram dog."

Marcus checked two different books on dog care. From the first book he learned that very active dogs need about 110 calories a day for each kilogram of weight. Inactive dogs—dogs that lie around most of the time—need only about 80 calories a day for each kilogram. In the second book Marcus found the graph shown on this page. It told how many calories a day an average dog needs, depending on how much it weighs.

Recommended Number of Calories per Day

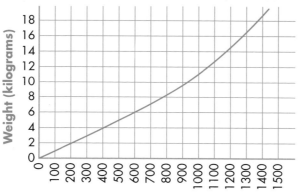

Recommended Number of Calories per Day

"I'm in trouble, Dad," Marcus said. "I have three different answers to how many calories a day Tiny should eat."

. . . to be continued

Work in groups. Discuss your answers and how you figured them out. Then compare your answers with those of other groups.

1 What are the three answers that Marcus got?

2 Which do you think is the best answer? Why?

3 How could you explain the fact that the graph gives an answer that is between the other two answers?

4 According to the graph, about how many calories a day should a dog eat for each kilogram of its weight? Is it the same for dogs of all sizes?

Graphing Composite Functions

Sometimes a function can involve more than one operation. In this lesson you'll learn about using rules with more than one step.

We call a function a **composite function** if two (or more) rules are put together to make its rule.

Example: x ——(×2)——▶ n ——(+5)——▶ y

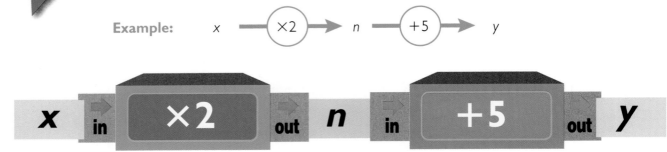

This composite rule says to first multiply the number x by 2 and then add 5 to the result to get y.

Suppose you start with 3.   3 ——(×2)——▶ n ——(+5)——▶ y

3×2 is 6. So n is 6.   3 ——(×2)——▶ 6 ——(+5)——▶ y

$6 + 5 = 11$. So y is 11.   3 ——(×2)——▶ 6 ——(+5)——▶ 11

If 3 is the first number, then 11 is the last number. The ordered pair (3, 11) satisfies the rule.

Use a computer or other means to draw the tables below, and complete the tables so that each ordered pair satisfies the given rule.

x ——(×2)——▶ n ——(+5)——▶ y x ——(×$\frac{1}{2}$)——▶ n ——(+3)——▶ y

1

x	3	2	0	−2	−3	−5
y	11	▪	▪	▪	▪	▪

2

x	0	2	5	−2	−4	−5
y	▪	▪	▪	▪	▪	▪

Graph each set of ordered pairs in problems 1 and 2.

◆   What do you think is true of the graph of each of these functions?

Answer the following.

3 On one sheet of graph paper, graph each of the following function rules. After the first two or three, you should be able to guess where the next graph will be.

a. $x \longrightarrow \boxed{\times 2} \longrightarrow n \longrightarrow \boxed{+1} \longrightarrow y$ **b.** $x \longrightarrow \boxed{\times 2} \longrightarrow n \longrightarrow \boxed{+3} \longrightarrow y$

c. $x \longrightarrow \boxed{\times 2} \longrightarrow n \longrightarrow \boxed{+5} \longrightarrow y$ **d.** $x \longrightarrow \boxed{\times 2} \longrightarrow n \longrightarrow \boxed{+7} \longrightarrow y$

e. $x \longrightarrow \boxed{\times 2} \longrightarrow n \longrightarrow \boxed{-1} \longrightarrow y$ **f.** $x \longrightarrow \boxed{\times 2} \longrightarrow n \longrightarrow \boxed{-3} \longrightarrow y$

4 On one sheet of graph paper, graph each of the following function rules. After the first two or three, you should be able to guess where the next graph will be.

a. $x \longrightarrow \boxed{\times \frac{1}{4}} \longrightarrow n \longrightarrow \boxed{+3} \longrightarrow y$ **b.** $x \longrightarrow \boxed{\times \frac{1}{2}} \longrightarrow n \longrightarrow \boxed{+3} \longrightarrow y$

c. $x \longrightarrow \boxed{\times 1} \longrightarrow n \longrightarrow \boxed{+3} \longrightarrow y$ **d.** $x \longrightarrow \boxed{\times 2} \longrightarrow n \longrightarrow \boxed{+3} \longrightarrow y$

e. $x \longrightarrow \boxed{\times 4} \longrightarrow n \longrightarrow \boxed{+3} \longrightarrow y$ **f.** $x \longrightarrow \boxed{\times 5} \longrightarrow n \longrightarrow \boxed{+3} \longrightarrow y$

5 Explain what the graph of the function rule $x \longrightarrow \boxed{\times 2} \longrightarrow n \longrightarrow \boxed{+2} \longrightarrow y$ will look like compared to the graphs in problem 3.

6 Explain the difference between the graphs of the function rules
$x \longrightarrow \boxed{\times 3} \longrightarrow n \longrightarrow \boxed{+1} \longrightarrow y$ and $x \longrightarrow \boxed{\times 3} \longrightarrow n \longrightarrow \boxed{+3} \longrightarrow y$.

7 Explain what the graph of the function rule $x \longrightarrow \boxed{\times 3} \longrightarrow n \longrightarrow \boxed{+3} \longrightarrow y$ will look like compared to the graphs in problem 4.

8 Explain the difference between the graphs of the function rules
$x \longrightarrow \boxed{\times 1} \longrightarrow n \longrightarrow \boxed{+5} \longrightarrow y$ and $x \longrightarrow \boxed{\times 2} \longrightarrow n \longrightarrow \boxed{+5} \longrightarrow y$.

Inverse Functions

You have learned how to find a value for *y* given a function rule and a value for *x*. In this lesson you'll review how to use **inverse operations** to find *x* when a value for *y* is given.

Suppose you have a function rule and you know a value for *y*. How can you find the corresponding value for *x*?

Example:

For this function rule, if *y* is 29, what is *x*?

First find *n* by using the inverse operation of −9.

Use +9.

$29 + 9 = 38$

So *n* is 38.

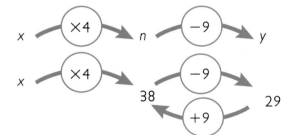

Find *x* by using the inverse operation of ×4.

Use ÷ 4.

$38 \div 4 = 9.5$

So *x* is 9.5.

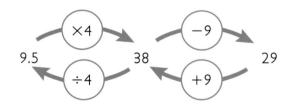

Let's check. If we use 9.5 for *x*, do we get 29 for *y*?

$9.5 \times 4 = 38$, and $38 - 9 = 29$. That checks.

1 Use a computer or other means to create the table below, and complete the table for the function rule *x* ×4 → *n* −9 → *y*.
Remember, when *x* is given, work the usual way. When *y* is given, work backward—undo each step in reverse order.

x	9.5	0.5	■	■	■	3	$2\frac{1}{2}$	$2\frac{3}{4}$	■	■
y	29	■	7	11	3	■	■	■	0	$2\frac{1}{4}$

Use a computer or other means to draw the tables below, and complete each table for the given function rule. Then graph the functions.

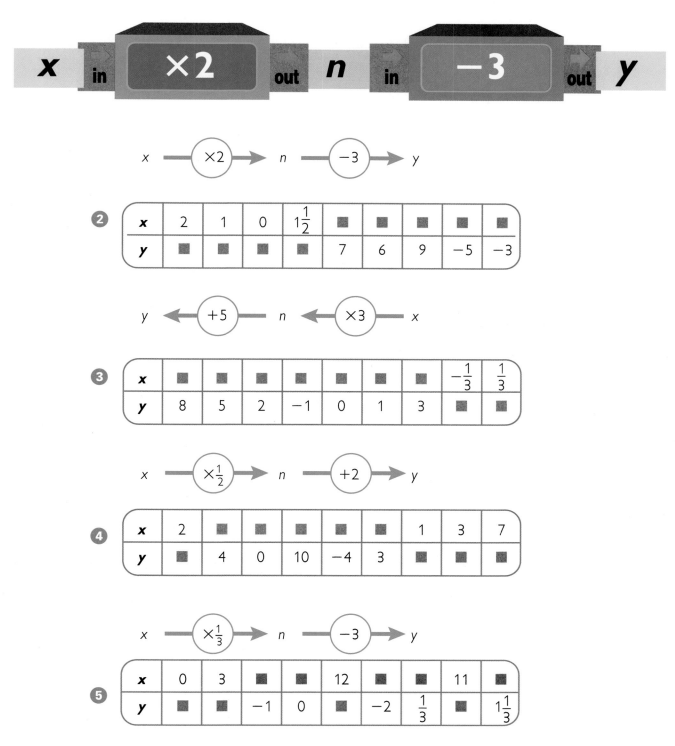

x —in— $\times 2$ —out— n —in— -3 —out— y

x —$\times 2$→ n —-3→ y

2

x	2	1	0	$1\frac{1}{2}$	■	■	■	■	■
y	■	■	■	■	7	6	9	−5	−3

y ←$+5$— n ←$\times 3$— x

3

x	■	■	■	■	■	■	■	$-\frac{1}{3}$	$\frac{1}{3}$
y	8	5	2	−1	0	1	3	■	■

x —$\times\frac{1}{2}$→ n —$+2$→ y

4

x	2	■	■	■	■	■	1	3	7
y	■	4	0	10	−4	3	■	■	■

x —$\times\frac{1}{3}$→ n —-3→ y

5

x	0	3	■	■	12	■	■	11	■
y	■	■	−1	0	■	−2	$\frac{1}{3}$	■	$1\frac{1}{3}$

LESSON 108

Keeping Sharp

Think. Work quickly. Watch the signs.

1. 30 + 40
2. 40 − 30
3. 400 + 300
4. 400 − 300
5. 3 + 4
6. 4 − 3
7. 3 × 4
8. 30 × 40
9. 300 × 400
10. 7 × 8
11. 70 × 80
12. 700 × 800
13. 70 + 80
14. 7 + 8
15. 700 + 800
16. 8 − 7
17. 800 − 700
18. 8 + 6
19. 8 − 6
20. 8 × 6
21. 80 − 60
22. 80 + 60
23. 80 × 60
24. 800 × 600
25. 800 − 600
26. 800 + 600
27. 9 × 7
28. 900 × 700
29. 900 + 700
30. 90 + 70
31. 17 − 8
32. 170 − 80
33. 1700 − 800
34. 7 + 5
35. 70 + 50
36. 500 + 700

Solve each chain calculation from left to right, unless you see a faster (and correct) way to get the answer. For example, to do 7 × 3 + 5 × 6, multiply 7 × 3 (to get 21), add 5 (to get 26), and multiply by 6 (to get 156). But to do 11 × 9 × 7 × 5 × 3 × 1 × 0, you should see that the answer must be 0.

37. 3 + 4 × 7 − 9 ÷ 8 + 5 × 7
38. 9 × 8 × 7 × 6 × 5 × 4 × 3 × 2 × 1 × 0
39. 10 + 9 + 8 + 7 + 6 + 5 + 4 + 3 + 2 + 1
40. 10 + 10 + 10 + 10 + 10 + 5
41. 10 + 9 + 1 + 8 + 2 + 7 + 3 + 6 + 4 + 5
42. What is the sum of the whole numbers from 1 through 10?
43. 20 + 20 + 20 + 20 + 20 + 20 + 20 + 20 + 20 + 10
44. What is the sum of the whole numbers from 1 through 19?

Solve these problems.

The average American uses 240 gallons of fresh water each day. Here's how the water is used.

45 Using a computer or other means, make and complete a chart like the following.

Use of Water	Approximate Percent of Use	Number of Gallons Used
Drinking and cooking	4	
Washing dishes	6	
Washing clothes	13	
Bathing	18	
Flushing toilet	22	
Outside the home (washing automobiles, watering lawns and flowers, and so on)	37	
Total	100	240

46 How average are you? Using a computer or other means, make a table like the one shown and estimate how much water you use for each item.

Many people believe that water needs to be conserved. That's especially true in parts of the country such as the dry regions in the southwest.

47 What are some ways you can conserve water? Discuss your answer.

48 It's not easy to measure how much water we use, but perhaps you can think of ways to measure some uses. Discuss ways you might do this.

49 If everyone in your class could conserve 2 gallons of water a day, how many gallons would be conserved in one year?

50 Suppose everyone in the country could conserve 2 gallons a day. How many gallons could be conserved in one year? (The U.S. population as of the 1990 census was about 249,000,000.)

51 Prepare a report to show how typical Americans can conserve 2 gallons of water every day. Show your data in chart or graph form.

◆ **LESSON 108** Keeping Sharp

Diet for a Small Terrier

Part 2

You may want to refer to the first part of this Thinking Story on pages 376–377.

Marcus figured out that the overweight toy terrier, Tiny, should have a diet of 550 calories a day. Then he had to figure out how much dog food that was. In a book on dog care Marcus read that each gram of protein or carbohydrate gives about 4 calories. Each gram of fat gives about 9 calories. Then he studied the labels on two kinds of dog food. Here is what he found:

Dry Dog Food
Each 100 Grams Contains
Protein 20 grams
Carbohydrate 55 grams
Fat 5 grams

Canned Dog Food
Each 100 Grams Contains
Protein 10 grams
Carbohydrate 20 grams
Fat 1 gram

. . . to be continued

Work in groups. Discuss your answers and how you figured them out. Then compare your answers with those of other groups.

1. How many calories are there in 100 grams of the dry dog food? How many in 100 grams of the canned dog food?

2. If Tiny is fed only dry dog food, how many grams of it should he get each day? How many grams should he get if he is fed only canned dog food?

3. How could you explain the fact that dry dog food contains so many more calories per 100 grams than canned dog food?

4. If you wanted a dog to get a greater ratio of protein to carbohydrate, which dog food would you feed it, the dry or the canned?

Determining Rules from Ordered Pairs

x	0	1	2	3	4	5	6	7	8	9	10
y	5	8	11	14	17	20	23	26	29		

Kwan made up the ordered pairs in this table by using a function rule. Using this table, can you find the function rule?

◆ How much does y increase each time x increases by 1?

◆ What is x multiplied by to get n?

◆ For each value of x, how much greater is y than n?

◆ What is the function rule?

◆ What values of y do you think should correspond to 9 and 10?

1 What rule could have produced the ordered pairs in this table?

x	0	1	2	3	4	5	6
y	1	3	5	7	9		

2 What values of y do you think should correspond to 5 and 6?

3 Look at the table below. What rule could have produced these ordered pairs?

4 What values of y do you think should correspond to 9, 11, and 13?

x	1	3	5	7	9	11	13
y	1	5	9	13			

Find the Function Rule Game

GAME

Players:	Two or more
Materials:	One calculator
Object:	To find the function rule put into the calculator
Math Focus:	Using a calculator, mental arithmetic (addition and multiplication), finding simple function rules, and mathematical reasoning

RULES

ALGEBRA READINESS

1. The lead player chooses an addition or multiplication rule (for example, ×8) and makes the calculator a function machine that uses that rule. To do this for ×8, for example, the lead player pushes ⑧, ✕, ⑧, ═ and then pushes ⓪, ═. The display should show ⎸ 0⎸. (Some calculators work differently.)

2. The second player puts a number into the calculator and sees what comes out. (For example, to put in the number 5, he or she would push ⑤, ═.)

3. The second player tries to figure out the function rule. If the player doesn't get it, he or she tries again. The player puts in another number, sees what comes out, and tries again to figure out the rule.

4. After the second player has found the rule, the lead shifts.

SAMPLE GAME

Luis was the first player. He decided to enter the function rule ×4.

Dory took the calculator. She decided to see what came out when she put in 1. The display read ⎸ 4⎸. Dory thought: "1 —(?)→ 4." Dory said that the function rule was +3.

Luis said no, so Dory tried again. She put in 10. The display read ⎸ 40⎸.

Dory figured out that the function rule was ×4. That was correct. It was Dory's turn to be lead player.

LESSON 110

Interpreting Data

SELECTED LIBRARY SYSTEMS IN THE UNITED STATES

Library Name and Location	Population Served	Number of Branches	Total Number of Books	Annual Circulation	Acquisition Expenditures
Atlanta-Fulton (GA)	714,418	31	1,950,552	2,104,745	$2,446,408
Buffalo & Erie County (NY)	968,584	52	4,000,000	8,500,000	$2,700,000
Chicago (IL)	2,783,726	82	11,463,011	7,156,442	$9,100,000
Detroit (MI)	1,027,954	25	1,680,000	1,267,000	$2,375,000
Miami-Dade (FL)	1,627,866	31	3,300,000	8,000,000	$5,000,000
Free Library of Philadelphia (PA)	1,585,577	53	5,129,439	6,178,951	$5,488,460
St. Louis County (MO)	842,936	17	2,013,472	9,456,114	$3,095,022
San Francisco (CA)	726,700	26	2,008,619	3,363,144	$1,015,855
Tucson-Pima (AZ)	734,247	18	1,138,300	5,200,000	$1,836,730

This chart gives information about selected library systems in the United States.

First study the chart. Then use the information in the chart to answer and discuss the questions below. Use a calculator. Try to support your answers.

1 Which city library is most likely to have a specific book?

2 Do you think that, on the average, the people in some cities read more than people in other cities? Which city do you think has a population that reads a lot?

3 Which library system do you think is the most efficient? Why?

4 If you know the population of a city, can you accurately predict how many branches or how many books its library will have? Why or why not?

5 Now use the information in the chart to make up questions. Discuss them with a friend.

In each problem two of the answers are obviously wrong and one is correct. Choose the correct answer without using pencil and paper and without using a calculator.

6. 4.2 × 7   **a.** 29.4   **b.** 36.4   **c.** 22.4

7. 6 × 10.5   **a.** 605   **b.** 6.105   **c.** 63

8. 3.1 × 3.1   **a.** 9.61   **b.** 21.1   **c.** 8.91

9. 7.5 × 2.2   **a.** 26.25   **b.** 16.5   **c.** 12.75

10. 1.05 × 25   **a.** 26.25   **b.** 23.25   **c.** 265.6

11. 32 × 2.15   **a.** 59.3   **b.** 68.8   **c.** 164.45

12. 1.2 × 1.2   **a.** 0.42   **b.** 1.44   **c.** 12.2

13. 1.02 × 1.05   **a.** 1.071   **b.** 0.152   **c.** 0.701

14. 9.8 × 22   **a.** 232.6   **b.** 215.6   **c.** 228.9

15. 0.19 × 15   **a.** 0.915   **b.** 19.5   **c.** 2.85

16. 0.05 × 3.5   **a.** 3.505   **b.** 4.05   **c.** 0.175

17. 0.13 × 0.21   **a.** 0.0273   **b.** 2.073   **c.** 0.273

In each problem decide which answer is correct or is the closest approximation.

18. 412 ÷ 16   **a.** 4.16   **b.** 25.75   **c.** 101.35

19. 108 ÷ 25   **a.** 4.32   **b.** 3.85   **c.** 10.85

20. 5700 ÷ 12   **a.** 475   **b.** 4750   **c.** 47.5

21. 72.5 ÷ 0.75   **a.** 67.25   **b.** 96.67   **c.** 62.75

22. 316 ÷ 36.1   **a.** 8.75   **b.** 10.15   **c.** 31.6

23. 1050 ÷ 2.62   **a.** 800.76   **b.** 100.76   **c.** 400.76

24. 1.82 ÷ 1.4   **a.** 2.3   **b.** 0.97   **c.** 1.3

25. 0.073 ÷ 0.071   **a.** 0.97   **b.** 10.83   **c.** 1.03

26. 882 ÷ 0.63   **a.** 600   **b.** 1400   **c.** 2200

Solve these problems.

27. The Wooden Soldier toy store had a sale on giant balloons—200 for $10.00. Ian thought, "Then one balloon will cost 50¢." Was he right?

28. The Wildlife Club is planning a trip for 20 people to the zoo. Admission costs $4.50. Will admission for the group cost less than $100?

LESSON
111

Using Formulas

Function rules are useful for many real-life applications. A formula is a function rule in which the letters stand for specific measurements. You can use any letters in a formula, but usually we use the first letter of the word describing the measurement for which the letter stands.

Some people use the formula C° —→ (×2) —→ n —→ (+30) —→ F°

to approximate a Celsius temperature given a Fahrenheit temperature.

◆ What does C° stand for?

◆ What does F° stand for?

◆ Why don't we use d to stand for degrees Celsius?

Solve these problems.

1 Use a computer or other means to make a table like the one below, and use the above formula to complete it.

C°	−10	0	10	20	30	40	50	60	70	80
F°	10	30								

2 The correct formula for getting exact values of Celsius temperature given a Fahrenheit temperature is C° —→ (×$\frac{9}{5}$) —→ n —→ (+32) —→ F°. Write and complete a table like the one for problem 1.

3 Look at the tables for problems 1 and 2.

a. For what values of F and C are the numbers fairly close?

b. For which values are they quite different?

Sometimes it is useful to convert from a Fahrenheit temperature to a Celsius temperature. Look at the function rule for converting from Celsius to Fahrenheit, and think about its inverse.

4 Write a formula for converting from Fahrenheit temperature to Celsius temperature.

5 Use the formula to complete the following table. Round your answers to the nearest degree.

F°	−10	0	10	20	30	40	50	60	70	80
C°										

6 You can tell how far a car or bicycle or other moving object has gone using the formula $t \xrightarrow{\times r} d$ where d is the distance the bicycle has gone, r is the average rate the bicycle went, and t is the time it was going. So, for example, if you ride at an average speed of 10 miles per hour for three hours, you will go 10 × 3 or 30 miles. Copy and complete the following chart for a rate of 10 miles per hour.

time traveled in hours	0	1	2	3	4	10	2.5
distance in miles	0						25

7 Mary rides her bicycle at an average rate of 15 miles per hour. Copy and complete the chart showing how far she will go for each of the given times.

time traveled in hours	1	3	5	10	20	100
distance in miles						

8 Do you think Mary could ride at an average speed of 15 miles per hour for 100 hours without stopping? If not, what could the figures in the table mean?

9 Ms. Smith is driving on an interstate highway at an average speed of 50 miles per hour. Make a chart showing how far she will travel for each hour from 0 through 10 hours.

10 The **perimeter**, or distance, around a rectangle is the sum of all four of its sides. So if the sides of a rectangle are 3 in., 7 in., 3 in., and 7 in., then the perimeter is 20 in.

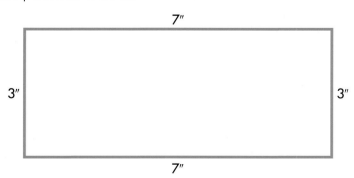

Write a formula for finding the perimeter of a rectangle if one side is 3 inches and another is w inches.

◆ **LESSON 111   Using Formulas**

Solve these problems.

11 The cost of a telephone call made on a weekend with a particular long distance company is 10 cents a minute. This can be shown using the formula $t \longrightarrow \boxed{\times 10} \longrightarrow c$, where t stands for the number of minutes talked and c stands for the cost in cents. Copy and complete the following chart:

time talked in minutes	0	1	2	3	4	10	2.5
cost in cents	0						25

12 Do you see any connection between your chart for problem 11 and your chart for problem 6?

13 On weekdays the same telephone company charges 15 cents a minute. Write a formula for calculating the cost of a telephone call on weekdays. Then copy and complete the table below.

time talked in minutes	1	3	5	10	20	100
cost in cents						

In the real world, telephone companies usually have a charge for a minute or any part of a minute. So if the company says they charge 10 cents a minute, they usually mean that as soon as you start talking, you will be charged 10 cents, and as soon as the call goes beyond one minute the charge goes up to 20 cents (but for exactly one minute the charge would still be 10 cents).

14 Would that fact change any of the numbers you have put in your charts for problem 11 or 13?

15 If the telephone company in problems 11–13 uses this method,

a. how much would you be charged for a weekend call that lasts 4 minutes, 15 seconds?

b. how much would you be charged for a weekday call that lasts 9 minutes, 53 seconds?

Solve these problems.

16 A parking garage charges $2.00 for the first hour a car is parked and $1.50 for each additional hour or part of an hour.

 a. How much will the garage charge for a car parked for two hours?

 b. How much will the garage charge for a car parked for four hours?

17 Write a formula to find the charge for a car parked for *h* hours if *h* is a whole number.

18 Use the formula to complete the following chart.

hours parked	1	3	5	8	10	14	24
charge							

19 Use the chart to help you answer these questions.

 a. How much will the garage charge for a car parked $2\frac{1}{2}$ hours?

 b. How much will the garage charge for a car parked 8 hours, 45 minutes?

 c. How much more would it cost to park a car for 2 hours, 10 minutes than to park a car for 45 minutes?

20 A taxi company charges 30¢ for every $\frac{1}{5}$ mile.

 a. How much will it cost to go 1 mile?

 b. How much will it cost to go 7 miles?

 c. How much will it cost to go $7\frac{2}{5}$ miles?

21 Write a formula to find the charge for *m* miles if *m* is a whole number.

22 Use the formula to complete the following chart.

miles traveled	2	3	5	8	10
cost					

Mid-Unit Review

Solve these problems.

The owner of Fred's Frozen Yogurt Factory surveyed his customers and then made the following table to show which of his five flavors sells the best.

Flavor Sold	Percent of Frozen Yogurt Sold
Vanilla Supreme	40
Chocolate Surprise	30
Strawberry Sundae	18
Just Peachy	7
Going Coconuts	5

1 To display these results, Fred decided to make a graph. Which kind of graph—bar graph or line graph—best shows the results of the survey? Why?

Miguel took over the Tasty Tortilla company in 1995. In 1997 he made the graph shown below to show how his profits have been increasing since he began running the company.

2 Approximately what were the profits for each of the years 1995, 1996, and 1997?

In the year 1999 Miguel made the graph shown below.

3 Approximately what were the profits for each of the years 1995 through 1999?

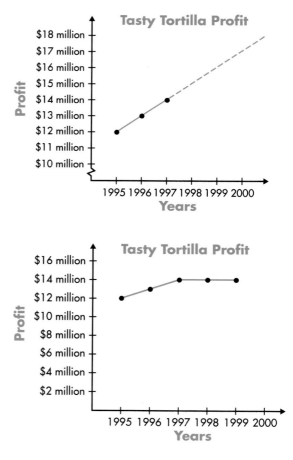

Solve these problems.

4 Miguel is planning to publish one of these graphs to show investors. Which one do you think is more honest? Why?

5 What do you think the dotted line in the first of Miguel's graphs indicates?

The chart below shows the weekly profits Anna made in her small dog-walking business.

Week	Profit	Week	Profit
1	$12.00	9	$25.00
2	$10.00	10	$24.00
3	$10.00	11	$25.00
4	$12.00	12	$28.00
5	$15.00	13	$25.00
6	$18.00	14	$24.00
7	$16.00	15	$20.00
8	$20.00	16	$25.00

6 Make a graph based on the data in Anna's table.

7 Anna says her business is booming. Do you agree? Why or why not?

On a sheet of graph paper draw coordinate axes so that each axis is at least 12 units long.

8 Plot and label the point (3, 7).

9 Plot and label the point (7, 3).

For each of the function rules in problems 10–12, make a set of five ordered pairs of numbers. (Use the number you choose for x as the input and the corresponding value of y as the output.)

10 $x \longrightarrow \boxed{\times 3} \longrightarrow y$ **11** $x \longrightarrow \boxed{+4} \longrightarrow y$ **12** $x \longrightarrow \boxed{-\frac{1}{2}} \longrightarrow y$

◆ UNIT 5 Mid-Unit Review

For each of the following, tell whether it is most like a rotation, a reflection, or a translation.

13 turning a page in a book

14 a hockey puck moving over the ice

15 twisting the lid on a jar

For each of the following figures, tell how many lines of symmetry the figure has.

16
17 **18**

Copy each ordered pair. Replace *x* or *y* with the correct number so that the pair satisfies the rule $x \longrightarrow \boxed{\times 4} \longrightarrow y$.

19 (2, *y*)   **20** (0.4, *y*)   **21** (2.5, *y*)   **22** (1.6, *y*)

23 (*x*, 20)   **24** (*x*, 2.4)   **25** (2.2, *y*)   **26** (*x*, 12)

Graph these functions.

27 $x \longrightarrow \boxed{+5} \longrightarrow y$ **28** $x \longrightarrow \boxed{-2} \longrightarrow y$ **29** $x \longrightarrow \boxed{\div 3} \longrightarrow y$

30 Ed rides his bicycle at an average rate of 16 miles an hour. Copy and complete the chart showing how far he will go for each of the given times.

time traveled in hours	0	1	2.5	4	10
distance in miles	▦	▦	▦	▦	▦

31 What rule could have produced the ordered pairs in this table?

x	0	1	2	3	4
y	−1	2	5	8	11

Aaron is exercising to keep fit. He has kept the following record of the number of push-ups he does each day.

Use the table below to answer the following questions.

Day	1	2	3	4	5	6	7	8	9	10	11
Push-ups	11	13	15	17	20	■	■	30	34	37	42

32 Describe the progress Aaron has made. How many push-ups would you predict Aaron might do on the 15th day?

33 About how many push-ups do you think Aaron might have done on days 6 and 7?

Copy and complete each table so that each ordered pair satisfies the given rule. Then graph each set of ordered pairs.

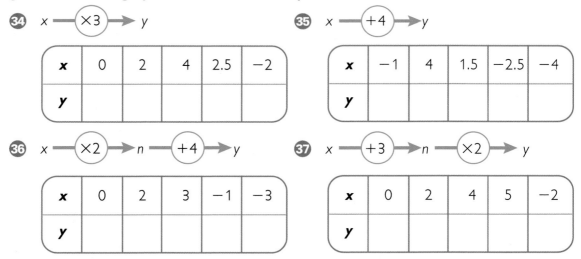

34 $x \longrightarrow \boxed{\times 3} \longrightarrow y$

x	0	2	4	2.5	−2
y					

35 $x \longrightarrow \boxed{+4} \longrightarrow y$

x	−1	4	1.5	−2.5	−4
y					

36 $x \longrightarrow \boxed{\times 2} \longrightarrow n \longrightarrow \boxed{+4} \longrightarrow y$

x	0	2	3	−1	−3
y					

37 $x \longrightarrow \boxed{+3} \longrightarrow n \longrightarrow \boxed{\times 2} \longrightarrow y$

x	0	2	4	5	−2
y					

In each problem two of the three answers are obviously wrong and one is correct. Choose the correct answer using mental arithmetic.

38 1.4 × 5

   a. 0.7

   b. 7

   c. 70

39 0.4 × 30

   a. 0.012

   b. 0.12

   c. 12

40 3.2 × 6.5

   a. 0.208

   b. 20.8

   c. 208

Standard Notation for Functions

You have learned one way to write a function rule. In this lesson you'll learn about another form—one that is more commonly used in algebra.

Function rules are usually written in a form shorter than the form we have been using.

For $x \xrightarrow{\times 2} n \xrightarrow{+5} y$, we could say, "Multiply x by 2 and add 5."

This could be written: $2 \times x + 5 = y$. Since the $\times$ sign and the x could easily be confused, it is customary to leave out the $\times$ sign if one number is represented by a letter. When we want to tell someone to multiply x by 2 and then add 5 to get y, we write:

$$2x + 5 = y$$

We read this as "two x plus 5 equals y."

If we want to tell someone to divide x by 4 to get y, we could write it in two ways:

$$x \div 4 = y \qquad \text{or} \qquad \frac{x}{4} = y$$

We would read these as "x divided by 4 equals y" and "x over 4 equals y."

Write each of these rules in the short form.

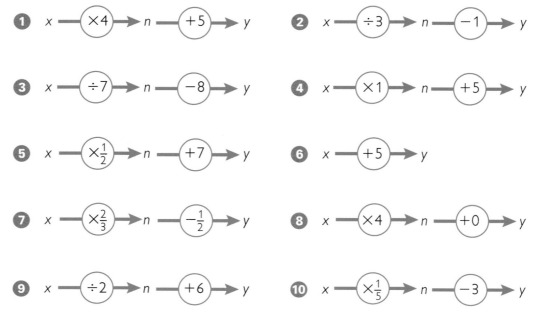

1 $x \xrightarrow{\times 4} n \xrightarrow{+5} y$ **2** $x \xrightarrow{\div 3} n \xrightarrow{-1} y$

3 $x \xrightarrow{\div 7} n \xrightarrow{-8} y$ **4** $x \xrightarrow{\times 1} n \xrightarrow{+5} y$

5 $x \xrightarrow{\times \frac{1}{2}} n \xrightarrow{+7} y$ **6** $x \xrightarrow{+5} y$

7 $x \xrightarrow{\times \frac{2}{3}} n \xrightarrow{-\frac{1}{2}} y$ **8** $x \xrightarrow{\times 4} n \xrightarrow{+0} y$

9 $x \xrightarrow{\div 2} n \xrightarrow{+6} y$ **10** $x \xrightarrow{\times \frac{1}{5}} n \xrightarrow{-3} y$

Write each rule in the longer form, using arrows.

⑪ $3x - 5 = y$

⑫ $\frac{1}{2}x + 4 = y$

⑬ $x - 8 = y$

⑭ $\frac{x}{2} = y$

⑮ $y = 5x$

⑯ $y = 5x + 3$

⑰ $y = \frac{2}{3}x - 8$

⑱ $y = \frac{x}{4} - 7$

⑲ $y = x + 1$

You may use the long form whenever you find it more convenient.

Use spreadsheet software or other means to complete each table and graph the function. You may use or think about the longer form for function rules, if that helps.

⑳ $y = 3x + 5$

x	0	1	2	3	−1	−2	−3
y	▪	▪	▪	▪	▪	▪	▪

㉑ $y = \frac{1}{2}x + 5$

x	0	2	4	−2	−4	1	−1
y	▪	▪	▪	▪	▪	▪	▪

㉒ $y = 2x - 7$

x	1	▪	▪	▪	▪	▪	▪
y	▪	−7	−1	3	5	0	1

㉓ $y = \frac{2}{3}x + 3$

x	▪	▪	▪	▪	▪	▪	▪
y	3	5	7	9	1	−1	0

LESSON
113

Finding Terms of Sequences

ALGEBRA READINESS

In each of the following sequences, there is a pattern that allows you to predict the next number or numbers by following that pattern. You may see several patterns that would give different results for missing numbers.

For each sequence, write the missing numbers according to your pattern. Tell what your pattern is.

Example: 1, 7, 3, 9, ___, ___, ___.
Answer: 5, 11, 7.
Pattern: Add 6, then subtract 4, alternately.

1. 20, 25, 30, ___, ___, ___, ___.

2. 1, 2, 4, 8, ___, ___, ___, ___.

3. 64, 32, 16, ___, ___, ___, ___, ___.

4. 0, 4, 2, 6, 4, 8, ___, ___, ___, ___.

5. 0, 0, 2, 6, 8, 24, ___, ___, ___.

6. 100, 95, 90, ___, ___, ___, ___.

7. 100, ___, 80, ___, 60, ___, ___.

8. 0, ___, 5, 20, 25, ___, 105, ___, 425.

9. 1, 4, 9, 16, ___, ___, ___, ___.

For each set of ordered pairs, give a function rule in the short form.

10.

x	0	1	2	3	-1	-2
y	3	7	11	15	-1	-5

11.

x	0	2	4	6	8	10
y	1	2	3	4	5	6

Think. Work quickly. Watch the signs.

12 40 + 50

13 50 − 40

14 500 − 400

15 500 + 400

16 5 + 4

17 5 − 4

18 5 × 4

19 500 × 400

20 50 × 40

21 7 × 6

22 70 × 60

23 700 × 600

24 7 + 6

25 600 + 700

26 700 − 600

27 7 − 6

28 70 + 60

29 8 + 4

30 8 − 4

31 8 × 4

32 15 − 8

33 150 − 80

34 1500 − 800

35 80 × 70

36 70 × 70

37 600 × 900

38 9 × 6

39 90 + 60

40 90 − 60

41 90 × 60

Do each chain calculation from left to right, unless you see a faster way. For example, to do 7 × 3 + 5 × 6, multiply 7 × 3 (to get 21), add 5 (to get 26), and multiply by 6 (to get 156).

42 5 × 8 ÷ 2 + 7 − 2

43 10 × 3 × 2 × 1 + 10

44 30 ÷ 5 × 6 − 6 + 7

45 50 + 50 + 50 + 50 + 50

46 8 + 1 + 2 + 3 + 5 + 7

47 4 × 9 × 2 × 5

48 7 × 8 − 6 ÷ 10 + 4 × 4 ÷ 6

49 5 × 9 + 3 ÷ 8 + 1 × 5 + 5 ÷ 5 − 5 − 5

50 10 × 9 × 8 × 7 × 6 × 5 × 4 × 3 × 2 × 1 × 0

51 12 × 9 × 6 × 3 × 0

52 9 + 8 + 7 + 6 + 5 + 4 + 3 + 2 + 1

53 10 + 10 + 10 + 10 + 5

54 9 + 1 + 8 + 2 + 7 + 3 + 6 + 4 + 5

55 20 + 20 + 20 + 20 + 20 + 20 + 20 + 20 + 20 + 20 + 10

56 What is the sum of the whole numbers from 1 through 20?

Graphing Linear Functions

You have learned how to satisfy a function rule by finding one coordinate given the other. In this lesson you'll practice graphing certain functions, and you'll discover what their graphs will look like.

To graph a function correctly, you must know where every point of the graph is. But often there is enough regularity so that a few points will determine where the others are.

Example: Graph the function $y = \frac{1}{2}x - 4$.

Choose some value of x.	Let's say 10.
Find the corresponding value of y.	$y = \frac{1}{2} \times 10 - 4 = 1$
Graph that point.	Graph (10, 1).
Choose another value of x.	Let's say 0.
Find the corresponding value of y.	$y = \frac{1}{2} \times 0 - 4 = (-4)$
Graph that point.	Graph (0, –4).

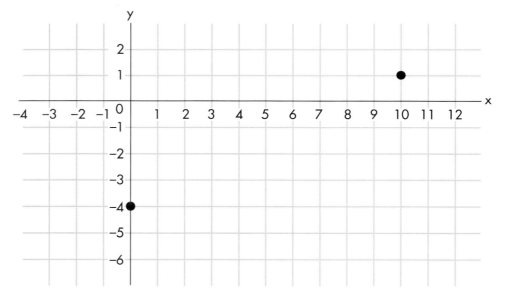

We have seen that functions with rules of the form $y = Ax + B$ have graphs that are straight lines.

◆   How many straight lines can you draw through one point?

◆   How many straight lines can you draw through two points?

Draw a line through (10, 1) and (0, −4). You can draw just one straight line through the two points you plotted for the function $y = \frac{1}{2}x - 4$.

If a function has the form $y = Ax + B$, you can draw the line if you know just two points.

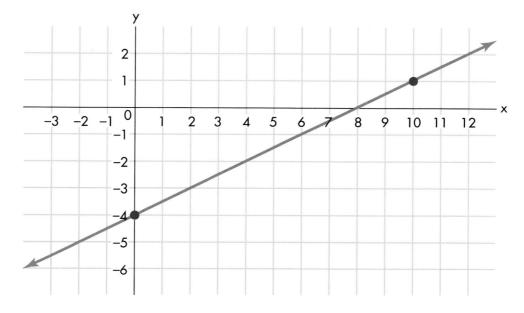

Let's check to see that it makes sense to say that this line is a graph of the function $y = \frac{1}{2}x - 4$.

◆   Choose any other value of x (besides 0 and 10). Find the corresponding value of y for the rule $y = \frac{1}{2}x - 4$. Are the numbers in the ordered pair the coordinates of a point on the line?

◆   Choose any point on the line. Do the coordinates of that point satisfy the rule $y = \frac{1}{2}x - 4$?

For each function rule, graph the function. (Choose any values you wish for x and find the corresponding values for y.)

1 $y = \frac{1}{2}x + 2$ **2** $y = 3x + 1$ **3** $y = 4x - 6$

4 $y = 2x - 7$ **5** $y = \frac{2}{3}x - 2$ **6** $y = \frac{3}{4}x + 5$

7   Were you able to graph each function using only two points?

8   When would it make sense to use more than two points when graphing a function?

◆ LESSON 114   Graphing Linear Functions

Some rules for functions are given in words rather than in symbols and numbers.

Example: Let x be the length of a side of an **equilateral triangle** and let y be the perimeter of the triangle. Try to write a function rule in the form $y = Ax + B$ for this function. Graph the function.

Remember, equilateral means all sides have the same length.

Draw a picture if it helps.

The length of each side of the triangle is x. Then the perimeter, y, is $x + x + x$, or 3 times x.

We can write this as $y = 3x$. We graph it by choosing some values for x and finding the corresponding values for y.

x	1	3			
y	3	9			

9   Choose at least three more values of x and find the corresponding values of y. Do these points fall on the graph of $y = 3x$?

10   Here is another function rule in words. Let x be the length of the short side of a rectangle and $3x$ be the length of the long side. Let y be the perimeter of the rectangle. Write the rule in the form $y = Ax + B$. Then graph the function.

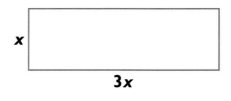

11   Choose at least three more values of x and find the corresponding values of y. Do these points fall on the graph you made for problem 10?

12   For the example and for problem 10, choose a point on the graph that has coordinates that have not been calculated yet. Do the coordinates of the point satisfy the function rule?

Function rules and graphs can be used to solve many kinds of problems. Here is one example of a situation that can be made clearer using functions.

Rita sells newspapers. She can usually sell 70 or 80 papers in a day. She sells the papers for 50¢ each. The newspaper company has offered her two different ways of getting paid.

The first choice is that they will give her as many papers as she wants, and she gets to keep 15¢ for each paper she sells. She would return the unsold papers to the company.

The second choice is that she will buy 100 papers from the company at the beginning of the day for $25. She gets to keep all the money people pay her for the papers and need not return any unsold papers. If she loses money, we would say that is a negative profit for the day, so she would have a profit of negative $25 (or –$25) if she sold no papers.

Solve the following problems.

13 Suppose Rita takes the first choice. Express her profit using a function rule in which x is the number of papers she sells and y is her profit.

14 Suppose Rita takes the second choice. Express her profit using a function rule.

15 If Rita sold 20 papers in a day, which choice would be better for her? What would her profit be with each choice?

16 How many papers must she sell to break even (have a "profit" of $0) with the second choice?

17 What would her profit be using the first choice if she sold 50 papers?

18 If she sold 80 papers, what would her profit be with each choice? Which is better?

19 Draw a double line graph showing her profit for different numbers of papers sold for each choice. About how many papers must she sell in order to do better with the second choice than with the first?

20 Given Rita's choice, what would you do? Why?

Order of Operations

Bill and Jordan each have a calculator. On his calculator Bill did the following problem: $3 + 5 \times 7 =$. The answer the calculator showed was 38. Jordan tried the same problem on her calculator. The answer the calculator showed was 56. They decided one of the calculators must be making a mistake.

◆   Which one do you think was making a mistake? Why?

◆   Solve the problem on your calculator. What answer do you get?

◆   Does anyone in your class get a different answer?

Many people solve problems like $3 + 5 \times 7$ from left to right and do the computations as they get to them. In this case, $3 + 5 = 8$ and $8 \times 7 = 56$. Others follow a rule that says that when there are multiplications and additions in the same problem, we should always do the multiplications first, and then the additions. They would first say $5 \times 7 = 35$, and then, $3 + 35 = 38$. Still a third rule might be to do additions first and then multiplications. With this method the answer would be 56.

For each of the following problems, find the answer using each of the three rules: (1) left to right; (2) multiplications first; (3) additions first.

1   $7 + 3 \times 10$ 2 $3 \times 10 + 7$ 3 $4 + 8 \times 5$

4   $8 \times 5 + 4$ 5 $73 + 27 \times 10$ 6 $10 \times 27 + 73$

7   $10 \times 7 + 3$ 8 $5 \times 8 + 4$ 9 $73 \times 10 + 27$

10   $5 + 5 \times 5$ 11 $5 \times 5 + 5$ 12 $10 + 10 \times 10$

If you know the situation that led to an arithmetic problem, you can find the answer. Otherwise, you will need some rule to follow. Sometimes we can eliminate confusion by using **parentheses** (always do the computations inside parentheses first). Sometimes we wish to use a different rule, but it is important that people reading our work use the same rule.

The two most common rules are to work from left to right and to do the multiplications (and divisions) before the additions (and subtractions).

Consider the short way of writing a function rule such as $7 + 3x = y$. If x is 2, what is y? Can you see why people who study algebra using this notation often use the convention of multiplication first, then addition?

Solve for *n*. Work from the inner parentheses to the outer parentheses.

13 $(3 + 4) \times 5 = n$

14 $3 + (4 \times 5) = n$

15 $(7 + 6) \times (3 + 4) = n$

16 $12 - (6 + 4) = n$

17 $(12 - 6) + 4 = n$

18 $(24 \div 3) + 5 = n$

19 $24 \div (3 + 5) = n$

20 $30 - (6 \times 2) = n$

21 $(30 - 6) \times 2 = n$

22 $34 - ((8 \times 2) + 3) = n$

23 $(34 - 8) \times (2 + 3) = n$

24 $((34 - 8) \times 2) + 3 = n$

25 $4 + ((16 \div 4) \times 5) = n$

26 $(4 + (16 \div 4)) \times 5 = n$

27 $((4 + 16) \div 4) \times 5 = n$

Solve for *n*. Use shortcuts when you can.

28 $100 \times 100 = n$

29 $99 \times 101 = n$

30 $3.1 \times 2.9 = n$

31 $2.9 \times 3.1 = n$

32 $100.1 \times 59.9 = n$

33 $6 \times 5 = n$

34 $60 \times 5 = n$

35 $61 \times 5 = n$

36 $61 \times 50 = n$

37 $610 \times 50 = n$

38 $75 \times 2 = n$

39 $75 \times 3 = n$

40 $75 \times 4 = n$

41 $75 \times 5 = n$

42 $75 \times 6 = n$

Watch the signs. If the answer is an improper fraction, you can leave it or change it to a mixed number.

43 $\frac{1}{2} + \frac{1}{2} = n$

44 $\frac{1}{2} - \frac{1}{2} = n$

45 $\frac{2}{2} - \frac{1}{2} = n$

46 $\frac{3}{2} - \frac{1}{2} = n$

47 $\frac{3}{2} - \frac{1}{4} = n$

48 $\frac{3}{2} - \frac{1}{8} = n$

49 $\frac{1}{2} \times \frac{1}{2} = n$

50 $\frac{1}{4} \div \frac{1}{2} = n$

51 $\frac{3}{8} + \frac{1}{4} = n$

52 $\frac{7}{8} + \frac{1}{4} = n$

53 $1\frac{1}{4} + 1\frac{1}{4} = n$

54 $1\frac{2}{3} + \frac{1}{3} = n$

55 $1\frac{2}{3} + \frac{2}{3} = n$

56 $1\frac{2}{3} + \frac{3}{3} = n$

57 $1\frac{2}{3} - \frac{3}{3} = n$

58 $\frac{3}{4} + \frac{2}{8} = n$

59 $7 \times \frac{2}{4} = n$

60 $7 \div \frac{2}{4} = n$

61 $\frac{1}{7} \div \frac{2}{4} = n$

62 $\frac{2}{7} \div \frac{2}{4} = n$

63 $\frac{3}{7} \div \frac{2}{4} = n$

64 $\frac{2}{3} \times 2 = n$

65 $\frac{2}{3} \times 3 = n$

66 $\frac{2}{3} \times \frac{1}{2} = n$

67 $\frac{2}{3} \times 2\frac{1}{2} = n$

68 $\frac{2}{3} \times 3\frac{1}{2} = n$

69 $2\frac{1}{2} - \frac{3}{8} = n$

70 $2\frac{1}{2} - \frac{5}{8} = n$

71 $2\frac{1}{2} - \frac{7}{8} = n$

72 $2\frac{1}{2} - 1\frac{1}{8} = n$

◆ **LESSON 115** Order of Operations

THINKING STORY

Diet for a Small Terrier

Part 3

You may want to refer to the earlier parts of this Thinking Story on pages 376–377 and 384–385.

After a week of exercise and dieting, Tiny was much livelier. But he was still a fat little terrier. When the owner came to visit, Marcus and Mr. Breezy put Tiny on the scale. He weighed 6.9 kilograms. "Why, Tiny has lost hardly any weight at all!" the owner said angrily. "He weighed 7 kilograms when I brought him to you, and he weighs about the same now. When I went on a diet last year I lost a kilogram a week. I thought you could do that well with a dog. I thought in just two weeks he'd be down to 5 kilograms. He'll never get there at this rate."

"I'm sorry we failed," said Mr. Breezy. "You can take Tiny back. I won't charge you for the week."

"Excuse me," said Marcus, "but I have a question. How much did you weigh when you started your diet?"

"About 70 kilograms, if you must know," said the owner.

"And how long did it take you to get down to 50 kilograms?"

"Well, I never actually got there," she said. "I quit dieting after ten weeks, when I was down to 60 kilograms."

"Then I think we may be doing as well with Tiny's diet as you did with yours," Marcus said.

. . . the end

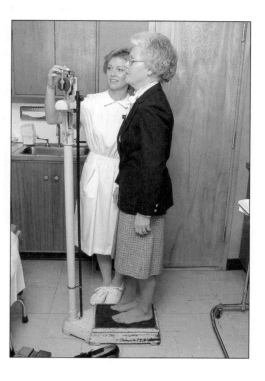

Work in groups. Discuss your answers and how you figured them out. Then compare your answers with those of other groups.

1 Is it reasonable to expect a small dog to lose as much weight in a week of dieting as a large person? Why or why not?

2 How much weight did Tiny lose in the first week? If he keeps losing that much every week, how long will it take him to get down to a weight of 5 kilograms?

3 How long would it have taken the owner to get down to a weight of 50 kilograms at the rate she was losing weight?

4 Try to show with numbers why you could say that Tiny's diet is going as well as his owner's diet did.

LESSON 116

Graphing Nonlinear Functions

Not all functions are in the form $y = Ax + B$. In this lesson you'll learn about other functions and the lines they form when their ordered pairs are graphed.

Here is a function rule in words. Let x be the length of the side of a square in centimeters. Let y be the area of the square in square centimeters.

Solve.

1 Use a computer or other means to draw and complete this table of ordered pairs for the function rule.

x	1	2	3	4	5	6	0.5	1.5	2.5	0.1
y	1	4	■	■	■	■	■	■	■	■

2 Copy and complete the graph of the function rule. (That is, graph the ordered pairs from problem 1.)

◆ Do the points you graphed fall on a straight line?

◆ Is it possible for x to be less than 0? Explain.

We call this kind of function nonlinear.

◆ What does nonlinear mean?

3 On your graph, connect the points with a smooth curved line.

4 Try to write a function rule in the short form, using x and y.

5 Would it be possible to draw a graph of this data based on only two ordered pairs?

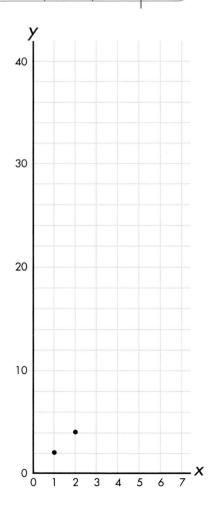

Think about the function that has this rule: x is the length (in centimeters) of the short side of a rectangle, $3x$ is the length (in centimeters) of the long side, and y is the area (in square centimeters) of the rectangle.

Here are three rectangles that meet these conditions.

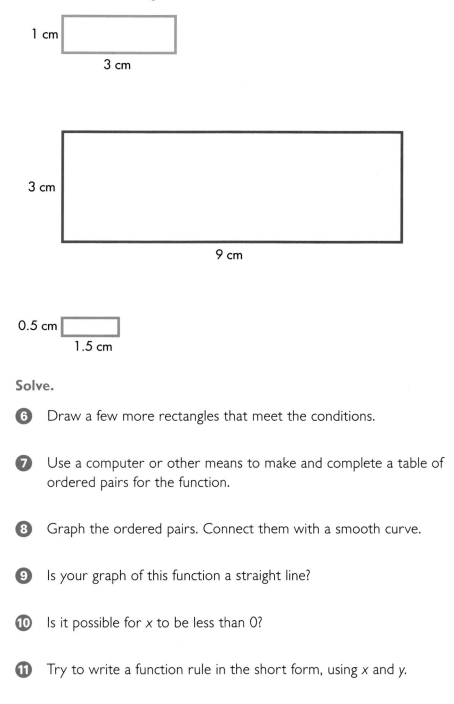

1 cm

3 cm

3 cm

9 cm

0.5 cm

1.5 cm

Solve.

6 Draw a few more rectangles that meet the conditions.

7 Use a computer or other means to make and complete a table of ordered pairs for the function.

8 Graph the ordered pairs. Connect them with a smooth curve.

9 Is your graph of this function a straight line?

10 Is it possible for x to be less than 0?

11 Try to write a function rule in the short form, using x and y.

More Nonlinear Functions

You've learned that functions of the form $y = Ax + B$ have graphs that are straight lines, while some other functions do not. In this lesson you'll graph more nonlinear functions.

Solve.

1 Use a computer or other means to make and complete this table of ordered pairs for the function rule $y = xx$.

x	0	1	2	■	■	5	0.1	0.2	0.3	0.4	0.5	0.6	0.7	0.8	0.9
y	■	■	4	9	16	25	■	■	■	■	■	■	■	■	■

A function rule such as $y = xx$ is more commonly written with exponents: $y = x^2$. (Remember, 3×3 can be written as 3^2, 5×5 as 5^2, and so on. So xx can be written as x^2.) We read $y = x^2$ as "y equals x squared."

To write $3xx$ with exponents, we write $3x^2$. The term $3x^2$ means to multiply 3 times x times x (the 3 is used as a factor only once). We read $y = 3x^2$ as "y equals three x squared."

2 Graph the function that has the rule $y = x^2$. You may copy and complete the graph that has been started here.

3 What is the relationship between this graph and the graph you drew for problem 2 on page 410?

4 What would the graph of $y = x^2 + 2$ look like?

5 What would the graph of $y = x^2 - 3$ look like?

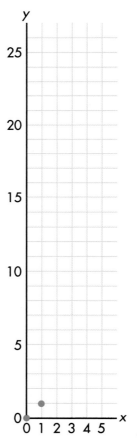

Look at this function rule: $y = 2x^2 + 5x + 5$.

If x is 3, what is y?

Here is how we can find out.

$y = 2x^2 + 5x + 5$

$y = (2 \times 3^2) + (5 \times 3) + 5$

$y = (2 \times 9) + (5 \times 3) + 5$

$y = 18 + 15 + 5$

$y = 38$

To avoid confusion when solving problems like this one, we agree that we will do all the multiplication and division first, then the addition and subtraction.

Solve.

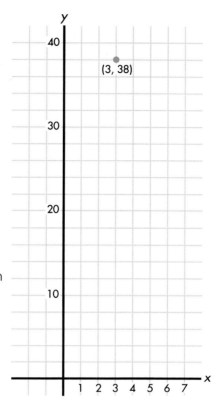

(3, 38)

⑥ Use a computer or other means to make and complete this table of ordered pairs for the function rule $y = 2x^2 + 5x + 5$.

x	0	1	2	3	0.5	1.5	2.5
y	■	■	■	■	■	■	■

⑦ Use the ordered pairs you found in problem 6 to graph $y = 2x^2 + 5x + 5$. You may copy and complete the graph that has been started here.

⑧ Why do we need to know what order of operations to use in finding ordered pairs for this function?

⑨ Use a computer or other means to make and complete this table of ordered pairs for the function rule $y = 3x^2 - 2x + 4$.

x	0	1	2	3	0.5	1.5	2.5
y							

⑩ Use the ordered pairs you found in problem 9 to graph the function $y = 3x^2 - 2x + 4$.

LESSON 118

Graphing a Perimeter Function

In this lesson you will learn whether there is a relationship between the length of a side and the perimeter of a square.

Side (*x*)															
Perimeter (*y*)															

Use a computer or other means to make a table like the one shown. In your table, record the results of the following measurements.

1 Measure the length of a side of each of the nine squares below. Then measure or calculate the perimeter of each square.

2 On a sheet of paper, draw at least six more squares of different sizes. Measure a side and either measure or calculate the perimeter of each square you draw.

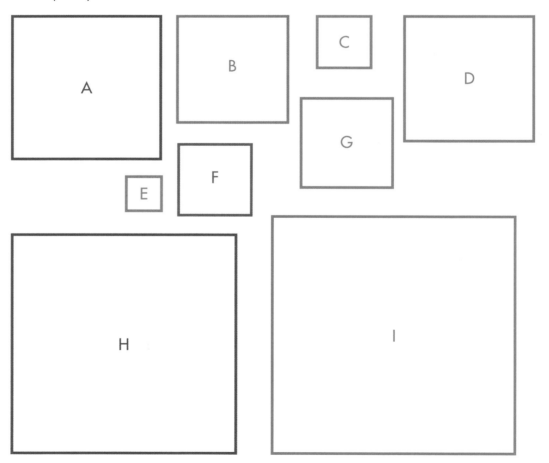

Graph the 15 ordered pairs from your table. Then answer these questions.

3 Do all the points fall on about the same straight line?

4 Does your graph look like the one to the right?

5 Can you tell from this graph what you multiply a side of a square by to find its perimeter?

Here is a closer look at part of the graph.

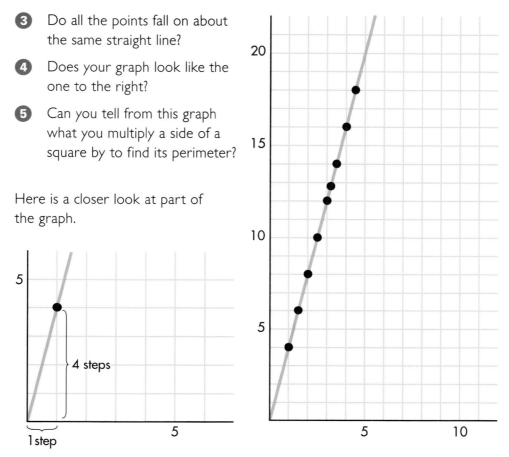

Draw a square that is 10 centimeters on a side. Measure or calculate its perimeter.

◆ Is the perimeter 40 centimeters?

◆ Is that 4 × 10?

The formula for finding the perimeter of a square can be written as:

$$y = 4x$$

with y as the perimeter and x as the length of a side. The formula is sometimes written this way:

$$p = 4s$$

with p as the perimeter and s as the length of a side.

Determining the Function Rule

In previous lessons you made graphs from function rules. In this lesson you'll figure out a function rule given a graph of that rule.

If you have a straight-line graph, you can figure out a rule for the function.

The number of steps up for each step to the right tells you what to multiply *x* by.

The place where the line crosses the *y*-axis tells you what to add (or subtract).

Example: Figure out a function rule for this graph.

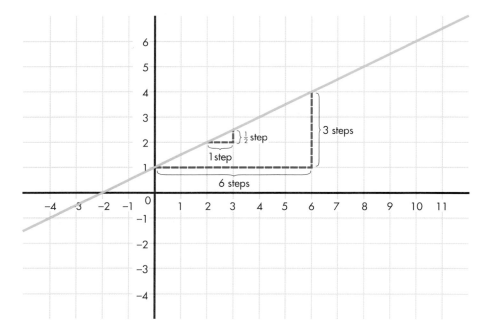

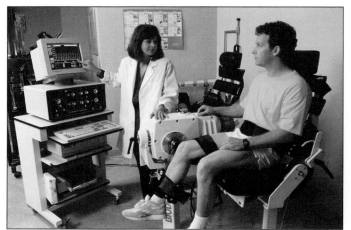

Here is a way to figure out a function rule for the graph.

First, figure out the number of steps up for each step to the right. Here are two ways to do this.

a. Choose a point on the line.
Go to the right one step.
How far up did the line go?

For example, (2, 2).

$\frac{1}{2}$ step

b. Choose a point on the line.
Go to the right any number
of steps.
How far up did the line go?

Divide to find out how many
steps up for each step to
the right.

For example, (0, 1).
Try 6 steps.

3 steps

$3 \div 6 = \frac{1}{2}$

The line goes up a half step for every step to the right. So the number x is multiplied by $\frac{1}{2}$. The function rule is $y = \frac{1}{2}x +$ "something." Remember that the "something" can be either positive or negative.

Second, find the point where the line crosses the y-axis. This is the point (0, 1). Because it is on the line, (0, 1) must satisfy the function rule. Since the graph is a straight line, we know that the rule is in the form $y = Ax + B$.

When $x = 0$, then $y = A \times 0 + B$, so $y = B$.

In this case, since $y = 1$ when $x = 0$, B must be 1.

You can do either of these steps first. B is always the value of y when $x = 0$. Another way to say this is that B is the y-coordinate of the point where the line crosses the y-axis.

So, the function rule for this graph must be $y = \frac{1}{2}x + 1$.

You can use these steps to find the function rule for any graph that is a straight line.

◆ LESSON 119 Determining the Function Rule

For each graph, determine a function rule.

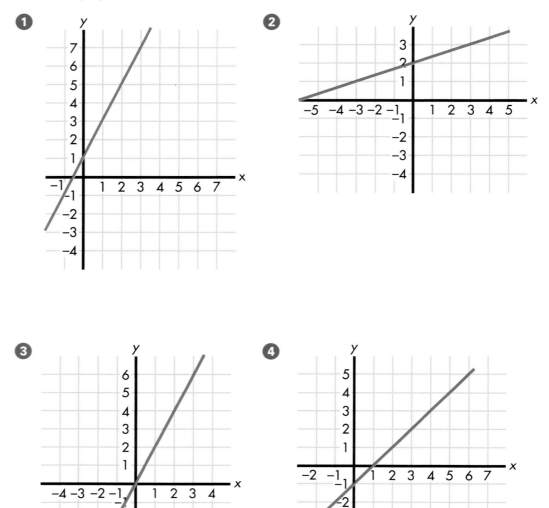

Hints: Write 1*x* as *x*.
To get from 0 to −1, subtract 1.

Solve for the variable. Use shortcuts when you can.

5 $n = 3 \times 20$

6 $4 \div \frac{1}{2} = w$

7 $6.1 \times 3.0 = n$

8 $w - 3.5 = 13.5$

9 $\frac{1}{2} \times \frac{3}{4} = n$

10 $16 \times 1000 = p$

11 $n \times 20 = 400$

12 $165.2 - 5.2 = n$

13 $25 \times 25 = t$

14 $x + 625 = 630.5$

15 $50 \times 50 = n$

16 $50 \times 51 = n$

17 $1000 \div t = 25$

18 $c \div 25 = 4000$

19 $n \times 6 = 36$

20 $15 \div n = 5$

21 $\frac{13}{13} \times \frac{57}{57} = n$

22 $30 \times w = 930$

23 $16.982 \times 100 = t$

24 $450 + 550 = n$

25 $5 + n = 7.45$

26 $\frac{16}{49} \times 1 = n$

27 $y \div 12 = 4$

28 $3\frac{1}{2} \times 4 = n$

29 $3\frac{1}{2} \times 40 = d$

30 $75 + \frac{35}{35} = n$

31 $169 \div 13 = t$

32 $\frac{19}{23} \times 0 = n$

33 $y \times 12 = 144$

34 $196 \div 14 = n$

Solve. Use shortcuts when you can.

35
$$\begin{array}{r} 750 \\ 750 \\ 750 \\ + 750 \\ \hline \end{array}$$

36
$$\begin{array}{r} 10,000 \\ - \ 9,950 \\ \hline \end{array}$$

37 $24\overline{)288}$

38 $12\overline{)288}$

39 $65\overline{)1235}$

40
$$\begin{array}{r} 16\frac{4}{5} \\ + 13\frac{3}{15} \\ \hline \end{array}$$

41 $19\overline{)1235}$

42 $1.9\overline{)123.5}$

Solve these problems.

43 Leah can swim 100 meters in 105 seconds. Can she swim 1000 meters in 17.5 minutes (1050 seconds)?

44 Today Leah swam 100 meters in $1\frac{2}{3}$ minutes. Was that a faster pace than 100 meters in 105 seconds?

Finding Circumference

In this lesson you'll investigate to discover whether there is a relationship between the **diameter** (the greatest distance across) and the **circumference** (the distance around) of a circle.

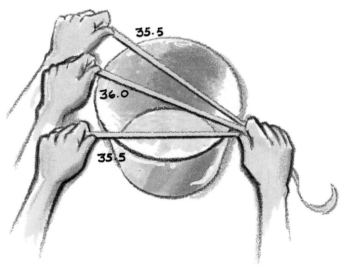

◆ Use a tape measure to measure the diameter and the circumference of at least five different circles or circular objects.

◆ Measure the diameter by holding one end of your tape measure (or ruler) at a point on the circle. Move the other end until the distance is the greatest. If you use a tape measure (or a string), be sure to pull it tight. In this picture, 36 centimeters is a good approximation of the diameter of the circle.

◆ Measure the circumference by wrapping a tape measure or string around the object. Measure as close to the edge as you can, particularly if the object has two bases of different sizes.

Write your measurements in a table like this one.

Circle	Diameter (cm) (x)	Circumference (cm) (y)
top of wastebasket	■	■
large jar	■	■
water glass	■	■
tire	■	■

Graph the ordered pairs from your table. Then answer these questions.

1 Are all the points you graphed approximately on a straight line?

2 About how many steps up does your graph go for each ten steps to the right? About how many steps up does it go for each step to the right?

3 Write a formula relating the circumference and the diameter of a circle.

4 The **radius** of a circle is the distance from the center to a point on the circle. What is the relationship between the radius and the diameter of a circle?

5 Rewrite your formula from problem 3 to use the radius instead of the diameter.

6 Use your formula from problem 3 to predict the circumference of a circle that is 50 centimeters in diameter.

7 If a circle is 50 centimeters in diameter, what is its radius?

8 Draw a circle 50 centimeters in diameter and measure its circumference. How close was your prediction?

◆ LESSON 120 Finding Circumference

The Greek letter π (pronounced "pī") is used to indicate the ratio of the circumference of a circle to its diameter.

$C = \pi d$ is the formula for finding the circumference (C) of a circle when the diameter (d) is known. To find the circumference, multiply d by π.

π is a definite fixed number between 3.141 and 3.142. The fraction $3\frac{1}{7}$ is a good approximation. The circumference (C) and diameter (d) of different circles vary, but π stays the same.

Answer the following questions.

9 In problems 2 and 3 on page 421, was your estimate of π about 3.14? An answer of 3 or more, but less than 3.3, would be considered close.

10 Use 3.14 for π to find the approximate circumference of a circle with a diameter of

   a. 10 centimeters   **b.** 20 meters   **c.** 25 centimeters

   d. 7 meters   **e.** 21 centimeters   **f.** 30 centimeters

11 Use $3\frac{1}{7}$ (or $\frac{22}{7}$) for π to find the approximate circumference of a circle with a diameter of

   a. 10 centimeters   **b.** 20 meters   **c.** 25 centimeters

   d. 7 meters   **e.** 21 centimeters   **f.** 30 centimeters

12 In finding a circumference, when is it easier to use 3.14 for π and when is it easier to use $3\frac{1}{7}$?

13 To seven places, the best approximation of π is 3.1415927. Use this number and a calculator to find the approximate circumference of each circle in problem 10.

14 Which approximations were closer to those in problem 13, those you found in problem 10 (using 3.14 for π) or those you found in problem 11 (using $3\frac{1}{7}$)? (Change your answers in problem 11 to decimals so you can compare them with your answers in problem 13.)

15 Is there a great difference in your answers for problems 10, 11, and 13?

16 Write a formula for finding the circumference of a circle when the radius is known.

Solve these problems. Try to do them in your head. Use shortcuts when you can.

17 9 × 8

18 9 + 8

19 9 − 8

20 90 × 800

21 6 × 7

22 7 × 60

23 420 ÷ 60

24 4200 ÷ 60

25 8 × 7

26 80 × 7000

27 80 − 70

28 6 × 3

29 6 ÷ 3

30 6 + 3

31 6 − 3

32 60 + 3

33 63 ÷ 7

34 630 ÷ 90

35 63 − 7

36 7 × 70

37 70 ÷ 7

38 7 + 70

39 70 − 7

40 490 ÷ 7

41 49 − 7

42 9 × 9

43 9 + 9

44 18 ÷ 9

45 810 ÷ 90

46 180 − 9

Multiply or divide. Watch the signs.

47 8.76 × 10

48 87.6 × 100

49 87.6 ÷ 10

50 0.876 × 1000

51 793.6 ÷ 100

52 79.36 × 10

53 0.7936 × 100

54 79.36 ÷ 10

55 8.457 × 10

56 8.457 × 1000

57 8.457 ÷ 100

58 845.7 ÷ 1000

59 1234 × 10

60 1234 ÷ 1000

61 12.34 × 100

62 1.234 × 100

63 0.5796 × 1000

64 57.96 ÷ 10

65 579.6 ÷ 10,000

66 5.796 × 100

67 0.5796 × 10

Solve these problems.

68 If hot dog buns come in packages of ten, how many packages are needed to get 75 buns?

69 One hot dog costs 75¢. How much will 100 hot dogs cost?

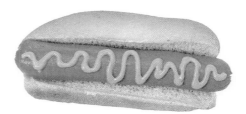

LESSON 121

Average Monthly Temperature

GEOGRAPHY CONNECTION

As you have seen throughout this unit, charts and graphs can help you analyze data and find patterns. Here is another example.

The following chart gives the average monthly temperatures (in degrees Celsius) in six cities.

	J	F	M	A	M	J	J	A	S	O	N	D
New York	0	1	5	11	17	22	25	24	20	14	8	2
Chicago	−4	−3	3	10	16	22	24	23	19	13	4	−2
Phoenix	11	14	14	19	27	31	34	34	29	23	16	13
San Francisco	9	11	12	13	14	17	14	17	18	16	13	10
Miami	19	20	22	24	26	27	27	28	28	26	22	20
Perth	24	25	23	20	16	15	15	16	17	18	20	22

Study the chart. Then discuss answers to these questions.

1 Which city has the greatest range in average monthly temperatures?

2 In which city do you think people need to spend the most money on clothing?

3 Which city would be likely to have the highest heating costs?

4 Which city has the warmest climate? Which has the coolest climate?

5 Perth is in Australia. Do you notice any difference between the temperature patterns in Perth and the patterns in the U.S. cities? Why is there a difference?

Work in groups to make up other questions from the chart. Discuss them with your group.

For each city in the chart on page 424, make a graph of the normal monthly temperatures. Repeat the data for two months at each end of the year, so that your graphs look like this:

City: _____

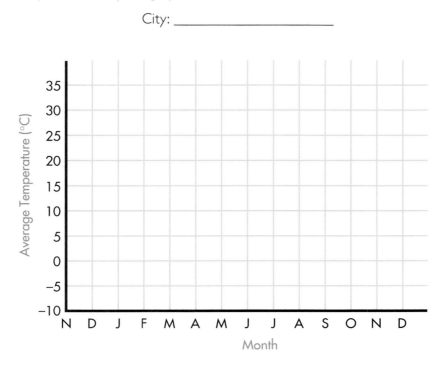

Look at the data and the graphs.

6 Try to explain why the temperatures change as they do.

7 Try to explain the differences among the graphs for different cities.

8 Is there any number in the chart that looks as if it might have been a mistake?

Functions that repeat themselves in a certain period are called *periodic functions*. The average monthly temperatures you graphed are periodic functions. Can you think of other periodic functions?

The hottest inhabited city on Earth is Djibouti, in the country of Djibouti in northeastern Africa, with an average temperature of 30°C (86°F).

LESSON 122

Unit 5 Review

Lessons 98, 101, and 104

What are the coordinates of

1 point A? **2** point B? **3** point C?

4 point D? **5** point E? **6** point F?

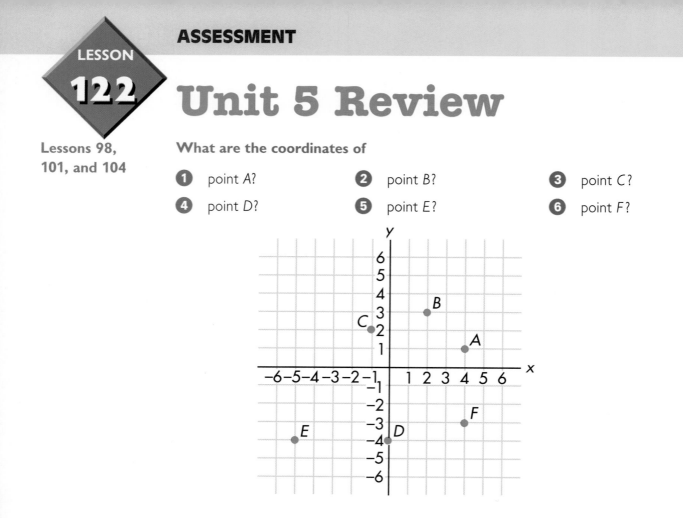

Lessons 99, 101, and 104

On your paper, graph the ordered pairs shown in the table. Label each point with its coordinates, for example (−3, −7).

7

x	−3	0	3	6	9
y	−7	−5	−3	−1	1

Lessons 101, 106, 112, 114, 116, and 117

Graph each of these functions.

8 $y = 2x + 1$ **9** $y = \frac{1}{2}x - 2$

10 $y = 2x^2$ (Graph this for values of x that are 0 or greater.)

Lesson 113

Find the next three terms of each sequence.

11 0, 6, 12, 18, ___, ___, ___

12 729, 243, 81, 27, ___, ___, ___

13 2, 5, 11, 23, ___, ___, ___

Lesson 109 Each of these tables of ordered pairs was made from a function rule of the form $y = Ax + B$ (**A** and **B** are numbers). In each case give the function rule.

14

x	0	5
y	−5	5

15

x	0	1
y	1	4

Lesson 120 Use 3.14 or $3\frac{1}{7}$ for π to find the approximate circumference of a circle with a diameter of

16 7 centimeters   **17** 10 centimeters   **18** 20 centimeters

Lesson 119 Give a function rule for each of these graphs.

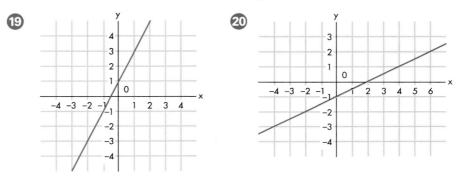

19   **20**

Lesson 100 For each pair of figures, tell whether a rotation, a reflection, or a translation could be used to fit one on top of the other.

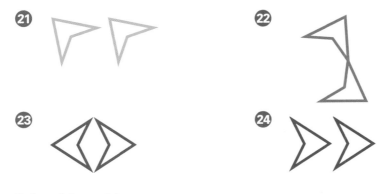

21   **22**

23   **24**

Lessons 95 and 96 Solve this problem.

25 Jeffrey is making a graph showing the amount of the time he spends on math, spelling, English, science, and social studies homework for one month. On which graph would it be easier to see the fraction of time he spent on each subject—a line graph or a circle graph?

LESSON 123

Unit 5 Practice

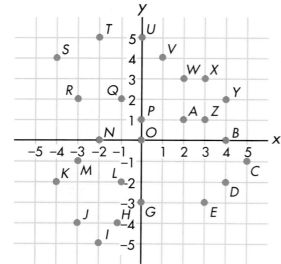

SOCIAL STUDIES CONNECTION

On your paper answer these questions by writing the correct letter for each of the coordinates on the graph above.

Lessons 99, 101, and 104

1 Who was the first United States president to die in office?

(2, 3), (−2, −5), (−1, −2), (−1, −2), (−2, −5), (2, 1), (−3, −1)
(−1, −4), (3, −3), (−2, 0), (−3, 2), (4, 2)
(−1, −4), (2, 1), (−3, 2), (−3, 2), (−2, −5), (−4, 4), (0, 0), (−2, 0)

2 Who was the first United States president to be born in the United States?

(−3, −1), (2, 1), (−3, 2), (−2, 5), (−2, −5), (−2, 0)

(1, 4), (2, 1), (−2, 0)   (4, 0), (0, 5), (−3, 2), (3, −3), (−2, 0)

3 Who was the first vice president to become president?

(−3, −4), (0, 0), (−1, −4), (−2, 0)

(2, 1), (4, −2), (2, 1), (−3, −1), (−4, 4)

4 Who was the only president to serve two terms that did not follow each other?

(0, −3), (−3, 2), (0, 0), (1, 4), (3, −3), (−3, 2)

(5, −1), (−1, −2), (3, −3), (1, 4), (3, −3), (−1, −2), (2, 1), (−2, 0), (4, −2)

Use this code to make up messages, questions, or riddles. Give them to a friend to decode.

Lessons 99, 101, 104, 109, and 119

Graph each set of ordered pairs. Decide whether each set of ordered pairs could have come from a function rule of the form $y = Ax + B$. (Are all the points on one straight line?) If the set could have come from a function rule of the form $y = Ax + B$, tell what the rule is.

5

x	0	1	2	3	4
y	1	2	4	8	16

6

x	0	1	2	3	4
y	−5	−2	1	4	7

7

x	0	1	2	3	4
y	0	2	4	6	8

8

x	0	2	6	−4	3
y	−2	−1	1	−4	$-\frac{1}{2}$

9

x	0	1	2	3	4
y	1	3	5	7	9

10

x	0	2	5	1.3	7
y	7	7	7	7	7

11

x	0	1	2	3	4
y	0	1	4	9	16

12

x	0	2	4	3	1
y	0	2	8	4.5	0.5

13

x	0	1	2	3	4
y	0	$\frac{1}{2}$	1	$1\frac{1}{2}$	2

14

x	0	3	−1.2	4	2.6
y	0	3	−1.2	4	2.6

Lesson 113

Give the next three terms of each sequence.

15 0, 1, 3, 6, 10, ___, ___, ___

16 4, 8, 12, 16, ___, ___, ___

17 3, 6, 12, 24, ___, ___, ___

◆ LESSON 123   Unit 5 Practice

Lessons 101, 106, 112, and 114

Graph each of these functions.

18 $y = x + 2$ **19** $y = x - 3$ **20** $y = x$

21 $y = x + 1$ **22** $y = x - 1$ **23** $y = 2x - 1$

24 $y = \frac{1}{2}x - 1$ **25** $y = 2x + 2$ **26** $y = 2x - 3$

27 $y = \frac{1}{2}x + 2$ **28** $y = \frac{1}{3}x - 2$ **29** $y = \frac{1}{3}x + 3$

Lessons 116 and 117

Graph each of these functions. (Use only values of x that are 0 or greater.)

30 $y = x^2$ **31** $y = \frac{1}{2}x^2 + 4x$ **32** $y = 2x^2 - 4x + 1$

Lesson 120

Use 3.14 or $3\frac{1}{7}$ for π to find the approximate circumference of a circle with a diameter of

33 7 cm   **34** 3.5 cm   **35** 14 cm   **36** 100 cm   **37** 10 cm

38 20 cm   **39** 1 cm   **40** 5 cm   **41** 6 cm   **42** 2 cm

43 0.5 cm   **44** 0.1 cm   **45** 9.1 cm   **46** 4 cm   **47** 23 cm

Lesson 120

Use 3.14 or $3\frac{1}{7}$ for π to find the approximate diameter of a circle with a circumference of

48 314 cm   **49** 62.8 cm   **50** 22 cm   **51** 44 cm   **52** 50 cm

Lesson 100

For each pair of figures, tell whether a rotation, a reflection, or a translation could be used to move one figure on top of the other.

53   **54**

Lesson 119   Give a function rule for each of these graphs.

55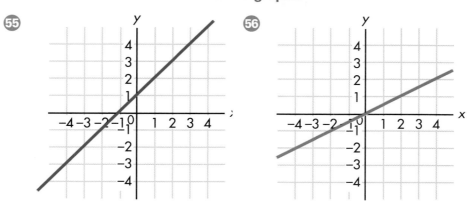

56

57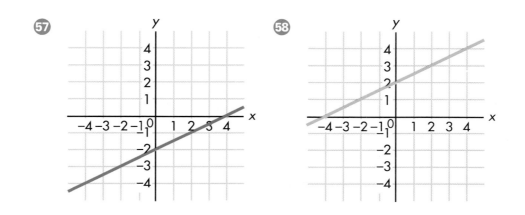

58

59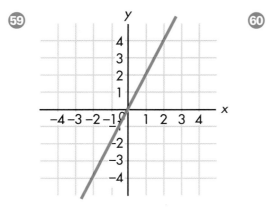

60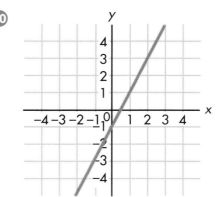

Unit Test

What are the coordinates of

1 point *A*?   **2** point *B*?   **3** point *C*?

4 point *D*?   **5** point *E*?   **6** point *F*?

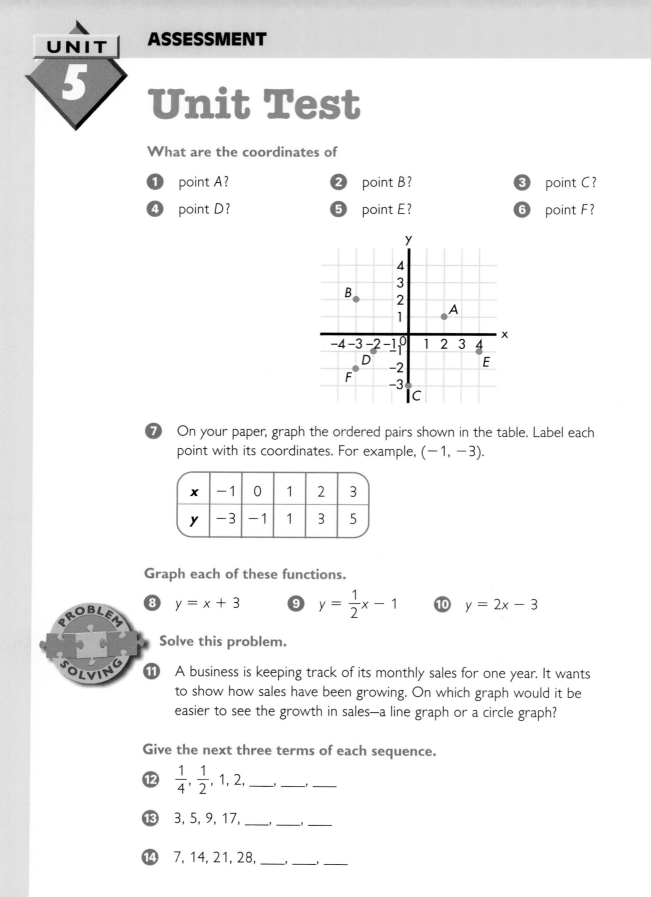

7 On your paper, graph the ordered pairs shown in the table. Label each point with its coordinates. For example, $(-1, -3)$.

x	−1	0	1	2	3
y	−3	−1	1	3	5

Graph each of these functions.

8 $y = x + 3$ **9** $y = \frac{1}{2}x - 1$ **10** $y = 2x - 3$

Solve this problem.

11 A business is keeping track of its monthly sales for one year. It wants to show how sales have been growing. On which graph would it be easier to see the growth in sales—a line graph or a circle graph?

Give the next three terms of each sequence.

12 $\frac{1}{4}, \frac{1}{2}, 1, 2,$ ___, ___, ___

13 3, 5, 9, 17, ___, ___, ___

14 7, 14, 21, 28, ___, ___, ___

Each of these tables of ordered pairs was made from a function rule of the form $y = Ax + B$. In each case, give the function rule.

⑮
x	−1	0
y	2	4

⑯
x	0	2
y	0	1

Use 3.14 or $3\frac{1}{7}$ to find the approximate circumference of a circle with a diameter of

⑰ 14 centimeters ⑱ 1 centimeter ⑲ 30 centimeters

Give a function rule for each graph.

⑳ 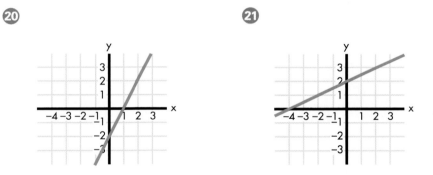 ㉑

For each pair of figures, tell whether a rotation, a reflection, or a translation could be used to move one figure on top of the other.

㉒ 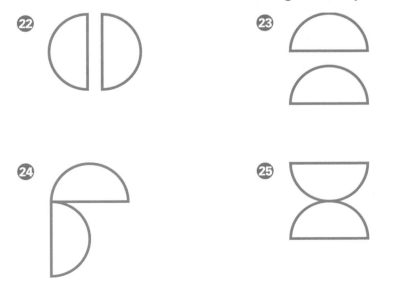 ㉓

㉔ ㉕

UNIT
5
WRAP-UP

Library Research

Collect information about your school library or your public library. Use the information you collect to complete the chart on page 435.

First estimate each answer, and record your estimates. Then think about how to find more precise answers. If you want to interview anyone, be sure to plan in advance what questions you will ask. You may want to make an appointment to be sure that the person you need to talk with will be available.

If you need to look up information in books or other records, think about where those resources might be found.

	FIRST ESTIMATE	ACTUAL OR SECOND ESTIMATE
Number of books in the library		
Annual circulation		
Number of people served by the library		
Annual budget		
Busiest day		
Least busy day		
Number of new books purchased in the past year		
Number of books discarded in the past year		

What are some other questions that will provide useful information?

Discuss the answers to these questions.

◆ About how much money is spent each year for each person served by the library?

◆ About how much money is spent each year for each book that is circulated?

Using the information you collect, compare your library with some of the library systems listed on page 388. Then make suggestions for making your library more effective.

UNIT 6

Geometry

PLANE AND SOLID FIGURES

- **perimeter and area**
- **polygons**
- **square roots**
- **measuring angles**
- **angle relationships**
- **compass constructions**

SCHOOL TO WORK CONNECTION

Architects use math . . .

An architect first makes sketches of what she wants to create. Then she uses her sketches to make a blueprint, or scale drawing, of the house. Using tools like the ones pictured, the architect draws angles, lines, and shapes on the blueprint to show the details of the house.

Area of a Rectangle

Luke has a tabletop that was made with small colored tiles that are 1 centimeter on a side.

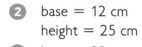
1 cm

The tabletop is 70 centimeters long and 50 centimeters wide. How many tiles does Luke need to make another tabletop just like the one he has?

◆ How do you find the area of a rectangle?

The formula that is most often used to find the area of a rectangle is this:

$$A = bh$$

In this formula b stands for the measure of the base, h stands for the measure of the height in the same units, and A stands for the area in square units.

Remember: We omit the × sign in written formulas to avoid confusion with the letter x. So bh means $b \times h$.

Example: Find the area of a rectangle with a base of 20 centimeters and a height of 9 centimeters.

$A = bh$
$A = 20 \text{ cm} \times 9 \text{ cm}$
$A = 180 \text{ cm}^2$

ALGEBRA READINESS

Find the area of the rectangles with these bases and heights. Be sure to include the correct unit in your answers.

1. base = 10 cm
   height = 25 cm

2. base = 12 cm
   height = 25 cm

3. base = 100 cm
   height = 100 cm

4. base = 99 cm
   height = 101 cm

5. base = 98 cm
   height = 102 cm

6. base = 97 cm
   height = 103 cm

7. base = 96 cm
   height = 104 cm

8. base = 95 cm
   height = 105 cm

9. base = 195 cm
   height = 205 cm

10. base = 295 cm
    height = 305 cm

Solve.

11. How many square tiles 1 centimeter on a side would be needed to cover a square tabletop 1 decimeter on a side? (10 cm = 1 dm)

12. How many square tiles 1 centimeter on a side would be needed to cover a square tabletop 1 meter on a side? (100 cm = 1 m)

Here are some symbols you should know:

cm^2 means "square centimeters"

dm^2 means "square decimeters"

m^2 means "square meters"

◆ The symbol for millimeters is *mm*. What do you think the symbol is for square millimeters? For square kilometers?

Find the area of each rectangle. Be sure to include the correct unit in your answers.

13 base = 12 cm, height = 14 cm

14 base = 1.2 cm, height = 1.4 cm

15 base = 0.12 cm, height = 0.14 cm

16 base = 7 cm, height = 4 cm

17 base = 7 cm, height = 0.4 cm

18 base = 0.7 cm, height = 0.4 cm

19 base = 1.5 cm, height = 3 cm

20 base = 1.5 cm, height = 0.3 cm

21 base = 4 cm, height = 5 cm

22 base = 4 cm, height = 0.5 cm

23 Look at problems 13–22 and their answers.

a. If you multiply two factors together, is the product always greater than either factor?
b. When is it greater?
c. When is it not greater?

24 The Up-Rise Company wants to build a large office building on a lot that it owns in Boomville. According to a Boomville law, you cannot put up an office building unless the lot is at least $\frac{1}{2}$ square kilometer. The dimensions of the rectangular lot are 0.82 kilometer and 0.55 kilometer.

a. Is the lot big enough?
b. How far would you have to walk to go all the way around the lot?

25 The High-Town Company owns a rectangular lot in Boomville that is 1.5 kilometers by 0.6 kilometer. How many smaller lots of at least 0.5 square kilometer can be made from this lot?

26 Research to find out building codes in your community.

LESSON
125

Surface Area

Buildings lose heat through their walls and windows. The heat lost from a building is greater if the surface area of the building is greater. So to find the expected heat loss, you must find the surface area of the building. The **surface area** of a three-dimensional (3-D) figure is the sum of the areas of all its faces.

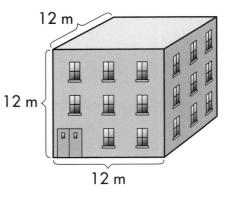

The illustration above shows the Big Block Company.

1 What is the area of the front of the Big Block Company's building?

2 What is the area of the back of the building?

3 What is the area of each side?

4 What is the area of the roof?

5 If no heat is lost through the ground, there are five faces (front, back, two sides, top) through which heat can be lost. What is the total area of these five faces?

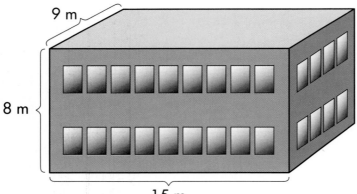

6 What is the total area of the top and four sides of the building above?

7 What is the total area of the top and four sides of a building that is 20 meters long, 12 meters wide, and 14 meters tall? (Draw a picture if it helps.)

8 What is the total area of the top and four sides of a building that is 25 meters long, 10 meters wide, and 8 meters tall?

Solve these problems.

9 If you could fold this figure along the dotted lines and glue the edges together, what solid figure would the pattern make?

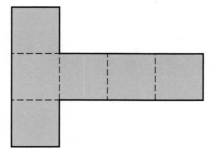

There are other patterns that would also make a cube if folded. Some people call such two-dimensional patterns for three-dimensional figures **nets**. For each of the following nets, decide whether you could fold it to make a cube. You may wish to make a pattern to see if it works.

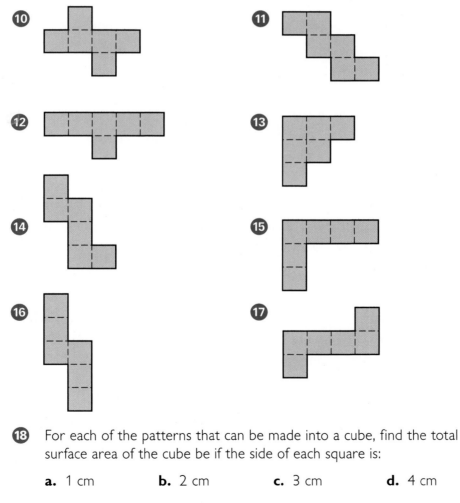

10

11

12

13

14

15

16

17

18 For each of the patterns that can be made into a cube, find the total surface area of the cube be if the side of each square is:

   a. 1 cm   **b.** 2 cm   **c.** 3 cm   **d.** 4 cm

◆ **LESSON 125 Surface Area**

THINKING STORY

On the Move

Part 1

Ferdie and Portia were going to move again. The apartment building where they lived was being torn down. Their mother had found another apartment on the other side of town. It was just like the one they were leaving. It had three small bedrooms, a tiny kitchen, and a living room in which three people were a crowd.

"Moving can cost a lot of money," their mother said. "Portia, would you call some movers? Find out which one will give us the best deal."

After a few phone calls Portia reported: "This is confusing. First I called Scratchit Brothers. They said they would charge us $60 an hour for the crew and the truck."

"Oh, dear," said their mother. "Last time it took the movers almost all day to move us. I think we have even more things now."

"Well," said Portia, "Aickenback Movers will move us for $160 per room. Rockyway Movers charges by weight—10¢ a pound. That sounds cheapest to me, but I'm not sure."

"We'll have to weigh everything in the house to figure it out," said Ferdie. He got out the bathroom scale and started piling dishes and cups on it. "After I weigh all the dishes, you can weigh all the books," he told Portia.

. . . to be continued

Work in groups. Discuss your answers and how you figured them out. Then compare your answers with those of other groups.

1 Which mover is likely to charge less, Scratchit Brothers or Aickenback? How do you know?

2 How do you know there will be such a large difference in what Scratchit Brothers and Aickenback would charge for this move? Can you think of a case in which the difference might be the other way around?

3 Do Portia and Ferdie have to weigh every single thing in the apartment to estimate what Rockyway Movers would charge? What is an easier way to estimate the weight?

4 In the apartment are two bookcases. Each bookcase has four shelves, and each shelf is 24 inches long. Three shelves are full of paperback books. The others are full of hardcover books. Estimate the total weight of books. Be prepared to defend your estimate. If possible, use a scale or a balance and weigh some real books to help you make a good estimate.

LESSON 126

Volume of a Rectangular Prism

In this lesson you'll learn a formula for finding the amount of space that a figure such as the one below contains.

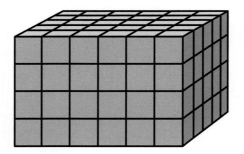

Solve the following problems.

1 Each small block shown above is 1 centimeter on a side. That is, each block is 1 cubic centimeter. How many cubic centimeters are in the entire stack above?

2 Is there a simple multiplication you can do to show how many cubic centimeters are in the bottom layer of blocks? What is it?

3 How many cubic centimeters are in the bottom layer?

4 Does each layer have the same number of cubic centimeters in it?

5 How many layers are there?

6 What simple multiplication can you do to show how many cubic centimeters are in the entire stack?

The number of cubic centimeters in the stack is its **volume** in cubic centimeters.

The volume of a box-shaped object (in cubic units) is equal to the product of the length, width, and height of the object (measured in the same units). This can be written in a shorter way with this formula:

$$V = lwh$$

Remember: *lwh* means *l* × *w* × *h*, or length × width × height.

7 When determining volume, does it make a difference which measure we call the width and which we call the length?

To find the volume of a **rectangular prism** (a box-shaped object), multiply the length by the width by the height.

$$V = lwh$$

Find the volume of boxes with the following dimensions. In each case, be sure to include the correct unit in your answer.

8   length = 4 cm, width = 5 cm, height = 6 cm

9   length = 10 cm, width = 20 cm, height = 2 cm

10   length = 4 cm, width = 2 cm, height = 1 cm

11   length = 2 dm, width = 2 dm, height = 2 dm

12   length = 1 dm, width = 1 dm, height = 1 dm

13   length = 10 cm, width = 10 cm, height = 10 cm

14   There are 10 centimeters in 1 decimeter. How many cubic centimeters are in 1 cubic decimeter? (Hint: Look at problems 12 and 13.)

Now find the volume of these boxes.

15   length = 1 m, width = 1 m, height = 1 m

16   length = 10 dm, width = 10 dm, height = 10 dm

17   There are 10 decimeters in 1 meter. How many cubic decimeters are in 1 cubic meter?

18   How many cubic centimeters are in 1 cubic meter? (There are 100 centimeters in 1 meter.)

Here are some symbols you should know:

cm^3 means "cubic centimeters"

dm^3 means "cubic decimeters"

m^3 means "cubic meters"

◆ LESSON 126 Volume of a Rectangular Prism

The Brick-Box Building Company wants to build a storage house that has at least 1000 cubic meters of space. To reduce heat loss and building costs, the total exposed area (four walls and the roof) should be as small as possible.

Calculate the volume and the exposed area for each of these sets of dimensions.

19 height (h) = 10 m, length (l) = 20 m, width (w) = 5 m

20 h = 20 m, l = 10 m, w = 5 m

21 h = 40 m, l = 5 m, w = 5 m

22 h = 10 m, l = 10 m, w = 10 m

23 h = 5 m, l = 20 m, w = 10 m

24 h = 5 m, l = 25 m, w = 8 m

25 h = 5 m, l = 15 m, w = 14 m

26 h = 6 m, l = 13 m, w = 13 m

27 h = 7 m, l = 12 m, w = 12 m

28 h = 7 m, l = 16 m, w = 9 m

29 Look at your results for problems 19–28. Which storage house would you build? Why?

Use a calculator to help you with these problems.

30 Can you give the dimensions of a building that has a volume of at least 1000 cubic meters and an exposed area less than 480 square meters?

a. Can you find an answer using a whole number of meters for each dimension?

b. Can you give dimensions that are not whole numbers of meters? What would the dimensions be?

c. Compare your answers with those of your classmates. Did everyone find the same answer?

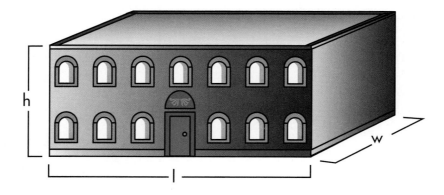

Work in small groups of three or four to answer these problems. You may use a calculator. Give your answers to the nearest tenth of a meter.

31 A builder would like to build a storage facility with a volume of 8000 cubic meters and the least possible total surface area. What should be the length, width, and height of the building? Try different possible values and compare your answer with those of other groups.

32 The builder wants to change the plans so that the volume of the building is 15,625 cubic meters. What length, width, and height would give the least possible total surface area?

33 Another builder would like to build a storage facility with a volume of 8000 cubic meters and the least possible area for the walls and ceiling (there will be no floor). What should be the length, width, and height of the building?

34 This builder wants to increase the volume of the planned building to 12,000 cubic meters. What length, width, and height would give the least possible area for the walls and ceiling?

Hint: Try different lengths, widths, and heights that give the volume you need, then find the surface area.

For problem 31, for example, if we choose 100 for length and 80 for width, then since volume = length × width × height, the height will be 8000 ÷ (80 × 100) = 8000 ÷ 8000, which is 1. The surface area would be 2 × [(100 × 800) + (100 × 1) + (80 × 1)] = 16,360 m².

If we choose 23 for length and 13 for width, then the height will be 8000 ÷ (23 × 13) = 26.76. The surface area would be about 2524.72 m².

Try to find dimensions that give a still smaller surface area.

In your Math Journal write about the strategies your group used for solving these problems.

LESSON 127

Area and Volume

You can apply what you know about perimeter, area, and volume to calculate these measurements for your classroom.

COOPERATIVE LEARNING

Work in groups of three or four. Find the perimeter and area of the floor of your classroom. (Use centimeters and square centimeters or inches and square inches—the class should decide on one unit of measure before you begin.)

1 Draw a rough map of the room.

2 Measure the length of each wall and label your map with these dimensions.

3 Calculate the perimeter and area using a calculator.

4 By how much do you think your perimeter measure might differ from those of other groups? less than 10 units? between 10 and 100 units? between 100 and 1000 units? between 1000 and 10,000 units? more than 10,000 units?

5 By how much do you think your area measure might differ from those of other groups?

Calculate the perimeter and area using the given measurements.

6 length = 45 cm, width = 20 cm, perimeter = ■, area = ■

7 length = 110 cm, width = 90 cm, perimeter = ■, area = ■

8 length = 200 cm, width = 150 cm, perimeter = ■, area = ■

9 length = 1400 cm, width = 700 cm, perimeter = ■, area = ■

10 length = 2000 cm, width = 2000 cm, perimeter = ■, area = ■

11 length = 275 cm, width = 75 cm, perimeter = ■, area = ■

12 length = 51 cm, width = 49 cm, perimeter = ■, area = ■

13 length = 1350 cm, width = 150 cm, perimeter = ■, area = ■

Calculate the volume using the given measurements.

14 length = 200 cm, width = 150 cm, height = 200 cm, volume = ■

15 length = 150 cm, width = 150 cm, height = 200 cm, volume = ■

16 length = 300 cm, width = 200 cm, height = 150 cm, volume = ■

17 length = 300 cm, width = 195 cm, height = 155 cm, volume = ■

18 length = 300 cm, width = 205 cm, height = 145 cm, volume = ■

Use a calculator to help solve these problems.

19 Work in small groups of three or four. Measure or estimate the height of your classroom. Using the measurements you found for problem 2 on page 448 and your figure for the height of the room, calculate the volume of the room.

20 Calculate the surface area of the room (the sum of the areas of the floor, ceiling, and all of the walls, including doors, windows, and so on).

Discuss these questions with the members of your group.

21 By how much do you think your volume figure might differ from those of other groups?

22 By how much do you think your surface area figure might differ from those of other groups?

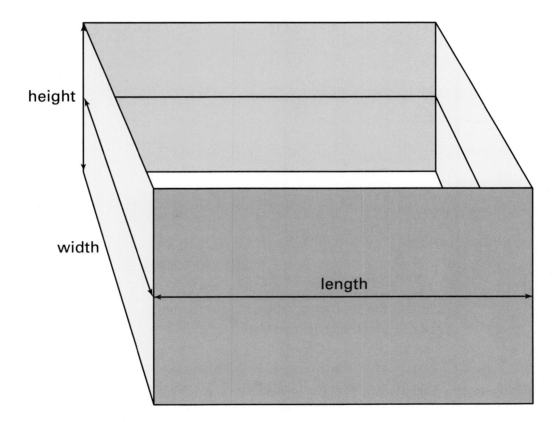

◆ LESSON 127   Area and Volume

In one class the map of the room looked like this:

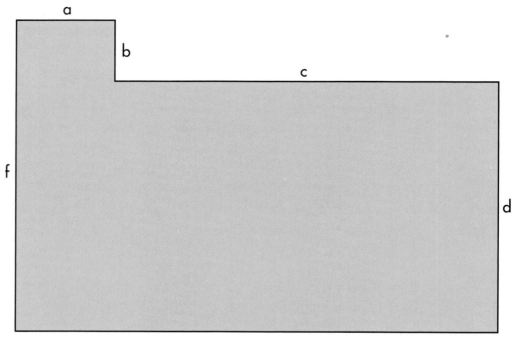

Ashley's group made the following measurements:

a = 183 cm	*b* = 122 cm	*c* = 731 cm
d = 488 cm	*e* = 914 cm	*f* = 610 cm

Maria's group measured:

a = 180 cm	*b* = 122 cm	*c* = 731 cm
d = 485 cm	*e* = 911 cm	*f* = 607 cm

Peter's group measured:

a = 184 cm	*b* = 122 cm	*c* = 731 cm
d = 490 cm	*e* = 915 cm	*f* = 612 cm

Solve.

㉓ Calculate the perimeter and area of the room using each group's measurements and compare them.

㉔ Compare the perimeter, area, and volume calculated by your group with those of other groups in your class. Write one or two sentences about what you think is interesting.

Solve.

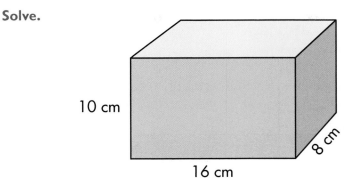

10 cm

8 cm

16 cm

25 Calculate the volume of a box 16 cm long, 8 cm wide, and 10 cm tall.

26 If each of the measures in problem 25 may be as much as 0.5 cm too low or too high, what are the greatest and least possible volumes for the box?

27 Find the surface area of the box in problem 25.

28 Find the greatest and least possible surface areas for the box if each measure may be up to 0.5 centimeter too low or too high.

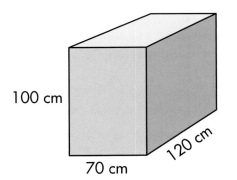

100 cm

120 cm

70 cm

29 Calculate the volume of a box that is 70 cm long, 120 cm wide, and 100 cm tall.

30 If each of the measures in problem 29 may be as much as 1 cm too low or too high, what are the greatest and least possible volumes for the box?

31 Find the surface area of the box in problem 29.

32 Find the greatest and the least possible surface areas for the box if each measure may be up to 1 cm too low or too high.

LESSON 128

Area of a Right Triangle

Areas of right triangles are related to areas of rectangles.

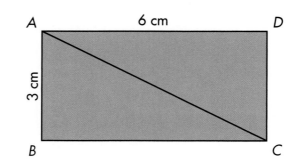

◆ What is the area of rectangle *ABCD* in square centimeters?

◆ The area of triangle *ABC* is what fraction of the area of *ABCD*?

◆ What is the area of triangle *ABC*?

Remember: A right angle is an angle that has a measure of 90°, like the corner of this page.

Angles *A*, *B*, *C*, and *D* are right angles.

A **right triangle** is a triangle that has a right angle.

Triangles *ABC* and *CDA* are both right triangles.

◆ Can we think of every right triangle as having half the area of a rectangle that shares two of the triangle's sides?

You can determine the area of a right triangle by taking one half the area of the corresponding rectangle.

Example: What is the area of triangle *EFG*?

Since *F* is a right angle, you can draw a rectangle with *EF* and *FG* as its height and base. The area of the rectangle is 3 × 4, or 12, square centimeters. So the area of triangle *EFG* is one half of 12, or 6, square centimeters.

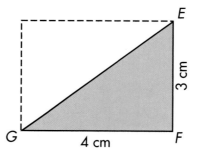

The area of a right triangle is one half the length of the base times the height.

$$A = \frac{1}{2}bh$$

(The base and height are measured on lines that meet in a right angle.)

$\angle C$ is a right angle.

Area of $\triangle ABC$

$$= \frac{1}{2} bh$$

$$= \frac{1}{2} (10 \times 7.5)$$

$$= 37.5 \text{ cm}^2$$

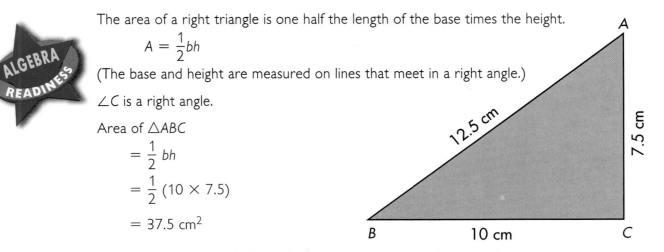

Remember, the symbol $\angle$ stands for angle, the symbol $\triangle$ stands for triangle, and cm^2 stands for square centimeters.

For each of these right triangles, name the right angle, the base, and the height.

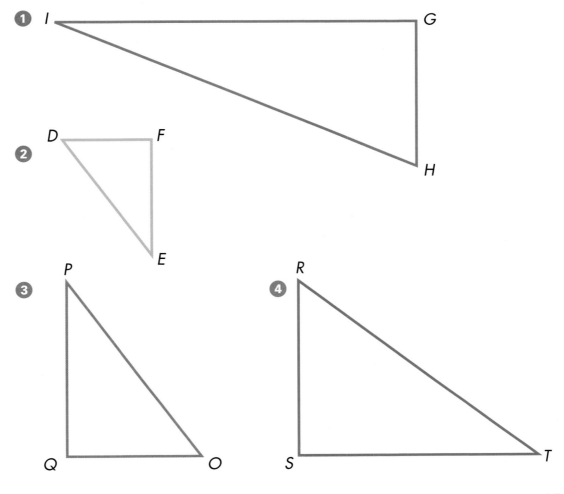

◆ **LESSON 128   Area of a Right Triangle**

Find the area of each of the right triangles shown below using the measurements given.

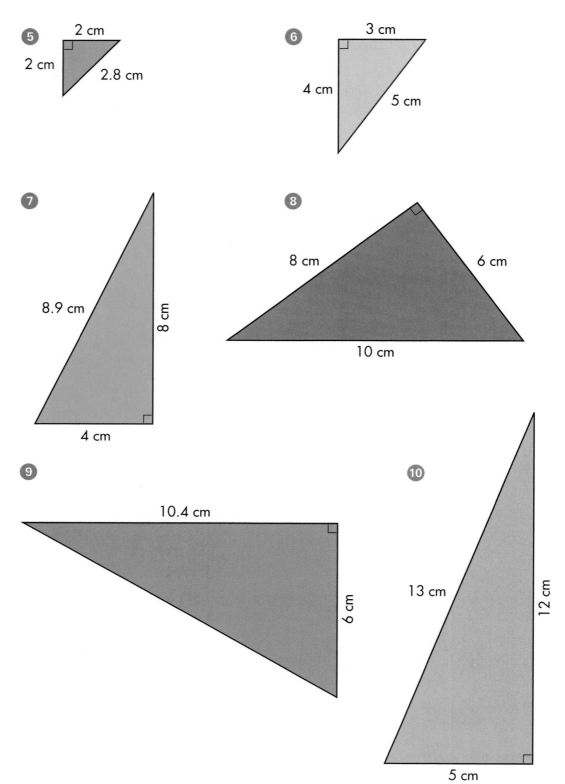

5
2 cm
2 cm
2.8 cm

6
3 cm
4 cm
5 cm

7
8.9 cm
8 cm
4 cm

8
8 cm
6 cm
10 cm

9
10.4 cm
6 cm

10
13 cm
12 cm
5 cm

Add or subtract. Watch the signs.

11 738
   − 265

12 831
   + 694

13 1979
   − 1492

14 13,875
   + 8,238

Multiply. Use shortcuts when you can.

15 50
   × 50

16 49
   × 51

17 70
   × 70

18 71
   × 69

Divide. Round decimal quotients to the nearest tenth when necessary.

19 7)315

20 9)1850

21 21)476

22 54)612

23 8)625

24 38)829

25 25)750

26 82)933

27 40)640

28 45)180

29 11)100

30 63)1979

Solve.

31 $\frac{1}{3}$ of 15

32 $\frac{1}{6}$ of 24

33 $\frac{3}{4}$ of 8

34 $\frac{1}{5}$ of 20

35 $\frac{2}{3}$ of 15

36 $\frac{1}{4}$ of 8

37 $\frac{1}{7}$ of 21

38 $\frac{2}{5}$ of 20

In each problem two of the answers are clearly wrong and one is correct. Choose the correct answer.

39 12.3 × 2.1   **a.** 25.83   **b.** 258.3   **c.** 2583

40 2.5 × 7.5   **a.** 0.1875   **b.** 1.875   **c.** 18.75

41 5.6 × 23.1   **a.** 12.936   **b.** 129.36   **c.** 1293.6

42 0.54 × 1.13   **a.** 0.06102   **b.** 0.6102   **c.** 6.102

43 8.3 × 6.47   **a.** 53.701   **b.** 537.01   **c.** 5370.1

44 936 × 0.28   **a.** 26.208   **b.** 262.08   **c.** 2620.8

45 49.7 × 5.6   **a.** 27.832   **b.** 278.32   **c.** 2783.2

Parallelograms

Lines are **parallel** if they go in the same direction and are the same distance apart at all points. Two parallel lines are in the same plane and never meet. These two lines are parallel.

Of course, we can draw only a small part of a line since a line goes on forever in both directions.

Although these lines do not meet on this page, they are not parallel because we know they will meet to the right when extended.

1 Look around your classroom. Find some examples of parallel lines (really, parts of parallel lines).

2 Think of examples of parallel lines that are not in your classroom.

A **quadrilateral** is a figure that has four sides (*quadri-* means "four," and *lateral* means "of the side" or "sided"). Figure *ABCD* is a quadrilateral.

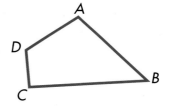

If both pairs of opposite sides of a quadrilateral are parallel, the figure is a **parallelogram**. Figure *JKLM* is a parallelogram.

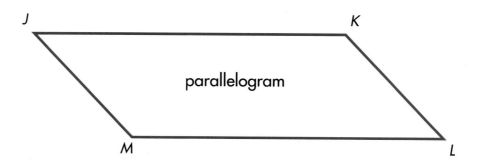

parallelogram

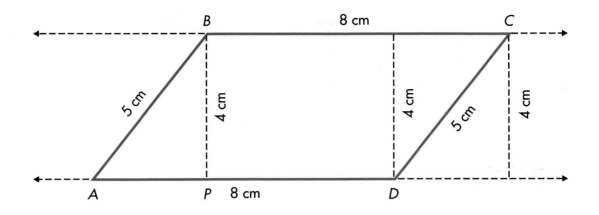

In parallelogram *ABCD*, *AB* is 5 centimeters, *BC* is 8 centimeters, *CD* is 5 centimeters, and *DA* is 8 centimeters long. The shortest distance between lines *AD* and *BC* is 4 centimeters.

◆   Can you figure out what the area of parallelogram *ABCD* is? (Hint: See if you can make it equal to the area of some rectangle.)

◆   What is the area of parallelogram *EFGH*? Explain how you got your answer.

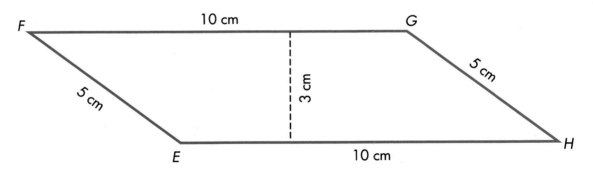

The area of a parallelogram is equal to the length of the base times the height.

$$A = bh$$

Remember, the height is measured on a line segment that is **perpendicular** to the base. Perpendicular lines intersect at right angles. So in parallelogram *EFGH*, if you choose *EH* as the base, the height is 3 centimeters (not 5 centimeters).

◆   Could we have chosen a different side as the base?

◆ **LESSON 129 Parallelograms**

Find the area of each of these parallelograms in square centimeters. A right angle (for example, ⌐ or ⌐) drawn at the intersection of two lines means that the lines are perpendicular.

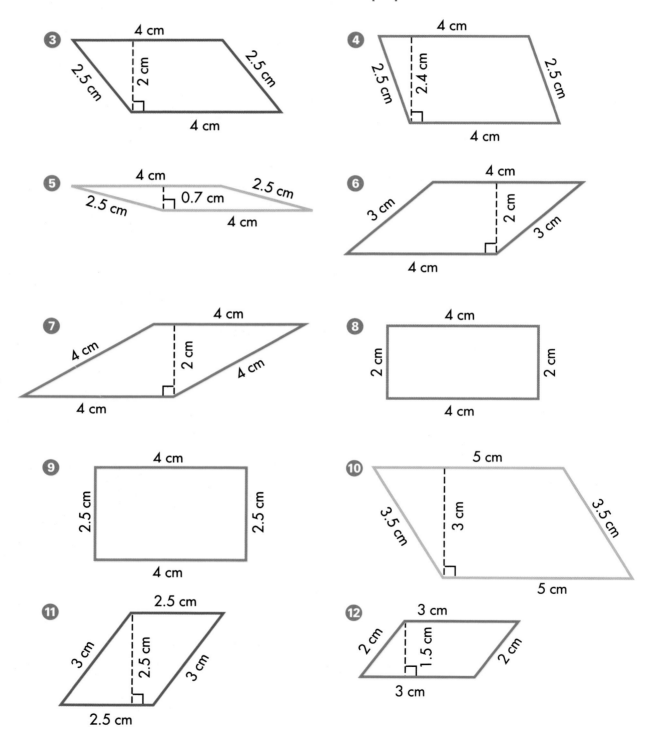

Find the perimeter or circumference of each of the following figures, using the measurements given (lines that look parallel are parallel; use either 3.14 or $\frac{22}{7}$ as your value for π).

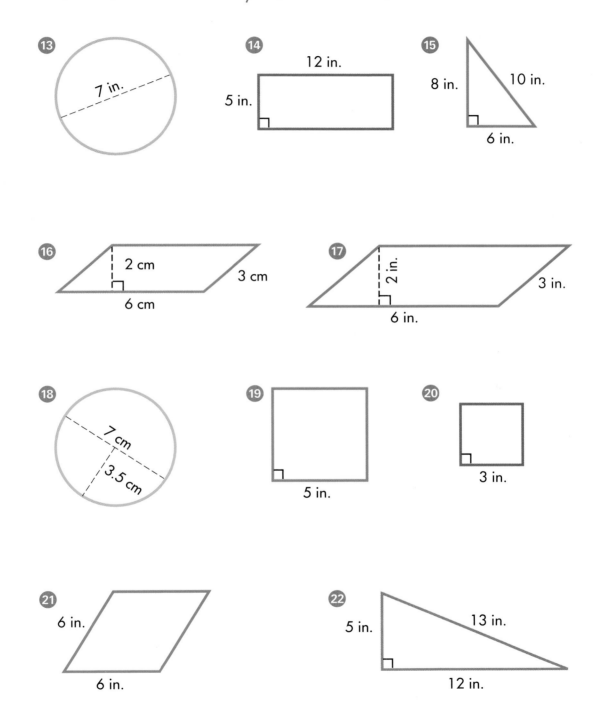

13

7 in.

14

12 in.

5 in.

15

8 in.   10 in.

6 in.

16

2 cm

3 cm

6 cm

17

2 in.

3 in.

6 in.

18

7 cm

3.5 cm

19

5 in.

20

3 in.

21

6 in.

6 in.

22

5 in.   13 in.

12 in.

Area of a Triangle

In this lesson you will review how to use the relationship between parallelograms and triangles that have the same base and height to come up with a formula for finding the area of triangles.

◆ What is the area of parallelogram *ABCD*?

◆ Is △*DBC* the same shape and size as △*BDA*? (Imagine cutting out the parallelogram and then cutting along *DB* to make two separate triangles. Would you be able to fit △*DBC* exactly on △*BDA*?)

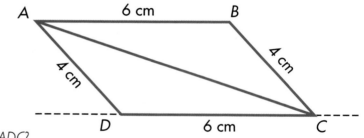

◆ What fraction of the area of *ABCD* is the area of △*DBC*?

◆ What is the area of △*DBC*?

◆ Suppose you cut parallelogram *ABCD* from *A* to *C*. What fraction of the area of *ABCD* is the area of △*ADC*?

◆ What is the area of △*ADC*?

◆ Is there more than one way to draw a parallelogram that shares two sides with a triangle?

◆ Do all of the parallelograms that share two sides with a triangle have the same area?

The area of a parallelogram is equal to the length of the base times the height.

$$A = bh$$

The area of a triangle is equal to one half the length of the base times the height.

$$A = \frac{1}{2}bh$$

The height of a parallelogram is measured on a line perpendicular to a base. The height of a triangle is measured on a line perpendicular to a base. In both cases we must choose a side to be the base.

Find the area of each of the following figures using the measurements given. Sides that look parallel are parallel.

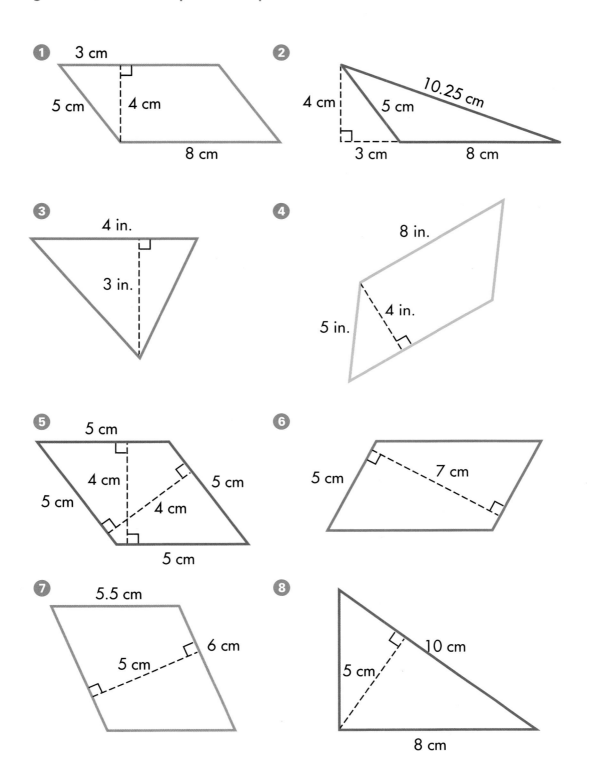

1
3 cm
5 cm
4 cm
8 cm

2
4 cm
5 cm
10.25 cm
3 cm
8 cm

3
4 in.
3 in.

4
8 in.
4 in.
5 in.

5
5 cm
4 cm
5 cm
5 cm
4 cm
5 cm
5 cm

6
5 cm
7 cm

7
5.5 cm
6 cm
5 cm

8
10 cm
5 cm
8 cm

◆ LESSON 130 Area of a Triangle

Sometimes we can find the area of a complicated figure by breaking it up into smaller parts. For example, in this figure you can see a square (red), a triangle (green), and a parallelogram (blue).

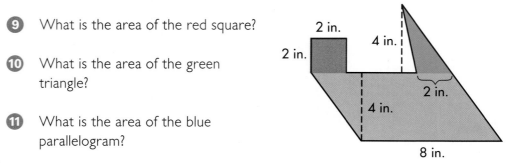

9 What is the area of the red square?

10 What is the area of the green triangle?

11 What is the area of the blue parallelogram?

12 What is the area of the entire figure?

Determine the area of each of these figures. For some of these you will need to divide the figure into triangles, parallelograms, and rectangles, and then find the sum of these areas.

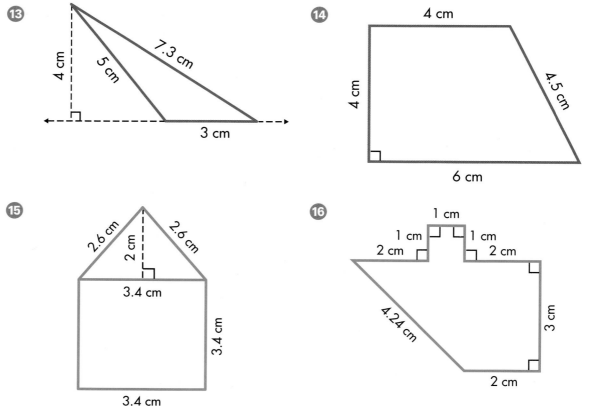

Determine the area of each of these figures by dividing the figures into triangles, parallelograms, and rectangles, and then find the sum of these areas. (If you draw lines to divide a figure, first copy the figure onto a sheet of paper. Or you can simply imagine the lines.)

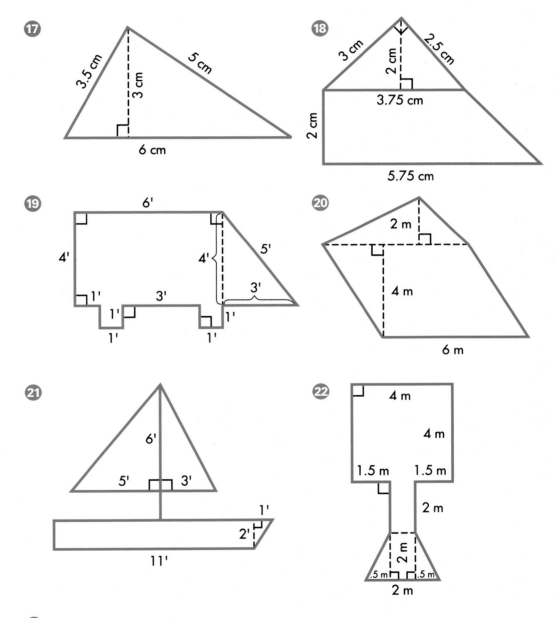

23 Draw two interesting pictures using only triangles, squares, parallelograms, and rectangles. Measure the needed lengths, and figure out the area of your picture.

Area of a Trapezoid

A **trapezoid** is a quadrilateral with exactly one pair of parallel sides.

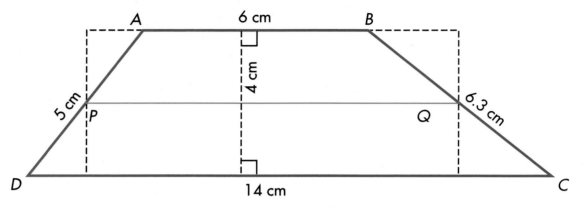

Figure *ABCD* is a trapezoid. Line *AB* is parallel to line *CD*.

◆ What do you think is the length of segment *PQ*? Why did you make that estimate? Measure to see how close your estimate is.

◆ The bases of a trapezoid are the two parallel sides. If the two bases of a trapezoid measure 4 centimeters and 8 centimeters, what is the length of the "middle" segment corresponding to *PQ* in the figure above?

For problems 1–8, *B* is the length of the longer base of a trapezoid and *b* is the length of the shorter base. The length of the "middle" segment is *m*, halfway between the bases and on a line parallel to them. In each case tell what *m* is.

1. $B = 10$ cm, $b = 6$ cm, $m = ?$ 2. $B = 20$ cm, $b = 14$ cm, $m = ?$

3. $B = 25$ cm, $b = 15$ cm, $m = ?$ 4. $B = 19$ cm, $b = 17$ cm, $m = ?$

5. $B = 5$ cm, $b = 4$ cm, $m = ?$ 6. $B = 17$ cm, $b = 14$ cm, $m = ?$

7. $B = 173$ cm, $b = 115$ cm, $m = ?$ 8. $B = 2.6$ cm, $b = 1.4$ cm, $m = ?$

9. $B = 16$ cm, $b = 14.2$ cm, $m = ?$ 10. $B = 92$ cm, $b = 87$ cm, $m = ?$

11. Try to find the area of trapezoid *ABCD* at the top of the page. (Hint: The broken lines may help.)

A way to find the area of a trapezoid is to multiply the height by the average of the bases.

The formula for this is the following:

$$A = h\left(\frac{b + B}{2}\right) \text{ or } \frac{h}{2}(b + B)$$

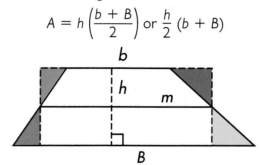

In the figure above, the green triangle is the same size as the red triangle. If you cut off the red triangle and put it where the green triangle is, the areas will match. This is also true for the blue and yellow triangles. So the area of the trapezoid is the same as the area of the rectangle with m as base and h as height: $A = hm$. But m is the average of b and B, so

$$m = \frac{b + B}{2} \text{ and } A = h\left(\frac{b + B}{2}\right)$$

Find the area of each trapezoid.

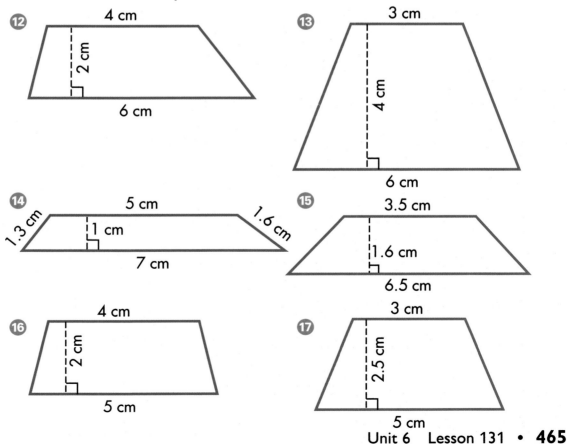

⑫ 4 cm / 2 cm / 6 cm

⑬ 3 cm / 4 cm / 6 cm

⑭ 1.3 cm / 5 cm / 1 cm / 7 cm

⑮ 3.5 cm / 1.6 cm / 1.6 cm / 6.5 cm

⑯ 4 cm / 2 cm / 5 cm

⑰ 3 cm / 2.5 cm / 5 cm

Area of Figures on a Grid

If a figure is drawn on squared paper, you can estimate the area of the figure by counting squares and parts of squares. Sometimes you can use the squares to calculate the exact area.

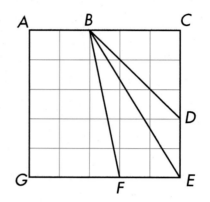

Calculate the area in square centimeters of each of these figures in the above square. Assume one square represents 1 square centimeter.

1 square *ACEG*

2 triangle *BCD*

3 triangle *BDE* (Hint: Think of *DE* as the base of this triangle. Then the height is the perpendicular distance from *B* to the line *EC*.)

4 triangle *BEF*

5 trapezoid *ABFG*

6 The figures in problems 2, 3, 4, and 5 cover the entire square exactly. So the sum of your answers for problems 2, 3, 4, and 5 should equal your answer for problem 1. Check to see if this is true.

Calculate the area in square centimeters of each of these figures.

7 triangle A

8 triangle B

9 trapezoid C

10 trapezoid D

11 triangle E

12 Do your answers for problems 7 through 11 add up to the total area of the square?

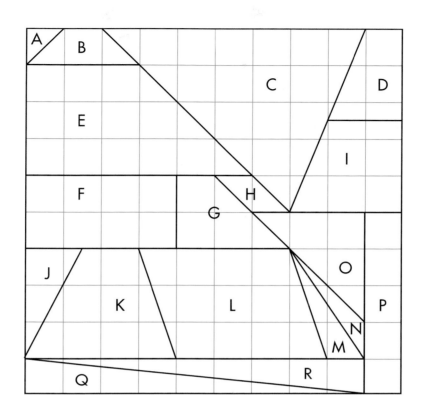

Calculate the area in square centimeters of each of these figures in the above square.

13 A   14 B   15 C

16 D   17 E   18 F

19 G   20 H   21 I

22 J   23 K   24 L

25 M   26 N   27 O

28 P   29 Q   30 R

Answer these questions.

31 What is the area of the entire square?

32 What is the sum of the areas you calculated for problems 13–30?

In your Math Journal record the strategies you used to find the areas of figures on the grids. How did you decide which lengths to use as bases? Were there any figures that had bases that were not whole centimeter lengths?

LESSON 133

Triangles and Quadrilaterals

There are names for special kinds of triangles. You already know that if one angle of a triangle is a right angle, the triangle is called a **right triangle**.

Examples:

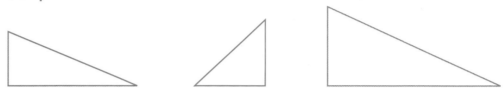

If two sides of a triangle are the same length, the triangle is called an **isosceles triangle.**

Examples:

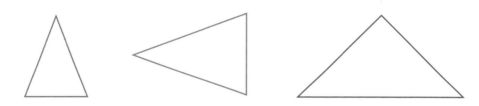

If all three sides are the same length, it is an **equilateral triangle**.

Examples:

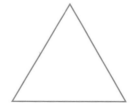

If no two sides are the same length, the triangle is **scalene**.

Examples:

Solve these problems.

1 Draw a triangle that is not a right triangle or an isosceles triangle.

2 Is every equilateral triangle an isosceles triangle?

3 Draw an isosceles triangle that is not an equilateral triangle.

4 Can a triangle have two right angles? If you think so, then try to draw such a triangle.

For problems 5–13, decide which triangles are scalene, isosceles, equilateral, and right triangles. Is it possible for a triangle to be more than one of these?

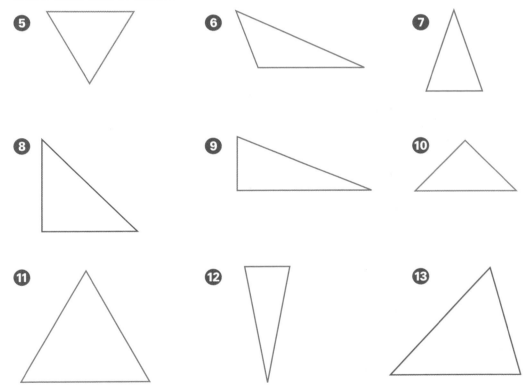

5 **6** **7**

8 **9** **10**

11 **12** **13**

Answer the following questions.

14 If a triangle is a right triangle, could it also be an isosceles triangle?

15 If a triangle is an equilateral triangle, could it also be a right triangle?

16 If a triangle is a scalene triangle, could it also be an isosceles triangle?

17 If a triangle is a scalene triangle, could it also be a right triangle?

◆ **LESSON 133   Triangles and Quadrilaterals**

We have names for special kinds of quadrilaterals. If exactly two sides of a quadrilateral are parallel, it is a **trapezoid**. If both pairs of opposite sides are parallel, the quadrilateral is a **parallelogram**.

A parallelogram in which all four angles are right angles is a **rectangle**. A rectangle with all four sides the same length is a **square**. A parallelogram with all four sides the same length is a **rhombus**.

QUADRILATERALS

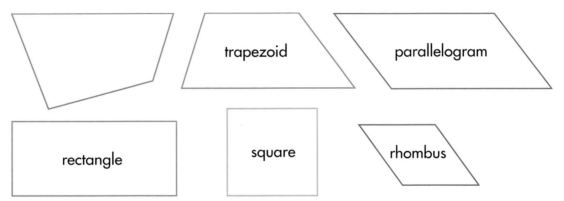

18   Try to draw a quadrilateral that has exactly one right angle.

19   Try to draw a trapezoid that has exactly one right angle.

20   Try to draw a parallelogram that has exactly one right angle.

21   Were you able to draw the figures described in problems 18–20?

22   Is every square a rectangle?

23   Is every rectangle a parallelogram?

24   Is every square a parallelogram?

25   Is every parallelogram a square?

26   Is every rhombus a trapezoid?

27   Is every trapezoid a rhombus?

28   What figure can be described as a rhombus-rectangle?

Answer the following questions. Assume that angles that look like right angles are right angles.

29 In the figure shown below, try to find as many squares as you can. Compare your answer with those of your classmates. Did you count large squares that had other figures inside them?

30 How many rhombuses can you find that are not squares?

31 How many rectangles can you find that are not squares?

32 How many parallelograms can you find that are neither rhombuses nor rectangles?

33 How many trapezoids can you find?

34 How many quadrilaterals can you find that are not any of the above?

35 How many right isosceles triangles can you find?

36 How many other triangles can you find?

37 Compare all your answers with those of your classmates. If there are differences, try to find out why, and decide which figures should be counted.

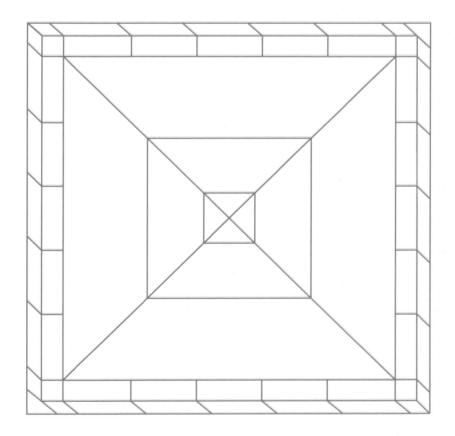

LESSON 134

Classifying Figures

As you play the "Three Questions" game on page 473, you may want to find characteristics that help you sort the remaining possible figures into two approximately equal sets. The following questions may help you.

Answer these questions.

1 Suppose that on the first question, you discover that the figure is a triangle. Considering the rules, how many different kinds of triangles are possible?

2 Can you think of a question that allows you to narrow the number of possible triangles to two or three, depending on the answer? Can you think of another question that would narrow the number of possibilities to two or three but with different triangles in the two groups? Explain.

3 Suppose that from the first answer you know that the figure is a quadrilateral. Then you ask whether the quadrilateral has two pairs of parallel sides.

   a. If the answer is "no," how many figures are possible? What are they?

   b. If the answer is "yes," how many figures are possible? What are they?

4 Suppose you ask whether a figure has at least one right angle.

   a. How many figures are possible if the answer is "yes"? What are they?

   b. How many figures are possible if the answer is "no"? What are they?

5 Suppose you ask whether the figure has four sides the same length.

   a. For an answer of "yes," what are the possible figures?

   b. For an answer of "no," what are the possible figures?

6 Suppose on the first question you ask whether the figure has at least two sides of equal length. If the answer is "yes," which figures are possible? Would this help you guess the figure in three questions?

Three Questions Game

Players: Two

Materials: Paper, pencil

Object: After asking three questions, to identify a figure the other player has drawn

Math Focus: Describing properties of geometric shapes and mathematical reasoning

RULES

1. The first player draws a figure and writes the name of it on a sheet of paper, making sure the second player cannot see it. The figure must be a triangle, quadrilateral, or one of the specific figures mentioned in bold on pages 468 and 470.

2. The figure may not have any extra properties not indicated by its name. For example, a quadrilateral with one right angle is not permitted.

3. The second player asks three questions, one at a time, to which the first player must answer *yes* or *no* truthfully.

4. The second player tries to name the figure the first player has drawn.

5. To win the round, the second player must correctly describe the figure as completely as possible. For example, if the figure is a rhombus and the second player says it is a parallelogram, the statement is true but not complete. So the first player would win.

SAMPLE GAME

Lena drew a trapezoid.

Harvey said:

Does it have four sides?

Does it have two pairs of parallel sides?

Does it have one pair of parallel sides?

It's a trapezoid.

Lena said:

Yes.

No.

Yes.

That's right.

Harvey won the round.

◆ **LESSON 134   Classifying Figures**

THINKING STORY

On the Move

Part 2

You may want to refer to the first part of this Thinking Story on pages 442–443.

Portia, Ferdie, and their mother were still trying to figure out the weight of everything they had to move. The heaviest piece of furniture was the couch. It took all three of them to lift it, and there was no way they could get it on the scale.

"I have an idea," said Portia. "Let's lift the couch. Then while we keep it level, we'll move around and take turns standing on the scale."

"That's stupid," said Ferdie. "While one person is getting weighed, the others are holding up part of the couch that is getting weighed too."

"It's not stupid," said Portia. "Between us we'll be holding up the whole weight of the couch. If we find out how much weight each one is holding, it should add up to the weight of the couch."

They decided to try it. Portia and Ferdie each lifted a back corner of the couch. Their mother held up the front of the couch. Here is what they found out:

	Portia	Ferdie	Mother
Normal weight	79 lbs.	95 lbs.	134 lbs.
Weight while holding couch	132 lbs.	148 lbs.	196 lbs.

. . . to be continued

Work in groups. Discuss your answers and how you figured them out. Then compare your answers with those of other groups.

1. According to the figures given, who is carrying more of the weight of the couch, Portia or Ferdie? How could you explain this?

2. Which part of the couch is heavier, the front or the back? How do you know?

3. About how much does the whole couch weigh?

Determining Lengths from Given Areas

ALGEBRA READINESS

The area of a certain rectangle is 56 square centimeters. The base is 8 centimeters.

◆ What is the height?

A farmer wants to plant 40,000 square meters of land with rows of corn. He wants each row to be 800 meters long, so the cornfield should be 800 meters long.

◆ How wide should the field be?

Answer the questions below. These formulas may help you.

Area of a parallelogram = base × height $A = bh$
Area of a triangle = $\frac{1}{2}$(base × height) $A = \frac{1}{2}bh$
Area of a trapezoid = height (average of bases) $A = h\left(\frac{b + B}{2}\right)$
Perimeter of any figure = side + side + side, and so on.

❶ The area of a right triangle is 24 square centimeters. The height is 8 centimeters. What is the base?

❷ A trapezoid has bases that are 10 and 20 centimeters long. The area of the trapezoid is 60 square centimeters. What is the height of the trapezoid?

❸ The area of a parallelogram is 48 square centimeters. The base is 6 centimeters. What is the height?

❹ A trapezoid has a height of 8 centimeters and an area of 80 square centimeters. One base is 12 centimeters. What is the other base?

❺ What is the height of an isosceles right triangle that has an area of 50 square centimeters?

❻ The height of a right scalene triangle is 5 centimeters and its area is 30 square centimeters. What is the base?

❼ What is the height of a trapezoid that has one base that is 14 centimeters and an area of 66 square centimeters? The other base is 8 centimeters.

Solve these problems.

8 A rectangular garden is 20 meters long and 35 meters wide. What is its area?

9 Triangle Park is shaped like an equilateral triangle with sides that are 250 meters long. What is its perimeter?

10 A parallelogram has a base of 15 centimeters. Its area is 150 square centimeters. What is its height?

11 A parallelogram has one side that is 15 centimeters. A second side is 10 centimeters. What is its area?

12 The area of a right triangle is 30 square centimeters. The base is 10 centimeters. What is the height?

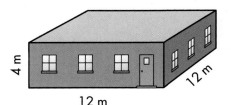

12 m

Mr. Gonzales's House

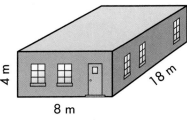

8 m

Mr. Culyer's House

13 What is the surface area of Mr. Gonzales's house?

14 How many square meters of living space does Mr. Gonzales's house have?

15 What is the surface area of Mr. Culyer's house?

16 How many square meters of living space does Mr. Culyer's house have?

17 Mr. Culyer and Mr. Gonzales like to keep the temperature in their houses the same. Both houses use the same kind of heating and cooling. Whose house will be more expensive to heat and cool? Explain your answer.

18 Find the volume of each house.

a. Which has the greater volume?

b. Could you answer problem 18a without multiplying?

LESSON
136

Square Roots

What is the length of one side of a square that has an area of 20 cm^2? You can use a calculator to help you find the answer.

The area of the square is 20 square centimeters. So if s is the length of one side, s times s must be 20. Since $4 \times 4 = 16$ and $5 \times 5 = 25$, the answer must be between 4 centimeters and 5 centimeters.

Then, since $4.5 \times 4.5 = 20.25$, the answer must be less than 4.5. But $4.4 \times 4.4 = 19.36$, so the answer must be greater than 4.4.

Notice that 20.25 is closer to 20 than 19.36 is. So the answer is probably closer to 4.5 than to 4.4. Try 4.47.

By now, you should be using a calculator. Multiply 4.47 by itself. If you continue making approximations this way, you will get to 4.472136.

If you multiply 4.472136 by itself on paper, you get 20.000000402496. If the calculator shows only the first eight digits, it will show 20 as the answer.

If you had been asked to find the length of the side to the nearest hundredth of a centimeter, you could have stopped when you realized that 4.47×4.47 (which is 19.9809) is closer to 20 than is 4.48×4.48 (which is 20.0704). So the answer to the nearest hundredth of a centimeter is probably 4.47 centimeters. To be sure, you'd multiply 4.475 by 4.475. Since the product is greater than 20, the answer to the nearest hundredth is 4.47.

1 Use a computer or other means to draw and complete this chart. For each area of a square, estimate the length in centimeters of a side of that square to the nearest whole centimeter, tenth of a centimeter, and hundredth of a centimeter.

Area of square (cm²)	Nearest whole number (cm)	Nearest tenth (cm)	Nearest hundredth (cm)
10			
30			
2			
3			
4			
5			
8			
9			
15			
50			

We call a number that can be multiplied by itself to give a second number the square root of the second number. For example, $4 \times 4 = 16$, so 4 is the square root of 16, and $5 \times 5 = 25$, so 5 is the square root of 25.

The symbol for square root is $\sqrt{}$. Your calculator may have a square root key.

◆ LESSON 136 Square Roots

For the following areas of a square (in square inches), try to estimate a number that would be very close to the length (in inches) of the side of the square. Do not use a calculator.

2 64   **3** 100   **4** 36   **5** 144   **6** 25

7 81   **8** 121   **9** 49   **10** 10,000   **11** 169

12 72   **13** 110   **14** 42   **15** 156   **16** 83

In your Math Journal write about the strategies you used to make your estimates.

17 Using your calculator, find the lengths for problems 2–16 to the nearest hundredth of an inch.

18 How good were your estimates?

19 For each of the areas in the chart, find the corresponding length to the nearest thousandth of a centimeter.

Area of square in square centimeters	2	20	200	2000	20,000	200,000
Length of side of square in cm	■	■	■	■	■	■

20 Do you see any interesting patterns in your answers to problem 19?

21 For each of the areas in the chart, find the corresponding length to the nearest thousandth of a centimeter.

Area of square in square centimeters	3	30	300	3000	30,000	300,000
Length of side of square in cm	■	■	■	■	■	■

22 Do you see any interesting patterns in your answers to problem 21? How do those relate to your answer for problem 20? Did they help you fill out the table for problem 21?

Solve these problems.

23 For each of the areas in the chart, find the corresponding length to the nearest thousandth of a centimeter.

Area of square in square centimeters	4	40	400	4000	40,000	400,000
Length of side of square in cm	▪	▪	▪	▪	▪	▪

24 What was different about the answers to problem 23 compared to the answers to problems 19 and 21?

25 What is the length of a side of a square that has an area of 100 square inches?

26 What is the length of a side of a square that has an area of 169 square centimeters?

27 A square field has an area of 576 square meters. What is the length of a side of that field?

28 A farmer's field has an area of 42,436 square yards. What is the length of a side of that field?

29 A parallelogram has a base the same length as its height. The area of the parallelogram is 225 square inches. What is its height?

30 A triangle has a base the same length as its height. The area of the triangle is 32 square centimeters. What is its height?

31 A rectangle's width is twice as great as its length. The area of the rectangle is 50 square centimeters. What is its length?

32 What is the perimeter of a square park with an area of 900 square feet?

LESSON 137

Estimating Measures

We frequently need to estimate distances, times, and other measurements. In this lesson you'll practice some everyday estimating.

1 Nancy knows that Lee is about 5 feet tall. She wants to estimate the height of the gymnasium wall that Lee is standing against. About how tall do you think the wall is?

2 Noah walks about 4 miles in an hour. He usually takes about 24 minutes to walk to school from his home. About how far do you think it is from Noah's home to school?

3 Tasha has noticed that she can fill four drinking glasses with a liter container of milk. She plans to have four friends over for lunch. If she and each of her friends usually drink about two glasses of milk with lunch, about how many liters of milk should Tasha have for five people?

4 Alex knows that a pair of his father's shoes weighs about 2.2 pounds. He thinks a pair of his own shoes weighs about as much as one of his father's shoes. If this is true, about how much does a pair of Alex's shoes weigh?

5 Janet measured the width of her desk in hand lengths. It was five hands long plus a few inches more. Janet's hand is about 5 inches long. How wide is her desk?

6 Rosemary is nine years old and weighs 75 pounds. She thinks her father weighs about twice as much as she does. If this is true, about how many pounds does her father weigh?

7 Water freezes at 0° Celsius (0°C) and boils at 100°C. A comfortable room temperature for most people is about 20°C. Normal human body temperature is 37°C. Sara wore her jacket yesterday because the weather was cool, but it was not cold enough to freeze water. About what do you think the temperature was?

8 Estimate at least 20 measures yourself and then check to see what the real measures are. (Include at least two lengths, two weights, two volumes, and two temperatures.) Here are some examples of measures to estimate:

a. length or width of the classroom

b. a friend's height in meters and centimeters

c. the length of this book

d. the weight of this book

e. the weight of your pencil

f. the weight of a jar of paste or paint

g. the temperature in your classroom (°C)

h. the temperature outside today (°C)

i. the temperature in a working refrigerator (°C)

j. the temperature in a working freezer (°C)

k. the volume of water in a large pitcher (in liters)

l. the volume of a container of dish detergent

m. the volume of water in a fish tank (in gallons)

UNIT 6

Mid-Unit Review

Find the area of each rectangle. Be sure to include the correct unit in your answers.

1 base = 14 cm, height = 11 cm

2 base = 1.5 cm, height = 1.1 cm

3 base = 1.4 cm, height = 12 cm

4 base = 0.3 cm, height = 1.3 cm

5 base = 24 cm, height = 61 cm

6 base = 0.22 cm, height = 0.5 cm

7 What is the total area of the top and four sides of a building that is 25 meters long, 12 meters wide, and 7 meters tall?

Calculate the volume and the total surface area for each of these sets of dimensions.

8 $h = 20$ m, $l = 10$ m, $w = 6$ m

9 $h = 5$ m, $l = 12$ m, $w = 8$ m

10 $h = 7$ m, $l = 11$ m, $w = 9$ m

11 $h = 12$ m, $l = 8$ m, $w = 15$ m

12 $h = 8$ m, $l = 13$ m, $w = 10$ m

Calculate the perimeter and area of each of these rectangles.

13 length = 25 cm, width = 30 cm

14 length = 40 cm, width = 35 cm

15 length = 275 cm, width = 200 cm

Calculate the the volume of a box with the following dimensions.

16 h = 10 cm, l = 15 cm, w = 7 cm

17 h = 80 cm, l = 40 cm, w = 60 cm

Find the area of each of the right triangles shown below.

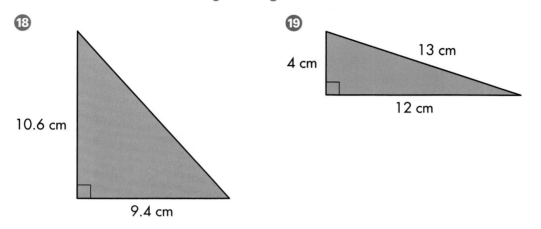

18

10.6 cm

9.4 cm

19

4 cm

13 cm

12 cm

Find the area of each of these parallelograms.

20

3 cm

7 cm

21

4 cm

12 cm

22

2 in.   3 in.

6 in.

23

4.5 cm

8 cm

24   Determine the area of the figure.

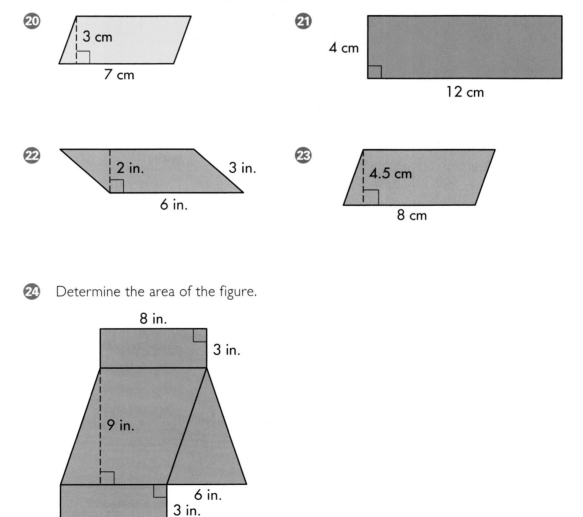

8 in.

3 in.

9 in.

6 in.

3 in.

8 in.

◆ UNIT 6 Mid-Unit Review

Find the area of each trapezoid.

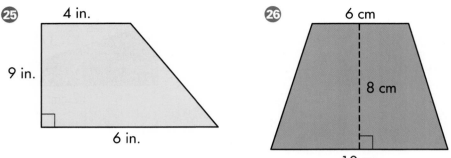

25 4 in.

9 in.

6 in.

26 6 cm

8 cm

10 cm

Answer these questions.

27 Can a right triangle be isosceles?

28 Can a trapezoid have two sides the same length?

29 If a triangle is isosceles, can it also be scalene?

30 Is every square a parallelogram?

31 Can a trapezoid have three right angles?

A group of students measured their classroom, which had a rectangular floor. They found that the length was 810 cm and the width was 680 cm. They believe their measurements are no more than 5 cm too high or too low.

Solve.

32 Find the perimeter and area of the classroom floor according to the students' measurements.

33 Find the greatest and the least possible perimeters if the measurements are off by 5 cm.

34 Find the greatest and the least possible areas if the measurements are off by 5 cm.

35 A rectangle has an area of 48 square meters. The base is 12 meters. What is the height?

36 The area of a parallelogram is 60 square centimeters. The height is 5 centimeters. What is the base?

Solve these problems.

37 The area of a right triangle is 42 square centimeters. The base is 14 centimeters. What is the height?

38 A trapezoid has bases that are 12 inches and 20 inches. The area of the trapezoid is 160 square inches. What is the height?

39 A garden is in the shape of an equilateral triangle. Each side is 15 meters long. What is its perimeter?

40 What is the height of an isosceles right triangle that has an area of 32 square feet?

41 What is the length of a side of a square that has an area of 144 square centimeters?

42 A square field has an area of 1296 square meters. What is the length of a side of that field?

43 Gregory rides his bicycle at an average speed of about 12 miles per hour. It usually takes him about 18 minutes to ride from his home to piano practice. About how far does he live from his piano teacher's house?

44 Anna weighs about 85 pounds. She thinks that her baby brother weighs about half as much as she does. If she is right, about how many pounds does her baby brother weigh?

Find the area in square units of each of the figures in the rectangle below.

45 A

46 B

47 C

48 D

49 E

50 F

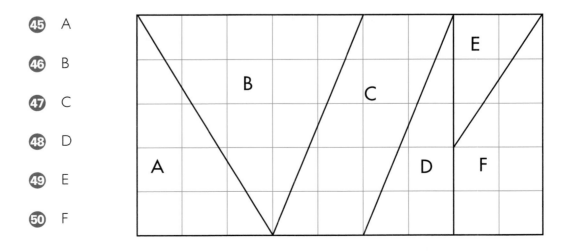

Multiplying and Dividing by Powers of 10

When we convert from one metric measurement to another, we need to multiply or divide by a power of 10. Keep in shape by practicing these computing shortcuts.

Do you remember the short way for multiplying or dividing by numbers such as 10, 100, and 1000? Look at these examples:

10 × 6.54	⟶	6.5 4 ⟶	65.4
100 × 6.54	⟶	6.5 4 ⟶	654
1000 × 6.54	⟶	6.5 4 0 ⟶	6540
87.5 ÷ 10	⟶	8 7.5 ⟶	8.75
87.5 ÷ 100	⟶	8 7.5 ⟶	0.875
87.5 ÷ 1000	⟶	0 8 7.5 ⟶	0.0875

Multiply.

1 2.5 × 10   **2** 2.5 × 100   **3** 2.5 × 1000

4 2.5 × 10,000   **5** 2.5 × 100,000   **6** 3.47 × 10

7 100 × 3.47   **8** 3.47 × 1000   **9** 10 × 0.6

10 100 × 0.6   **11** 1000 × 97   **12** 9.7 × 1000

13 0.97 × 1000   **14** 0.08 × 1000   **15** 100 × 0.08

16 9.3 × 10   **17** 0.93 × 1000   **18** 93 × 100

Divide.

19 6.2 ÷ 10   **20** 6.2 ÷ 100   **21** 6.2 ÷ 1000

22 6.2 ÷ 10,000   **23** 6.25 ÷ 10,000   **24** 34 ÷ 10

25 34 ÷ 100   **26** 34 ÷ 1000   **27** 873 ÷ 100

28 873 ÷ 10   **29** 69.1 ÷ 10   **30** 9.1 ÷ 100

31 10.5 ÷ 10   **32** 0.7 ÷ 100   **33** 0.7 ÷ 10

Multiply or divide. Watch the signs.

③④ 4.1 ÷ 100	③⑤ 6.9 × 10	③⑥ 100 × 87
③⑦ 87 ÷ 100	③⑧ 5 ÷ 10	③⑨ 5 ÷ 100
④⓪ 5 × 1000	④① 100 × 50	④② 50 ÷ 100
④③ 5 ÷ 1000	④④ 5.5 ÷ 10	④⑤ 0.2 × 100
④⑥ 0.2 ÷ 10	④⑦ 1000 × 0.08	④⑧ 0.08 ÷ 10
④⑨ 0.1 × 10	⑤⓪ 0.1 ÷ 10	⑤① 1.5 × 100
⑤② 10,000 × 1.5	⑤③ 1.5 × 100,000	⑤④ 0.75 × 100
⑤⑤ 0.75 ÷ 10	⑤⑥ 75 ÷ 1000	⑤⑦ 75 ÷ 100,000

Solve. Watch the signs.

⑤⑧ 35 + 10	⑤⑨ 35 − 10	⑥⓪ 108 ÷ 10
⑥① 108 + 100	⑥② 108 + 10	⑥③ 650 ÷ 100
⑥④ 650 − 100	⑥⑤ 650 × 100	⑥⑥ 0.7 + 10
⑥⑦ 0.7 × 10	⑥⑧ 3.6 + 10	⑥⑨ 3.6 × 10
⑦⓪ 3.6 ÷ 10	⑦① 62.5 × 100	⑦② 62.5 + 100
⑦③ 462.5 − 100	⑦④ 0.15 × 1000	⑦⑤ 0.15 + 1000
⑦⑥ 100 × 27.42	⑦⑦ 27.42 + 10	⑦⑧ 115 ÷ 100
⑦⑨ 0.115 × 100	⑧⓪ 0.115 + 10	⑧① 967.14 × 1000

Solve these problems.

⑧② The Drama Club is selling tickets to their play for $2.50 each. They hope to sell 100 tickets. How much money would that bring in for the club?

⑧③ Rebecca measured a stack of 100 identical workbooks. It was 46.2 centimeters thick. How thick was each workbook?

⑧④ How much would a $100 pair of boots cost if sales tax is 6%?

The Metric System

In the history of the world, many systems of measurement have been used. Today almost all the world's population uses some form of the metric system.

One advantage of the metric system is that conversions from one unit to another are very easy. For example, there are 100 centimeters in a meter, so if you are 1.45 meters tall, you are 145 centimeters tall. Multiplying by powers of 10 (0.1, 1, 10, and 100, for example) is easier than multiplying by any other numbers.

The prefix in a metric unit tells you what power of 10 is involved. For example, a kilogram is 1000 grams, and a kilometer is 1000 meters.

◆   How many liters are in a kiloliter?

A centimeter is one hundredth of a meter.

◆   What fraction of a gram is a centigram?

There are 1000 milliliters in 1 liter.

◆   How many millimeters are in a meter?

Some common and less common metric prefixes are listed below.

Table of Metric Prefixes

Prefix	Symbol	Power of 10	Meaning in Words
mega-	M	$1{,}000{,}000\ (10^6)$	one million
kilo-	k	$1000\ (10^3)$	one thousand
hecto-	h	$100\ (10^2)$	one hundred
deka-	da	$10\ (10^1)$	ten
—	—	1	one
deci-	d	0.1	one-tenth
centi-	c	0.01	one-hundredth
milli-	m	0.001	one-thousandth
micro-	μ	0.000001	one-millionth

Use the table on page 490 to solve these problems.

1. How many meters are in a **kilo**meter?

2. How many grams are in a **kilo**gram?

3. How many **centi**meters are in a meter?

4. How many **milli**meters are in a meter?

5. How many **milli**grams are in a gram?

6. How many **milli**liters are in a liter?

7. How many liters are in a **deka**liter?

8. Which is larger, a **deka**meter or a **deci**meter?

9. How many **deci**meters are in a **deka**meter?

10. How many **deci**liters are in a **deka**liter?

11. How many **deci**grams are in a **deka**gram?

12. Which is longer, a **centi**meter or a **milli**meter?

13. How many **milli**meters are in a **centi**meter?

14. How many **milli**grams are in a **centi**gram?

15. How many **milli**liters are in a **centi**liter?

16. How many **centi**meters are in a **hecto**meter?

17. How many **centi**grams are in a **hecto**gram?

18. How many **milli**meters are in a **kilo**meter?

19. How many **micro**meters are in a **mega**meter?

20. How many **micro**liters are in a **mega**liter?

◆ LESSON 139 The Metric System

To convert from one unit to another, multiply or divide by the appropriate number. In the metric system this means multiplying or dividing by some power of 10 (see the table on page 490). You can do this by simply moving a decimal point (and writing in extra 0s when needed).

Example: Change 3.758 meters to centimeters.

1 meter is 100 centimeters. So 3.758 meters is 3.758 × 100 centimeters.

You can multiply 3.758 by 100 by moving the decimal point two places to the right (because there are two 0s in 100).

3.7 5 8 ⟶ 375.8

So 3.758 meters = 375.8 centimeters.

Example: Change 35 grams to kilograms.

1 kilogram is 1000 grams. So 35 grams is 35 ÷ 1000 kilograms.

You can divide 35 by 1000 by moving the decimal point three places to the left (because there are three 0s in 1000).

0 3 5 ⟶ 0.035

So 35 grams = 0.035 kilogram.

Convert these measurements.

21 5.68 meters to centimeters

22 5.68 grams to centigrams

23 5.68 liters to centiliters

24 834 meters to kilometers

25 574.2 millimeters to meters

26 43.2 kilograms to grams

27 23 kilometers to meters

28 0.023 kilometer to meters

29 0.023 kilogram to grams

30 3 dekaliters to liters

31 0.12 kilogram to grams

32 1.2 kilograms to grams

33 0.12 kilometer to meters

34 12 kilometers to meters

35 7.9 liters to milliliters

36 79 meters to kilometers

37 416 centigrams to grams

38 135 centimeters to meters

39 753 meters to kilometers

40 753 milligrams to grams

41 753 liters to milliliters

42 14 decimeters to meters

43 2408 grams to milligrams

44 2408 kilometers to meters

Solve these problems.

45 Melissa and her friends wanted to hang a swing from a branch of a strong old oak tree in her backyard. The friends knew that the branch was 4.5 meters high. They wanted the swing to be 30 centimeters above the ground.

a. How much rope must the friends buy?

b. If they buy too little rope, will the swing be higher or lower than they had planned?

46 Sally is 148 centimeters tall. Her bookcase is 178 centimeters tall. Can Sally reach a book on the top shelf without standing on something?

47 Mr. Foster has a board that is 2.75 meters long. He cut two equal pieces off of the board. Now his board is only 2.35 meters long.

a. How many centimeters long were the pieces he cut from the board?

b. Can Mr. Foster get ten more 20-centimeter pieces from the board?

c. If so, how much board will remain?

48 Mackenzie and Spencer were preparing for a large picnic. They had four tables that were each 183 centimeters long. They placed the tables end to end to create one large serving table.

a. How many meters long was that table?

b. Could those tables, placed end to end, fit in your classroom?

49 One hectare is equal to 10,000 square meters.

a. If a square lot of land has an area of 1 hectare, how many meters long is it on each side?

b. What is the perimeter of that lot?

The Customary System

The customary system is a set of measurement units commonly used in the United States. Unlike the metric system, the customary system uses many unrelated conversions. There are separate sets of conversions for capacity, length, and weight.

Answer the questions based on each set of conversions.

There are 8 fluid ounces in 1 cup.

There are 2 cups in 1 pint.

There are 2 pints in 1 quart.

There are 4 quarts in 1 gallon.

1 How many fluid ounces are in 1 pint?

2 How many fluid ounces are in 1 quart?

3 How many fluid ounces are in 1 gallon?

There are 12 inches in 1 foot.

There are 3 feet in 1 yard.

There are 1760 yards in 1 mile.

4 How many feet are in 1 mile?

There are 16 ounces in 1 pound.

There are 2000 pounds in 1 ton.

5 How many ounces are in 1 ton?

There are 60 seconds in one minute.

There are 60 minutes in one hour.

There are 24 hours in one day.

There are 7 days in one week.

There are about 52 weeks in one year.

There are 10 years in one decade.

There are 10 decades in one century.

There are 10 centuries in one millennium.

6 How many seconds are in one day?

7 How many minutes are in one week?

8 How many decades are in one millennium?

Solve these problems.

9 Suki is 63 inches tall. How many feet tall is Suki?

10 A bag of grapes weighs 3 pounds. How many ounces is that?

11 A recipe calls for 13 cups of apple juice. How many quarts is that?

12 Megan is planting crocuses in late fall. The directions say that the flowers will bloom in about 100 days. How many weeks is that?

13 How many seconds old are you?

14 How much older will you be when you finish this problem?

15 Standard years have 365 days. Leap years have 366 days.

    a. How often do we have leap years?

    b. What is the exception to this rule? You may need to do research to find the answer.

16 How many days are in one century? Keep in mind your answer to problem 15.

17 How many hours will be in the twenty-first century?

Estimating Volume

Making good estimates takes practice. The more practice you get, the more reasonable estimates you'll be able to make.

How well can you estimate relative volume? See if you get better at it as you do this activity.

Look at a group of containers of different sizes and shapes.

1 Write down which container you think holds the least amount. Then write which one you think holds the next least amount. Keep going until you have listed all the containers in order from least to greatest volume in the table on page 497.

2 Estimate how many times you would have to fill up the smallest container to equal the volume of the largest container. Record your estimate in the table.

3 Use water to check your estimate for problem 2. Fill the smallest container and pour the contents into the larger container. Record how many times you did this before the large container was full. You may need to estimate a fraction of the smaller container for the last pouring. Record your result in the table.

4 Estimate how many times you would have to fill up the smallest container to equal the volume of each of the other containers. Record your estimates in the table.

5 Use water to check your estimates. Record your results in the table.

6 Use these results to see if you put the containers in the right order from smallest to largest.

Use a computer or other means to draw a table like this. Make one row for each container.

Container	Estimated volume (in smallest containers)	Actual volume (in smallest containers)

How good were your estimates? Did they become more accurate as you measured more containers? How did you make your estimates? Record your answers in your Math Journal.

Discuss this question with your classmates.

Why do you think some things that we buy in the supermarket come in odd-shaped bottles?

Make a bottle display for your class or school. Collect different kinds of empty bottles and wash off their labels. Determine exactly how many ounces each contains and then label each bottle. Put the bottles in order from least to greatest capacity.

When you get a new bottle, estimate how many ounces it contains before measuring to find out. Then put the new bottle into your collection.

Keeping Sharp

Keep in shape by practicing these computations with fractions.

Completely reduce each fraction.

1. $\frac{2}{4}$ 2. $\frac{3}{9}$ 3. $\frac{3}{12}$ 4. $\frac{12}{15}$ 5. $\frac{4}{6}$

6. $\frac{8}{24}$ 7. $\frac{6}{8}$ 8. $\frac{6}{12}$ 9. $\frac{3}{15}$ 10. $\frac{4}{10}$

11. $\frac{6}{24}$ 12. $\frac{12}{24}$ 13. $\frac{10}{24}$ 14. $\frac{15}{18}$ 15. $\frac{12}{20}$

Add. Completely reduce each answer.

16. $\frac{1}{2} + \frac{1}{2}$ 17. $\frac{1}{3} + \frac{1}{2}$ 18. $\frac{2}{5} + \frac{1}{3}$ 19. $\frac{3}{4} + \frac{1}{3}$

20. $\frac{7}{12} + \frac{1}{3}$ 21. $\frac{3}{4} + \frac{3}{4}$ 22. $\frac{2}{3} + \frac{1}{4}$ 23. $\frac{1}{4} + \frac{1}{5}$

24. $\frac{2}{3} + \frac{1}{2}$ 25. $\frac{1}{6} + \frac{1}{3}$ 26. $\frac{1}{4} + \frac{1}{2}$ 27. $\frac{1}{5} + \frac{1}{3}$

Subtract. Completely reduce each answer.

28. $\frac{3}{4} - \frac{1}{2}$ 29. $\frac{2}{3} - \frac{1}{6}$ 30. $\frac{2}{5} - \frac{1}{10}$ 31. $\frac{5}{6} - \frac{2}{3}$

32. $\frac{7}{8} - \frac{3}{8}$ 33. $\frac{3}{4} - \frac{1}{8}$ 34. $\frac{2}{3} - \frac{1}{4}$ 35. $\frac{3}{5} - \frac{1}{3}$

36. $\frac{5}{8} - \frac{1}{4}$ 37. $\frac{2}{3} - \frac{1}{2}$ 38. $\frac{5}{9} - \frac{1}{3}$ 39. $\frac{7}{10} - \frac{2}{5}$

Solve the following problems.

40. Pedro asked each of his classmates what his or her favorite sport was. Here is what Pedro's list looked like.

Favorite Sport	Number of People
basketball	8
football	4
swimming	4
baseball	3
soccer	3
tennis	2

a. What fraction of the students liked basketball best? What fraction liked tennis best?

b. If you made a fraction for each sport and added the fractions, what would the total be?

Solve the following problems.

41 Many books are published with pages that are $8\frac{1}{2}$ inches wide and 11 inches long.

  a. What is the area of each page?

  b. An artist is designing a page. She knows that she will need $\frac{5}{8}$-inch margins on all four sides of the page. About what area will she have with which to work?

42 Hector's garden measures about 4 yards by $2\frac{1}{2}$ yards.

  a. What is the area of Hector's garden?

  b. How many square feet is that?

  c. Compare your answers to problems a and b. Do you see a short way to convert square yards to square feet? Does your way work in other examples?

43 Mr. and Mrs. Harkary are measuring their den for carpeting. The room measures $9\frac{1}{2}$ feet by $13\frac{1}{2}$ feet.

  a. What is the area of the room in square feet?

  b. What is the area of the room in square yards?

44 Here is a scale drawing of the forest preserve in Small County.

  a. What is its area?

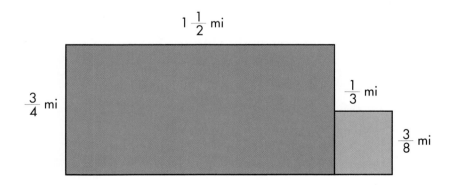

  b. The people of Small County are thinking of using about $\frac{1}{5}$ of the preserve to build a botanical garden. If they do, how much area will remain in the preserve?

◆ **LESSON 142** Keeping Sharp

THINKING STORY

On the Move

Part 3

You may want to refer to the earlier parts of this Thinking Story on pages 442–443 and 474–475.

While Ferdie and his mother were still weighing everything in their apartment, Portia called another moving company. "Spaceway Movers charges by how much space your things take up in the moving van," she reported. "They charge $50 per cubic yard."

"Oh, no!" said Ferdie. "Now we have to measure everything to figure out how much it will cost."

Just then Ms. Eng stopped by to visit. She knew a lot about moving. "On the average these moving companies charge about the same," she said. "If you have an average house, it will cost you about the same no matter which mover you use. But if your things are light for their size, you're better off paying by weight. If your things are heavier than average, Spaceway Movers is probably your best bet."

. . . the end

Work in groups. Discuss your answers and how you figured them out. Then compare your answers with those of other groups.

1 If all your furniture were made of very light plastic foam, would Spaceway Movers be a good choice? Why or why not?

2 Make a list of common household things that are heavy for their size.

3 Make a list of common household things that are very light for their size.

Angles and Rotation

GEOGRAPHY
CONNECTION

People find it useful to talk about directions and to measure differences between directions.

On a compass, north is the direction toward the North Pole. South is the opposite direction.

The east-west line is perpendicular to the north-south line.

Northeast is halfway between north and east. Southeast is halfway between south and east, and so on.

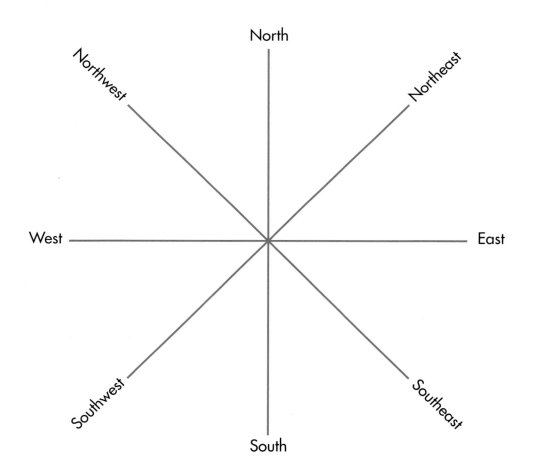

Suppose you are facing north and want to face west. To do that with the least possible change in your position, you would make $\frac{1}{4}$ of a complete turn. That's the least turn you could make.

What fraction of a complete turn do you need to make to go from

1 facing north to facing south?

2 facing south to facing east?

3 facing north to facing east?

4 facing east to facing north?

5 facing north to facing northwest?

6 facing east to facing northwest?

7 facing west to facing northeast?

8 facing northwest to facing southeast?

9 facing north to facing northeast?

10 facing south to facing northeast?

An angle that is less than $\frac{1}{4}$ of a complete turn is an **acute angle.**

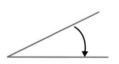

An angle that is $\frac{1}{4}$ of a turn is a **right angle.**

An angle that is between $\frac{1}{4}$ of a turn and $\frac{1}{2}$ of a turn is an **obtuse angle.**

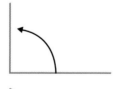

11 What would an angle that is $\frac{1}{2}$ of a complete turn look like?

12 What is the least turn that would leave you facing the same direction as $\frac{3}{4}$ of a complete turn?

Unit 6   Lesson 143 • **503**

◆ LESSON 143 Angles and Rotation

Discuss these with your classmates.

13 Look around your classroom. Do you see any right angles? Describe several right angles in your classroom.

14 Think about angles that are formed by things outside your classroom, such as street intersections, the sides of objects such as rugs, and so on. Describe several that are right angles.

15 Are there any acute angles in your classroom or hallway? Describe at least five acute angles that are either inside or outside your classroom.

16 Describe at least five obtuse angles that are formed by real objects.

17 Consider the following letters:

a. List the letters that have acute angles.

b. List the letters that have obtuse angles.

c. List the letters that have right angles.

d. Can a letter have more than one kind of angle?

Tell whether each angle is acute, right, or obtuse.

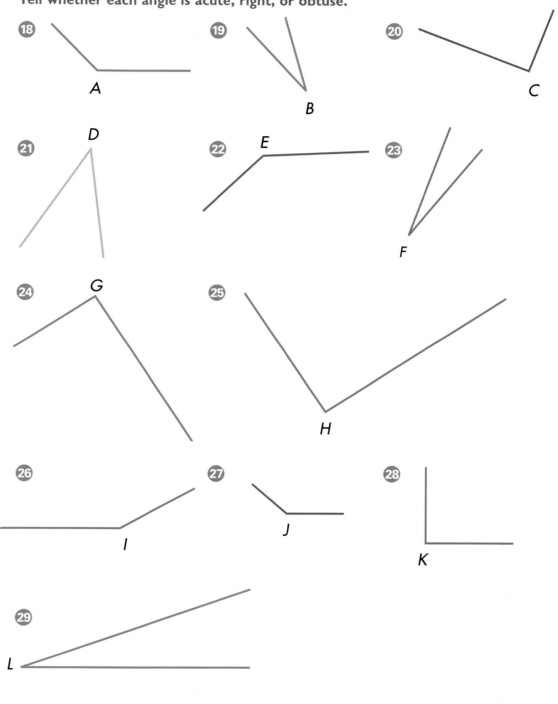

Solve.

30 Which is larger, ∠J or ∠K? Remember, when we talk about the size
of an angle, we are talking about how far you must turn if you are
facing along one side and you want to face along the other side.

Measuring Angles

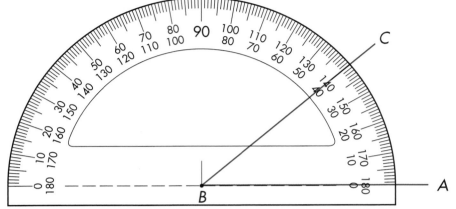

We measure angles with a *protractor*. To measure ∠ABC with the protractor shown above, follow these steps:

A. Place the protractor as shown. The small hole is over the **vertex** of the angle (point *B*). The broken line on the protractor lies on one side of the angle (side *BA*).

B. Look at the number through which the other side of the angle (*BC*) passes. There are two numbers, 40 and 140. If the angle is acute, use the lesser number (40). If the angle is obtuse, use the greater number (140). Since this angle is acute, we use the lesser number (40).

C. The number you found in step B is the measure of the angle in degrees. So the measure of ∠ABC is 40 degrees (40°).

Your protractor may look a little different from the one above, but the steps in using it should be almost the same. Be sure that one side of the angle is passing through 0°.

Remember, we can label an angle by its vertex (for example, ∠*B*). But we can also use three points to label an angle. The vertex must be the middle letter in the angle's name. The angle shown on this page could be called ∠*B* or ∠*ABC* or ∠*CBA*. We say its measure is 40° by writing ∠*B* = 40° or ∠*ABC* = 40° or ∠*CBA* = 40°.

Measure each of these four angles to the nearest degree.

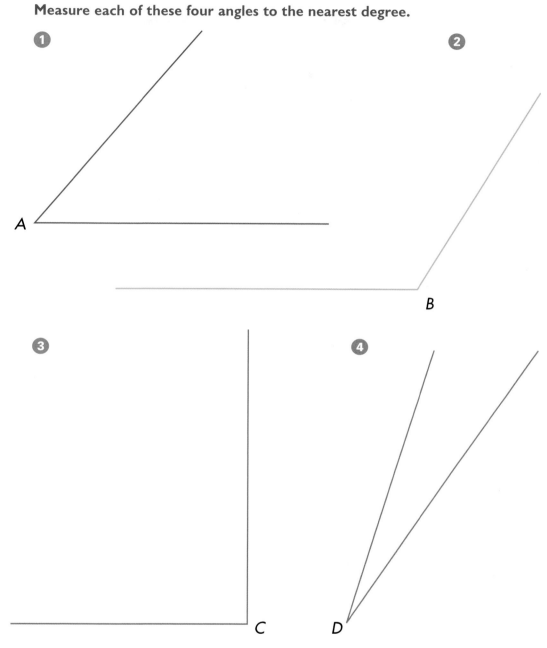

1

2

A

B

3

4

C

D

The most densely populated country on earth is Monaco, with a population of 31,719 and an area of 0.75 square miles. If the United States were as densely populated as Monaco, the population would be over 140 billion.

◆ LESSON 144 Measuring Angles

Measure the three angles in each triangle.

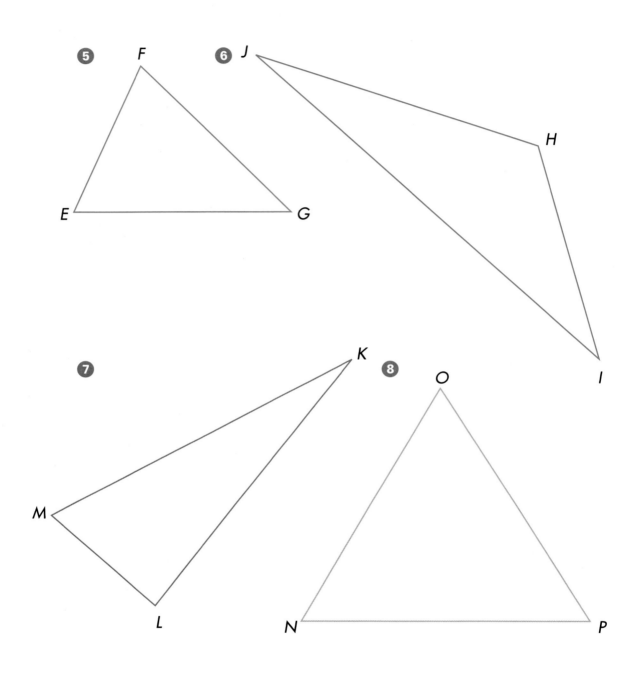

⑤ F ⑥ J H I E G

⑦ K ⑧ O M L N P

⑨ Add the measures of the three angles in △EFG. What is the sum?

⑩ What is the sum of the measure of the angles of △HIJ? of △KLM? of △NOP?

Assume the sum of the angles of a triangle is always 180 degrees. You will see why this must be so in Lesson 146.

11 If one of the angles of a triangle is obtuse, what can you say about the other two angles of the triangle?

12 If one of the angles of a triangle is a right angle, what can you say about the other two angles?

13 If one of the angles of a triangle is acute, what can you say about the other two angles of the triangle?

Any triangle that has an obtuse angle in it is called an **obtuse triangle**. Any triangle that has a right angle in it is called a right triangle. If a triangle has no obtuse angle and no right angle (that is, it has three acute angles) it is called an **acute triangle**.

Look at the triangles below, and complete the following exercises.

14 Make a list of the triangles that are obtuse triangles.

15 Make a list of the triangles that are right triangles.

16 Make a list of the triangles that are acute triangles.

17 Did any triangle appear in more than one list? Can you draw a triangle that would appear in more than one of the lists? Explain.

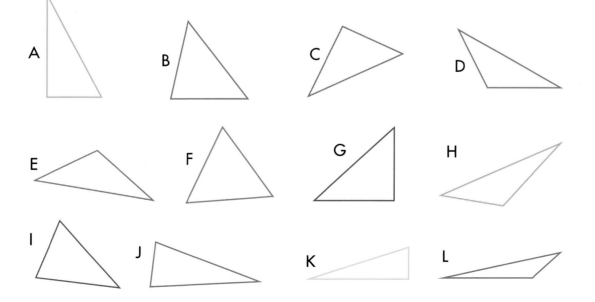

Corresponding Angles and Vertical Angles

Remember: Two lines that "go in the same direction" are called parallel lines.

Because we cannot draw an entire line on a sheet of paper, we indicate a line with an arrow at each end of a line segment to show that it goes on forever in both directions.

If a line crosses two parallel lines, the angles formed in corresponding positions have the same measure. These pairs of angles are called *corresponding angles*.

Look at angles *DEB* and *GHB*. These angles are in corresponding positions. Here ∠*DEB* has the same measure (about 58°) as ∠*GHB*. If two angles have the same measure we write = between them

$$\angle DEB = \angle GHB$$

and say, "Angle *DEB* equals angle *GHB*."

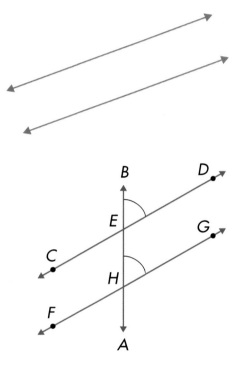

◆   Can you name some other pairs of corresponding angles?

If two lines cross, four angles are formed. Angles that are formed in this way and are opposite to each other are called *vertical angles*. For example, ∠*AEC* and ∠*BED* are vertical angles.

◆   What other pair of vertical angles is formed by lines *AB* and *CD*?

◆   What do you think is true of vertical angles?

∠*AED* and ∠*BEC* are vertical angles.

◆   Do they have the same measure?

◆   What can you now tell about ∠*CEH* and ∠*BHG*?

◆   How can you show that ∠*BEC* and ∠*AHG* are equal?

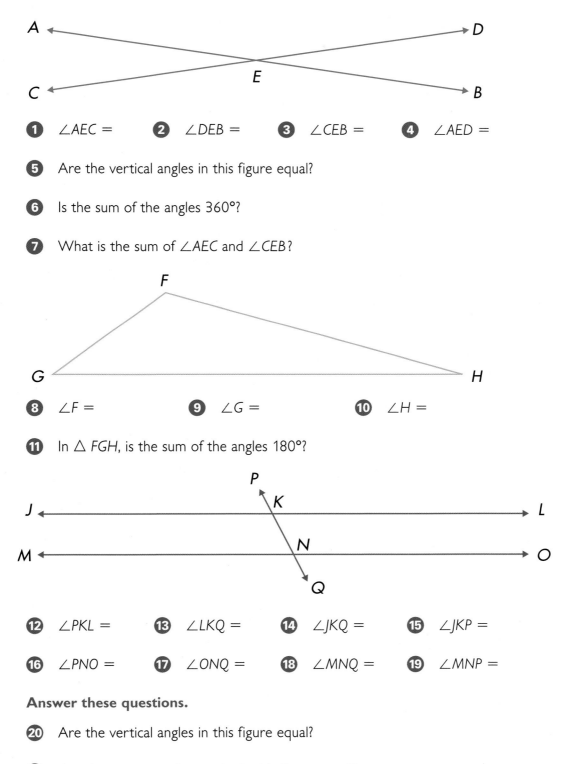

Measure each angle in each figure. Then answer the questions.

1 ∠AEC =   **2** ∠DEB =   **3** ∠CEB =   **4** ∠AED =

5 Are the vertical angles in this figure equal?

6 Is the sum of the angles 360°?

7 What is the sum of ∠AEC and ∠CEB?

8 ∠F =   **9** ∠G =   **10** ∠H =

11 In △ FGH, is the sum of the angles 180°?

12 ∠PKL =   **13** ∠LKQ =   **14** ∠JKQ =   **15** ∠JKP =

16 ∠PNO =   **17** ∠ONQ =   **18** ∠MNQ =   **19** ∠MNP =

Answer these questions.

20 Are the vertical angles in this figure equal?

21 Are the corresponding angles in this figure equal?

◆ **LESSON 145   Corresponding Angles and Vertical Angles**

In the figure below, lines *AB*, *CD*, and *EF* are parallel to each other.

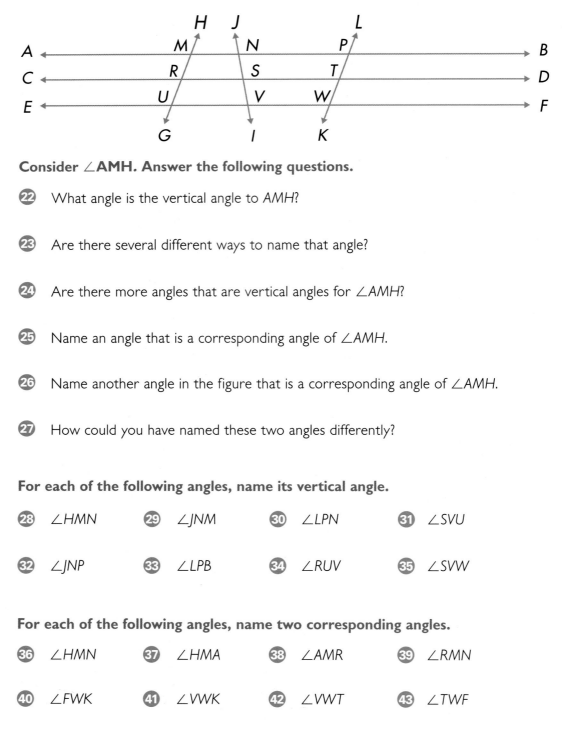

Consider ∠AMH. Answer the following questions.

22   What angle is the vertical angle to *AMH*?

23   Are there several different ways to name that angle?

24   Are there more angles that are vertical angles for ∠*AMH*?

25   Name an angle that is a corresponding angle of ∠*AMH*.

26   Name another angle in the figure that is a corresponding angle of ∠*AMH*.

27   How could you have named these two angles differently?

For each of the following angles, name its vertical angle.

28   ∠*HMN*   **29**   ∠*JNM*   **30**   ∠*LPN*   **31**   ∠*SVU*

32   ∠*JNP*   **33**   ∠*LPB*   **34**   ∠*RUV*   **35**   ∠*SVW*

For each of the following angles, name two corresponding angles.

36   ∠*HMN*   **37**   ∠*HMA*   **38**   ∠*AMR*   **39**   ∠*RMN*

40   ∠*FWK*   **41**   ∠*VWK*   **42**   ∠*VWT*   **43**   ∠*TWF*

44   ∠*NST*   **45**   ∠*NSR*   **46**   ∠*VSR*   **47**   ∠*VST*

In the figure below, lines *AB*, *CD*, and *EF* are parallel. Also, line *HG* is parallel to line *JI*.

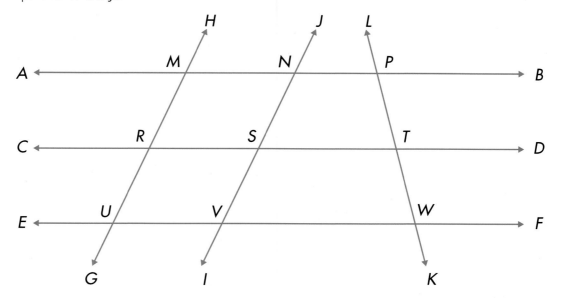

Because lines *HG* and *JI* are parallel, angles *AMH* and *MNJ* are corresponding angles. Because lines *AB* and *CD* are parallel, angles *AMH* and *CRM* are corresponding angles.

48 Since you know that corresponding angles are equal, and both *MNJ* and *CRM* are corresponding angles of ∠*AMH*, what can you say about angles *MNJ* and *CRM*?

49 Using your knowledge of vertical and corresponding angles, list all the angles in the figure that are equal to ∠*AMH*. How many are there?

50 List all the angles that are equal to ∠*HMN*. How many are there?

51 List all the angles that are equal to ∠*LPB*. How many are there?

52 List all the angles that are equal to ∠*LPN*. How many are there?

Astronauts traveling on board the space shuttle can see a sunrise every 90 minutes.

Straight and Supplementary Angles

In addition to finding corresponding angles and vertical angles, you can use other angle relationships to find measures of unlabeled angles.

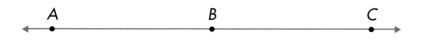

An angle whose sides go in opposite directions on a straight line is called a **straight angle.** Here $\angle ABC$ is a straight angle.

◆ What is the measure of $\angle ABC$?

◆ Do you think that every straight angle has the same measure?

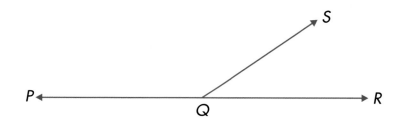

◆ Without measuring, what do you think is the sum of the measures of $\angle SQR$ and $\angle PQS$?

Measure $\angle SQR$ and $\angle PQS$. Then add the measures.

◆ Is the sum about 180°?

The angles $\angle PQS$ and $\angle SQR$ are called *supplementary angles* because their measures add up to 180°.

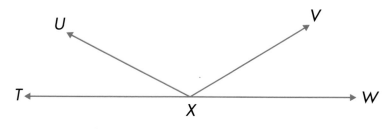

◆ Without measuring, what do you think is the sum of the measures of $\angle TXU$ and $\angle UXV$ and $\angle VXW$?

Measure $\angle TXU$, $\angle UXV$, and $\angle VXW$. Then add the measures.

◆ Is the sum about 180°? If it is not exactly 180°, why might it be off a little?

In the figure below, lines *AB*, *CD*, and *EF* are parallel. Also, line *HG* is parallel to line *JI*.

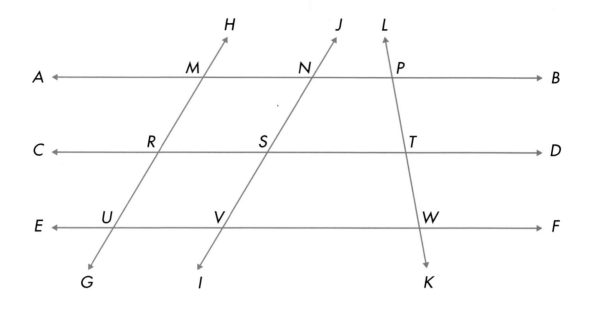

1 Name a supplementary angle of ∠*HMN*.

2 Name another angle that is supplementary to ∠*HMN*.

3 If the measure of ∠*HMN* is 60°, what is the measure of ∠*HMA*?

4 What is the measure of ∠*RMN*?

For the following, assume the measure of ∠*HMN* is 60° and the measure of ∠*LPB* is 100°. (We usually write these facts: ∠*HMN* = 60° and ∠*LPB* = 100°.)

Determine the measure of each of the following angles.

5 ∠*HMA*	**6** ∠*VSR*	**7** ∠*SVE*	**8** ∠*IVF*
9 ∠*AMR*	**10** ∠*VWK*	**11** ∠*PTS*	**12** ∠*LTD*
13 ∠*RMN*	**14** ∠*FWK*	**15** ∠*VUG*	**16** ∠*JNM*
17 ∠*RUV*	**18** ∠*LPN*	**19** ∠*VST*	**20** ∠*MRS*

◆ **LESSON 146 Straight and Supplementary Angles**

In the figure below, **AC** and **DG** are parallel. Answer the following questions based on the figure.

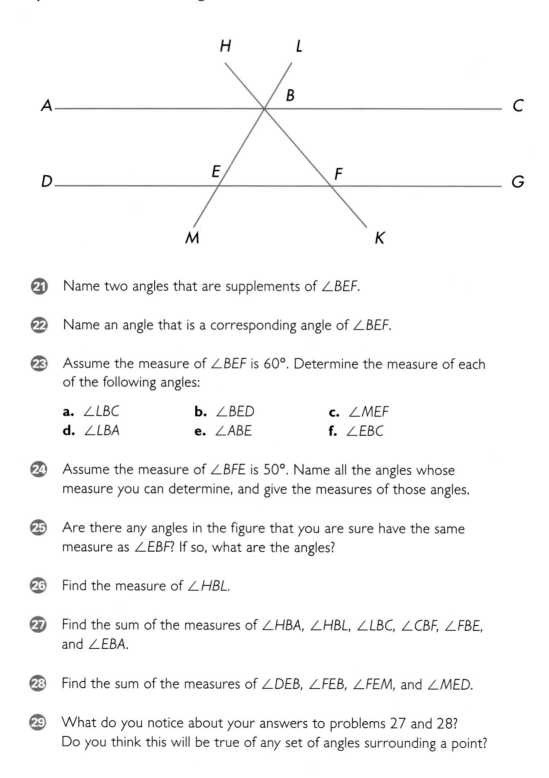

21 Name two angles that are supplements of ∠BEF.

22 Name an angle that is a corresponding angle of ∠BEF.

23 Assume the measure of ∠BEF is 60°. Determine the measure of each of the following angles:

    a. ∠LBC   **b.** ∠BED   **c.** ∠MEF
    d. ∠LBA   **e.** ∠ABE   **f.** ∠EBC

24 Assume the measure of ∠BFE is 50°. Name all the angles whose measure you can determine, and give the measures of those angles.

25 Are there any angles in the figure that you are sure have the same measure as ∠EBF? If so, what are the angles?

26 Find the measure of ∠HBL.

27 Find the sum of the measures of ∠HBA, ∠HBL, ∠LBC, ∠CBF, ∠FBE, and ∠EBA.

28 Find the sum of the measures of ∠DEB, ∠FEB, ∠FEM, and ∠MED.

29 What do you notice about your answers to problems 27 and 28? Do you think this will be true of any set of angles surrounding a point?

Look at △ABC.

Line *DE* is parallel to line *FG*.

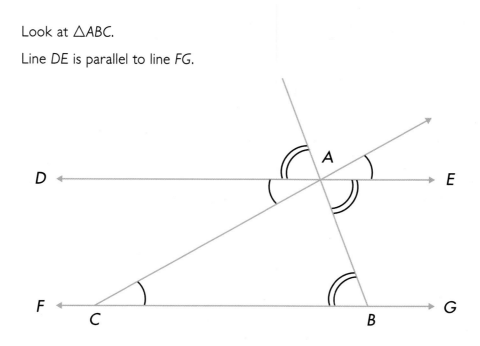

◆ If you measure ∠ACB and ∠DAC, what would you expect to find?

Measure the angles to check.

◆ If you measure ∠ABC and ∠BAE, what would you expect to find?

Measure the angles to check.

◆ What is the sum of the measures of ∠DAC, ∠CAB, and ∠BAE?

You know ∠DAC = ∠ACB and ∠BAE = ∠ABC.

◆ What do you think is the sum of the measures of ∠ACB, ∠CAB, and ∠ABC?

Since these questions would be answered the same way for any triangle, we can consider this a proof that the sum of the angles of any triangle is 180°.

The Pyramids of Giza in Egypt are the only one of the Seven Wonders of the Ancient World that still exist. The largest, sometimes called the Great Pyramid, was built over 4000 years ago out of more than 2,000,000 stone blocks. Each of the blocks weighs about 2.3 tons—that's about the weight of 19 baby elephants.

Angles of Polygons

For each triangle you are given the measure of two angles. Find the measure of the third angle. Then, measure the angles to check your answers.

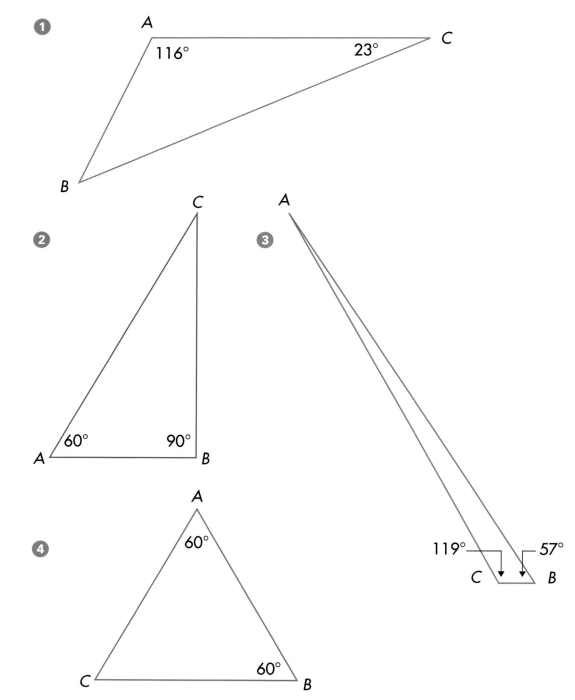

1

A
116°   23°   C

B

2

C

60°   90°
A   B

3

A

119°┐   ┌57°
    C ↓ ↓ B

4

A
60°

60°
C   B

◆ What do you think is the sum of the angles of quadrilateral *ABCD*?

Measure ∠*A*, ∠*B*, ∠*C*, and ∠*D*. Ignore the dotted line for now. Then add the angles to check your answer to the first question.

Imagine you draw line *BD*.

◆ What is the sum of the angles of △ *ABD*?

◆ What is the sum of the angles of △ *CBD*?

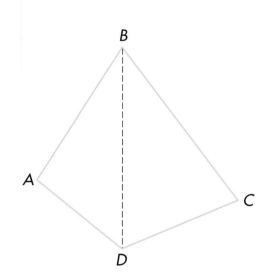

◆ Try to explain why the sum of the angles of quadrilateral *ABCD* is equal to the sum of the angles of two triangles.

The sum of the angles of any quadrilateral is 360°.

◆ What do you think is the sum of the measures of the angles of a **pentagon** (five-sided figure)? Explain why. (Hint: Look at how lines *GE* and *GJ* divide the pentagon into triangles.)

5 What do you think is the sum of the measures of the angles of a **hexagon** (six-sided figure)?

6 What is the sum of the measures of the angles of a heptagon (seven-sided figure)?

7 What is the sum of the measures of the angles of an **octagon** (eight-sided figure)?

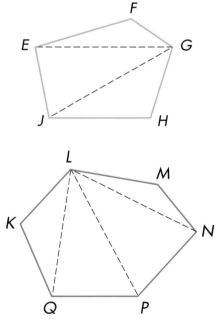

8 Write a function rule or formula for finding the sum of the measures of the angles of a **polygon**, given the number of sides. Use *s* for number of sides and *m* for the sum of the measures of the angles.

9 Can you draw a figure for which the rule will not work?

◆ LESSON 147 Angles of Polygons

Andrew says, "I am thinking of a quadrilateral in which all the angles are the same size."

◆ What is the measure of each angle? (Remember, the sum of the angles of a quadrilateral is 360°.)

◆ What do we call the figure that Andrew is thinking of?

Solve the following problems.

10 In a **regular polygon** the sides are all the same size and the angles are all the same size. The sum of the angles of a pentagon is 540°. What is the measure of each angle of a regular pentagon?

11 Use your protractor and ruler to draw a regular pentagon. (Make each side 6 centimeters long.)

12 The sum of the angles of a hexagon is 720°. In a regular hexagon all six angles are the same size. What is the measure of each angle of a regular hexagon?

13 Use your protractor and ruler to draw a regular hexagon. (Make each side 5 centimeters long.)

14 Draw a regular triangle. What do we usually call this figure?

15 Draw a regular quadrilateral. What do we usually call this figure?

16 Draw a regular octagon (a regular eight-sided polygon).

17 Use the formula you found for problem 8 on page 519 to find the sum of the measures of the angles of a 20-sided figure.

18 What is the measure of each angle in a regular 20-sided figure?

19 What is the sum of the measures of the angles of a 100-sided figure?

20 What is the measure of each angle in a regular 100-sided figure?

There are two kinds of line segments in this pentagon. One kind is a side. The other kind, which crosses the inside of the pentagon, is a **diagonal**.

Solve the following problems.

side

diagonal

21 All possible diagonals have been drawn in this pentagon. How many diagonals are there?

22 Draw a quadrilateral. What is the greatest number of diagonals you can draw in a quadrilateral?

23 How many diagonals can you draw in a triangle?

24 Use a computer or other means to draw a chart like the following, and then complete it. You might not have to draw the diagrams.

Name	Number of Sides	Number of Diagonals
Triangle	3	0
Quadrilateral	4	2
Pentagon	5	5
Hexagon	6	
Heptagon	7	
Octagon	8	
Nonagon	9	
Decagon	10	

25 If three people meet and each person shakes everybody else's hand, how many handshakes will there be?

26 If four people meet and each person shakes everybody else's hand, how many handshakes will there be?

27 If five people meet and each person shakes everybody else's hand, how many handshakes will there be?

28 What is the same about the diagonal problems and the handshake problems? What is different about them?

29 If ten people meet and each person shakes everybody else's hand, how many handshakes will there be?

Points, Lines, and Planes

Look at points *P* and *Q*.

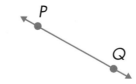

◆ How many straight lines could you draw through both *P* and *Q*?

Mathematical lines go on forever in both directions. Any line we draw is really a **line segment** or part of a line.

Look at lines *AB* and *CD*.

◆ If these line segments were extended, would they meet?

◆ At how many points will the lines meet?

◆ Is it possible to draw two lines that do not meet at all?

◆ How would you describe those lines?

◆ Is it possible to choose two points so that no straight line can go through both points?

◆ Can you think of two lines that do not meet but are not parallel? (Remember, the lines extend forever.)

Look at the line that is made where the ceiling of your classroom meets the front wall. (This line runs across the front of the room.) Now look at the line that is made where the floor meets a side wall. (This line runs across the side of the room.)

◆ Do these two lines go in the same direction?

◆ Are they parallel?

◆ Do the two lines meet?

Lines that are not parallel and do not meet are called **skew lines**.

If you think of the shape of a flat ceiling, extended forever in all directions (forward, backward, left and right, but not up or down), you are thinking of a **plane**.

◆ Do you think the plane of your classroom ceiling and the plane of the floor meet? If not, the planes are parallel.

Think of two planes that meet. (For example, think of the plane of a ceiling and the plane of a wall it meets.)

◆ Do they have more than one point in common? (Is more than one point in both planes?)

◆ How would you describe the set of all points that the two planes have in common?

Think of any line and any plane. Both go on forever.

◆ Do they meet?

If they do meet, they are not parallel. If they do not meet, they are parallel.

◆ If the line and plane are parallel, is the line parallel to every line in the plane or just to some of them?

Think of a line and a plane that do meet.

◆ How many points do the line and plane have in common?

◆ If a line and a plane have more than one point in common, what is true of the line and plane?

Give examples of each of these.

◆ a line and a plane that are parallel

◆ a line and a plane that meet at one point

◆ a line and a plane that have more than one point in common

Think of two points and a plane that contains both points.

◆ Can you think of another plane that contains both points?

◆ How many planes can you think of that contain both points?

LESSON 148 Points, Lines, and Planes

Answer these questions.

1 Think of any three points. Is there a straight line that contains all three points?

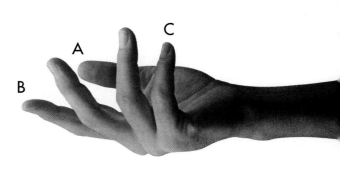

If your answer to this question is yes, then think of three points that are not on the same straight line.

Now think of a plane that goes through all three points. (For example, hold up two fingers and a thumb and imagine the tips to be points. Then place a book or piece of cardboard on the fingers and thumb to show the plane that contains those three points.)

2 Is it possible to find more than one plane through the three points?

Think of three points through which there is more than one plane.

3 What is true of the three points?

4 Can you think of three points not on the same straight line that have more than one plane through them?

Look at the point in your classroom where the ceiling, the side wall, and the front wall meet. Let's call that point *P*. Now look at the point beneath that where the floor, the side wall, and the front wall meet. Let's call that point *Q*.

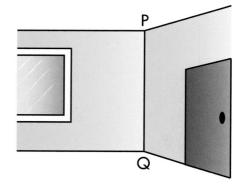

The line *PQ* where the two walls meet is perpendicular to the plane of the floor.

Now think of any line in the plane of the floor that goes through point *Q*.

5 What angle is made by line *PQ* and your new line?

6 If you measured the angle with your protractor, what would its measure be?

7 Would the measure be the same for every line on the floor that goes through point *Q*?

524 • Geometry

Sometimes we wish to talk about the part of a line that starts at a point and goes in only one direction. You might think of it as a half-line. Such a half-line is usually called a **ray.**

P

The mathematical objects we call points, lines, rays, and angles are ideal versions of things we see in everyday life. In mathematics we think of a point as something that has no width, depth, height, color, weight, and so on. In the real world, there isn't any such object, but there are things that are very similar to that.

We think of the mathematical points, lines, rays, and angles as models of things in the real world. We can study the mathematical objects, and they will often tell us something about how the real objects behave.

◆ Think of examples of rays in everyday life. One example is a ray of light. In your Math Journal name at least five other things from the real world that remind you of a ray.

◆ Think of things that remind you of a line in real life. Name five things from the real world that remind you of a line. Record these in your Math Journal.

◆ Name five things in the real world that remind you of a point. Record these in your Math Journal.

◆ On your paper draw a picture of a ray that starts at some point (label the point *P*) and goes in only one direction from that point. Now draw a second ray that starts at the same point *P* but goes in a different direction. What does the drawing look like? Sometimes an angle is defined to be two rays with the same starting point.

LESSON 149

Congruent and Similar Figures

Look at the two figures shown here.

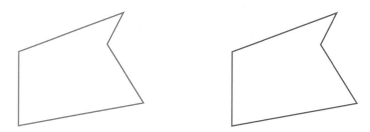

What do you think is true of the two figures? Get a piece of lightweight paper that you can see through. Trace one of the figures. Move your tracing so that it fits on top of the other figure. Does it fit exactly?

When two figures fit exactly on each other, we say they are *congruent*.

1   Think of some objects in everyday life that you would describe as congruent to each other. In the case of three-dimensional objects, you will not be able to put them exactly on each other, but you can think about whether they are exactly the same size and shape. Would two new automobiles of the same model from the same plant seem congruent (before any extra equipment is added)? List ten congruent pairs of objects.

2   From the figures below, choose the ones that appear to be congruent. It is all right to turn the tracing paper over, so figures *A* and *B* are considered to be congruent.

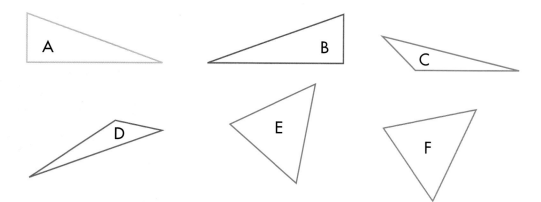

Sometimes two figures have exactly the same shape but not the same size. An architect's scale model of a building should be exactly the same shape but be smaller than the building when it is completed. A map is supposed to be just like the cities and towns that are shown on it, with streets going at the same angles to each other and distances between objects proportional to the real distances.

The two figures shown here are similar to each other. Corresponding angles are equal and corresponding sides are proportional (the sides of the larger figure are four times the length of those on the smaller figure).

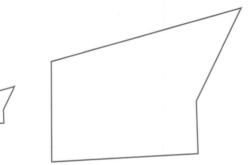

Solve.

③ Think of some objects in everyday life that you would describe as similar to each other. List ten pairs of similar objects.

④ From the figures below, choose the ones that appear to be similar to each other.

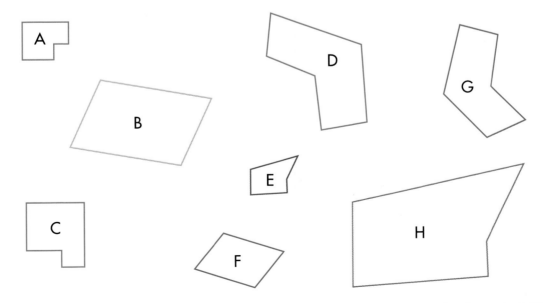

Compass Constructions

A **circle** is the set of all points that are the same distance from a point called the center. Circles are hard to draw free-hand.

You can use a compass to draw a circle. If you are using a compass with a sharp point, put cardboard or something like it under your paper so that you do not make a hole in your desk.

Each point on the circle you draw with the compass is the same distance from the center. This distance is called the *radius* of the circle.

◆   How does the radius relate to the diameter?

Solve.

1   Draw three circles that have the same center. Make one circle with a radius of 3 centimeters, one with a radius of 2 centimeters, and one with a radius of 4 centimeters.

2   Do the circles meet at any point?

3   Assuming two circles do not overlap completely, what is the greatest number of points at which they could meet?

4   Can two circles meet at exactly one point?

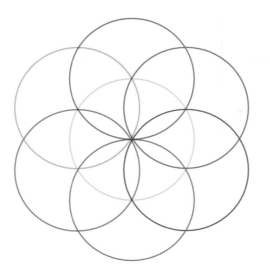

5 Make a design like the one above. Here's how:

A. Draw a circle with about a 3-centimeter radius.

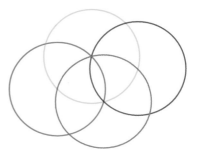

B. Draw another circle of the same size but with its center on a point of the first circle.

C. Draw a third circle (same size) with the center where the first and second circles meet.

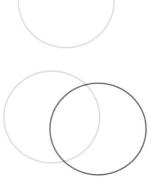

D. Draw a fourth circle with the center where the first and third circles meet.

E. Continue in this way until you have a design like the one shown.

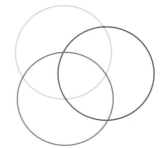

◆ LESSON 150 Compass Constructions

Centuries ago, Greek mathematicians challenged themselves to draw angles and geometric figures using only an unmarked straightedge and a compass.

You can copy angles and lines segments with a compass and a straightedge (a ruler, for example). You could do it more easily with a straightedge and a protractor, but it is interesting to see how to do it with only a compass, just as the Greeks did.

To copy ∠ABC, you would follow these steps:

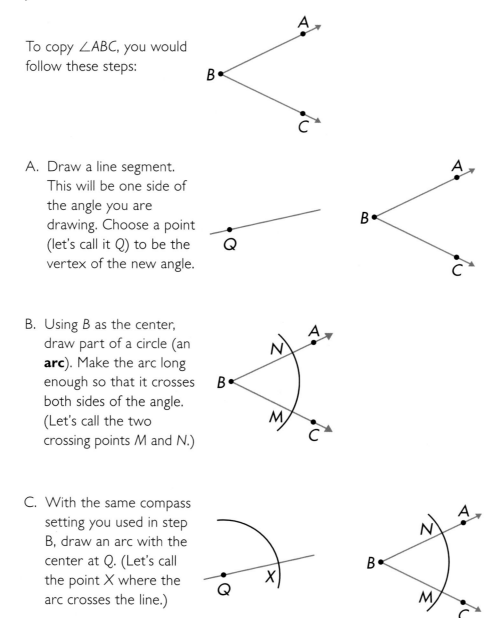

A. Draw a line segment. This will be one side of the angle you are drawing. Choose a point (let's call it Q) to be the vertex of the new angle.

B. Using B as the center, draw part of a circle (an **arc**). Make the arc long enough so that it crosses both sides of the angle. (Let's call the two crossing points M and N.)

C. With the same compass setting you used in step B, draw an arc with the center at Q. (Let's call the point X where the arc crosses the line.)

D. Put the point of the compass at M. Set the compass so that the pencil point just touches N. Using this new setting, draw an arc with the center at X. Make sure the arc crosses the arc you drew in step C. (Let's call the point where the arcs meet P.)

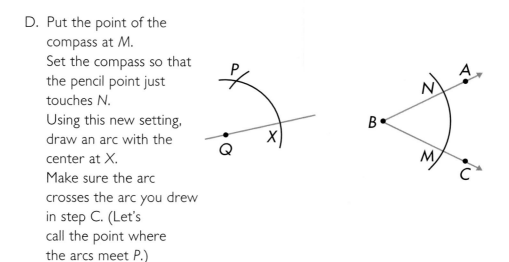

E. Draw line QP.
Then ∠ABC = ∠PQX.

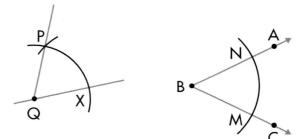

6 Draw any angle.

a. Copy the angle with a compass and a straightedge.

b. Measure both angles with your protractor.

c. Do they have about the same measure?

7 Use your protractor to draw a 120° angle.

a. Copy it with a compass and a straightedge.

b. Measure the new angle.

c. Is it about 120°?

8 Trace or use your protractor to draw a 90° angle.

a. Copy the angle.

b. Copy the angle again on each side of the angle you drew in step a.

c. Look at the figure created by the sides of the angles. What is the name of this figure?

◆ **LESSON 150** **Compass Constructions**

Remember, congruent figures are figures that would exactly fit on each other if you cut one out and placed it on the other.

Two triangles are congruent if their corresponding angles and corresponding sides are the same size.

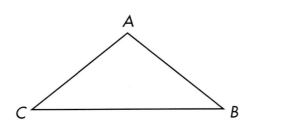

To construct a triangle congruent to triangle *ABC*, you would follow these steps:

A. Draw a line (call it *PX*).

B. Set your compass by placing its point at *C* and the pencil at *B* on the triangle. With this setting draw an arc with *P* as the center. Mark point *Q*. (*PQ* corresponds to side *CB* of triangle *ABC*.)

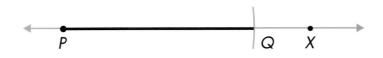

C. Copy ∠*C* with *P* as the vertex and *PQ* as one side. (Pages 530–531 show you how to copy an angle.) You may extend side *CA* a bit to make this easier.

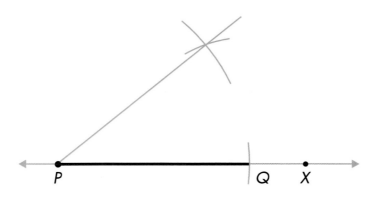

D. Mark off *PR* so that it is the same length as *AC*.

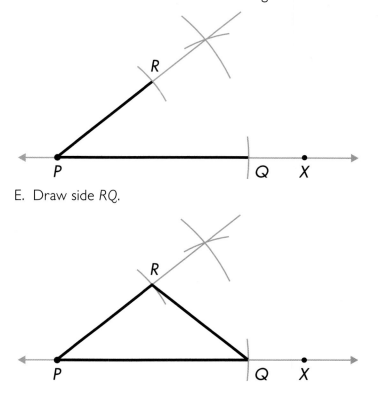

E. Draw side *RQ*.

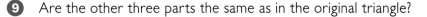

Notice that we copied only three parts of the triangle: a side, a vertex, and another side.

9 Are the other three parts the same as in the original triangle?

10 Draw any triangle. Label it *ABC*. Use a compass and a straightedge to draw a congruent triangle.

    a. To check that the triangles are congruent, measure all three sides and all three angles of each triangle.

    b. Are the corresponding parts the same size?

11 Now you know how to make a congruent triangle by copying two sides and the angle between them. Try to make a congruent triangle by copying two angles and the side between them. Measure the other parts to check.

12 Try to copy a triangle by copying three sides and no angles. (Hint: Copy one side. From each endpoint, draw an arc with a radius equal to the length of the corresponding side.) Measure the angles to check that the triangles are congruent.

Circle Graphs

Circle graphs are often used to show information. They are especially used to show what fraction or percent of the whole certain parts are. For example, this circle graph gives a picture of what fraction of our presidents belonged to each political party.

Political Parties of United States Presidents, 1787–1996

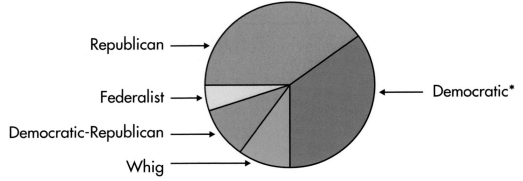

Republican ⟶

Federalist ⟶

Democratic-Republican ⟶

Whig ⟶

⟵ Democratic*

* Grover Cleveland was counted twice because his terms of office were not consecutive.

◆ Which of the five political parties shown has had the fewest presidents?

Two United States presidents belonged to the Federalist party.

◆ How many presidents do you think belonged to the Democratic-Republican party?

◆ About how many belonged to the Democratic party?

◆ To which two parties did the same number of presidents belong?

◆ About what fraction of presidents belonged to either the Democratic or the Republican party?

◆ Do you know which two of our presidents were members of the Federalist party? If you do not, research to find the answer.

To make a circle graph, follow these steps:

A. Decide what fraction (or percent) of the circle should be used for each category. We call a fraction or part of a circle a **sector**.

B. Decide how many degrees should be in each sector of the circle. There are 360 degrees in a circle.

C. Draw a circle and locate its center. Then use a protractor to measure off each sector.

For example, here is how one of the sectors in the circle graph on page 534 might have been made. Let's take the Democratic party sector.

A. There are 42 presidents in all shown on the graph. If 15 of them belonged to the Democratic party, then we can say that $\frac{15}{42}$ were Democrats. We can also say that about 36% were Democrats. (Remember that to express a fraction as a percent, you divide the numerator by the denominator and multiply the resulting decimal by 100.)

B. The sector for the Democratic party should be 36% of 360° or about 129°.

Use a computer or other means to make and complete this chart. Consider using spreadsheet software. Then use the chart to make a circle graph like the one on page 534.

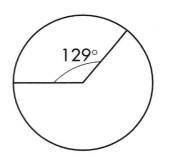

129°

Political Party	Number of Presidents Who Belonged	Fraction of Presidents Who Belonged	Percent of Presidents Who Belonged	Number of Degrees in Sector of Circle
Republican	17	▦	▦	▦
Democratic	15	$\frac{15}{42}$	36%	129
Whig	4	▦	▦	▦
Democratic-Republican	4	▦	▦	▦
Federalist	2	▦	▦	▦
Total	42	▦	▦	▦

◆ LESSON 151   Circle Graphs

Kamal collected data to see what color shirts students wore to school.
Kamal counted 400 people the first day. He recorded his results in a table.

Use the table to solve the following problems.

Shirt Color	Number of Children
Brown or tan	80
White	100
Blue	60
Green	60
Yellow	40
Other	60
Total	400

1. Use a computer or other means to make a circle graph to show the information in the chart.

2. If someone wore a blue and red striped shirt, did Kamal count it as both blue and red? How can you tell?

3. Suppose the school has 800 students. Do you think Kamal's results would be about the same if he had counted all 800 students? Why or why not?

4. If Kamal counted 400 students the following day, would his results be the same? Why or why not?

5. If Kamal counted students and made circle graphs each day for a week, would the graphs look very different or about the same? Explain.

6 This chart shows the number of cars made by major manufacturers in the United States during a recent year. (The numbers are rounded to the nearest thousand.)

Manufacturer	Number of Cars
Honda®	499,000
Chrysler® Corporation	551,000
Ford Motor® Corporation	1,221,000
General Motors® Corporation	2,720,000
Toyota®	399,000
Total	5,390,000

7 Make a circle graph to show this information.

8 What other kinds of graphs would be appropriate for this information?

Find a graph in a newspaper or magazine. In your Math Journal explain why that type of graph was chosen to represent the data.

LESSON
152

Right Triangles: Squares of Sides

Look at △ABC. The length of AC is 1 centimeter, and the length of CB is 1 centimeter.

1 What is the area of the red square?

2 What is the area of the green square?

3 What is the area of the blue square? (Hint: Add the areas of the four triangles that make up the blue square.)

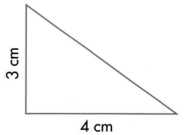

4 Is it true that the sum of the areas of the squares on the two short sides of right triangle ABC is the same as the area of the square on the long side?

On your paper very carefully draw a right triangle in which the two shorter sides are 3 centimeters long and 4 centimeters long.

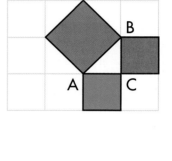

3 cm

4 cm

5 Measure the length of the longest side.

6 What is the area of a square with each side 3 cm long?

7 What is the area of a square with each side 4 cm long?

8 What is the area of a square with each side 5 cm long?

9 Is it true in your right triangle that the area of the square on the longest side equals the sum of the areas of the squares on the shorter sides?

The long side of the right triangle is called the **hypotenuse.** More than 2500 years ago, a Greek mathematician named Pythagoras proved that for any right triangle, the area of the square of the hypotenuse is equal to the sum of the areas of the squares of the other two sides.

The statement that Pythagoras proved is called the **Pythagorean theorem.** You can use the Pythagorean theorem to find the length of one side of a right triangle if you know the lengths of the other two sides.

Example:

Antonio walked 2 kilometers south and then 3 kilometers east. About how far will he have to go if he walks directly back to his starting point?

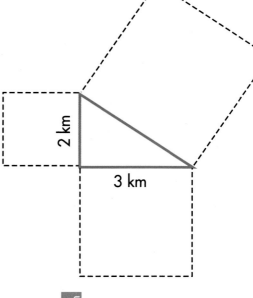

$$2 \times 2 = 4$$

$$3 \times 3 = 9$$

$$4 + 9 = 13$$

So the area of the big square is 13 square kilometers. Using a calculator, we can find a number that we can multiply by itself to get about 13.

$$3.605 \times 3.605 = 12.996025$$

$$3.606 \times 3.606 = 13.003236$$

(We could also have found the square root of 13 using the □ key.)

A side of the big square is a bit more than 3.6 kilometers. So Antonio must walk a bit more than 3.6 kilometers back to the starting point.

10 In each case the lengths of the two shorter sides of a right triangle are given. Find the length of the hypotenuse. Use the Pythagorean theorem. Give answers to the nearest tenth of a centimeter.

a. 6 cm, 8 cm   **b.** 5 cm, 12 cm   **c.** 9 cm, 12 cm

d. 1 cm, 1 cm   **e.** 4 cm, 6 cm   **f.** 2 cm, 3 cm

g. 3 cm, 6 cm   **h.** 1 cm, 2 cm   **i.** 2 cm, 2 cm

11 Use a protractor and a ruler to carefully draw each right triangle described in problem 10. Then measure the length of each hypotenuse. Are these measurements the same as the calculations you made in problem 10?

12 Crystal is walking around a park by going 40 feet west and 30 feet north. How much shorter would her walk be if she cut through the park diagonally?

13 Is it possible for a hypotenuse to be one of the sides of the right angle in a right triangle?

LESSON
153

Unit 6 Review

Find the area in square centimeters of each of these figures.

Lessons 128–131

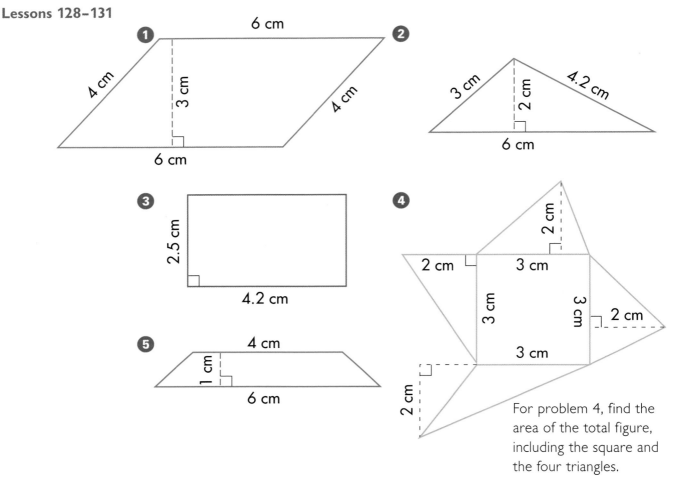

For problem 4, find the area of the total figure, including the square and the four triangles.

Lessons 125, 126, 135, and 136

Solve the following problems.

6 The area of a rectangle is 28 square centimeters, and its base is 7 centimeters long. What is its height?

7 The area of a square is 81 square centimeters. What is the length of a side?

8 The area of a square is 10 square centimeters. To the nearest tenth of a centimeter, how long is a side?

9 A rectangular box is 7 centimeters long, 3 centimeters wide, and 4 centimeters tall. What is the volume of the box in cubic centimeters?

10 What is the total area of the six faces of the box in problem 9?

Lesson 139   **Answer the following questions.**

**Remember: There are 100 centimeters in a meter.
                 There are 1000 meters in a kilometer.**

⑪   How many grams are in a kilogram?

⑫   How many centigrams are in a gram?

⑬   How many centimeters are in a kilometer?

⑭   How many centiliters are in a kiloliter?

⑮   At which of these outdoor temperatures would you be most
       comfortable?

       a. 0°C   **b.** 20°C   **c.** 50°C   **d.** 70°C   **e.** 100°C

Lesson 144   **Use your protractor to measure each of these angles.**

⑯ ∠A   ⑰ ∠B   ⑱ ∠C   ⑲ ∠JEF

⑳ ∠JHI   ㉑ ∠DEH   ㉒ ∠FEH   ㉓ ∠GHE

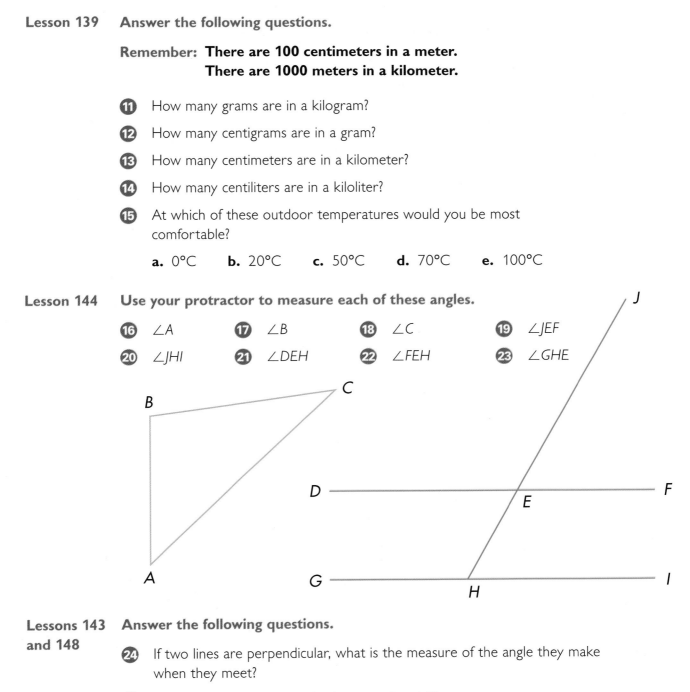

**Lessons 143
and 148**   **Answer the following questions.**

㉔   If two lines are perpendicular, what is the measure of the angle they make
       when they meet?

㉕   How many planes contain both points A and B?

LESSON
154

Unit 6 Practice

Lessons 128–131   Find the area in square centimeters of each of these figures.

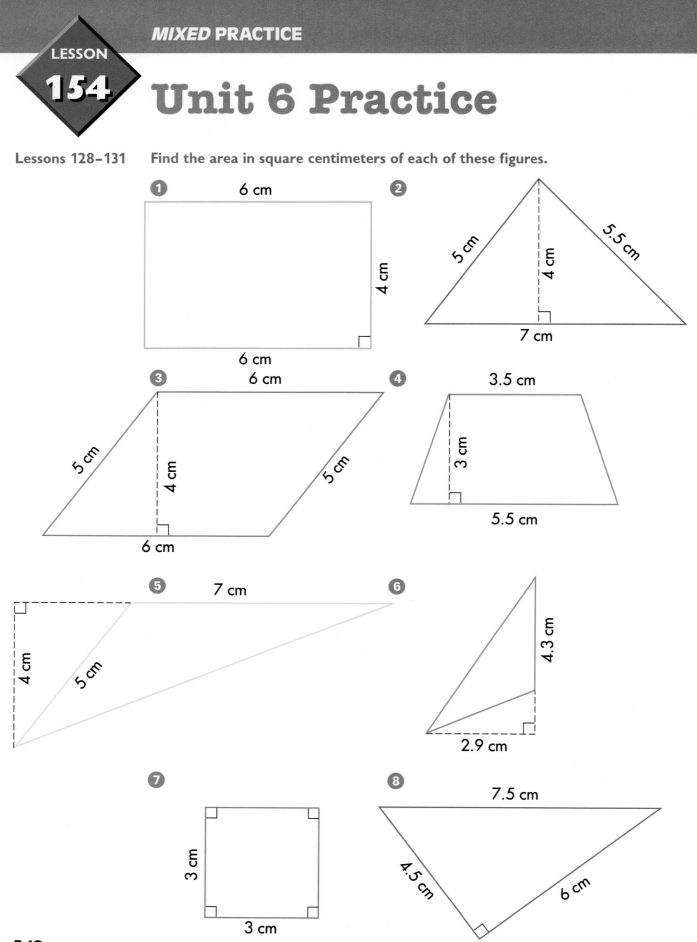

1   6 cm
4 cm
6 cm

2   5 cm   4 cm   5.5 cm
7 cm

3   6 cm
5 cm   4 cm
6 cm

4   3.5 cm
3 cm
5.5 cm

5   7 cm
4 cm
5 cm

6   4.3 cm
2.9 cm

7   3 cm
3 cm

8   7.5 cm
4.5 cm   6 cm

Lessons 124, 128, 131, and 152

Answer the following questions.

9 Find the area in square centimeters of each of the three squares and the triangle.

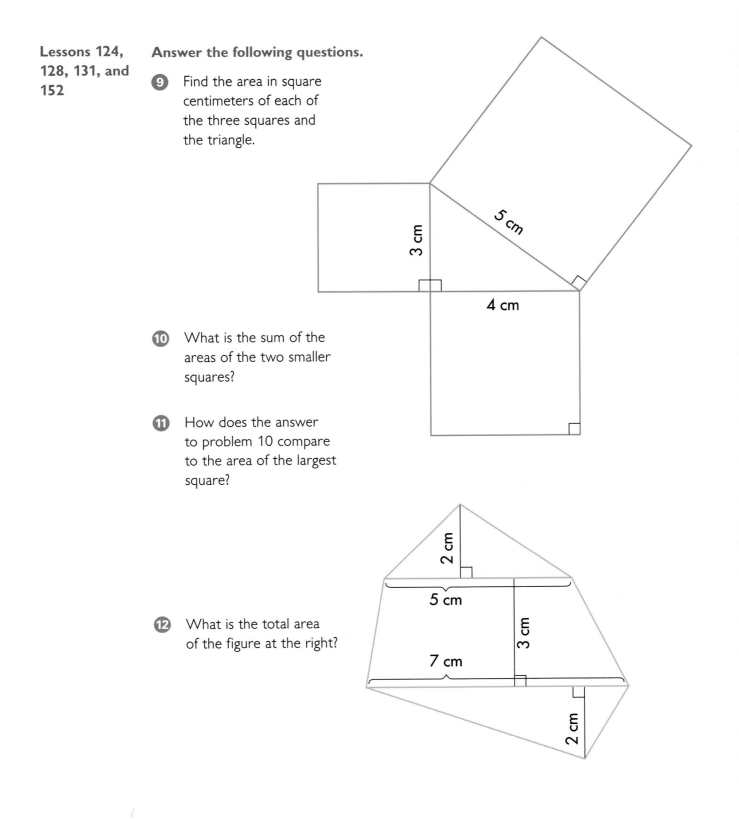

3 cm

5 cm

4 cm

10 What is the sum of the areas of the two smaller squares?

11 How does the answer to problem 10 compare to the area of the largest square?

12 What is the total area of the figure at the right?

2 cm

5 cm

3 cm

7 cm

2 cm

More Practice

Lessons 125, 126, 135, and 136

Solve the following problems.

1 The area of a rectangle is 56 square centimeters. The length of its base is 8 centimeters. What is its height?

2 The area of a triangle is 56 square centimeters. The length of its base is 8 centimeters. What is its height?

3 The area of a square is 100 square centimeters. What is the length of a side?

4 The area of a square is 169 square centimeters. What is the length of a side?

5 The area of a square is 2 square centimeters. To the nearest tenth of a centimeter, what is the length of a side?

6 What is the volume in cubic centimeters of a rectangular box that is 4 centimeters long, 4 centimeters wide, and 4 centimeters tall?

7 What is the volume in cubic centimeters of a rectangular box that is 3 centimeters long, 2 centimeters wide, and 1 centimeter tall?

8 What is the volume in cubic centimeters of a rectangular box that is 3.2 centimeters long, 1.5 centimeters wide, and 5 centimeters tall?

9 What is the total area of the six faces of the box

   a. in problem 6?

   b. in problem 7?

   c. in problem 8?

Lesson 139

If necessary, use the table on page 490 to help solve these problems.

10 ▓ grams = 1 kilogram

11 ▓ meters = 5 kilometers

12 ▓ meters = 1 kilometer

13 ▓ meters = 4.7 kilometers

14 ▓ grams = 5 kilograms

15 ▓ milligrams = 8.64 grams

16 ▓ grams = 4.7 kilograms

17 ▓ millimeters = 8.64 meters

18 ▓ liters = 2500 milliliters

19 ▓ centimeters = 3.6 meters

Lesson 137 **Answer the following questions.**

⑳ Lola and Omar were ice-skating outside on a frozen pond. They looked at a thermometer. Which of these temperatures might they have seen? (More than one answer may be correct.)

a. −20°C   **b.** −5°C   **c.** 15°C   **d.** 25°C   **e.** 35°C

㉑ At which of these temperatures would it generally be most comfortable to go swimming?

a. 10°C   **b.** 16°C   **c.** 27°C   **d.** 50°C   **e.** 80°C

㉒ What is the normal boiling point of water?

a. 51°C   **b.** 100°C   **c.** 168°C   **d.** 212°C   **e.** 508°C

㉓ How many feet are in 12 yards?

㉔ How many pounds are in 192 ounces?

Lesson 148 **Use the figures at the right to answer these questions.**

㉕ How many lines can be drawn through the points M and N?

• N

㉖ How many planes could go through the points M and N?

• M

㉗ Suppose two lines meet at point M. Will they meet at any other points?

• A

㉘ Suppose two planes meet at point M. Will they meet at any other points?

p

㉙ Line AB is perpendicular to plane p. What is the relationship of line AB to a line in plane p that meets AB? What is the relationship of line AB to a line in plane p that does not meet AB?

• B

Practice

Lessons 144–147   **Find the measure of each angle. If you can do this without actually measuring in some cases, do so.**

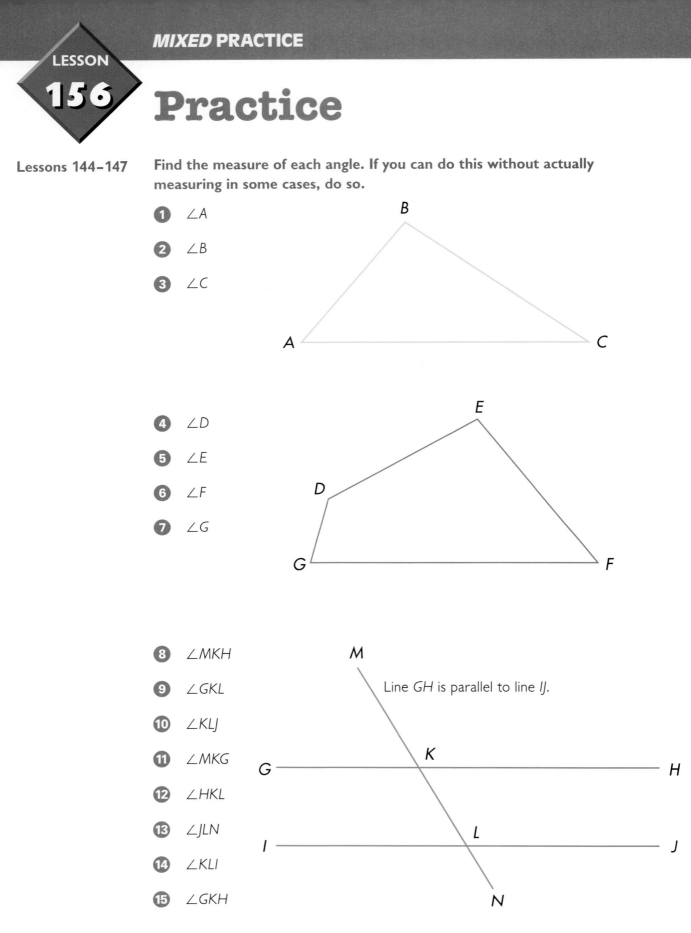

1 ∠A

2 ∠B

3 ∠C

4 ∠D

5 ∠E

6 ∠F

7 ∠G

8 ∠MKH

9 ∠GKL

10 ∠KLJ

11 ∠MKG

12 ∠HKL

13 ∠JLN

14 ∠KLI

15 ∠GKH

Line *GH* is parallel to line *IJ*.

Lesson 151

Study this circle graph. Then answer the questions.

16 In 1995 what percent of the government's money came from individual income taxes?

17 In 1995 the government received about $1519 billion (including money it borrowed). How many dollars came from

   a. individual income taxes?

   b. social insurance taxes and contributions?

   c. corporation income taxes?

   d. borrowing?

   e. excise taxes?

18 This chart shows how our government spent its money in fiscal year 1995. Use a computer or other means to draw and complete the chart. You may also want to use a calculator.

Where Our Government Gets Its Money Fiscal Year 1995
(Oct. 1, 1994–Sept. 30, 1995)

- Corporation Income Taxes 10%
- Borrowing 11%
- Individual Income Taxes 39%
- Other 4%
- Excise Taxes 4%
- Social Insurance Taxes and Contributions 32%

Spending Category	Amount (billions of dollars)	Percent
Income security	556.3	
National defense	272.0	
Other	29.7	
Health	275.3	
Net interest	232.3	
Education, training, and social services	54.2	
Veterans	38.0	
Transportation	39.3	
Natural resources and environment	22.1	

19 Work in groups to make a circle graph to show this information.

Unit Test

Find the area in square centimeters of each of these figures.

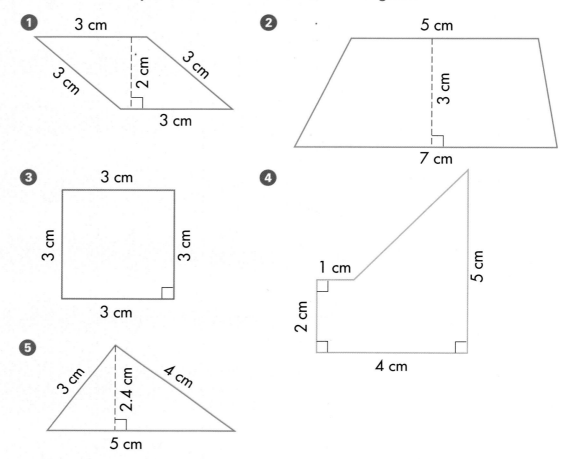

1 3 cm / 3 cm / 2 cm / 3 cm / 3 cm

2 5 cm / 3 cm / 7 cm

3 3 cm / 3 cm / 3 cm / 3 cm

4 1 cm / 2 cm / 4 cm / 5 cm

5 3 cm / 2.4 cm / 4 cm / 5 cm

Solve the following problems.

6 The area of a rectangle is 35 square centimeters, and its height is 7 centimeters. What is the length of its base?

7 The area of a square is 49 square centimeters. What is the length of a side?

8 The area of a square is 5 square centimeters. To the nearest tenth of a centimeter, how long is a side?

9 Each side of a cube is 3 centimeters long. What is the volume of the cube in cubic centimeters?

10 What is the total area of the six faces of the cube in problem 9?

Answer the following questions.

Remember: There are 1000 millimeters in a meter. There are 10 meters in a dekameter.

⑪ How many milligrams are in a gram?

⑫ How many grams are in a dekagram?

⑬ How many milligrams are in a dekagram?

⑭ How many milliliters are in a dekaliter?

⑮ At which of these room temperatures are most people comfortable?

    a. 0°C   **b.** 19°C   **c.** 37°C   **d.** 64°C   **e.** 98°C

Use your protractor to measure each of these angles.

⑯ ∠A   **⑰** ∠B   **⑱** ∠C   **⑲** ∠DEG

⑳ ∠IJG   **㉑** ∠HJK   **㉒** ∠GJK   **㉓** ∠GEF

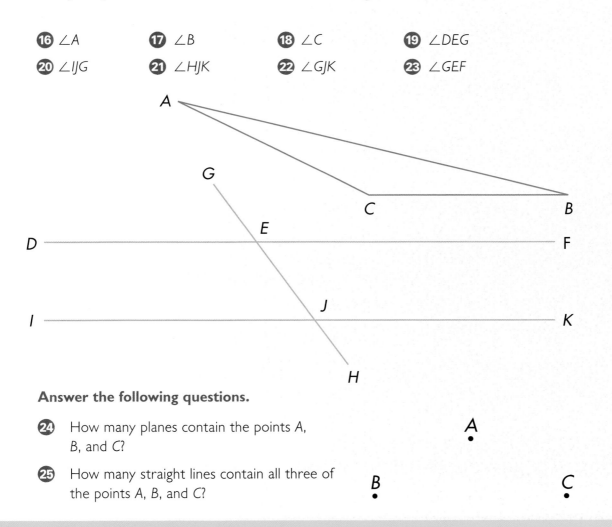

Answer the following questions.

㉔ How many planes contain the points A, B, and C?

㉕ How many straight lines contain all three of the points A, B, and C?

Melting Ice Cubes

◆ Does the shape that ice is in affect the time it takes to melt?

To find out, have an ice cube melting contest.

Here are the rules.

A. Each person is allowed to freeze 2 ounces of water.

B. You can freeze it in any shape.

C. Everyone's ice is put into and taken out of the freezer at the same time.

D. The person whose ice lasts the longest is the winner.

Record the results in a table such as the one shown below.

Description of containers	Time taken from freezer	Time ice becomes water	Time to thaw	Comment

Here are some things to consider before beginning.

Since water expands when it freezes, don't use closed containers or glass containers to freeze your ice.

Let your ice melt in a place where the water will be collected in a pan.

Think about the possible effects of surface area and volume.

Repeat the contest. Work in small groups to design your shapes. Is there a "best shape" that allows the ice to last the longest?

In your Math Journal write an explanation of why you think a particular shape is the best or why you think the shape doesn't make a difference.

Cumulative Review
Use after Lesson 4

Write the numbers in standard form.

1 4000 + 700 + 60 + 5

2 8000 + 200 + 70 + 6

3 3000 + 50 + 1

4 40,000 + 600 + 70

5 5 + 600 + 40,000

6 300,000 + 4000 + 70

7 3 tenths, 2 hundredths, 5 thousandths

8 0.6 + 0.08 + 0.003

9 0 tenths, 4 hundredths, 2 thousandths

10 0.04 + 0.002 + 0.1

11 0.005 + 0.4 + 0.02

12 0.004 + 0.06

Copy each pair of numbers but replace ■ with <, >, =.

13 3.7 ■ 2.9

14 0.4 ■ 0.04

15 0.678 ■ 0.7

The point A is the number 0, and the point B is the number 1.

16 What fraction tells us where point R is?

    a. $\frac{1}{2}$ **b.** $\frac{1}{3}$ **c.** $\frac{2}{3}$

17 What fraction tells us where point S is?

    a. $\frac{1}{4}$ **b.** $\frac{9}{10}$ **c.** $\frac{3}{4}$

Solve these problems.

18 Of the 32 students in Juan's class, 18 are wearing sneakers today. Are the majority of his classmates wearing sneakers?

19 A CD player that regularly sells for $80 is on sale for $62.95. Is that more than $\frac{1}{5}$ off the usual price?

Solve for n.

20 6 + 7 = n

21 15 − 4 = n

22 n = 9 + 4

23 n = 12 − 8

24 11 − 5 = n

25 n = 16 − 7

Cumulative Review
Use after Lesson 8

Write the numbers in standard form.

1 4 + 700 + 600,000

2 0.3 + 0.05 + 0.009

3 30 + 8000 + 20,000 + 700,000

4 0.004 + 0.5 + 0.08

5 4000 + 20 + 7

6 0.03 + 2 + 0.006

Copy each pair of numbers but replace ■ with <, >, or =.

7 0.7 ■ 0.69

8 0.42 ■ 0.042

9 9.0 ■ 0.9

Solve for *n*. Watch the signs.

10 $27 \div 9 = n$

11 $6 \times 9 = n$

12 $n = 49 \div 7$

13 $n = 80 \times 5$

14 $210 \div 3 = n$

15 $n = 70 + 80$

Add. Use shortcuts when you can.

16
$$\begin{array}{r} 45 \\ + 45 \\ \hline \end{array}$$

17
$$\begin{array}{r} 73 \\ + 98 \\ \hline \end{array}$$

18
$$\begin{array}{r} 84 \\ + 15 \\ \hline \end{array}$$

19
$$\begin{array}{r} 4000 \\ + 26 \\ \hline \end{array}$$

20
$$\begin{array}{r} 269 \\ +331 \\ \hline \end{array}$$

21
$$\begin{array}{r} 784 \\ + 6 \\ \hline \end{array}$$

22
$$\begin{array}{r} 72 \\ + 72 \\ \hline \end{array}$$

23
$$\begin{array}{r} 8000 \\ +3000 \\ \hline \end{array}$$

24
$$\begin{array}{r} 2003 \\ +3000 \\ \hline \end{array}$$

25
$$\begin{array}{r} 500 \\ +700 \\ \hline \end{array}$$

26
$$\begin{array}{r} 3814 \\ +4186 \\ \hline \end{array}$$

27
$$\begin{array}{r} 4032 \\ +7153 \\ \hline \end{array}$$

Solve these problems.

28 A sports arena has 15,000 seats. About two–thirds of the seats are sold for each event. If tickets cost $15 each, about how much money would the arena collect for 10 events?

29 Mara was on vacation with her family for two weeks. There she found 17 new soft drink labels for her collection. If she had 97 labels before the vacation, how many does she have now?

30 Mr. Takamura worked 38 hours last week and 43 hours this week. How many hours has he worked over the past two weeks?

Cumulative Review
Use after Lesson 12

Solve for *n*.

1 $60 + 7 = n$

2 $150 \div 3 = n$

3 $n = 9 \times 4000$

Add. Use shortcuts when you can.

4 $67 + 32 + 48$

5 $3000 + 2000 + 6000$

6 $250 + 150 + 350$

Solve these problems. Use shortcuts when you can.

7 $82 - 27$

8 $100 - 7$

9 $1000 - 6$

10 $4027 + 3026$

11 $4002 + 2740 + 2000 + 3317$

GEOGRAPHY CONNECTION

Use the map to answer these questions.

12   How many miles is it from Miami to Daytona Beach if you go through Vero Beach?

13   How many miles is a round trip between Tampa, Daytona Beach, and Vero Beach?

14   Which round trip is longer:

    a. Miami–Gainesville–Miami?

    b. Miami–Vero Beach–Tampa–Ft. Myers–Miami?

Map of Florida with cities: Gainesville, Daytona Beach, Tampa, Vero Beach, Ft. Myers, Miami. Distances: 129 mi, 138 mi, 333 mi, 131 mi, 164 mi, 130 mi, 136 mi, 152 mi.

Multiply.

15 30×70

16 800×60

17 200×700

18
$$\begin{array}{r} 78 \\ \times\ 6 \\ \hline \end{array}$$

19
$$\begin{array}{r} 624 \\ \times\ 5 \\ \hline \end{array}$$

20
$$\begin{array}{r} 800 \\ \times\ 7 \\ \hline \end{array}$$

21
$$\begin{array}{r} 420 \\ \times\ 8 \\ \hline \end{array}$$

22
$$\begin{array}{r} 615 \\ \times\ 90 \\ \hline \end{array}$$

23
$$\begin{array}{r} 300 \\ \times\ 70 \\ \hline \end{array}$$

24
$$\begin{array}{r} 700 \\ \times\ 9 \\ \hline \end{array}$$

25
$$\begin{array}{r} 3500 \\ \times\ 400 \\ \hline \end{array}$$

Cumulative Review
Use after Lesson 15

Copy each pair of numbers but replace ■ with <, >, or =.

① 0.06 ■ 0.059   **②** 0.72 ■ 0.072   **③** 9.1 ■ 0.199

Solve for *n*. Watch the signs.

④ $2700 \div 90 = n$ **⑤** $600 \times 9 = n$ **⑥** $n = 420 \div 7$

⑦ $5124 + 6387 = n$ **⑧** $416 \times 2 = n$ **⑨** $6947 - 3258 = n$

⑩ $937 \times 4 = n$ **⑪** $250 \div 5 = n$ **⑫** $500 - 6 = n$

Choose the correct answer.

⑬ 17×48 **a.** 816   **b.** 416   **c.** 1480

⑭ $7105 - 2929$ **a.** 3276   **b.** 10,034   **c.** 4176

⑮ 326×311 **a.** 10,138   **b.** 101,386   **c.** 11,386

⑯ $9472 + 6314$ **a.** 1586   **b.** 13,986   **c.** 15,786

Divide.

⑰ $6\overline{)48}$ **⑱** $3\overline{)15}$ **⑲** $4\overline{)36}$ **⑳** $9\overline{)54}$

㉑ $7\overline{)567}$ **㉒** $6\overline{)2436}$ **㉓** $3\overline{)25,578}$ **㉔** $8\overline{)76,144}$

㉕ $321,088 \div 2$ **㉖** $9880 \div 4$ **㉗** $33,264 \div 9$

Solve these problems.

㉘ Mr. Wang is buying carpet for his home office. The office is 4 meters wide and 8 meters long. The carpeting he likes is 4 meters wide and costs $109.95 a meter. How much carpeting should he buy, and how much will it cost?

㉙ Forty students from Rugged High are going on a camping trip. If six students can fit in a van, how many vans will they need to take?

㉚ Claudia's team cycled 457 kilometers in six days. If they rode about the same distance each day, about how many kilometers did they ride each day?

Cumulative Review
Use after lesson 19

Solve for *n*. Watch the signs.

1 $2400 \div 60 = n$ **2** $2500 \times 4 = n$ **3** $n = 2025 \div 25$

Divide.

4 $32\overline{)960}$ **5** $42\overline{)252}$ **6** $90\overline{)90,900}$

7 $87\overline{)609}$ **8** $28\overline{)12,068}$ **9** $250\overline{)7500}$

10 $198\overline{)64,350}$ **11** $770\overline{)15,400}$ **12** $74\overline{)30,710}$

Choose the correct answer.

13 57×1247 **a.** 7109 **b.** 71,079 **c.** 717,079

14 83×69 **a.** 5727 **b.** 4727 **c.** 3727

15 $2845 - 391$ **a.** 2645 **b.** 2556 **c.** 2454

Solve these problems.

16 Fred's travel club is planning a hiking trip to Scotland. There are 36 members of the club, who will share the cost equally. If the total cost of the trip is $21,672, how much will each member pay?

17 Carlos earns $7.25 an hour fixing bicycles. How much will he earn for 12 hours of work?

18 Ms. Chen earns $39,000 a year. She is paid every week. About how much is she paid each week?

19 Willy's checking account has $1145.89 in it. If he writes four checks, each for $150, how much will he have left in the account?

20 Which job pays the highest salary, one that pays $40,000 a year, one that pays $3500 a month, or one that pays $850 each week?

Cumulative Review
Use after Lesson 23

Copy and complete the number sequences.

1 3997, 3998, 3999, ■, ■, ■, ■, 4004

2 99,996; 99,997; ■; ■; ■; ■; ■; 100,003

Round each number to the nearest ten.

3 58 **4** 84 **5** 22 **6** 97

Round each number to the nearest hundred.

7 237 **8** 444 **9** 877 **10** 550

Round each number to the nearest thousand.

11 1045 **12** 1382 **13** 6500 **14** 7596

Round each number to the nearest whole number.

15 71.3 **16** 54.9 **17** 87.5 **18** 39.6

Write the missing items.

	Temperature	Change	New Temperature
19	15°C	down 20°	■
20	−10°C	down 5°	■

Add or subtract. Watch for negative numbers.

21 $100 - 200$ **22** $(-100) + 50$ **23** $(-150) - 50$

Solve these problems.

24 Miranda is driving to Jerome, 1977 kilometers away. She wants to spend four days driving and drive about the same distance each day. About how far should she plan to drive each day?

25 Jared has $43.75 in his checking account. Does he have enough money in his account to buy six paperbacks that are on sale for $6.95 each? Can he buy seven paperbacks?

Cumulative Review
Use after Lesson 26

Solve these problems. Watch the signs.

1 745
+ 248

2 1073
× 98

3 8400
− 15

4 3)4050

5 6741
× 63

6 784
× 126

7 8072
+ 725

8 8000
× 3000

9 70)2240

10 2500
− 700

11 932
+ 359

12 208
× 34

13 13)5226

14 600
− 207

15 24,067
− 15,315

Round each number to the nearest whole number.

16 7.3

17 54.5

18 82.4

19 59.6

Add or subtract. Watch for negative numbers.

20 200 − 200

21 (−10) + 15

22 (−15) − 15

23 7 − 15

Multiply. Watch for negative numbers.

24 −5 × 8

25 10 × −6

26 −12 × 4

27 7 × 7

Divide. Round decimal quotients to the nearest whole number.

28 2496 ÷ 60

29 25,000 ÷ 48

30 50,622 ÷ 78

31 522 ÷ 6

Solve these problems.

32 Maria had a checking account balance of $183. What would her new balance be after writing a check for $200?

33 At Frank's Fruit Market, apples are $0.79 a pound and melons cost $1.29 each. How much will Simone pay for two pounds of apples and three melons?

34 A Landrider holds seven passengers. How many Landriders are needed to transport 30 people?

35 Thirty-six golf balls sell for $54 at Sid's Sports. Do you think Sid will sell you a ball for $1.25?

Cumulative Review
Use after Lesson 30

Round each number to the nearest whole number.

1   14.3   **2**   5.4   **3**   40.45   **4**   9.67

Choose the correct answer. Watch the signs.

5   34 × 50   **a.** 170   **b.** 1700   **c.** 17,000

6   3000 − 127   **a.** 1873   **b.** 2873   **c.** 1730

7   42,000 ÷ 300   **a.** 140   **b.** 1400   **c.** 14,000

Add or subtract.

8   0.8 − 0.2   **9**   0.75 + 0.25   **10**   0.5 − 0.44   **11** 7.6 − 1.5

Multiply.

12   10 × 2.7   **13**   100 × 0.06   **14**   1.726 × 1000

Divide.

15   24 ÷ 10   **16**   2.5 ÷ 1000   **17**   314.2 ÷ 100

Complete.

18   2 m = ■ cm   **19**   0.6 L = ■ mL   **20**   4000 g = ■ kg

Multiply.

21   7.1 × 4   **22**   5.5 × 8   **23**   0.8 × 7   **24**   0.04 × 6

25   15.3 × 9   **26**   2.84 × 12   **27**   32 × 5.8   **28**   41 × 0.06

Solve these problems.

29   Emma's gerbil weighs 140 grams. What is its weight in kilograms?

30   Phillip went to the grocery store and bought a carton of juice for $2.49, a loaf of bread for $2.19, and a box of cereal for $2.99. How much change should he receive if he pays with a $10 bill?

Cumulative Review
Use after Lesson 36

Copy each pair of numbers but replace ■ with <, >, or =.

① 0.006 ■ 0.058   **②** 1.72 ■ 1.720   **③** 9.1 ■ 1.99

Multiply or divide.

④ 7.1 × 100   **⑤** 25.5 ÷ 10   **⑥** 1000 × 0.06   **⑦** 0.05 ÷ 100

Complete.

⑧ 2000 cm = ■ m   **⑨** 600 mL = ■ L   **⑩** 4.5 kg = ■ g

Multiply.

⑪ 4.1 × 1.8   **⑫** 0.5 × 6   **⑬** 1.01 × 0.09   **⑭** 305 × 3.3

For each of the following problems, write two more problems that would have the same answer

⑮ 0.41)‾8.88   **⑯** 0.065)‾4.178   **⑰** 0.12)‾41.3   **⑱** 30.5)‾0.056

Divide. Round quotients to the nearest hundredth.

⑲ 0.8)‾14   **⑳** 0.045)‾5   **㉑** 0.75)‾200   **㉒** 400)‾6252

Add or subtract.

㉓ 35 − 65   **㉔** (−20) + 7   **㉕** (−5) − 9   **㉖** −4 + 12

Solve these problems.

㉗ Jonathan measured the length of a rectangular field to be 200 m and the width to be 50 m. If the true length and width of the field are 0.5 m greater than his measurements, what are the true perimeter and area?

㉘ Suppose the true length and width are 0.5 less than Jonathan's measurements. What are the true perimeter and the true area?

㉙ Ralph had a $20 bill. After shopping, he had $5.75 left. How much did he spend shopping?

㉚ Alana wants to buy six jars of peanut butter that cost $2.79 each. What will the total cost be?

Cumulative Review
Use after Lesson 41

Solve for *n*. Watch the signs.

① $240 \div 80 = n$ **②** $2.5 \times 4 = n$ **③** $n = 2.25 \div 25$

Divide. Round quotients to the nearest hundredth.

④ $33\overline{)9.9}$ **⑤** $2.4\overline{)9600}$ **⑥** $60\overline{)606}$ **⑦** $83\overline{)1410}$

Solve. Do as many as you can without paper and pencil.

⑧ $20 \times 20 = \blacksquare$ **⑨** $\blacksquare = 6 \times 7$ **⑩** $4 \times 800 = \blacksquare$

⑪ $\blacksquare = 19 \times 100$ **⑫** $\blacksquare = 160 + 129$ **⑬** $540 \div 6 = \blacksquare$

Write in exponential form.

⑭ $4 \times 4 \times 4 \times 4$ **⑮** $12 \times 12 \times 12 \times 12 \times 12 \times 12$

⑯ $6 \times 6 \times 6 \times 6 \times 6$ **⑰** $205 \times 205 \times 205 \times 205$

Write in standard form.

⑱ 10×4^3 **⑲** 6×7^2 **⑳** 3×10^5 **㉑** 4×10^4

㉒ 2×10^6 **㉓** 10^3 **㉔** 9×10^2 **㉕** 58×10^5

Solve these problems.

㉖ The floor of a rectangular room is 3.5 meters long and 2.6 meters wide. How many 0.1-meter square tiles are needed to cover this rectangular floor?

㉗ Megan is choosing one photograph and one painting to hang on the wall. She has ten photographs and six paintings from which she can choose. How many different combinations could she choose?

㉘ Olga works part-time at the florist, where she earns $5.50 an hour. She has forgotten how many hours she worked last week, but her paycheck was $71.50. How many hours did she work?

㉙ Jason is saving money for a new pair of tennis shoes that costs $64. If he saves $7 a week, how many weeks will it be before he can buy the shoes?

㉚ Apples are on sale for 59¢ a pound. How much will 5 pounds cost?

Cumulative Review
Use after Lesson 47

Complete.

1 200 cm = ■ dm   **2** 0.6 kg = ■ g   **3** 300 mL = ■ L

Add or subtract. Watch the signs.

4 $(-5) + 10$ **5** $(-2) + 2$ **6** $10 - 15$ **7** $(-2) - 2$

Write in standard form.

8 5×10^4 **9** 10^8 **10** $10^5 \times 4$ **11** 7×10^3

Multiply or divide. Watch the signs.

12 $10^3 \times 10^4$ **13** $10^8 \div 10^6$ **14** $10^{12} \div 10^5$ **15** $9^2 \times 10^2$

16 $5^3 \times 5^3$ **17** $6^3 \div 6^2$ **18** $8^5 \div 8^3$ **19** $2^3 \times 2^5$

Approximate. Use exponential notation.

20 318×687 **21** 8499×6499 **22** $220 \times 55{,}012$

Choose a reasonable approximation for each problem.

23 $3.876 - 2.138$ **a.** 0.7   **b.** 1.7   **c.** 0.17

24 $784.1 \div 36.5$ **a.** 36   **b.** 210   **c.** 21

25 14.8×26.3 **a.** 3900   **b.** 390   **c.** 450

26 $50.38 \div 0.765$ **a.** 65   **b.** 6.5   **c.** 650

Solve these problems.

27 Jessica usually earns $6 an hour. On holidays she earns time and a half. How much does she earn per hour on a holiday?

28 A stack of 100 cardboard sheets is 3.8 cm thick. How thick is each sheet?

29 How many hours will you sleep in your lifetime? Make an estimate.

30 On the average the moon is about 238,857 miles from Earth. How many baseball bats would be needed to reach the moon if they could be placed end to end?

Cumulative Review
Use after Lesson 51

For each of the following problems, write three more problems that would have the same answer.

1 $0.32\overline{)6.88}$ **2** $0.0005\overline{)41.22}$ **3** $50.3\overline{)12.62}$

Multiply or divide. Write answers in exponential form.

4 $10^3 \times 10^4$ **5** $10^8 \div 10^6$ **6** $10^7 \div 10^2$

7 $(4 \times 10^6) \times (4 \times 10^5)$ **8** $(12 \times 10^{11}) \div (3 \times 10^7)$ **9** $(3 \times 10^6) \times (2 \times 10^4)$

Multiply.

10 4.4×3.8 **11** 0.5×0.6 **12** 1.11×0.003 **13** 3.05×33

Change each percent to a decimal.

14 20%   **15** 6.4%   **16** 55%   **17** 0.4%   **18** 95.5%

Change each decimal to a percent.

19 0.45   **20** 0.5   **21** 0.06   **22** 0.025   **23** 0.668

Find each amount.

24 6% of 100   **25** 5% of 6   **26** 12.5% of 24   **27** 25% of 60

28 50% of 50   **29** 7% of 56   **30** 8% of 40   **31** 75% of 30

Solve these problems.

32 There is a 25% discount on large cactus plants at the Green Thumb nursery. The regular price is $16. What is the sale price?

33 Loretta wants to buy a personal stereo that lists for $32. If the sales tax is 5%, how much will she have to pay for it?

34 A $60 atlas is on sale at a 10% discount. The sales tax is 6%. With the discount and the tax, what is the cost of the atlas?

35 Ed has $50 to spend at a local music store, where everything is on sale for 25% off. Can he afford to buy both the new Rolling Pebbles double CD that regularly sells for $32 and the new Blueberries three-CD set that usually sells for $30?

Cumulative Review
Use after Lesson 55

Change each percent to a decimal.

1 20% **2** 6.4% **3** 55% **4** 0.4% **5** 95.5%

Change each decimal to a percent.

6 0.65 **7** 0.04 **8** 2.5 **9** 0.175 **10** 0.8

Multiply. Watch for negative numbers.

11 4×-7 **12** 9×-6 **13** 8×5 **14** -3×4

Find each amount.

15 12% of 100 **16** 10% of 45 **17** 4% of 60 **18** 75% of 20

19 90% of 50 **20** 25% of 70 **21** 35% of 200 **22** 3% of 25

In each case calculate the amount of money you would have.

	Principal	Rate of Interest	Number of Years	Amount
23	$100	6%	1	■
24	$100	7%	2	■
25	$200	8%	5	■
26	$200	6%	10	■

Solve these problems.

27 Mr. Yang put $100 in a bank at 5% interest for ten years. Ms. Van Wyck put $80 in a bank at 7% interest for ten years. Who will have more money in the bank after ten years?

28 Ms. Gomez put $500 in the bank at 6% interest. How long must she leave the money in the account in order to double the amount she deposited?

29 The Generosity Bank pays 5% interest compounded quarterly. If you were to deposit $1000 in that bank, how much money will you have after one-quarter of a year? How much will you have after six months? After one year?

30 Adam bought a baseball glove on sale for $60. That was 25% less than the regular price. What was the regular price of the glove?

Cumulative Review
Use after Lesson 59

Write in standard form.

1 10×5^3 **2** 2×7^3 **3** 5×10^4 **4** $10^2 \times 2^3$

Multiply.

5 4.5×20 **6** 0.5×0.006 **7** 1.01×0.95 **8** 105×3.03

Solve for _n_. Watch the signs.

9 $4800 \div 80 = n$ **10** $2.5 \times 400 = n$ **11** $n = 62.5 \div 50$

Choose the correct answer. Watch the signs.

		a.	**b.**	**c.**
12	24×500	120	1200	12,000
13	$4000 - 4$	3600	3960	3996
14	$120,000 \div 400$	30	300	3000
15	27×53	761	981	1431
16	$4973 + 8412$	13,385	13,985	14,285

Which of these numbers are divisible by 2? by 5? by both 2 and 5?

17 20   **18** 64   **19** 55   **20** 400   **21** 95

Which of these numbers are divisible by 3? by 6? by both 3 and 6?

22 27   **23** 66   **24** 54   **25** 213   **26** 954

PROBLEM SOLVING

Solve these problems.

27 A $300 stereo is on sale at a 20% discount. The sales tax is 6%. How much will the stereo cost?

28 Carlos deposited $5000 in a bank to open an account. The bank pays 4% interest compounded quarterly. How much will he have in the account in a year?

29 Which costs less, a stereo system regularly priced at $289 on sale at $50 off or on sale at 20% off?

30 A stack of ten identical calculators weighs 1.1 kg. About how much does each calculator weigh?

Cumulative Review
Use after Lesson 64

Divide. Round decimal quotients to the nearest whole number.

1 $4410 \div 70$ **2** $35,000 \div 72$ **3** $16,308 \div 27$

4 $592 \div 8$ **5** $23,874 \div 46$ **6** $1671 \div 31$

Write in standard form.

7 5×10^4 **8** 10^8 **9** $10^5 \times 4$ **10** 7×10^3 **11** $10^4 \times 2$

List the factors for each number.

12 20 **13** 64 **14** 556 **15** 140 **16** 1548

Show the prime factorization for each number.

17 20 **18** 64 **19** 556 **20** 140 **21** 1548

Change each percent to a decimal and each decimal to a percent.

22 40% **23** 0.064 **24** 0.55 **25** 0.8% **26** 78.6

Find the cost, with tax, of each item.

27 an $80 jacket with 5% sales tax

28 a $59.95 fishing rod with 7% sales tax

Find the discount price of each item.

	Regular Price	Discount	Discount Price
29	$25	10%	▦
30	$1.75	20%	▦
31	$150	20%	▦
32	$84	25%	▦
33	$195	10%	▦
34	$62.50	10%	▦
35	$75	20%	▦

Cumulative Review
Use after Lesson 68

Round each number to the nearest whole number.

1 24.3   **2** 5.47   **3** 400.65   **4** 99.499

Copy each pair of numbers but replace ● with <, >, or =.

5 0.6 ● 0.58   **6** 2.62 ● 2.620   **7** 9.1 ● 9.09

Complete.

8 5000 mL = ■ L   **9** 600 mm = ■ m   **10** 6.25 kg = ■ g

11 2.4 m = ■ cm   **12** 325 mg = ■ g   **13** 4.7 L = ■ mL

Solve these problems.

14 $\frac{1}{3}$ of 15   **15** $\frac{2}{5}$ of 25   **16** $\frac{4}{5}$ of 40   **17** $\frac{5}{6}$ of 12

18 $\frac{2}{3}$ of $\frac{3}{4}$ **19** $\frac{1}{2}$ of $\frac{5}{6}$ **20** $\frac{1}{4}$ of $\frac{1}{3}$ **21** $\frac{3}{8}$ of $\frac{1}{2}$

Complete.

22 $\frac{1}{4} = \frac{?}{8}$ **23** $\frac{2}{5} = \frac{?}{15}$ **24** $\frac{2}{3} = \frac{?}{9}$ **25** $\frac{4}{5} = \frac{16}{?}$

PROBLEM SOLVING

Solve these problems.

26 A $250 ping-pong table is on sale at a 10% discount. The sales tax is 8%. How much will the table cost?

27 Hakim deposited $2000 in a bank to open an account. The bank pays 5% interest compounded monthly. How long will it take Hakim to earn over $100 in interest?

28 A motorcycle discounted 20% is on sale for $1600. What is the regular price of the motorcycle?

29 Mrs. Pulaski earns about $650 a week. What is her annual pay?

30 A school band is selling concert tickets for $3.50. If they sell 150 tickets, how much money will they raise?

Cumulative Review
Use after Lesson 72

Add or subtract. Watch the signs.

1 $(-4) + 5$

2 $(-2) + 4$

3 $7 - 12$

4 $20 - 10$

5 $(-20) - 20$

6 $(-15) + 6$

Multiply or divide. Watch the signs.

7 $10^3 \times 10^2$

8 $10^8 \div 10^1$

9 $10^{10} \div 10^4$

10 $10^{12} \div 10^7$

11 $10^2 \times 10^1$

12 $10^5 \times 10^3$

Reduce each fraction completely.

13 $\frac{6}{10}$

14 $\frac{4}{6}$

15 $\frac{5}{100}$

16 $\frac{21}{60}$

17 $\frac{30}{96}$

Find the greatest common factor of each pair of numbers.

18 10 and 12

19 8 and 20

20 5 and 15

21 48 and 54

Find the least common multiple of each pair of numbers.

22 2 and 5

23 4 and 10

24 8 and 12

25 9 and 12

Copy each pair of numbers but replace ● with <, >, =.

26 $\frac{2}{3}$ ● $\frac{3}{8}$

27 $\frac{2}{5}$ ● $\frac{5}{6}$

28 $\frac{5}{12}$ ● $\frac{1}{2}$

Add or subtract. Watch the signs.

29 $\frac{2}{3} + \frac{3}{4}$

30 $\frac{5}{8} - \frac{1}{3}$

31 $\frac{7}{10} - \frac{2}{5}$

32 $\frac{1}{2} + \frac{5}{7}$

Solve these problems.

33 Before her trip the odometer on Elena's car read 8507 miles. After the trip it read 9225 miles. How far did she drive on the trip?

34 Alex bought two boxes of cereal at $3.79 each and 4 pounds of grapes at $0.89 a pound. He paid with a $20 bill. How much change should he get?

35 Donna earns $6.50 an hour at her part-time job. How much will she earn if she works 15 hours?

Cumulative Review
Use after Lesson 76

Add or subtract. Watch the signs.

❶ $\dfrac{2}{5} + \dfrac{1}{4}$

❷ $\dfrac{7}{8} - \dfrac{2}{3}$

❸ $\dfrac{9}{10} - \dfrac{1}{5}$

❹ $\dfrac{3}{4} - \dfrac{1}{3}$

Change each percent to a decimal.

❺ 30%

❻ 5.6%

❼ 55.5%

❽ 2.91%

Change each decimal to a percent.

❾ 0.0007

❿ 0.85

⓫ 4.5

⓬ 0.038

Find the least common multiple of each set of numbers.

⓭ 3, 6, and 12

⓮ 2, 3, and 8

⓯ 2, 4, 6, and 9

Add.

⓰ $\dfrac{1}{4} + \dfrac{2}{3} + \dfrac{1}{6}$

⓱ $\dfrac{3}{5} + \dfrac{1}{3} + \dfrac{2}{15}$

⓲ $\dfrac{3}{8} + \dfrac{1}{4} + \dfrac{1}{12}$

Solve these problems.

⓳ If you roll a 0–5 number cube, what is the probability of getting a 3?

⓴ If you roll a 0–5 cube, what is the probability of getting a number greater than 3?

㉑ If you roll a 0–5 cube, what is the probability of getting a 7?

㉒ You roll a 0–5 cube 60 times. About how many times would you expect to roll a 4? a number other than 4?

㉓ You roll a 5–10 cube 90 times. About how many times would you expect to roll either a 9 or a 10?

㉔ Of the 25 students in a kindergarten class, $\dfrac{3}{5}$ are boys. How many boys are in the class?

㉕ To override the governor's veto in a certain state, the State Senate must pass a bill with a $\dfrac{2}{3}$ vote. If there are 49 members of the State Senate, how many must vote for the bill to override the veto?

Cumulative Review
Use after Lesson 81

Copy each pair of numbers but replace ● with <, >, or =.

1. $\frac{2}{3}$ ● $\frac{14}{21}$

2. $\frac{4}{5}$ ● $\frac{5}{6}$

3. $\frac{7}{12}$ ● $\frac{1}{2}$

Watch the signs and reduce your answers.

4. $\frac{2}{3} + \frac{1}{4}$

5. $\frac{3}{8} \times \frac{1}{3}$

6. $\frac{3}{10} - \frac{1}{5}$

7. $\frac{3}{4} \times \frac{1}{5}$

8. $0.5 + 0.45$

9. $0.73 - 0.11$

10. $0.75 - 0.5$

11. 0.5×0.47

Change each improper fraction to a mixed or whole number.

12. $\frac{3}{2}$

13. $\frac{5}{4}$

14. $\frac{18}{5}$

15. $\frac{10}{7}$

16. $\frac{25}{10}$

Find the decimal equivalent or an approximation to the nearest hundredth.

17. $1\frac{1}{4}$

18. $\frac{5}{6}$

19. $\frac{8}{5}$

20. $\frac{7}{10}$

21. $5\frac{1}{3}$

Add or subtract.

22. $2\frac{2}{5} + 1\frac{1}{5}$

23. $5\frac{7}{8} - 2\frac{2}{3}$

24. $9\frac{7}{10} - 7\frac{2}{5}$

25. $4\frac{3}{4} + 2\frac{1}{3}$

PROBLEM SOLVING

Solve these problems.

26. You roll a 0–5 number cube 120 times. About how many times would you expect to roll an even number?

27. A school van holds eight band members and their instruments. How many vans are needed to transport the 44 members of the band to their concert in Little Falls?

28. You open a savings account with a $2000 deposit. How much money will you have in your account after one year if the bank pays 4% interest compounded semi-annually?

29. If it takes $1\frac{1}{2}$ hours to clean your room and $2\frac{1}{4}$ hours to mess it up properly again, how long does it take to clean and then mess up your room again?

30. A recipe calls for $1\frac{1}{2}$ cups of olive oil. You need to triple the recipe but you only have $\frac{3}{4}$ cups of olive oil at home. How much more olive oil do you need to buy?

Cumulative Review
Use after Lesson 86

Copy each pair of numbers but replace ● with <, >, or =.

1 $\frac{2}{5} \bullet \frac{4}{10}$

2 $\frac{4}{7} \bullet \frac{5}{6}$

3 $\frac{7}{8} \bullet \frac{11}{12}$

4 $0.02 \bullet 0.14$

5 $0.4 \bullet 0.04$

6 $7.2 \bullet 7.20$

Find the least common multiple of each set of numbers.

7 2 and 7

8 8 and 12

9 3, 4, and 5

10 4, 6, and 10

Solve for *n*.

11 $\frac{1}{7} \times 14 = n$

12 $\frac{2}{3} \times 24 = n$

13 $n = \frac{3}{4} \times 16$

Complete.

14 $500 \text{ cm} = \blacksquare \text{ m}$

15 $0.65 \text{ kg} = \blacksquare \text{ g}$

16 $3000 \text{ mL} = \blacksquare \text{ L}$

Divide. Reduce when possible.

17 $12 \div \frac{1}{4}$

18 $\frac{3}{8} \div \frac{1}{2}$

19 $\frac{3}{5} \div \frac{1}{5}$

20 $\frac{3}{4} \div \frac{1}{4}$

The Scale and Fin Highway runs from Tuna to Pompano.

Tuna —4 km— Mackerel —7.5 km— Salmon —13 km— Sea Bass —7 km— Flounder —16 km— Pompano

How many kilometers is it from

21 Tuna to Salmon?

22 Mackerel to Flounder?

23 Sea Bass to Pompano and back?

24 Flounder to Tuna, then back to Sea Bass?

Solve this problem.

25 At Best Deal Rent-a-Car, you can rent a small car for $25.95 a day with 500 free miles and $0.10 a mile for any miles over 500. What will it cost to rent for three days and drive for 750 miles?

Cumulative Review
Use after Lesson 90

Find the greatest common factor of each set of numbers.

1 12 and 16

2 8 and 11

3 2, 4, and 10

4 4, 16, and 20

Write in standard form.

5 10×3^2

6 $6^2 \times 7^2$

7 5×10^5

Solve for n.

8 $12 \div \frac{1}{2} = n$

9 $\frac{2}{5} \times 20 = n$

10 $n = \frac{3}{4} \div \frac{1}{6}$

Change each improper fraction to a mixed or whole number.

11 $\frac{6}{2}$

12 $\frac{5}{3}$

13 $\frac{12}{5}$

14 $\frac{16}{7}$

15 $\frac{25}{15}$

For each set of numbers, find the mean, median, and mode.

16 2, 3, 5, 8, 10, 2

17 4, 4, 7, 10, 10, 10, 11

18 1, 1, 5, 2, 15, 18, 7

19 5.5, 6.5, 8, 8, 9.5, 10.5

20 15, 12.5, 8, 12.5, 12.5, 5.5, 3, 3, 0

Solve these problems.

21 Arturo starting riding his bike at 9:45 A.M. and finished at 12:20 P.M. For how long did he ride?

22 Cassie bought 50 comic books for $0.25 each and sold them all for $0.60 each. How much profit did she make?

23 Which is the better buy, a 10-kilogram bag of Doggie Delights that sells for $14.95, or a 7-kilogram bag of the same product that sells for $9.79?

24 Mackenzie can do 20 sit-ups in 30 seconds. If she keeps up that rate, how many sit-ups would she do in three minutes?

25 Kyle took six tests and got these scores: 90, 70, 69, 60, 95, and 75. Then he scored 90 on the next three tests. What was his mean score for the tests? What was his median score? What was the mode of his scores? Which measure of average best represents his test performance?

Cumulative Review
Use after Lesson 94

Write three fractions equal to the given fraction.

1 $\frac{2}{3}$ **2** $\frac{8}{5}$ **3** $\frac{4}{7}$ **4** $\frac{5}{5}$

For each set of numbers, find the mean, median, and mode.

5 12, 3, 5, 14, 10, 9, 10   **6** 4, 4, 9, 12, 10, 12, 12

7 1, 1, 5, 2, 2, 5, 8, 1, 7   **8** 2, 7, 4, 5, 8, 1, 8

ALGEBRA READINESS

Solve each proportion.

9 $\frac{2}{5} = \frac{n}{10}$ **10** $\frac{3}{8} = \frac{n}{24}$ **11** $\frac{4}{9} = \frac{24}{n}$ **12** $\frac{1}{8} = \frac{n}{32}$

Each pair of figures is similar. Give the missing side lengths.

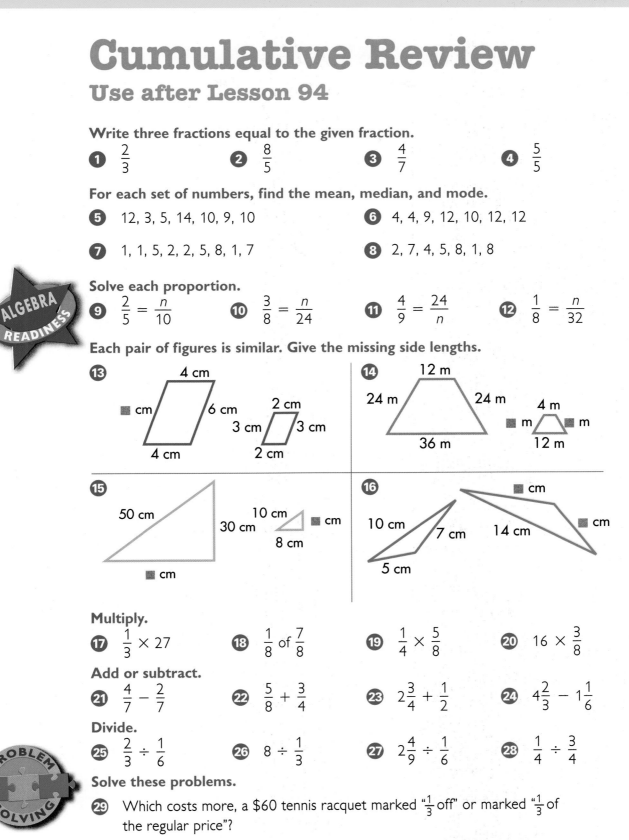

13 4 cm, ■ cm, 6 cm, 4 cm / 2 cm, 3 cm, 3 cm, 2 cm

14 12 m, 24 m, 24 m, 36 m / 4 m, ■ m, ■ m, 12 m

15 50 cm, 30 cm, ■ cm / 10 cm, 8 cm, ■ cm

16 ■ cm, 10 cm, 7 cm, 14 cm, 5 cm, ■ cm

Multiply.

17 $\frac{1}{3} \times 27$ **18** $\frac{1}{8}$ of $\frac{7}{8}$ **19** $\frac{1}{4} \times \frac{5}{8}$ **20** $16 \times \frac{3}{8}$

Add or subtract.

21 $\frac{4}{7} - \frac{2}{7}$ **22** $\frac{5}{8} + \frac{3}{4}$ **23** $2\frac{3}{4} + \frac{1}{2}$ **24** $4\frac{2}{3} - 1\frac{1}{6}$

Divide.

25 $\frac{2}{3} \div \frac{1}{6}$ **26** $8 \div \frac{1}{3}$ **27** $2\frac{4}{9} \div \frac{1}{6}$ **28** $\frac{1}{4} \div \frac{3}{4}$

PROBLEM SOLVING

Solve these problems.

29 Which costs more, a \$60 tennis racquet marked "$\frac{1}{3}$ off" or marked "$\frac{1}{3}$ of the regular price"?

30 On a map with a scale of 1 inch = 22 miles, how far apart are two cities that are 6 inches apart on the map?

Cumulative Review
Use after Lesson 99

Find the greatest common factor of each set of numbers.

1 12 and 18

2 9 and 10

3 2, 5, and 10

4 4, 12, and 16

Solve for *n*.

5 $16 \div \frac{1}{2} = n$

6 $\frac{4}{5} \times 15 = n$

7 $n = \frac{3}{8} \div \frac{1}{4}$

Solve each proportion.

8 $\frac{2}{7} = \frac{n}{21}$

9 $\frac{3}{4} = \frac{n}{24}$

10 $\frac{3}{8} = \frac{n}{20}$

11 $\frac{1}{6} = \frac{n}{36}$

12 The table below shows sales of widgets by the Wee Widget Division of International Gadget. Use the data to make two bar graphs—one to show a rapid increase in sales from year to year, and one to show a more modest growth in sales. Then write an explanation of your strategy for showing the sales in two different lights.

Year	Widget Sales	Year	Widget Sales
1993	125,000	1996	155,000
1994	130,000	1997	160,000
1995	140,000	1998	175,000

On a sheet of graph paper draw coordinate axes so that each is at least six units long. Then plot and label each of these points:

13 (3, 4)

14 (4, 3)

15 (5, 0)

16 (0, 3)

Solve these problems.

17 Which costs more, an $80 CD player marked "$\frac{1}{4}$ off" or the same player on sale for 20% off? How much more?

18 At the same time a flag pole that is 28 feet tall casts a 16-foot shadow, a road sign nearby casts a 4-foot shadow. How tall is the sign?

19 Angela started hiking at 11:40 A.M. and finished at 1:25 P.M. She hiked at a rate of 3.5 miles an hour. For how long did she hike?

20 Rashid bought a bicycle for $120 and sold it for 15% less than he paid. For how much did he sell it?

Cumulative Review
Use after Lesson 103

For each of the following figures, tell how many lines of symmetry there are.

1 △   **2** ▱   **3** (trapezoid)   **4** (octagon)

Copy each pair of numbers, but replace ● with <, >, or =.

5 $\frac{2}{5}$ ● $\frac{4}{10}$ **6** $\frac{4}{7}$ ● $\frac{5}{6}$ **7** $\frac{7}{8}$ ● $\frac{11}{12}$

8 0.02 ● 0.14   **9** 0.4 ● 0.04   **10** 7.2 ● 7.20

Copy each ordered pair. Replace x or y with the correct number so that the ordered pair satisfies the rule x ──(×4)──> y.

11 (2, y)   **12** (4.5, y)   **13** (x, 12)   **14** (x, 2.4)

Alan Isleshoot is a professional basketball player. The table shows some of his shooting statistics.

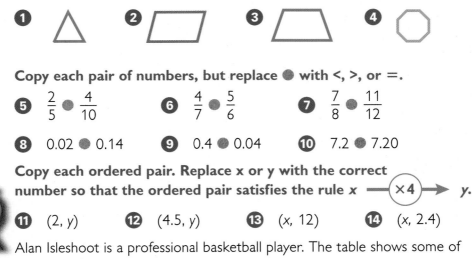

Game	1	2	3	4	5
Shot Attempts	19	13	22	16	11
Shots Made	12	8	14	10	7

Make a graph using this information. Then use the graph to estimate the number of shots Alan might expect to make if the number of shots he attempts is

15 25?   **16** 8?   **17** 32?   **18** 35?

19 Make a line graph of the temperatures shown in the table below.

Day	1	2	3	4	5	6	7	8	9
Temperature (°C)	4	3	5	−1	0	−2	−3	1	3

Solve this problem.

20 Which is the better buy, a 12-ounce bottle of shampoo that sells for $8.95 or a 32-ounce bottle of the same shampoo that sells for $26.95?

Cumulative Review
Use after Lesson 108

Add or subtract.

1 $\dfrac{4}{11} - \dfrac{2}{11}$ **2** $1\dfrac{5}{8} + 2\dfrac{3}{4}$ **3** $5 - \dfrac{3}{8}$ **4** $3\dfrac{2}{5} - 1\dfrac{5}{6}$

For each of the following problems, write two more problems that would have the same answer.

5 $0.12\overline{)4.8}$ **6** $0.003\overline{)47.25}$ **7** $10^1 \times 10^4$ **8** $10^7 \div 10^5$

List the factors of each number.

9 201   **10** 64   **11** 516   **12** 1160   **13** 2096

Copy and complete the tables so that each ordered pair satisfies the given rule.

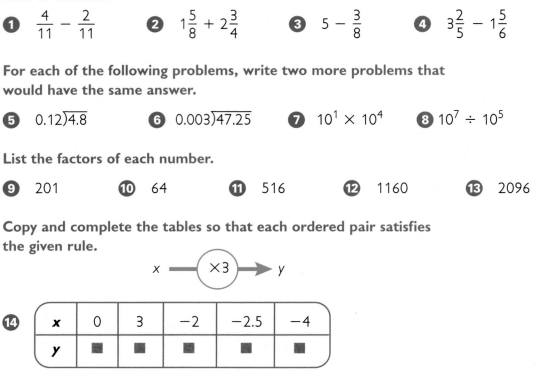

$$x \longrightarrow \boxed{\times 3} \longrightarrow y$$

14

x	0	3	-2	-2.5	-4
y	■	■	■	■	■

15 Graph each set of ordered pairs in the above table.

Do each chain calculation from left to right, unless you find a faster way to get the answer.

16 $4 + 2 \times 6 - 12 - 4 \div 5$

17 $10 + 9 + 3 + 7 + 1 + 10 + 10 + 10$

18 $1 \times 2 \times 3 \times 4 \times 5 \times 6 \times 0$

Solve these problems.

19 You roll a 5–10 number cube 90 times. About how many times would you expect to roll a number greater than 5?

20 Janine wants to buy a coat that regularly sells for $80 but is now on sale for 20% off. If the sales tax is 6%, what will the coat cost her?

Cumulative Review
Use after Lesson 113

Solve. Watch the signs.

1 $700 - 600$ **2** 700×600 **3** $6 \times 10^2 \times 70$

Choose the correct answer without calculating.

4 1.2×1.2 **a.** 0.144   **b.** 1.44   **c.** 14.4

5 24×2.5 **a.** 6   **b.** 60   **c.** 600

6 0.15×0.15 **a.** 0.0225   **b.** 0.225   **c.** 2.25

7 3.2×0.8 **a.** 0.256   **b.** 2.56   **c.** 25.6

Copy each pair of numbers, but replace ● with <, >, or =.

8 2.5 ● 2.25   **9** 0.047 ● 0.074   **10** 0.875 ● 0.9

For each sequence write the missing terms. Tell what your pattern is.

11 1, 5, 9, 13, _____ , _____ , _____

12 2, 3, 5, 9, 17, _____ , _____ , _____

13 1, 3, 7, 15, _____ , _____ , _____

14 40, 37, _____ , 31, _____ , _____ , 22

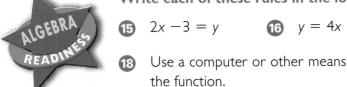

Write each of these rules in the long form, using arrows.

15 $2x - 3 = y$ **16** $y = 4x$ **17** $\frac{1}{2}x + 3 = y$

18 Use a computer or other means to complete the table and graph the function.

$$y = 2x - 5$$

x	1	4	■	■	■	■	■
y	■	■	7	−9	1	9	−7

Solve these problems.

19 You roll a 5–10 number cube. What is the probability of getting a 5 or a 6?

20 A taxi cab company charges $2 for the first mile of a trip and $0.35 for each additional one fourth of a mile. What is the cost of a 2.5 mile trip?

Cumulative Review
Use after Lesson 118

Change each improper fraction to a mixed or whole number.

1 $\frac{5}{2}$ **2** $\frac{7}{4}$ **3** $\frac{18}{7}$ **4** $\frac{10}{3}$ **5** $\frac{25}{25}$

Find the decimal equivalent or a decimal approximation to the nearest thousandth.

6 $1\frac{1}{5}$ **7** $\frac{5}{8}$ **8** $\frac{8}{7}$ **9** $\frac{9}{10}$ **10** $6\frac{2}{3}$

Write three fractions equal to the given fraction.

11 $\frac{2}{5}$ **12** $\frac{9}{4}$ **13** $\frac{5}{7}$ **14** $\frac{15}{5}$ **15** $\frac{8}{12}$

ALGEBRA READINESS

Graph the function for each function rule.

16 $2x + 4 = y$ **17** $y = 3x - 2$ **18** $\frac{1}{2}x + 5 = y$

Solve for n.

19 $8 \times 8 = n$ **20** $60 \times 60 = n$ **21** $39 \times 41 = n$

22 $75 \times 7 = n$ **23** $81 \times 5 = n$ **24** $810 \times 5 = n$

25 Use a computer or other means to complete the table and graph the function.

$$y = 2x^2 + 3x + 2$$

x	0	1	2	3	0.5	1.5	2.5
y	■	■	■	■	■	■	■

26 Draw three rectangles that meet the conditions of the function $y = 3x + 1$, where x is the length of the shorter side and y is the length of the longer side.

For each pair of figures, tell whether a rotation, a reflection, or a translation could be used to move one figure on top of the other.

27   **28**

29   **30**

Cumulative Review
Use after Lesson 123

Write in standard form.

1 10×3^3

2 $8^2 \times 5^2$

3 25×10^3

Add or subtract. Watch the signs.

4 $\dfrac{2}{5} + \dfrac{3}{4}$

5 $\dfrac{5}{8} - \dfrac{1}{6}$

6 $\dfrac{7}{10} - \dfrac{3}{5}$

7 $\dfrac{3}{8} + \dfrac{5}{12}$

ALGEBRA READINESS

For each graph determine a function rule.

8

9

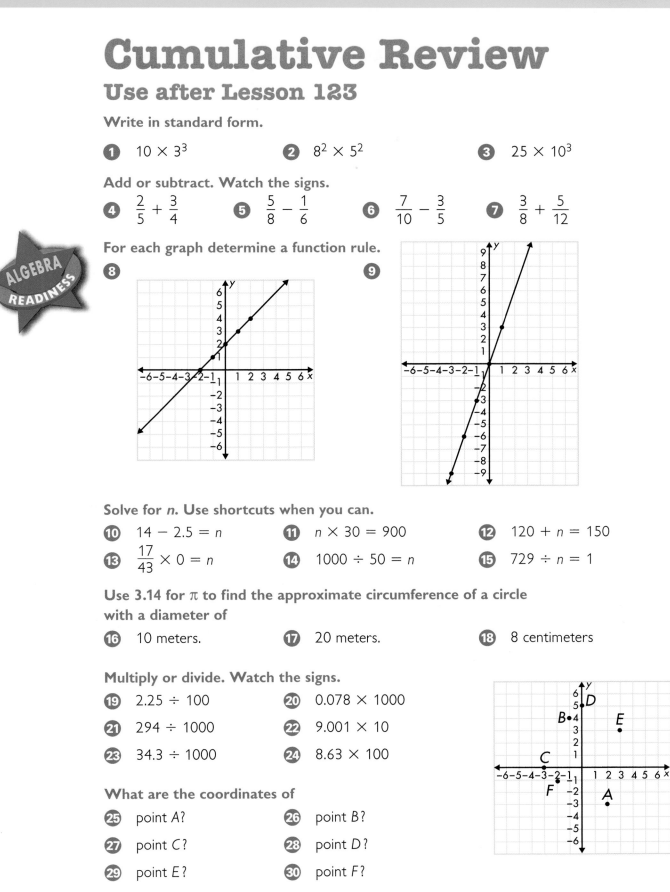

Solve for *n*. Use shortcuts when you can.

10 $14 - 2.5 = n$

11 $n \times 30 = 900$

12 $120 + n = 150$

13 $\dfrac{17}{43} \times 0 = n$

14 $1000 \div 50 = n$

15 $729 \div n = 1$

Use 3.14 for π to find the approximate circumference of a circle with a diameter of

16 10 meters.

17 20 meters.

18 8 centimeters

Multiply or divide. Watch the signs.

19 $2.25 \div 100$

20 0.078×1000

21 $294 \div 1000$

22 9.001×10

23 $34.3 \div 1000$

24 8.63×100

What are the coordinates of

25 point *A*?

26 point *B*?

27 point *C*?

28 point *D*?

29 point *E*?

30 point *F*?

Cumulative Review
Use after Lesson 126

Solve for *n*. Use shortcuts when you can.

1 $30 - 12.9 = n$

2 $n \times 40 = 1600$

3 $50 \times 50 = n$

4 $100 \div 0.20 = n$

Graph the function for each function rule.

5 $x + 3 = y$

6 $y = 2x - 4$

7 $2x + 5 = y$

Copy each pair of numbers but replace ● with <, >, or =.

8 $\frac{1}{2}$ ● $\frac{12}{24}$

9 $\frac{7}{8}$ ● $\frac{20}{24}$

10 $1\frac{5}{6}$ ● $\frac{13}{6}$

Find the area of the rectangles with these bases and heights.

11 base = 10 cm, height = 30 cm

12 base = 48 cm, height = 60 cm

13 base = 1.5 m, height = 0.5 m

14 base = 0.14 m, height = 0.4 m

Find the volume of boxes with the following dimensions.

15 length = 5 cm, width = 6 cm, height = 8 cm

16 length = 4 m, width = 6 m, height = 3 m

17 length = 10 cm, width = 12 cm, height = 8 cm

18 length = 2 dm, width = 2 dm, height = 3 dm

Solve these problems.

19 What is the total area of the top and four sides of a building that is 22 meters long, 18 meters wide, and 11 meters tall?

20 What is the total price, including tax, of a mountain bike that regularly sells for $240, but is now on sale for 25% off? The sales tax is 6.5%.

Cumulative Review
Use after Lesson 129

For each sequence write the missing terms. Tell what your pattern is.

1 1, 4, 8, 13, ___ , ___ , ___

2 2, 3, 5, 6, 8, ___ , ___ , ___

3 1, 3, 7, 13, ___ , ___ , ___

4 50, 45, ___ , ___ , ___ , 25, 20

Choose the correct answer without calculating.

5 1.1 × 1.1   **a.** 0.121   **b.** 1.21   **c.** 12.1

6 20 × 0.35   **a.** 7   **b.** 70   **c.** 700

7 0.25 × 0.25   **a.** 0.0625   **b.** 0.625   **c.** 6.25

Calculate the perimeter and the area of a rectangle having the given measurements.

8 length = 25 cm, width = 30 cm, perimeter = ■, area = ■

9 length = 40 cm, width = 500 cm, perimeter = ■, area = ■

10 length = 80 cm, width = 120 cm, perimeter = ■, area = ■

For each of these right triangles name the right angle, base, and height.

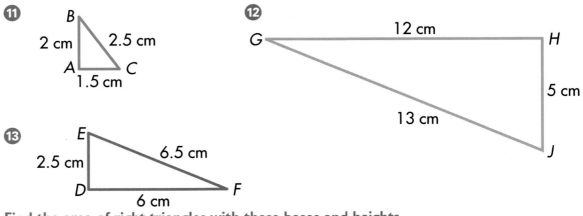

Find the area of right triangles with these bases and heights.

14 base = 10 cm, height = 15 cm

15 base = 22 cm, height = 30 cm

Cumulative Review
Use after Lesson 134

Divide. Round decimal quotients to the nearest tenth when necessary.

① $305 \div 7$ ② $952 \div 21$ ③ $320 \div 20$ ④ $1658 \div 96$

⑤ $2652 \div 13$ ⑥ $814 \div 6$ ⑦ $450 \div 90$ ⑧ $3072 \div 64$

Multiply. Use shortcuts when you can.

⑨ 30×30 ⑩ 81×79 ⑪ 500×50 ⑫ 60×60

⑬ 93×10 ⑭ 250×40 ⑮ 302×7 ⑯ 41×300

ALGEBRA READINESS

Graph the function for each function rule.

⑰ $x + 6 = y$ ⑱ $y = 2x - 2$ ⑲ $3x + 4 = y$

Find the area of each trapezoid.

⑳ 12 cm, 8 cm, 20 cm

㉑ 9 cm, 3 cm, 10 cm

㉒ 4 cm, 4.8 cm, 5 cm

㉓ 2 cm, 12 cm, 5.5 cm

For problems 24 and 25, *B* is the length of the longer base of a trapezoid, and *b* is the length of the shorter base. The length of the segment halfway between the bases and parallel to them is *m*. Find *m*.

㉔ $B = 10$ cm, $b = 6$ cm, $m = ?$ ㉕ $B = 25$ cm, $b = 12$ cm, $m = ?$

㉖ Draw a right scalene triangle.

㉗ Is every rhombus a square?   ㉘ Is every square a rhombus?

㉙ Is every quadrilateral a parallelogram?   ㉚ Is every trapezoid a quadrilateral?

Cumulative Review
Use after Lesson 139

Use 3.14 for π to find the approximate circumference of a circle with a diameter of

① 12 meters. **②** 15 meters. **③** 6 centimeters.

Multiply or divide. Watch the signs.

④ 2.25 ÷ 100 **⑤** 0.078 × 1000 **⑥** 9.001 × 10

⑦ 34.3 ÷ 1000 **⑧** 5.1 ÷ 1000 **⑨** 200.5 ÷ 100

⑩ 0.003 × 100 **⑪** 25 × 100,000 **⑫** 10,000 × 0.002

⑬ 10 ÷ 20 **⑭** 25 ÷ 100,000 **⑮** 2.5 × 10,000

⑯ Use a computer or other means to draw and complete this chart. Round each length to the nearest hundredth of a centimeter.

Area of square (cm²)	10	20	40	2	4	6	12
Length of side (cm)	■	■	■	■	■	■	■

Convert these measurements.

⑰ 3.82 meters to centimeters

⑱ 472.5 meters to kilometers

⑲ 0.24 kilograms to grams

⑳ 0.034 kilometers to meters

Solve these problems.

㉑ Draw a right isosceles triangle with an area of 32 cm². Use a centimeter ruler or centimeter grid paper.

㉒ A trapezoid has bases that are 14 and 18 centimeters long. If the area of the figure is 320 cm², what is its height?

㉓ What is the length of one side of a square that has an area of 625 m²?

㉔ Rachel walks about 4 kilometers in an hour. It usually takes about 28 minutes to walk from her house to her piano teacher's house. About how far is it from Rachel's house to her teacher's house?

㉕ Jack measured a stack of 50 identical magazines. It was 38.8 centimeters high. How thick was each magazine?

Cumulative Review
Use after Lesson 144

What are the coordinates of

① point *A*?   **②** point *B*?

③ point *C*?   **④** point *D*?

⑤ point *E*?

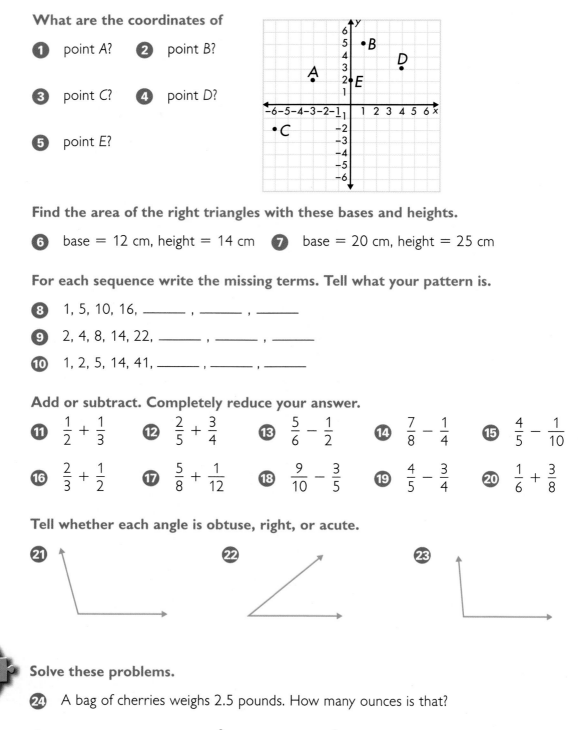

Find the area of the right triangles with these bases and heights.

⑥ base = 12 cm, height = 14 cm   **⑦** base = 20 cm, height = 25 cm

For each sequence write the missing terms. Tell what your pattern is.

⑧ 1, 5, 10, 16, _____ , _____ , _____

⑨ 2, 4, 8, 14, 22, _____ , _____ , _____

⑩ 1, 2, 5, 14, 41, _____ , _____ , _____

Add or subtract. Completely reduce your answer.

⑪ $\frac{1}{2} + \frac{1}{3}$ **⑫** $\frac{2}{5} + \frac{3}{4}$ **⑬** $\frac{5}{6} - \frac{1}{2}$ **⑭** $\frac{7}{8} - \frac{1}{4}$ **⑮** $\frac{4}{5} - \frac{1}{10}$

⑯ $\frac{2}{3} + \frac{1}{2}$ **⑰** $\frac{5}{8} + \frac{1}{12}$ **⑱** $\frac{9}{10} - \frac{3}{5}$ **⑲** $\frac{4}{5} - \frac{3}{4}$ **⑳** $\frac{1}{6} + \frac{3}{8}$

Tell whether each angle is obtuse, right, or acute.

㉑   **㉒**   **㉓**

Solve these problems.

㉔ A bag of cherries weighs 2.5 pounds. How many ounces is that?

㉕ A rectangular room is $17\frac{3}{4}$ feet long and $10\frac{1}{2}$ feet wide. What is the area of the floor of the room?

584 • Cumulative Review

Cumulative Review
Use after Lesson 148

For each sequence write the missing terms. Tell what your pattern is.

1 1, 8, 15, 22, _____ , _____ , _____

2 2, 5, 11, 23, 47, _____ , _____ , _____

3 1, 4, 16, 64, _____ , _____ , _____

Add or subtract. Completely reduce your answer.

4 $\frac{1}{5} + \frac{1}{3}$ **5** $\frac{2}{3} + \frac{3}{8}$ **6** $\frac{5}{6} - \frac{1}{4}$ **7** $\frac{7}{9} - \frac{2}{5}$ **8** $\frac{4}{5} - \frac{7}{10}$

Tell whether each triangle is obtuse, right, or acute.

9 **10** **11**

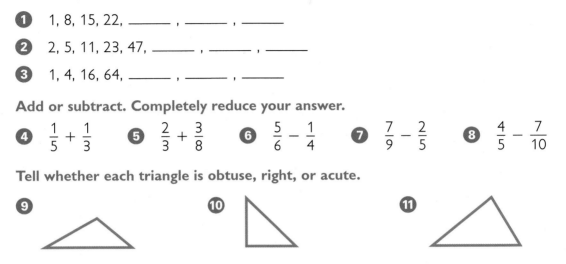

In the figure below, lines *AC*, *DF*, and *JK* are parallel to each other. The measure of ∠1 is 50 degrees.

Determine the measure of each of the following angles.

17 ∠2 **18** ∠4 **19** ∠3 **20** ∠9 **21** ∠6

Determine the measure of the third angle.

22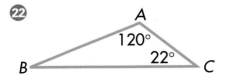

23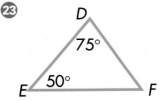

Give examples of each of these.

24 A line and a plane that meet at one point

25 A line and a plane that are parallel

Cumulative Review
Use after Lesson 151

Multiply or divide. Watch the signs.

1 $1.25 \div 1000$ **2** 0.078×10 **3** 5.001×100

4 $44.4 \div 1000$ **5** $5.5 \div 1000$ **6** $500.5 \div 10{,}000$

7 0.005×100 **8** $5 \times 100{,}000$ **9** $999 \div 1000$

Convert these measurements.

10 3.12 decimeters to centimeters   **11** 76.5 meters to kilometers

12 0.744 kilograms to grams   **13** 0.0834 kilometers to meters

14 5 feet to inches   **15** 80 ounces to pounds

16 4 quarts to cups   **17** 14 minutes to seconds

Graph the function for each function rule.

18 $x - 3 = y$ **19** $y = \frac{1}{2}x + 3$ **20** $3x - 2 = y$

Find the area of the triangles with these bases and heights.

21 base = 12 m, height = 8.5 m   **22** base = 2.2 cm, height = 3 cm

23 Dave and Belinda recorded the number and kinds of vehicles that passed through an intersection of their town. The table shows their results. Use a computer or other means to make a circle graph to show the information in the chart.

Type of vehicle	Number seen
Sedan	55
Coupe	24
Station wagon	8
Van	18
Sports utility	27
Sports car	12
Truck	6

Solve.

24 List five pairs of similar objects from everyday life.

25 Draw any triangle. Use a compass and a straightedge to construct a triangle congruent to it.

Cumulative Review
Use after Lesson 156

Tell whether each triangle is obtuse, right, or acute.

①   **②**   **③**

Find the decimal equivalent or an approximation to the nearest hundredth.

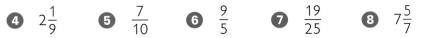

④ $2\frac{1}{9}$ **⑤** $\frac{7}{10}$ **⑥** $\frac{9}{5}$ **⑦** $\frac{19}{25}$ **⑧** $7\frac{5}{7}$

Choose the correct answer without using paper or a calculator.

⑨ 11×1.1 **a.** 1.21   **b.** 12.1   **c.** 121

⑩ 30×0.25 **a.** 7.5   **b.** 75   **c.** 750

⑪ 0.5×0.05 **a.** 0.025   **b.** 0.25   **c.** 2.5

In each case the lengths of the two shorter sides of a right triangle are given. Find the length of the hypotenuse. Give answers to the nearest tenth of a centimeter.

⑫   4 cm, 6 cm   **⑬**   2 cm, 5 cm   **⑭**   7 cm, 10 cm

Find the area in square centimeters of each of these figures.

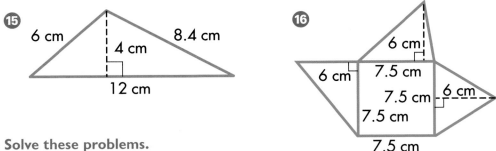

⑮   6 cm   8.4 cm   4 cm   12 cm

⑯   6 cm   7.5 cm   6 cm   7.5 cm   7.5 cm   6 cm   7.5 cm   7.5 cm

Solve these problems.

⑰   The area of a square is 256 cm². What is the length of a side?

⑱   What is the volume in cubic centimeters of a rectangular box that is 5.6 centimeters long, 2.2 centimeters wide, and 4.0 centimeters tall?

⑲   The formula for converting between degrees Celsius (C) and degrees Fahrenheit (F) is $F = \frac{9}{5} C + 32$. Water boils at 100°C. What is the boiling point of water in degrees Fahrenheit?

⑳   How many milliliters are in a centiliter?

Metric System

Length		Weight (mass)		Liquid Volume (capacity)	
millimeter (mm)	0.001 m	milligram (mg)	0.001 g	milliliter (mL)	0.001 L
centimeter (cm)	0.01 m	centigram (cg)	0.01 g	centiliter (cL)	0.01 L
decimeter (dm)	0.1 m	decigram (dg)	0.1 g	deciliter (dL)	0.1 L
meter (m)	1 m	gram (g)	1 g	liter (L)	1 L
dekameter (dam)	10 m	dekagram (dag)	10 g	dekaliter (daL)	10 L
hectometer (hm)	100 m	hectogram (hg)	100 g	hectoliter (hL)	100 L
kilometer (km)	1000 m	kilogram (kg)	1000 g	kiloliter (kL)	1000 L

◆ **Units of area are derived from units of length.**

square centimeter (cm^2) $1\ cm^2 = 0.0001\ m^2$

square meter (m^2) $1\ m^2 = 10{,}000\ cm^2$

square kilometer (km^2) $1\ km^2 = 1{,}000{,}000\ m^2$

◆ **Units of volume can also be derived from units of length.**

cubic centimeter (cm^3) **cubic meter** (m^3) $1\ m^3 = 1{,}000{,}000\ cm^3$

◆ **Descriptions of some common units:**

kilometer *You can walk a kilometer in about 12 minutes.*

meter *Most classroom doors are about 1 meter wide.*

centimeter *This line segment is 1 centimeter long.* ━━━

millimeter *This line segment is 1 millimeter long.* ▪

liter *Four average-sized glasses hold about 1 liter of liquid all together.*

milliliter *This cube holds about 1 milliliter of liquid.*

kilogram *A pair of size-10 men's shoes weighs about 1 kilogram.*

gram *A nickel weighs about 5 grams.*

Customary System

◆ Length

inch (in.)   1 in. = $\frac{1}{12}$ ft

$\frac{1}{36}$ yd

foot (ft)   1 ft =   12 in.

$\frac{1}{3}$ yd

yard (yd)   1 yd =   36 in.

3 ft

mile (mi)   1 mi =   5280 ft

1760 yd

◆ Area

square inch (sq in. or in.^{2})

square foot (sq ft or ft^2)   1 ft^2 =   144 in.^{2}

square yard (sq yd or yd^2) 1 yd^2 = 9 ft^2

acre (A)   1 A =   4840 yd^2

square mile (sq mi or mi^2) 1 mi^2 = 640 A

◆ Weight

ounce (oz)   1 oz = $\frac{1}{16}$ lb

pound (lb)   1 lb =   16 oz

ton (T)   1 T =   2000 lb

◆ Volume

cubic inch (cu in. or in.^{3})

cubic foot (cu ft or ft^3)   1 ft^3 = 1728 in.^{3}

cubic yard (cu yd or yd^3)   1 yd^3 = 27 ft^3

◆ Liquid Volume (capacity)

fluid ounce (fl oz) 1 fl oz = $\frac{1}{8}$ cup

cup (c)   1 c =   8 fl oz

$\frac{1}{2}$ pt

pint (pt)   1 pt =   16 fl oz

2 c

$\frac{1}{2}$ qt

quart (qt)   1 qt =   32 fl oz

4 c

$\frac{1}{4}$ gal

gallon (gal)   1 gal =   128 fl oz

16 c

8 pt

4 qt

Formulas

Circle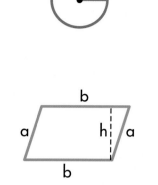

area $= \pi r^2$

diameter $= 2r$

circumference $= \pi d$

Parallelogram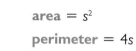

area $= bh$

perimeter $= 2a + 2b$

Square

area $= s^2$

perimeter $= 4s$

Rectangle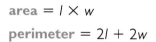

area $= l \times w$

perimeter $= 2l + 2w$

Triangle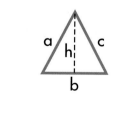

area $= \frac{1}{2}bh$

perimeter $= a + b + c$

Trapezoid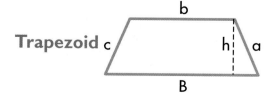

area $= \dfrac{h\,(B + b)}{2}$

perimeter $= a + b + c + B$

Volume $V = lwh$

Interest $I = prt$ (principal × rate × time)

Probability $\dfrac{\text{number of favorable outcomes}}{\text{number of possible outcomes}}$

Temperature Conversions   Fahrenheit to Celsius $C° = (F° - 32) \times \frac{5}{9}$
Celsius to Fahrenheit $F° = \frac{9}{5}C° + 32$

Finding Total Degrees of Angles of Regular Polygons $180 \times (n - 2)$, where $n =$ number of sides

Pythagorean Theorem $a^2 + b^2 = c^2$, where c is the hypotenuse of a right triangle and a and b are the other sides

Formula for a Straight Line $y = Ax + B$, where A is the number of steps to the right for each step up, and B is the y-coordinate for $x = 0$

A

acute angle An angle that measures less than 90°. These are acute angles:

These are not acute angles:

acute triangle A triangle with three acute angles.

addend A number that is added to another number to make a sum. For example:

$$\begin{array}{r} 35 \text{ —— addend} \\ + 48 \text{ —— addend} \\ \hline 83 \text{ —— sum} \end{array}$$

7 + 8 = 15 —— sum

—— addend

—— addend

algorithm A step-by-step procedure for solving a certain type of problem.

angle Two rays with a common endpoint.

approximation An answer to a mathematical problem that is close enough for the purpose. Sometimes an approximate answer is more appropriate than an exact answer. (See *estimate*.)

arc A part of a circle.

area The number of square units enclosed by a figure. The area of this rectangle is 6 square centimeters:

3 cm
2 cm

arrow operation A notation for showing an action of a function machine. In 7 ——(× 8)——▶ 56 , 7 goes in and is multiplied by 8 to give 56. The function rule in this case is ×8. In the operation

6 ◀——(− 5)—— 11 , 11 goes in and 5 is subtracted from it to give 6. The function rule in this case is −5.

average A number that can sometimes be used to represent a group of numbers. To find one kind of average of a set of numbers, commonly called the *mean*, add the numbers and divide the sum by how many numbers were added. The average of 5, 6, 6, 8, and 10 is 7 (5 + 6 + 6 + 8 + 10 = 35, and 35 ÷ 5 = 7). (The *median* and *mode* are also sometimes called the average.)

axes (of a graph) The two zero lines of a graph that give the coordinates of points. The horizontal axis is the *x*-axis. The vertical axis is the *y*-axis.

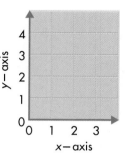

B

balance 1. The amount of money remaining in a bank account. 2. A double-pan balance is an instrument used to measure weight.

bar graph A graph in which quantities are shown by bars. Each bar in this bar graph shows the average number of rainy days per year in a selected United States city.

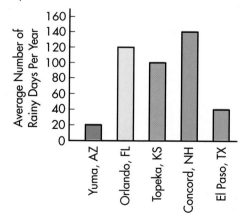

base 1. A side of a polygon or a surface of a space figure.

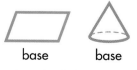

2. The number to be raised to a power. In the expression 3^4, 3 is the base.

bound

cube

bound A number that an answer must be greater than or less than. For example, 36 × 21 must be less than 40 × 30, or 1200. So 1200 is an upper bound. The answer to 36 × 21 must be greater than 30 × 20, or 600. So 600 is a lower bound.

C

Celsius (C) A temperature scale named after a Swedish astronomer, in which 0° is the temperature at which water freezes and 100° is the temperature at which water boils under standard conditions.

circle A figure (in a plane) in which all points are the same distance from a point called the center. In this figure, for example, points A, B, and C are the same distance from point O, the center of the circle:

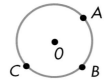

circumference The distance around a circle.

clipped range In a set of numbers, the range calculated without the greatest and least values.

common denominator A common multiple of two or more denominators. For example, 56 is a common denominator of $\frac{1}{7}$ and $\frac{3}{8}$.

composite function A function with two or more operations. For example:

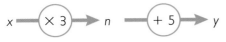

composite number A whole number having factors other than 1 and itself.

compound interest Interest that is paid on the previous interest as well as on the principal.

concave Shape of a figure in which there exists a line segment between two points of the figure that goes outside the figure.

cone A figure made by connecting every point of a circle to a point not in the plane of the circle.

congruent Figures that are the same size and same shape; that is, they fit perfectly when placed on top of each other.

These triangles are congruent:

These are not:

convex Shape of a figure in which every line segment between two points of the figure remains entirely inside the figure. (See *concave*.)

coordinates Numbers that give the position of a point on a graph. In the figure shown, for example, the coordinates of point A are (2,3). The x-coordinate is 2. The y-coordinate is 3.

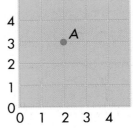

cube A solid figure with six congruent square faces. For example:

cylinder A figure with two parallel bases that are usually congruent circles.

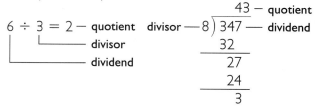

dividend A number that is divided by the divisor. (See *divisor*.) For example:

$$6 \div 3 = 2 \text{ — quotient}$$

divisor, dividend, quotient, dividend, 32, 27, 24, 3

D

decimal point A dot used to separate the ones digit from the tenths digit.

degree 1. A unit for measuring temperature. 2. A unit for measuring angles.

denominator The part of a fraction written below the line. The part written above the line is called the numerator. The denominator tells how many equal parts something is divided into; the numerator tells how many of those parts are being referred to. In the fraction $\frac{3}{4}$ the denominator (4) indicates that something is divided into four equal parts. The numerator (3) says to consider three of those parts.

deposit To add money to a bank account. (Also, the amount of money added.)

diagonal A segment that joins two nonadjacent vertices of a polygon.

diameter A line segment, going through the center of a circle, that starts at one point on the circle and ends at the opposite point on the circle. (Also, the length of that line segment.) *AB* is a diameter of this circle.

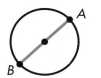

difference The amount by which one number is greater or less than another number. For example:

43 — minuend
− 16 — subtrahend
27 — difference

10 − 7 = 3 — difference
subtrahend
minuend

digit Any of the numbers 0, 1, 2, 3, 4, 5, 6, 7, 8, and 9. The two digits in 15 are 1 and 5.

divisor A number that the dividend is divided by. (See *dividend*.)

E

equation A mathematical statement with an equal sign stating that two quantities are equal. For example, $4 + 2 = 6$ and $6 + n = 10$ are equations.

equilateral triangle A triangle with all three sides the same length. For example:

equivalent fractions Fractions that have the same value. The fractions $\frac{2}{6}$, $\frac{4}{12}$, and $\frac{1}{3}$ are equivalent fractions.

estimate A judgment about the size or quantity of something. (Also, to make such a judgment.) (See *approximation*.)

even number Any multiple of 2. The numbers 0, 2, 4, 6, 8, and so on are even numbers.

exponent A number written slightly above and to the right of the base. It tells how many times the base is to be used as a factor. In the expression 3^4, 4 is the exponent.

F

factor 1. A whole number that divides evenly into a given second whole number. 2. One of the numbers multiplied to give a product.

Fahrenheit (F) A temperature scale named for a German physicist, in which 32° is the temperature at which water freezes and 212° is the temperature at which water boils under standard conditions.

fraction

fraction Examples of fractions are $\frac{1}{2}$, $\frac{3}{4}$, and $\frac{7}{8}$. The fraction $\frac{3}{4}$ means that something is divided into four equal parts and that we are considering three of those parts. (See *denominator* and *numerator*.)

function machine A device (sometimes imaginary) that does the same thing to every number that is put into it. (See *arrow notation*.)

function rule See *arrow notation*.

G

greatest common factor The greatest number that divides two or more numbers with no remainders.

H

hexagon A polygon with six sides.

hundredth If a whole is divided into 100 equal parts, each part is one hundredth of the whole.

hypotenuse The longest side of a right triangle.

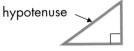

hypotenuse

I

identity function A function that always gives back the same number that is put in.

improper fraction A fraction in which the numerator is greater than or equal to the denominator.

inequality A statement that tells which of two numbers is greater. For example, $4 > 3$ is read "4 is greater than 3." The expression $3 + 6 < 10$ is read "3 plus 6 is less than 10."

interest The payment made by a bank to those who have deposited money there.

line

intersecting lines Lines that meet. In this figure, lines *AB* and *CD* intersect at point *E*:

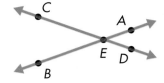

inverse operation An operation that undoes the results of another operation. Multiplication and division are inverse operations; addition and subtraction are inverse operations.

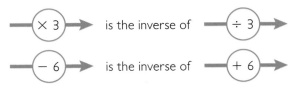

isosceles trapezoid A trapezoid with two equal sides. This is an isosceles trapezoid:

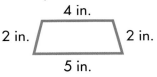

isosceles triangle A triangle with two equal sides. These are isosceles triangles:

L

least common multiple (LCM) The least number (except 0) that is a multiple of two or more numbers.

line A set of points continuing without end in both directions.

line graph A graph made up of lines. This line graph shows John's height at different times in his life. The marked points show his height at the times when he was measured.

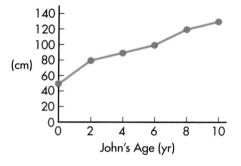

line of symmetry A line on which a figure can be folded so that one half of the figure overlaps exactly with the other.

line segment A part of a line with two endpoints. For example, *AB* is a line segment; points *A* and *B* are its endpoints.

M

mean See *average.*

median The middle number in a group of numbers when they are listed in order from least to greatest. If there are two numbers in the middle, their average is the median. The median of 2, 3, 4, 5, and 6 is 4.

minuend A number from which another number is subtracted. (See *difference.*)

mixed number A number made up of a whole number and a fraction. For example, $1\frac{1}{2}$, $2\frac{3}{4}$, and $7\frac{7}{8}$ are mixed numbers.

mode The number that occurs most often in a set of numbers. The mode of 1, 2, 3, 1, 4, and 1 is 1.

multiple A number that is some whole number times another number. For example, 12 is a multiple of 3 because $3 \times 4 = 12$.

multiplicand A number that is multiplied by another number, the multiplier. For example:

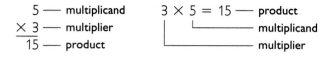

The multiplier and multiplicand are also called the factors of the product.

multiplicative inverse See *reciprocal.*

multiplier See *multiplicand.*

N

net A two-dimensional figure that, when folded along particular lines, makes a three-dimensional figure.

numerator The part of a fraction written above the line. (See *denominator.*)

O

obtuse angle An angle that measures between 90° and 180°. These angles are obtuse:

These are not:

obtuse triangle A triangle with one obtuse angle.

octagon A polygon with eight sides.

odd number A whole number that is not a multiple of 2. All whole numbers that are not even are odd. The numbers 1, 3, 5, 7, 9, 11, and so on are odd numbers.

ordered pair Two numbers written so that one is considered before the other. Coordinates of points are written as ordered pairs, with the *x*-coordinate written first, then the *y*-coordinate. For example: (3, 4). (See *coordinates.*)

P

parallel lines Lines in a plane that do not intersect. Lines *AB* and *CD* are parallel:

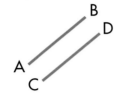

Lines *EF* and *GH* are not parallel:

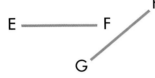

parallelogram A quadrilateral with opposite sides parallel and congruent.

parentheses A pair of symbols ( ) used to show in which order operations should be done. For example, (3 × 5) + 7 says to multiply 5 by 3 and then add 7; the expression 3 × (5 + 7) says to add 5 and 7 and then multiply by 3.

partial product The product that comes from multiplying the multiplicand by one of the digits of the multiplier. For example:

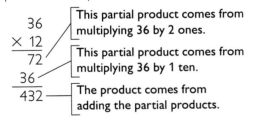

```
    36
  × 12
  ─────
    72     This partial product comes from
           multiplying 36 by 2 ones.
    36     This partial product comes from
  ─────    multiplying 36 by 1 ten.
   432     The product comes from
           adding the partial products.
```

pentagon A polygon with five sides.

percent A word meaning "per hundred" or hundredths. The % symbol is used to represent percent.

perimeter The distance around a figure. The perimeter of this rectangle is 6 centimeters:

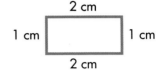

2 cm
1 cm   1 cm
2 cm

perpendicular lines Lines that intersect at right angles.

These lines are perpendicular:

So are these:

But these are not:

place value The value of a digit in a number. The value of 7 in 27 is 7 ones; in 74 its value is 70, or 7 tens; and in 726 its value is 700, or 7 hundreds.

plane An endless, flat surface that extends in all directions.

point An exact location in space.

polygon One of a certain type of figure. These figures are polygons:

These are not:

Here are the names of some common polygons and their number of sides:

Number of Sides	Name
3	triangle
4	quadrilateral

5   pentagon—a regular
                     pentagon has five equal sides:

6   hexagon—a regular hexagon
                     has six equal sides:

8   octagon—a regular octagon
                     has eight equal sides:

prime number A whole number divisible only by 1 and itself.

principal The amount of money deposited in a bank or invested.

prism A space figure with two parallel, congruent faces called bases. These are prisms:

probability How likely it is that something will happen. The probability that some particular thing will happen is a fraction. The denominator is the total number of possible things that can happen and the numerator is the number of ways this particular thing can happen. The probability that an ordinary coin will land on heads when it is flipped is about $\frac{1}{2}$.

product The result of multiplying two numbers together. (See *multiplicand*.)

profit In a business, the money that is left after all expenses have been paid.

pyramid A figure formed by connecting all points of a polygon to a point not in the plane of the polygon. These are pyramids:

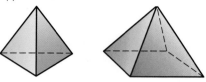

Pythagorean theorem Named for the Greek mathematician Pythagoras. For any right triangle, the square of the length of the hypotenuse is equal to the sum of the squares of the lengths of the other two sides. It is written as $a^2 + b^2 = c^2$, where c is the length of the hypotenuse.

Q

quadrilateral A polygon with four sides.

quotient The result (other than the remainder) of dividing one number by another. (See *dividend*.)

R

radius A line segment that goes from the center of a circle to a point on the circle. (Also, the length of such a segment.) *OA* is a radius of the circle shown here. The radius of this circle is 1 centimeter:

range In a set of numbers, the difference between the greatest and least values.

rate A ratio written with units, as in 20 miles per hour.

ratio The comparison of two numbers by division.

ray A set of points that has one endpoint and extends without end in one direction. *OA* is a ray. *OB* is a ray.

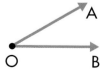

reciprocal Two fractions whose product is 1. For example, $\frac{3}{4}$ and $\frac{4}{3}$ are reciprocals of each other.

rectangle A quadrilateral in which all four angles are right angles.

reflection A change in the location of a figure in which it is flipped over a line.

regroup To rename a number to make adding and subtracting easier.

Example of regrouping in subtraction:

$$\begin{array}{r} {}^{1}\ ^{15} \\ \cancel{25} \\ 17 \\ \hline 8 \end{array}$$

(To subtract in the ones column, 2 tens and 5 is regrouped as 1 ten and 15.)

Example of regrouping in addition:

$$\begin{array}{r} ^{1} \\ 296 \\ +\ 442 \\ \hline 738 \end{array}$$

(After the tens column is added, 13 tens is regrouped as 1 hundred and 3 tens.)

regular polygon A polygon with all sides congruent and all angles equal.

relation signs The three basic relation signs are $>$ (greater than), $<$ (less than), and $=$ (equal to). (See *inequality.*)

remainder A number less than the divisor that remains after the dividend has been divided by the divisor as many times as possible. For example, when 25 is divided by 4, the quotient is 6 with a remainder of 1:

$$\begin{array}{r} 6\ \ \textbf{R1} \\ 4\overline{)25} \\ 24 \\ \hline 1 \end{array}$$

rhombus A parallelogram with four congruent sides.

right angle An angle that forms a square corner. These are right angles:

These are not:

right triangle A triangle with one right angle.

rotation A change in the location of a figure when it is turned in a circle around a point.

rounding Changing a number to another number that is easier to work with and that is close enough for the purpose. (See *approximation.*)

S

scalene triangle A triangle that has no congruent sides. For example:

scientific notation A method of expressing a number as the product of two factors, one of which is a number of greater than or equal to 1 but less than 10, and the other of which is a power of 10. This notation is used to convert, indicate, or evaluate very great numbers. For example, $35{,}897 = 3.5897 \times 10^{4}$.

sector A section of the inside of a circle.

similar figures Figures with the same shape but not necessarily the same size.

These triangles are similar:

skew lines Lines that are not parallel and do not meet. Lines *LM* and *TV* in the figure below are skew lines.

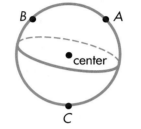

sphere A space figure with all points the same distance from a point called the center. This is a sphere:

square A quadrilateral with four congruent sides and four equal angles.

straight angle An angle that measures 180°.

180°

subtrahend A number that is subtracted from another number. (See *difference*.)

sum The result of adding two or more numbers. (See *addend*.)

surface area The sum of the areas of the faces of a space figure.

symmetrical figure A figure that has a line of symmetry. (See *line of symmetry*.)

T

tenth If a whole is divided into ten equal parts, each part is one tenth of the whole.

thousandth If a whole is divided into 1000 equal parts, each part is one thousandth of the whole.

translation A change in the location of a figure in which it is slid without being turned.

trapezoid A quadrilateral with exactly one pair of parallel sides.

triangle A polygon that has three sides.

U

unit 1. An amount used as a standard for measuring. For example, meters, liters, and kilograms are units in the metric system of measure, and feet, quarts, and pounds are units in the traditional system of measure. Sometimes nonstandard units are used for measuring. See pages 588 and 589 for tables of metric and customary measures. 2. One of anything.

unit cost The cost of one item or one specified amount of an item. If 20 pencils cost 40¢, then the unit cost is 2¢ for each pencil. If dog food costs $9 for 3 kilograms, then the unit cost is $3 per kilogram.

V

vertex 1. The point where two rays meet. 2. The point of intersection of two sides of a polygon. 3. The point of intersection of three edges of a space figure. (The plural is vertices.)

volume The number of cubic units needed to fill a space figure.

W

whole number The numbers that we use to show how many (0, 1, 2, 3, and so on). For example, 3 is a whole number, but $3\frac{1}{2}$ and 4.5 are not whole numbers.

Z

zero The number that tells how many things there are when there aren't any. Any number times 0 is 0, any number plus 0 is that number: $0 \times 3 = 0$, and $0 + 3 = 3$.

ACKNOWLEDGMENTS

Photo Credits

Unit Openers/Table of Contents
pp. 2-3, ©Donald Smetzer/Tony Stone Images; **100-101, 174-175, 236-237, 340-341, 436-437,** ©SuperStock.

Unit 1
p. 7, ©Fotosmith; **13, 20,** ©SuperStock; **24,** ©Fotosmith; **25, 27,** ©SuperStock; **28,** ©Fotosmith; **29, 31, 37(br),** ©SuperStock; **37(tr),** ©Fotosmith; **39,** ©Mark Richards/PhotoEdit; **40,** ©Fotosmith; **41,** ©SuperStock; **42,** ©Fotosmith; **43,** ©Tony Freeman/PhotoEdit; **45,** ©Rob Downey Photo/Cards courtesy of Donruss and Topps; **50,** ©PhotoDisc, Inc.; **51,** ©SuperStock; **53,** ©PhotoDisc, Inc.; **55,** ©SuperStock; **56,** ©Fotosmith; **57, 62, 64, 65,** ©SuperStock; Jerry Howard/Stock Boston; **66,** ©PhotoDisc, Inc.; **68, 69,** ©SuperStock; **77,** ©PhotoDisc, Inc.; **80,** Mike Legendre; **81,** ©Bonnie Kamin/PhotoEdit; **83,** ©PhotoDisc, Inc.; **87, 88,** ©PhotoDisc, Inc.; **91, 98,** ©SuperStock; **99,** ©PhotoDisc, Inc.

Unit 2
p. 103, 106, ©SuperStock; **108,** ©PhotoDisc, Inc.; **119,** ©SuperStock; **124, 125,** ©Rob Downey Photo; **128,** ©PhotoDisc, Inc.; **129, 131,** ©Fotosmith; **132,** ©SuperStock; **133,** ©David Young-Wolff/PhotoEdit; **135,** ©1997 Aaron Haupt; **137,** ©Fotosmith; **143,** ©SuperStock; **144,** ©Fotosmith; **145,** ©Robert Brenner/PhotoEdit; **148,** ©Fotosmith; **149(bl),** ©PhotoDisc, Inc.; **149(br),** ©SuperStock; **151,** ©Bill Hickey/The Image Bank; **153, 155, 158,** ©SuperStock; **161,** FOTOfactory; **165, 169, 171, 172, 173,** ©SuperStock.

Unit 3
p. 177, ©SuperStock; **178, 180,** ©PhotoDisc, Inc.; **184,** ©SuperStock; **186,** ©Photo Disc, Inc.; **191,** ©David Young-Wolff/PhotoEdit; **192,** ©Fotosmith; **193,** ©SuperStock; **194,** ©David Young-Wolff/PhotoEdit; **195, 196, 197, 198,** ©SuperStock; **201, 202,** ©PhotoDisc, Inc.; **203, 208,** ©SuperStock; **215,** ©Fotosmith; **216,** ©Billy E. Barnes/PhotoEdit; **218, 227,** ©Fotosmith; **228,** ©John Boykin/PhotoEdit; **229,** ©SuperStock; **235,** ©PhotoDisc, Inc.

Unit 4
p. 240, ©SuperStock; **241, 244, 250,** ©Fotosmith; **255,** ©SuperStock; **257,** ©Tony Freeman/PhotoEdit; **260, 263, 265,** ©Fotosmith; **267,** ©SuperStock; **268,** ©Alan Oddie/PhotoEdit; **273,** FOTOfactory; **281,** ©Fotosmith; **285,** ©Mary Kate Denny/PhotoEdit; **287, 289,** ©Fotosmith; **290, 298,** ©SuperStock; **305,** ©James Shaffer/PhotoEdit; **311,** ©SuperStock; **313,** ©Tom McCadhy/PhotoEdit; **314, 316,** ©SuperStock; **317,** ©SuperStock; **321,** ©PhotoDisc, Inc.; **322,** ©SuperStock; **323,** ©SuperStock; **325,** ©PhotoDisc, Inc.; **327,** ©E. Zuckerman/PhotoEdit; **331,** ©SuperStock; **335,** ©Fotosmith; **337,** ©PhotoDisc, Inc.

Unit 5
p. 345, ©Myrleen Ferguson/PhotoEdit; **347,** ©PhotoDisc, Inc.; **358(t)** ©PhotoDisc, Inc., **358(b)** ©Shinichi Kanno/FPG; **361,** ©Fotosmith; **364, 367,** ©SuperStock; **368,** ©PhotoDisc, Inc.; **370,** ©David Young-Wolff/PhotoEdit; **372,** ©PhotoDisc, Inc.; **373,** ©SuperStock; **374,** ©Fotosmith; **376,** ©PhotoDisc, Inc.; **382,** ©Fotosmith; **385,** ©PhotoDisc, Inc.; **401,** ©Fotosmith; **405(t), 405(b), 408,** ©PhotoDisc, Inc.; **409,** ©SuperStock; **416,** ©PhotoDisc, Inc.; **417,** ©Fotosmith; **420,** ©SuperStock; **423,** ©PhotoDisc, Inc.; **424,** ©SuperStock; **428, 434, 435,** ©PhotoDisc, Inc.

Unit 6
p. 439, ©SuperStock; **443,** ©Robert Brenner/PhotoEdit; **445,** ©Fotosmith; **447,** ©Michael Newman/PhotoEdit; **470, 472,** ©Fotosmith; **475,** ©Robert Brenner/PhotoEdit; **476, 478,** ©SuperStock; **479,** ©Fotosmith; **483,** ©Jeffrey Sylvester/FPG; **489,** ©PhotoDisc, Inc.; **491,** ©SuperStock; **493, 494, 495, 496, 497, 500, 501, 502(t), 502(c), 502(b),** ©PhotoDisc, Inc.; **503,** ©Fotosmith; **520,** ©SuperStock; **522, 524,** ©PhotoDisc, Inc.; **525,** ©SuperStock; **528,** ©PhotoDisc, Inc.; **532,** ©Fotosmith; **536,** ©PhotoDisc, Inc.; **537, 551,** ©SuperStock.

Technical Illustration Credits

Units 1, 2, 3, and 6 Ruttle Graphics, Inc.; **Units 4 and 5** Dipherent Strokes, Inc.

Illustration Credits

pp. 4, 5, 12, 44, 52, 78, 318, Jane Caminos; **13, 146, 189, 206, 214, 221, 225, 329, 338, 349, 357,** John Edwards & Associates; **76,** Joel Snyder; **233,** Katy Farmer; **238, 242, 278,** Donna Perrone; **420,** Bob Berry; **482,** Mimi Powers.

Cover Credits

Front cover photo, Fotosmith; **Design and Illustration front cover,** Morgan-Cain & Associates; **Back cover photo,** Timothy Fuller and Fotosmith.